EXPOSED

Before the first story was off the air, the WRC switchboard was besieged with calls. Dozens of patients with similar stories described their desperate attempts to have children and said they had consulted Dr. Jacobson as a last resort. They were led to believe they were pregnant, many of them multiple times, only to be told they were miscarrying and would resorb. For years they had suffered in silence—each woman believed her problem was unique to herself—but now, after seeing other women with identical stories, they wanted to talk. The memories came flooding back. Some reacted with tears; others with rage. Some accused him of fraud. Others described stunning incompetence.

By the end of the week forty-one women had called the station to report questionable pregnancies. Together they had experienced more than seventy resorptions.

One of the last calls would prove to be the most significant of all. It wasn't from a patient. It was from one of Cecil's former employees. Her name was Donna Kessler, and she had worked at the clinic as a laboratory technician during the early 1980s. She said she was shocked by what she'd seen on TV, but she wasn't calling about the resorptions. She had information on what would prove to be an even more explosive topic. She wanted to talk about Dr. Jacobson's sperm bank.

THE BABYMAKER

Fertility Fraud and the Fall of Dr. Cecil Jacobson

Rick Nelson

BANTAM BOOKS

New York · Toronto · London · Sydney · Auckland

THE BABYMAKER
A Bantam Book / December 1994

ISBN 0-553-56162-6
Published simultaneously in the United States and Canada

Bantam Books are published by Bantam Books, a division of Bantam Dou-
bleday Dell Publishing Group, Inc. Its trademark, consisting of the words
"Bantam Books" and the portrayal of a rooster, is Registered in U.S. Patent
and Trademark Office and in other countries. Marca Registrada. Bantam
Books, 1540 Broadway, New York, New York 10036.

PRINTED IN THE UNITED STATES OF AMERICA
OPM   0   9   8   7   6   5   4   3   2   1

The reporting for this book began eight years before its publication with a tip about an infertility doctor who was preying on the vulnerability of his patients. Since then I have interviewed more than 300 people—patients, friends, enemies, and colleagues of Dr. Cecil Jacobson—who unselfishly gave of their time.

I especially wish to thank the many infertility patients who agreed to reopen old wounds and discuss the most traumatic event of their lives. Without their assistance this book and the original stories that exposed Dr. Jacobson would not have been possible. I also wish to acknowledge the help of Carol Laws and the vast contributions of my editor at Bantam Books, Ilene Block, whose guidance was felt on every page.

The names of the insemination patients who testified during Dr. Jacobson's trial have been changed to protect their privacy and, especially, the identity of their children who still don't realize that he is their biological father.

Chapter One

October 3, 1987

Debbie Gregory fought back tears as she lay on the examination table waiting for the doctor's diagnosis. The life of her unborn child was in danger—she was four months pregnant and the doctor couldn't hear the baby's heartbeat, an ominous sign that she was preparing to miscarry again.

Just getting pregnant had been struggle enough. After nearly two years of treatments and dozens of visits to her infertility specialist, she had conceived twice already and lost them both. Now keeping this baby meant more to her than anything in the world.

This was only her second visit to Dr. John Doppelheuer, and Debbie didn't know what to make of the young obstetrician. He had performed a cursory exam, and now he wanted to check her more thoroughly. Despite her protests he was performing a pelvic examination.

Her infertility specialist, a renowned medical pioneer, Dr. Cecil Jacobson of Vienna, Virginia, had warned her that allowing other doctors to do a pelvic could jeopardize the pregnancy. It was dangerous, he'd said, and could cause a miscarriage. But the new doctor was insistent. He sensed a serious problem and wanted to investigate.

Just the previous afternoon Dr. Jacobson had told Debbie that her pregnancy was progressing as expected. He had performed an ultrasound exam and said the baby's growth was normal and its heartbeat, which he pointed out on the sonogram screen, was strong and steady. "There's Junior," he'd said as he showed Debbie and her husband the pulsating blip on the screen. But now, less than twenty-four hours later, this new doctor couldn't hear a thing.

1

Debbie's husband, Steven, stood off to the side, the concern registered on his face. He'd never been to an ob/gyn's office before. He felt helpless and out of place. He'd accompanied Debbie to the doctor's office that Saturday morning only so he could meet the man who would eventually deliver their child. It was supposed to be a routine prenatal visit, but now Steven wasn't sure which doctor to believe—the one who had been treating them for so long and was saying everything was fine, or the one they had just met who was acting as if their baby was dying.

The exam seemed to drag on forever, and they could tell from the doctor's silence that he wasn't pleased with his findings. When he finally concluded, he told Debbie to get dressed and said he wanted to see them in his office.

Dr. Doppelheuer wasted no time in getting to the point. "There is no baby," he said.

Debbie had expected the worst. She had lost another one. "The baby has died?" she asked, starting to cry. Already she was blaming herself for having killed another baby.

But the doctor said that's not what he meant. "No, there is no baby," he said. "You're not pregnant."

Debbie said she didn't understand. Of course she was pregnant. She was *four months* pregnant. She explained how her doctor had seen the heartbeat the day before. She even had a sonogram photo of the baby and pulled it from her purse to show him.

But Dr. Doppelheuer said there was no mistake. He was quite sure of his findings. "I'm sorry," he said, as if it were his fault. "But there is no baby." And as far as he could tell—Debbie had not been pregnant anytime in the recent past.

Chapter Two

As President Jimmy Carter was taking the oath of office in January 1977, Steven Gregory sought refuge from the bone-chilling Washington weather to watch the historic event on television. He and a friend had ordered drinks and were watching the big-screen TV over the bar at Joe Theismanns restaurant, a popular watering hole and sports bar owned by the Washington Redskins quarterback, when two stunning women came in from the cold.

Steven's friend knew one of them. When she came over to thaw out and say hello, Steven was introduced to the other one. Her name was Debbie Smith, and their attraction was instant and mutual. They talked, they drank, and before the night was over, they went to dinner and a movie. They hit it off so well that Debbie invited Steven back to her apartment for a cup of coffee. Then he ruined everything when he told Debbie about his fiancée.

He was engaged to be married, a detail he'd failed to mention until he was comfortably settled in Debbie's living room. She promptly poured his coffee into a Styrofoam cup, walked him to the door, and said it had been a pleasure to meet him. He called several times during the next few days and asked to see her again, but Debbie said she didn't date soon-to-be-married men. The next time she heard from him, he was standing on her doorstep—suitcase in hand, a pair of tennis shoes slung over his shoulder, and a sheepish grin on his face. He said the wedding was off. When he'd told his fiancée about his infatuation with Debbie, and admitted that he wanted to see Debbie again, she booted him out. Now he had nowhere to stay. He asked if he could sleep on Debbie's couch until he got settled.

Against her better judgment she opened the door and let him in. Her friends would say she was out of her mind—he could be Jack the Ripper, for all she knew about him—but Debbie had a premonition about the guy, and once he moved in, he didn't move out.

By the fall of 1985 Debbie and Steven had been married for seven years. They lived in a comfortable subdivision of winding streets and tree-shaded yards in Fairfax, Virginia. Their neighbors were mostly young families and upwardly mobile Washingtonians who commuted every morning into the nation's capital, just ten miles away.

Debbie worked in graphic sales; Steven sold floor space for conventions. Their friends thought they led an idyllic life. They took spur-of-the-moment vacations and dined out whenever they wanted. They could sneak off to their favorite bed-and-breakfast hideaway in the country, and their annual spring parties were the social event of the year. They had money in the bank and two cars in the driveway. They seemed to have it all—everything except children.

Every year or so another one of Debbie's friends was getting pregnant, until pretty soon she was the last one without a baby. It wasn't that she and Steven didn't want children; they had never really tried. From the way they doted on their friends' children, there was no question they would make wonderful parents. The kids called Steven "Mr. Bear," and Debbie never forgot a birthday or holiday. But sometimes when they were home alone, and the house seemed too quiet, they talked about what it would be like to have kids of their own. They had a spoiled, overgrown dog and a batch of cats that had the run of the house, but it wasn't the same. By 1985 Debbie was thirty-four years old and knew that if they were going to start a family, they had to start soon. So she put away her diaphragm, went to bed with her husband, and waited.

When nothing happened after a few months, she consulted her doctor. She had been seeing the same gynecologist, Dr. Robert Barter, since she was a teenager. He was from the old school of medicine, when doctors' opinions were unquestioned. Sometimes gruff and surly, he was more comfortable issuing commands than providing explanations. He'd operated on Debbie twice already—once to remove an ovarian cyst and another time to extract a dislodged IUD—and when she went to him with her infertility questions, his solution was another surgery. She needed a laparoscopy, he said, to clear out her fallopian tubes. He didn't assess the risks or describe the benefits. But if she wanted a baby, she needed the operation. End of discussion.

A few days later she told a friend about her growing dissatisfaction with her doctor. She wanted someone who would discuss her problems, not just bark orders. She wanted a baby, not surgery.

Her friend said she knew just the man. "This guy is incredible," she said. He was friendly, easy to talk with, and had a great personality. Debbie's friend had gone to him for an amniocentesis before one of her three children was born. She said the doctor was not only an expert at performing the procedure to diagnose birth defects, but he'd invented it. "You'll love him."

Her friend said his name was Dr. Cecil Jacobson.

In many respects selecting a new doctor is no different from hiring a plumber, or finding an honest car mechanic. If Debbie had questions about a repairman, she would call the Better Business Bureau. But what about doctors? Who kept tabs on them?

She concluded that the best source of information was the county medical society, so she found the number in the phone book and called. She wasn't sure what to ask, but she figured if there were some problems with the doctor, the medical society would tell her. The clerk checked the files for information about Dr. Cecil Jacobson and returned with his résumé. He specialized in reproductive genetics, ob/gyn, and infertility. He was a doctor in good standing, licensed in the District of Columbia since 1965 and in Virginia since 1976. He was a graduate of George Washington University in the District and had taught at a number of other medical schools, including as a guest scientist at Cambridge University in England. He'd been a member of the President's Committee on Mental Retardation, a Rhodes-scholar finalist, and a member of more than a dozen scientific societies. Debbie was impressed. So was the clerk.

When Debbie called the doctor's office to make an appointment, the receptionist said she would mail Debbie a packet of information. That night, when she told Steven what she'd done, he wasn't enthused. He didn't mind if Debbie went to her own gynecologist, but going to an infertility specialist was something different. It had the same social stigma of seeing a psychiatrist.

Debbie described the doctor's impeccable credentials and told Steven about the rave reviews her friend had given him. "What have we got to lose?" she said. "Let's go for a consultation and see what this guy has to say." If they didn't like it, they could leave.

Steven finally relented, but only because Debbie was so excited. He felt he didn't need any help in getting his wife pregnant, but if he had to expose his bruised male ego, he might as well do it in front of the best doctor they could find.

The Reproductive Genetic Center was located near Tyson's Corner, a congested crossroads of shopping malls and office buildings that commuters knew best to avoid in northern Virginia. The clinic was on the fifth floor of a professional office complex called Tycon 1.

Long before their appointment Debbie had started pestering Steven to fill out the information the clinic had sent them. He was supposed to complete a genealogy report and draw a detailed family tree, complete with drawings and coded markings to signify which ancestors had birth defects, miscarriages, or hereditary diseases. Debbie was supposed to fill out a report, too, plus record her basal body temperature when she woke up each morning. Steven had dabbled at one set of questions and had given a token effort at the family-history stuff, but never completed either one. Debbie didn't push him—just getting him to the clinic was enough for the time being.

Steven nearly canceled the appointment when he learned he had to produce a semen sample for the doctor to analyze. Now, on the drive to the clinic, he kept the sample warm in a vial cradled under his armpit. "I feel like an idiot," he said, threatening to turn around and go home.

Fortunately for him, the clinic was empty. The receptionist told them to take a seat, then went to get the doctor. When he walked into the waiting room, they were stunned at his appearance.

He's as big as a house, Debbie thought to herself. Dr. Cecil Jacobson was a huge man, not much taller than Debbie, but weighing more than 250 pounds. He had a huge head with multiple chins and was so heavy he wheezed as he breathed. He was wearing a blue short-sleeve shirt, like something a hospital orderly would wear, but otherwise he didn't look much like a doctor. His curly gray hair was badly in need of a comb, and his clothes could have used a trip to the dry cleaner's.

Debbie was a little put off by his appearance, especially when she considered he'd be putting his hands all over her, but once he started talking, he quickly put her at ease. He welcomed them to his clinic, just as pleasant as her friend had described him. As he escorted them to his private office, he gave them a brief tour of his cramped quarters.

Like the doctor, his clinic was informal and casual, more like a well-worn living room than a sterile medical office. And the place had the feel of home. His wife was working at the front desk, and one of his daughters was in the laboratory peering through a microscope.

He was obviously an important man. Impressive-looking plaques and citations were all over the place. There were pictures of the doctor posing with President Richard Nixon and hobnobbing with Washington power brokers. But the most impressive display of all was on the wall for all the patients to see. Baby pictures—hundreds of them tacked to bulletin boards—attesting to his success at helping infertile couples. "My babies," he called them with obvious pride.

As they settled into his tiny office, he worked his way around his desk until he sat facing the Gregorys like a Buddha, with his arms folded across his ample stomach. A portrait of his wife and seven children was displayed prominently on his desk. When he noticed Steven and Debbie looking at his family, he joked that he obviously knew something about treating infertility—and had the track record to prove it.

He was relaxed and informal as he explained his method of treating infertility. It was very simple, he said. He didn't believe in subjecting his patients to expensive tests, or powerful drugs, or risky surgeries. He preferred a natural approach. He treated each patient with a natural hormone that would help her ovulate. Then, when the timing was right each month, he would send the woman to bed with her husband. There was nothing magical about it, but he guaranteed for Debbie that it would work. Eighty-five percent of his patients had gotten pregnant, he said, and if Steven and Debbie stayed with him long enough, they would go home with a baby too—just like the ones on the bulletin board.

To be successful, they had to promise to follow his regimen precisely. "No cheating," he said. If they weren't going to follow his rules, then he didn't want to treat them. He was in the midst of a sensitive, clinical study, he said, and the results were very important to him. He didn't want anyone messing up his statistics because they wouldn't follow his rules.

He made it clear he wanted Steven included in all the treatments, too. Although Debbie was the one who would be receiving the hormone injections, he wanted Steven to be present whenever possible. He treated them as a couple, he said, not individually.

He told them he wanted to work on the sexuality of their marriage. His goal was to get them into bed together every night—and he knew it wouldn't be easy. He suggested they take a warm bath together, or seduce each other over a bottle of champagne. He realized his program of timed intercourse could be a tremendous burden and could even strain their marriage, but he vowed to make it as pleasant as possible.

For nearly an hour he spoke to them practically nonstop, sometimes lecturing, sometimes bantering, sometimes joking, but always talking. They noticed an aura of brilliance about him as he discussed the scientific aspects of pregnancy, explaining functions of a woman's reproductive cycle that Debbie, much less Steven, had never heard of. He spoke in medical jargon that was way beyond them, yet he made it all sound so simple—just take a few of his hormone shots, make love when he told them, and they would have a baby. He guaranteed it.

When he finally paused to see if either of them had any questions, Debbie asked if he wanted to see her medical records. He said it wasn't necessary.

She told him she had been seeing Dr. Robert Barter and detailed her two previous operations and Dr. Barter's recommendation for a third. Dr. Jacobson scoffed. Debbie didn't need surgery, he said. Too many doctors used needless surgeries and unnecessary tests to pad their bills, he claimed, and left the records on his desk as he took the Gregorys to his lab to analyze Steven's semen specimen.

He poured a sample of sperm onto a slide and examined it under his microscope. After a few moments he announced the sperm wasn't the problem. The motility was good and the count was adequate, he said, and invited them to see for themselves.

When they returned to his office, he filled out a report on his assessment of the couple's problem. Debbie was suffering from what he called a "major risk of fetal defect" for which he prescribed injections of his miracle hormone, human chorionic gonadotropin, commonly known as HCG.

The HCG helped a woman ovulate, he explained, so he could time intercourse to coincide with the release of a ripened egg. If the HCG didn't work, he said they might add another fertility drug, Clomid. And if neither was successful, they would try artificial insemination. As a last resort they could try one of the new high-tech treatments, like in-vitro fertilization, but for the time being he preferred the most conservative, and least expensive, course of treatment—injections of HCG and daily sex.

Debbie was so impressed with her new doctor that she didn't stop to consider how easily he had arrived at the diagnosis. He never examined her or even glanced at her medical records. He didn't check the genealogy report they were supposed to fill out—Steven hadn't completed it anyway. The only test he performed was looking through a microscope at Steven's sperm for a few seconds. Yet after sitting across the desk and talking with them for an hour, he concluded she had a major risk of fetal defect. He was telling them everything they wanted to hear. Steven and Debbie thought he was a genius.

On the way out he walked them past the bulletin board and showed them the baby pictures again. Debbie looked at them closely. She couldn't wait to have one of her own. And this unconventional doctor was going to help her do it.

"He was everything you would want in a doctor," Debbie would say after that first visit. Personable. Friendly. Always accessible. He reminded Debbie of a down-home country doctor who was willing—even anxious—to take whatever time was necessary to answer her questions. He told Debbie to call him anytime, day or night. He would always be available. "You won't get a nurse," he said, "you'll get me." He was exactly what she was searching for.

Once Steven got over his initial reservations, he conceded that it wasn't as dreadful as he'd expected. "What can be so bad about being required to have sex with your wife every day?" he said.

They started the doctor's program right away. Before getting out of bed each morning, Debbie was supposed to take her temperature with a rectal thermometer and dutifully mark the result on a chart Dr. Jacobson had given her. Fluctuations in the basal body temperature chart would signify when she ovulated each month.

Debbie's treatments started a week after that first visit, on December 2, 1985, when the temperature chart signified the time was right. She and Steven arranged to leave work early and meet at the clinic. They were surprised to find the place was packed with women waiting for their HCG shots. When it was Debbie's turn, she was escorted to an examination room. In a moment the doctor breezed in, with a syringe protruding from his shirt pocket. Debbie unceremoniously lowered her slacks, the doctor injected her in the hip with ten thousand units of HCG, and as quick as that, he was off to see the next patient.

As instructed, they made love that night, and every night for the rest of the week. "This is great," Steven said after the first few days. They were like honeymooners again. No headaches. No excuses. No complaints about being too tired.

For each day of intercourse Debbie was supposed to draw an arrow on her temperature chart, then bring the chart to the clinic so Dr. Jacobson could inspect it. If everything was filled out correctly, he would draw a star on it at the end of the month, like a teacher approving her homework.

During the first month Debbie had seven HCG injections and marked her chart with fourteen consecutive arrows. But by the middle of their second week, their vision of sexual nirvana wasn't as blissful as Steven had imagined.

Their lovemaking was predetermined by ovulation schedules and temperature charts. They were both working long hours and were exhausted at the end of the day, yet they were obligated to perform every night, whether they were in the mood or not. Debbie wondered how many people besides newlyweds, or couples on a Caribbean vacation, actually slept together fourteen nights in a row.

When she finally had her period, announcing that the first month of treatments hadn't worked, she was secretly relieved. She needed a break—and so did Steven. But soon enough it was time to start the next month of treatments—and they felt they were becoming trapped in a vicious cycle.

Debbie got up every morning, jabbed herself with a thermometer, then rushed off to work, where she felt guilty for lying to her boss about her reasons for leaving early three times a week. She didn't want anyone at the office to know she was consulting an infertility doctor, so she claimed she was making a sales call when she was actually sneaking off for a shot in the hip. She usually met Steven at Dr. Jacobson's office, then went home to have sex. Just a few months earlier they had been uncertain about having a baby, but now they were trying harder than anyone they knew. "Our whole life is becoming, 'Let's have a baby,'" Debbie said one day in frustration. The strain was causing tension at home, and before long Debbie wasn't drawing arrows on her chart every night.

After the third month of injections they decided to postpone the treatments for a while. Despite the doctor's guarantee, the HCG shots weren't working. Debbie started to wonder if she was cut out to be a mother. There was a history of fertility problems in her family. She was an only child—her mother had tried for eight years to conceive her—and two of her aunts never had children. Over the years she had been less than conscientious about birth control without suffering the consequences.

As much as she wanted a child, the stress was becoming intolerable. Her life wasn't her own anymore. She was going to the clinic so often that she didn't have any free time for herself. She didn't see her friends. The infertility treatments were in control of their lives. The doctor set their schedules and told them when to make love.

When Debbie decided to stop, she was afraid to tell the doctor. She remembered his admonition about ruining his statistics. She worried that when she wanted to resume, he would banish her from the program forever and she would never get pregnant. Steven, at that point, didn't care. He thought it would be a blessing if the doctor dropped them. "Just call," he said.

Debbie phoned the doctor and apologized, explaining that the stress was wearing them down. "It's not that I don't want to have a child," she said. "But I'm working ten and twelve hours a day. This is just too difficult." She said she needed a break.

To her relief Dr. Jacobson couldn't have been more understanding. "No problem," he said. "A lot of women need to take a break from time to time." He told Debbie to call him in a few months when she was ready to resume.

Chapter Three

He was known to some as a pioneer, a genius, the preeminent expert in his field, the doctor whom other physicians called upon when their infertility cases were too tough to handle by themselves. One obstetrician would admit to keeping the easy cases for himself and referring the impossible ones to Cecil Jacobson. "Those are the kind he likes to treat," the obstetrician would say.

In many respects Cecil Bryan Jacobson was a simple country doctor who didn't mesh with the nuances of metropolitan medicine. He wasn't a member of the country-club set, and as a teetotaler and devout Mormon, he didn't travel the cocktail-party circuit. When he kept doctor's hours and closed his clinic on Tuesdays and Thursdays, he didn't head for the golf course—he went to the farm, where he raised food for the poor and conducted fertility experiments on animals.

His fascination with reproductive genetics began as a boy in Salt Lake City, Utah, where he was born October 2, 1936. His friends would remember how he caught frogs and small animals around the ponds near his home and watched intently as they reproduced—then dissected them to study their reproductive systems.

He was a fourth-generation Mormon, whose great-grandfather had fled religious persecution and trekked across the plains with other Mormon settlers in search of a new home out west. The Church of Jesus Christ of Latter Day Saints encouraged members to raise large families and considered children spiritual blessings, espousing that followers were "spirit children" before birth who were waiting to inhabit earthly bodies and then become "gods" or "goddesses" in the next life. For a young Mormon man

14

there was hardly a more noble profession than being a doctor who helped women produce humanly temples for spirit children to inhabit.

At the time Cecil was in school, the Mormons were more advanced in genetics than most scientists, as they conducted a massive genealogy project in Salt Lake City, where Church members were compiling genealogy charts on generations of ancestors. The information would be used to conduct religious ceremonies, like baptisms and marriages for long-dead relatives, but an outgrowth of the project was that it isolated major genetic disorders that were being passed from generation to generation. Cecil became involved in the genealogy project long before most people had even heard of the science of genetics, and when he enrolled as a premed student at Utah State University in 1954, he majored in genetics.

Before he earned his undergraduate degree, his schooling was interrupted when he was sent overseas to do missionary work for the Church. His mission took him to Germany, where he proselytized to strangers in the park or went door to door, trying to gain Mormon converts. When he returned to Utah, he got his degree, then moved to Washington, D.C., in 1960, where he enrolled in medical school at George Washington University.

From the beginning Cecil thrived in the academic environment. One of his classmates, Tom Jones, another young Mormon from Salt Lake City who was studying to be an obstetrician, would remember Cecil as "one of the smartest guys" in school. During lectures, while Jones and his classmates were furiously scribbling notes, he would glance over at Cecil and see him sitting back in his chair, occasionally jotting down something the professor said, and the rest of the time just listening as if he was bored. But when they later compared notes, Cecil's two pages covered the salient points better than Jones's fifteen pages. "He had an uncanny ability to abstract whatever was important," Jones would remember.

It wasn't long before Cecil was attracting the attention of his professors. "He had talents that far outstripped others in his class," his anatomy professor, Ira Pelford, would recall. Because the science of genetics was so new, GWU didn't have a genetics department, much less a genetics laboratory, where Cecil could perform his experiments. So he created one.

His area of expertise was cytogenetics—"just a fancy name for chromosomes," as he liked to say. In one of the early experiments in his new lab, he eclipsed anything that even his professors were doing. From a concoction of human tissue, bone marrow, and blood, he managed to grow chromosomes—twenty-three pairs of threadlike structures that resemble paper dolls within the nuclei of cells. He developed a method of harvesting them until they reached a stage where he could add a chemical to freeze them and stop their growth. Then he would spread the cells on a slide, stain them, and analyze them under a high-powered microscope. His discovery would become an essential cornerstone of future genetics work.

"He was far in advance of his time," remembered Dr. Robert Barter, who was chairman of the university's obstetrics and gynecology department, and who later would become Debbie Gregory's gynecologist. A meticulous surgeon, Dr. Barter was known as a gruff, no-nonsense disciplinarian who struck terror into the hearts of underlings. Whenever a resident stepped out of line in the operating room, he could expect to be scrubbing the next time with the authoritarian department chairman. "He would cut you down in a second," one of his students would say, "but he wasn't often wrong."

Although Dr. Barter didn't take a liking to many students, he recognized Cecil's extraordinary talents and took him under his wing. Cecil became known as one of "Barter's Boys" and was hired to teach genetics to older medical students. The university sent him to The Hague to attend the International Congress of Genetics, where his chromosome-harvesting technique was applauded by his fellow scientists. Before long he was becoming known outside the university as well.

Washington, D.C., in the early 1960's was an exciting and progressive place to be—the Kennedys had come to town, bringing with them a pioneering spirit for exploration and discovery, not to mention additional funding for research. Soon after taking office, President Kennedy, whose sister Rosemary was mentally retarded, announced a "comprehensive and coordinated attack on the problem of mental retardation" and formed a blue-ribbon panel for the prevention and cure of birth defects.

Cecil was hired as a consultant by the Food and Drug Administration to study how food additives affected chromosomal abnormalities, and he was called in as a technical adviser to the White House Conference on Mental Retardation. The military made him a consultant on a top-secret project to study the effects of radiation exposure on soldiers during the height of the Cold War. He conducted chromosomal studies on dogs to determine ways to save the bone marrow of the President, members of Congress, and other top government officials in the event of radiation exposure. The Navy asked him to set up a lab like the one he'd established at the university. And he was hired by the U.S. government in another top-secret study to determine the risk of genetic damage to U.S.-embassy personnel in Moscow who were being bombarded with sound waves. He got a paid fellowship from the National Science Foundation for Birth Defects to conduct research on the prevention of mental retardation, and the National Science Foundation funded a teaching position for him at GWU as a special lecturer in human genetics.

All of this before he even got his medical degree.

After his first year of medical school he had married a British-born stewardess, Joyce Kenyon, whom he'd met in Utah after returning from his missionary work. She was a non-Mormon who converted a few years later. Their friends would describe them as a stereotypical Mormon couple. He was domineering, she was submissive. He did the talking, she did the listening. He would make the money, she would raise the children. Their first child was born while he was still in school, and together they often worked late into the night harvesting his precious chromosomes. His friends would recall that after the birth of their son, they sometimes brought the baby into the lab and kept him warm in the lab incubator.

For Cecil these were the best of times. "We were flying by the seat of our pants," he would say, "but we were having successes." His greatest success, however, was about to come, and like so much of his work, it would set off a firestorm of controversy.

Cecil graduated from medical school in 1964 and enrolled in a graduate program at George Washington University for obstetrics and gynecology, but his medical career was nearly derailed before it got started. When he took his medical boards, he almost flunked. He passed by the slimmest margin, getting a 75.8 "general average" when a 75 was the minimum. He was spending so much time in the lab, rather than attending to patients like the other students in his class, that his lack of clinical training was evident. He scored well below average on several sections, like surgery and pediatrics. Nevertheless, he was licensed to practice medicine in the District of Columbia in 1965.

Even then Cecil didn't get the same practical experience as his classmates. While the rest of the ob/gyn department was completing a two-year internship and learning how to deliver babies, perform surgeries, and treat women for gynecological problems, Cecil took a "mixed internship" that afforded him more time for conducting research in the lab than for working in the delivery room.

He was a master of the microscope whose experiments were limited only by the bounds of his imagination. His colleagues marveled at his fearlessness but also worried about his recklessness. In those days, before the proliferation of medical malpractice suits, doctors were held in almost godlike esteem. Most hospitals had yet to establish medical-review committees, and physicians had virtual carte blanche to do whatever they deemed best for their patients—even without the patients' knowledge or permission. Cecil's daring and swashbuckling presence in the lab served him well in that casual climate.

While conducting a seemingly innocuous study of how a viral infection affects a pregnancy, he wondered whether a mother would pass along the virus to her fetus. As an experiment he stuck a blunted needle into the sac surrounding the fetus and extracted a sample of amniotic fluid. Considering his minimal obstetrical training, it was a tremendous risk. Fortunately, it was a success and led to a revolutionary discovery.

While analyzing the chromosomes he counted forty-seven, not forty-six, meaning the fetus had Down's syndrome. Even Cecil would acknowledge his discovery as "blind luck." He hadn't been looking for Down's, but his discovery would mean debilitating diseases could be diagnosed before birth through a procedure known as amniocentesis. Genetics counselors would no longer have to recommend sterilization for couples who had conceived one child with severe birth defects and feared their next would be born with abnormalities as well.

Amniocentesis itself was not a new discovery. Doctors and scientists had performed amnios since the late nineteenth century to relieve abdominal pressure in women, and since the 1950's amniocentesis had been used for gender determination and to diagnose Rh incompatibility, a potentially fatal mismatch of blood between the mother and baby. But Cecil was one of the first to stick a needle into a healthy, ongoing pregnancy. A British research team attempted it shortly before him, and a team from Northwestern University was close behind him, but Cecil would be credited with being the first American to perform amniocentesis for prenatal diagnosis.

Dr. Albert Gerbie was a member of the Northwestern University team that was conducting amniocentesis research, and was also sticking needles into pregnant women to withdraw amniotic fluid. He realized the risk he and Cecil were taking. "It takes guts, both for the doctor and the patient," he would say. But Dr. Gerbie's situation was different from Cecil's. Gerbie was a trained obstetrician who had been asked to assist the research project because his partner, a geneticist like Cecil, didn't feel qualified to be drawing the fluid himself. But Cecil didn't have that fear as he poked the unsuspecting patient with the needle. In later years he never would have gotten away with it. "You'd have to have an institutional review board, a human-subjects review committee, and then they would never approve it," Dr. Gerbie would say.

From the outset Cecil's work sparked debate. He was beset by critics who accused him of gross recklessness for tampering with an ongoing pregnancy. Puncturing the sac would lead to miscarriages and cause genetic disorders, they argued. Then theologians joined the fray and accused him of trying to play God by interfering with the miracle of human reproduction. His genetic diagnosis would prompt a woman to seek an abortion rather than give birth to a Down's syndrome child. Others said the experiment wouldn't work at all.

Cecil not only weathered the criticism, he seemed to revel in the controversy. He would say his most pressing concern was consulting his Church elders about the moral implications of performing a medical procedure that could promote abortions, but once he obtained their permission, he moved ahead with his amnio work. In later years his experiments would be expanded to include prenatal diagnosis of Tay-Sachs disease, spina bifida, and dozens of other genetic diseases, although it would take years for the safety and effectiveness of his amnio work to be authenticated.

Considered brilliant before his experiments with amniocentesis, Cecil Jacobson was now elevated to the status of genius. He was awarded a prestigious fellowship, the Josiah Macy Fellowship in Obstetrics, that allowed him to expand his laboratory research. While his classmates continued to pull all-night duty in the delivery room, Cecil was conducting extensive studies on the causes of repeated miscarriages and birth defects. He published heavily and presented his findings at medical and scientific expositions throughout America and overseas.

He was asked to set up genetics laboratories at several other hospitals in Washington. He conducted a chromosome survey of fifteen hundred newborns and a year-long study of deliveries at nearby Children's Hospital. He became one of the most prolific cytogenetic researchers in the country, authoring nearly fifty studies during the next six years, and his work was published in some of the top medical journals in America and Britain.

As the only geneticist in the ob/gyn department at GWU, Cecil was conducting most of his experiments without supervision. He was juggling so many research projects and experiments that no one could keep up with him. He wasn't subject to the same rules as the rest of the ob/gyn department, and in effect no one had a clue about what he was doing, or how he did it. "He was in there every day working on heaven only knows what," remembered a university colleague.

An imposing figure, he was usually the largest, and loudest, person in the room. "If you were ever in his presence, you wouldn't forget him," recalled a university colleague. Even as a young researcher he had the arrogance and swagger of a senior surgeon, was oblivious to the hospital pecking order, and never was cognizant of his place. He didn't endear himself to many of his peers, who toiled all night in the delivery room, then had to listen to Cecil boast about his latest trip to testify on Capitol Hill or his latest invitation to address some of the nation's top medical experts.

Never accused of being humble, he constantly touted his research projects, often considering them more important than anything his contemporaries were attempting. He seemed always to be working on an experiment he claimed would yield spectacular results, so most residents never gave it a second thought when he started pestering them to provide him with the ovaries of women who had undergone a hysterectomy in the university's hospital. Normally, the ovaries would be discarded, but Cecil explained he'd found a use for them. He wanted to retrieve the eggs from the ovaries and attempt to fertilize them in his laboratory. He provided some half-cocked explanation about developing the world's first test-tube baby.

One visitor to his lab during that time was Dr. Henry Nadler, one of the leading geneticists in the country, who had been part of the amniocentesis team at Northwestern University. Dr. Nadler had become a visiting professor at

GWU, and he would remember his first meeting with Dr. Jacobson, as Cecil invited him to peer through the microscope at his fledgling attempts to breed test-tube babies. Nadler had never seen anything like it. Cecil's work was years ahead of its time. Cecil later explained that he'd managed to get the eggs to reproduce to the four-cell stage, but no further. He was convinced the problem was with the medium in which he was cultivating the cells, but those who witnessed his work were duly impressed. "Some of the in-vitro work he was doing was really very dramatic," Dr. Nadler would recall. "He was certainly as knowledgeable in genetics as anyone in the OB field. No question about it."

In reality Cecil's genetics laboratory was little more than a closet containing a microscope and a dark room. One of his employees, Jadda Varhidy, a Hungarian immigrant, was surprised during her job interview to discover that Cecil was nearly twenty years younger than she was. He was only twenty-six at the time but was so sure of himself that he seemed much older. When he took her to his lab during the interview, he began dissecting a human placenta in a dish. He continued to slice it apart, then asked if she felt faint. When she said no, he hired her.

He liked Jadda, he said, because she was old enough that she wouldn't be quitting to have a baby, or constantly missing work to take care of her kids when the baby-sitter didn't show up. When he hired another lab assistant, Faye Redwine, he told her basically the same thing. One of his first questions to her concerned the type of birth control she was using. He said he was fed up with women getting pregnant and taking maternity leave. He often asked the lab assistants about their sex lives, inquiring whether they were "getting any" or if they "had fun" the previous night.

Despite his eccentricities his employees generally enjoyed working for him. He supported them and fought for their pay raises. He had a "good sense of humor" and was "extremely smart," Jadda Varhidy would remember. He trained her to grow amnio cultures from blood and body tissue.

Faye Redwine was one of his few undergraduate lab assistants who would become a geneticist in her own right, and later would head her own genetics laboratory at the Medical College of Virginia in Richmond. She would call Cecil "the most interesting person I've ever met," although the more she observed his work, the more she concluded he was a mediocre researcher, at best. "He didn't conduct research in the way it's normally conducted," she would say. "Not even close. He would do something and make a conclusion from it, whether or not the data was sound, or whether or not he had any data."

Faye was surprised at how little time he actually spent in the lab. He was supervising genetics laboratories at two hospitals, teaching a full slate of courses at the medical school, lecturing at seminars all over the country, juggling a host of research projects, applying for research grants, acting as lay leader of his church, and raising a family. He didn't have adequate time for any of them.

From what she saw, most of his lab work was being done by a small army of assistants. "He would breeze in, bless the operation, and leave," she remembered. He didn't provide much guidance or instruction for Faye or the other lab techs, and they learned to grow the amnio cultures by trial and error. Was an hour too long to leave the cultures in the oven? Was forty-two minutes too short? To the techs' amusement he sometimes performed the culture work himself, for the benefit of a class of students he was teaching. He presented a comical sight, wearing a surgical mask with a hole cut out for his nose, as he sweated profusely at the lab bench. The techs wondered why he bothered to wear a mask at all.

But most of all Faye was aghast at the "circus atmosphere" that surrounded some of his research studies. "Everything he did he made a big production out of," she would say. Most studies ended with a grand announcement that proclaimed some new and astounding results.

Because so many of his research projects had a flair for the sensational, he was often written up in the popular press, not just in medical journals. He appeared on television and was quoted in newspapers and magazines. Some of his critics would say his research seemed to have a hidden agenda, or to capitalize on whatever fad was in vogue at the time. Because Mormons didn't smoke tobacco, drink alcohol, coffee or tea, some people would find it curious that much of his research for a while set out to prove that tobacco, alcohol, and caffeine were responsible for birth defects.

Then, when pollution became a national concern, he announced studies linking birth defects with environmental problems. Although much of his work would prove to be true, his reasoning was considered by other geneticists to be overly simplistic. He theorized that the longer a woman lives, the higher the risk of producing defective offspring because she is exposed to mutagens in the environment that contaminate her eggs.

Then, during the height of the psychedelic drug culture, he declared he'd found a link between birth defects and the use of LSD.

He'd been asked to investigate why an unusually high number of women at a home for unwed mothers in Washington were giving birth to babies with spina bifida. He announced that the problem was drug use. He was invited to testify before Congress; then he and a GWU pediatrician were given a Justice Department grant to conduct an in-depth study. He began working with a group of young, pregnant LSD users, who answered ads in underground newspapers or who were referred to him by local physicians, clergy, and adoption agencies. Those who were working with him at the time recalled his genuine concern for the teenagers. He spent hours in counseling sessions with them, preaching against the evils of drugs and sounding more like a minister than a doctor.

Cecil was concerned that many of the teenagers were neglecting to get proper prenatal care, and he warned them they wouldn't be allowed to deliver the baby at the hospital unless they were first examined at the prenatal care clinic. The assertion wasn't true, but he used it as a means of making sure the teenagers got the proper medical attention. The ploy was successful for a while and led to more girls receiving complete examinations and blood work, but then someone realized that what Cecil was doing was illegal. Doctors couldn't offer a quid pro quo to coerce women into the clinic. Cecil, however, thought there was nothing wrong with it. As long as the teenagers received the necessary medical attention, he wasn't concerned how it was accomplished. He was a firm believer in the end justifying the means.

After two years his research study was released to the public in 1970 and billed as the "first extensive, long-term study" of the relationship between LSD and birth defects. A headline in *The New York Times* announced, "Study of LSD Spurs Suspicions of Drug's Link to Birth Defects."

The study group involved 112 women who had ingested LSD before, during, or after conception. Although the research was the ninth study on the subject—four had found a link, and five hadn't—Cecil's was the first to monitor the women during their pregnancy. He and a partner reported that the miscarriage rate was double the normal population, and the rate of children born with genetic abnormalities was 6 in 62, when the general population was 6 in 1,000.

The results were spectacular and alarming—except that Cecil's study was flawed. When other researchers tried to replicate his work, they couldn't do it. He had failed to sort out LSD from a wide range of other possible factors, such as poor nutrition, the history of previous illness, and venereal disease. When the Justice Department funding expired, the project wasn't renewed. But by then Cecil had moved on to a host of other projects, and a follow-up study was never conducted to determine the long-term effect on the women or their children.

When Faye Redwine heard about the study, she wasn't surprised. "He was long on show and short on substance," she said. "If he had channeled his brilliance into proper training and technique, he truly would have been a world leader."

Other geneticists who observed Cecil's work over the years would reach a similar conclusion.

"His work was never quite as thorough as many would have liked," recalled Dr. Joe Leigh Simpson, a GWU resident who later went on to head the genetics department at the University of Tennessee. Dr. Simpson thought Cecil's work in those days was "frenetic," as Dr. Jacobson jumped from one project to another, cranking out nearly a dozen studies a year in the late sixties and early seventies. "When someone is that energetic, it sometimes bothers people," Dr. Simpson would say.

Cecil was a much-sought-after speaker who never met an audience he didn't like. He could hold a meeting spellbound, especially in the often dry and stuffy world of reproductive medicine. Once, when he was invited to present a paper at a symposium, he was supposed to send the reviewer a copy in advance so a discussion could be prepared. But Cecil submitted his paper shortly before he walked to the podium. The reviewer would recall that the paper was incomplete and barely intelligible, yet Cecil's oral presentation was a huge success.

Another time, during the late 1960's, he was invited to deliver a key address on amniocentesis at a national forum sponsored by the National Institutes of Health. The invitation was a great honor, extended to only the best and brightest scientists in the country, and Cecil's presentation was well received, as usual. But behind the scenes his work wasn't so highly praised.

Before the conference each participant had agreed to submit a manuscript for inclusion in a textbook on amniocentesis. Cecil's chapter was supposed to explain how the procedure was performed, but when he finished his presentation, he was the only one who didn't turn in a paper.

The doctor in charge of the conference, Dr. Felix De la Cruz of the National Institutes of Health, hounded him for months. Meanwhile, publication of the textbook was delayed. "It was a horrendous experience," Dr. De la Cruz would remember, and he vowed never to invite Cecil to another meeting. Finally Dr. De la Cruz "trapped" Cecil at his office and extracted a "very brief manuscript." In the end the textbook, edited by Dr. Albert Dorfman of the University of Chicago, would remain the authoritative source on amniocentesis for years to come, even if it was nearly a year overdue. Cecil never explained his delay nor offered an apology. "That's beneath him," Dr. De la Cruz would scoff.

Despite all of Cecil's amniocentesis research, he didn't publish any of it in reputable, refereed journals, apart from some early papers to announce his Down's syndrome discovery. "Unless you publish and present your findings in a scientific forum, where there could be an exchange of opinion, where you could be queried and forced to respond, then everything gravitates to trust," Dr. De la Cruz said. "Scientists are a bunch of people who do not believe in trust. They want to see the data. And he never did that. He tends to publish his experience in amnio in the popular press, like *Parade* magazine."

One year in the late 1960's Cecil wrote several abstracts to be considered for publication by the American Society of Genetics. In a typical year five hundred abstracts might be submitted, with only fifty to seventy-five accepted for an oral presentation, and another one hundred to two hundred accepted for "posting" at the convention. The rest were included in a booklet as a courtesy.

That year, as Dr. Simpson leafed through the booklet of also-rans, he found three or four of Cecil's papers. Most researchers had faced similar rejections and didn't take them personally, but Cecil seemed insulted. He later would say he believed some people in the scientific community were out to get him, and he attributed these and other rejections to professional jealousy.

He withdrew from the genetics society, and over time he dropped his membership in most of the professional societies to which other leading geneticists belonged. "The organizations that Cecil should have been involved in, he wasn't involved in any of them," Dr. Simpson would say.

In 1969 Cecil's research took a dramatic turn that would lead to his most controversial work. He was awarded a grant to fund a sabbatical to Cambridge University, where he was named a "guest scientist" in the Reproductive Physiology Unit. Cambridge at the time was the Mecca

for fertilization research, and Cecil worked side by side
with the team of doctors who later developed the world's
first test-tube baby. Cecil's role was to do chromosomal
analysis on the ovum to detect defects caused by the fertilization attempts. But it wasn't the in-vitro fertility work
that fascinated him as much as the research he conducted
with Christopher Polge, the first scientist to freeze sperm
successfully.

Polge wasn't a physician; he was an animal scientist,
and Cecil collaborated with him in studying the ovulatory
cycle of pigs. The pigs were useful because their reproductive systems closely resembled humans. Cecil and Polge
artificially inseminated the pigs at different stages of the
ovulatory cycle, then analyzed how the timing affected
the ovum. The research was the precursor of Cecil's later
infertility work. It also was the beginning of his work with
human chorionic gonadotropin, HCG.

The hormone had been manufactured synthetically for
years, but a pharmaceutical company was finding it prof-
itable to extract the hormone from the urine of pregnant women. The HCG was being exported from Holland,
where little white vans and dog-drawn wooden carts traveled the Dutch cities and countryside collecting urine from
pregnant women. It was called the "Mooter to Mooter"
program, Dutch for going "mother to mother."

Cecil ostensibly had gone to Cambridge to complete work
toward his Ph.D. in reproductive genetics. As part of his
Ph.D. program he also was slated to study in Copenhagen,
under the tutelage of a noted Danish geneticist, but he
found his work with animals in England so fascinating—
he would call it "mind expanding"—that he didn't leave.
He got sidetracked and remained in England with his wife,
and by then three children, for another seven months. He
didn't complete his doctoral work.

When he returned to America, he was brimming with
fresh ideas. He bought nitrogen tanks and began his own
experiments with freezing sperm in his lab. For years he
had been doing research with semen from primates. He
liked to jolt listeners with his story about the time a fellow
researcher, who was collecting semen from a large ape, had

his arm ripped from its socket when the ape pulled him against the side of a hydraulic squeeze cage. The moral of his story was, "You want to be careful when you're collecting specimens from primates."

But now his research focused on his new theory—developed from the pigs—that the timing of ovulation was the key factor in a healthy pregnancy. The eggs had to be fertilized at the proper time during ovulation; otherwise, the sperm would inseminate an egg that was overcooked or undercooked and cause birth defects.

Cecil bought a farm in rural Virginia, near the Blue Ridge Mountains, where he raised pigs and other animals and expanded his barnyard experiments. He injected the swine with HCG so he could control the release of the egg; then he would artificially inseminate them with pig semen and later analyze the fertilized eggs.

His research with semen also expanded into another, more controversial area. He began experimenting with sex selection.

Through amniocentesis he already was able to predict the gender of a child before birth, but he told a colleague, Dr. Edward Gahres, that he was on the verge of being able to predict gender before conception. He claimed he could distinguish between sperm that produced a male and sperm that produced a female. By freezing a batch of male-producing sperm, he would be able to artificially inseminate a woman to produce a son. His research would be of great interest to people of countries, or of religions, that valued males over females.

Dr. Gahres realized the ramifications and warned his friend to move cautiously, but Cecil announced his potential discovery to others at the university as something that could be even bigger than the development of amniocentesis. Then it quietly went away. As far as anyone knew, he failed to refine his research before his attention was diverted elsewhere, and the project apparently got lost among his other unfinished studies.

About that time he was also doing experiments on a 256-cell conceptus, the stage at which an embryo can be removed from the test tube and implanted in the uterus.

In England he had been doing similar studies on animals, and he saw no reason why a human's surrogate mother had to be a human. He suspected a human embryo could be transplanted into animals as well. He often spoke of which animal would be most suitable—a pig, chimpanzee, or cow.

"He talked about it a lot," remembered his longtime friend, Dr. Tom Jones. Cecil believed that humans were descended from apes, and he told Jones he believed the experiment had already been proved successful. "How do you think Adam got here in the first place?"

Although Cecil talked openly about the possibility of using an animal surrogate, he kept the results, if any, to himself. He realized how controversial his project would be. "If he did the experiments, he didn't say," Jones remembered.

Dr. Henry Nadler, Cecil's amniocentesis colleague from Northwestern University, would also recall discussing the experimental possibilities with Cecil, but he never heard about the final outcome, either. "I have no idea whatever happened to that work," Nadler would say. "I don't remember what the legality or the ethics were at the time. He didn't publish much about it."

But some of those who knew Cecil well had little doubt that he attempted the experiment. Years later there would be considerable speculation about what other experiments he was conducting at his farm near the mountains.

Chapter Four

When Debbie Gregory was scheduled to resume her infertility treatments in the summer of 1986, she couldn't force herself to make the call. She had agreed with Dr. Jacobson to take a three-month respite, but when the deadline expired, she needed more time. She and Steven wondered whether having a child was worth the trouble. The doctor's program of hormone shots and prescription sex had so dominated their lives and strained their marriage that they wondered whether they wanted to continue. They finally decided that if they didn't do something soon, it would be too late. Debbie's biological clock was ticking and time was running out.

Debbie returned to Dr. Jacobson on October 1, 1986, almost eight months after her last visit. He greeted her like an old friend, making her feel as if she'd never left. He said he wanted to try something new this time—he would add another fertility drug, Clomid, to the hormone injections. The only drawback was a possibility of swollen ovaries, so he performed a brief pelvic examination to check her before administering the powerful drug.

The first month was easy. Debbie had three HCG injections and eight nights of intercourse, which didn't interfere with their lives at all. The second month was more rigorous—three consecutive weeks of shots every Monday, Wednesday, and Friday—until they felt they were becoming trapped in the same rut again. Just as they considered quitting again—Debbie's period was late.

She called the doctor, and he told her to bring in a urine sample on her next visit. He gave her specific instructions on how to collect it, telling her not to drink liquids the night before and to collect a sample of her first urine in the morning to ensure it was the most powerful concentrate.

On Monday, November 24, she left work early and went to the clinic. Steven was busy at work and couldn't get away. Instead of going to the examination room where she normally got her injections, Dr. Jacobson took her into his private office, where they had met for the initial consultation. He took the urine sample into the next room and returned with a pregnancy-test kit, then pulled up a chair so he could sit on the same side of the desk as Debbie.

Using an eye dropper, he collected a few drops of urine and mixed them with a solution from the pregnancy test, then placed the kit on his desk and waited. His test kit wasn't much different from the ones Debbie had seen at the grocery store, but Dr. Jacobson explained it was so sensitive, he could detect a pregnancy just two days after conception.

They exchanged small talk a while longer; then, suddenly, he said, "Look."

In the middle of the test pack was a plus sign, like the crosshairs of a target sight. It was vivid blue.

"Congratulations," Dr. Jacobson said, getting up from his chair to hug her. The test was positive.

Debbie couldn't believe it. She checked it again to make sure it was true.

"I told you if you stuck with the program, you'd get pregnant," he said. The layoff had obviously helped to relieve Debbie's tension, he said, which was the key to getting pregnant. Once she learned to relax, then everything clicked.

He said the deep-blue color of the test indicated Debbie's hormone levels were high. "That's a really strong one," he said, and drew three plus signs on her chart to signify the potency of the test. He calculated her due date on a form letter he said he would send to her obstetrician when it was time.

To the best of our estimate, this patient conceived on Nov. 13 and would be expected to deliver around Aug. 5. We thank you for referring this pleasant couple and share their joy in this pregnancy.

Cecil B. Jacobson, M.D.

As Debbie was leaving, he congratulated her again and gave her the pregnancy test to take with her. "Show it to your husband," he said. She looked at it again and smiled. The plus sign was shining bright as a beacon.

Once ambivalent about having a child, Debbie was now hooked on motherhood. She bought baby books, studied all there was to know about pregnancy and prenatal care, and started dreaming of names for the baby. She and Steven called practically everyone they knew to share the good news.

Dr. Jacobson said he would refer Debbie to an obstetrician at the end of her first trimester, but for the time being he wanted her to continue her hormone injections. "I want to make sure the pregnancy takes," he said. From the way he described the HCG, it was like a magic elixir. It not only aided ovulation, but it also, he said, reduced the chance of a miscarriage.

He warned Debbie that miscarriages in these early pregnancies were very common. According to his calculations, in the first week of pregnancy Debbie had a 95 percent chance of losing the baby; but the chances improved to 65-35 the second week, 50-50 the third week, 35-65 the fourth week, and by the sixth week she would be out of danger. That's when he would stop doing pregnancy tests and start performing ultrasounds.

Until then, however, he said he wanted her to have a pregnancy test every week. Because he was able to detect pregnancies much earlier than other doctors, he said the weekly pregnancy tests were the only way to monitor such an early pregnancy. It wouldn't even show up on the ultrasound yet.

Steven went with Debbie for her next pregnancy test and sat anxiously as the doctor mixed the urine and reagent solution. He would later call it "the happiest moment of my life" as he watched the plus sign turn blue. Once again Dr. Jacobson said the test was so strongly positive that he marked another three plus signs on Debbie's chart.

* * *

Debbie was less than three weeks pregnant when the trouble began. She started to bleed. At first she thought she was having her period; the timing was right, but the flow was different—it was lighter and spottier than normal—but she knew from her pregnancy books that any bleeding was a bad sign. She called Dr. Jacobson right away. He was seeing another patient, but he took Debbie's call.

"As long as you're not cramping, don't worry," he told her. "It's going to be fine." He said it was common for a woman to bleed during her pregnancy, but just to be sure, he wanted her to come in so he could do another pregnancy test. Steven went with her; she was so upset, she was in no condition to go by herself. To their relief the test registered positive. Dr. Jacobson told her to relax. The worst thing she could do was get upset, he said. The stress was bad for her.

Debbie was supposed to fly to California that weekend to visit an old friend, but she wondered if it would be safe. She wanted to cancel her trip, but Dr. Jacobson advised her to go. "It will be good for you," he said. "Relax and enjoy yourself." The worst thing she could do was stay home and worry. Even if she lost the baby, it wouldn't be the end of the world, he said. "These things happen. Don't worry, you'll get pregnant again."

He gave her another HCG shot and wrote out a prescription for progesterone suppositories, which he said would control the bleeding; then he sent her off to California. As soon as she boarded the plane, she knew she'd made a mistake. "I shouldn't be doing this," she told herself. She was a nervous wreck, still bleeding and worried that she was losing the baby. The progesterone suppositories were melting in her purse, so she asked the flight attendant if she could store them in the plane's refrigerator.

When she arrived in California, she was so upset, she couldn't enjoy herself, but by the time she returned home a few days later, the bleeding had stopped. When she told the doctor, he gave her an "I-told-you-so" speech. "Don't you trust me?" he asked. "If I thought there was something to worry about, wouldn't I tell you?"

* * *

The bleeding resumed a week later. Dr. Jacobson continued to insist Debbie was fine, that bleeding during early pregnancy was common, that she had nothing to worry about; but she suspected he was just trying to placate her. One of her books on prenatal care described a similar condition called a threatened abortion—it was said to be serious, but not critical as long as the bleeding and cramping didn't last more than a few days.

She canvassed her friends, wanting to know if anyone had experienced bleeding during pregnancy. She even asked women she barely knew. As long as the woman had delivered a baby, Debbie was interested in her opinion. One woman whom she met during a sales call to Fairfax Hospital said that she'd bled "until I thought I was going to die" and then had given birth to a healthy baby girl. Debbie was relieved to know that someone else had agonized through a troubled pregnancy and had come out of it all right.

Dr. Jacobson said he ordinarily wouldn't schedule Debbie's first sonogram until she was six weeks pregnant, but since she was experiencing so many problems, he moved up the exam to her fourth week, on December 17. Steven went with her. When they got to the clinic, the doctor told her to sit in the waiting room and drink water to expand her bladder. He said it would improve the resolution of the ultrasound and make the images sharper. Just when Debbie thought she was going to burst, the doctor finally called her into the examination room and told her to lie down on the table.

She lifted her blouse, and Dr. Jacobson smeared a jellylike substance on her stomach; then he picked up a device that looked like a microphone—he called it a transducer—and maneuvered it over her abdomen. He asked Steven to turn off the light, and they sat in the darkness a moment watching the machine.

Ghoulish shades of black, gray, and white flickered across the screen that was no bigger than a 1950's television set.

"Here's her bladder," Dr. Jacobson said to Steven, as if Debbie weren't there. He pointed out Debbie's internal organs, like a professor teaching an anatomy class. "And here's the uterus." The machine was positioned where Debbie couldn't see it, and a smaller screen overhead was too far away for her to see clearly.

As he adjusted the transducer, Dr. Jacobson zeroed in on a tiny undulating shadow in the center of the screen. "Here's the baby," he announced.

Steven stepped closer to get a better look. The screen was so fuzzy, he couldn't decipher anything except a field of moving shadows. He moved closer until he was standing almost ear to ear with the doctor, but he still couldn't see what Dr. Jacobson was talking about.

The doctor pointed to a dark, shaded area within a white cloud. "There's Junior," he said, explaining it was the gestational sac. Steven had to take the doctor's word for it—he couldn't tell on his own.

Dr. Jacobson adjusted some knobs and dials and began taking measurements. "It's right on schedule," he said, explaining he was very impressed with the progress. "The baby is growing at the rate it should be growing." The size of the sac was twenty-six by twenty-three by thirty centimeters. The measurements didn't mean anything to Debbie or Steven, but the doctor said it was the yardstick by which they would chart the future growth.

He pressed another button, and a Polaroid print emerged from the machine, offering three views of the sac. The measurements were denoted by large white numbers in each frame.

He handed the Polaroid to Debbie and showed her the sac. The resolution was even worse than what Steven had seen on the screen. The pictures looked more like clouds on the horizon than a view of her child, but the more she looked at it, the more visible the baby became. "Take it with you," Dr. Jacobson said. It was something they would look at often in the years ahead.

With each week Debbie was feeling more and more pregnant. She was gaining weight and her breasts were tender.

Despite the intermittent bleeding, she'd never felt better. She felt energized. She suspected the hormones coursing through her body were giving her strength as she prepared for the upcoming birth.

The Christmas holidays had always been a favorite time of year for her, but this year was extra special. She thought of Dr. Jacobson as a jolly Santa Claus who had given them a wonderful present. A special bond was forming between them. He was becoming more than their doctor—he was becoming their friend. She bought him a Christmas present and gave him a copy of an article from a women's magazine that listed his amniocentesis work among the top one hundred medical advances of all time. He laughed when she gave it to him and said several other women had brought him copies too.

She had been scheduled to visit her mother in Ohio, like every other year, but she was so involved in her treatments, and fearful that traveling again might cause her to bleed, that she canceled the trip. She celebrated Christmas with a sonogram on Christmas Eve.

During each sonogram Steven watched in fascination as the doctor wielded the transducer like a magic wand and made the child appear among the shadowy images that danced on the screen. He still couldn't see the baby by himself—Dr. Jacobson had to point it out for him—but the longer he stared at the screen, the more the shadowy shapes started to take the form of a tiny fetus.

Steven showed the sonogram photos to everyone he knew, like an obnoxious new father with a wallet full of baby pictures. He reminded Debbie of a woman she had known at work who was so proud of her sonograms that she had taped them on her desk. Debbie was a little more reserved, but not much.

The week after Christmas, Debbie started to bleed again. Dr. Jacobson gave her some more progesterone suppositories and assured her there was still nothing to worry about. As he predicted, the bleeding soon stopped and her prognosis brightened. On January 7, the eighth week, he detected fetal movement for the first time.

"There's Junior rolling over," he said. "He's moving around." According to the doctor's calculations, Debbie was past the point of danger. She was doing so well, he said, that he took her off the hormone shots. But within a few days she started bleeding again. He instructed her to collect a urine sample so he could perform another pregnancy test. Like the others, it was positive.

He continued the sonograms for the next two weeks and confirmed the sac was getting larger and the fetus was growing. The second week he said he could see the baby's arms and legs. When she went in for her regularly scheduled sonogram on February 4, she was ten weeks pregnant. She hadn't been bleeding lately, and the pregnancy finally seemed to be going smoothly.

As usual, she climbed on the examination table, and Steven took his customary position beside the doctor. Dr. Jacobson turned on the machine and ran the magic wand over Debbie's stomach, but this time the magic wasn't there. "It doesn't look good," he said solemnly. His tone was frightening.

"What's wrong?" Debbie asked.

The doctor didn't answer. He continued to move the transducer about in silence. Steven looked at the screen, but he didn't see anything different from before.

The doctor, usually upbeat and jovial, now was restrained and grim. "I have some bad news," he said finally.

"The sac is down," he said. "The baby has died."

Chapter Five

When Dr. Jacobson told Debbie that her baby was dead, she didn't believe him. "What do you mean?" she asked. She hadn't been bleeding in more than two weeks and believed the worst was behind her.

Dr. Jacobson asked if she'd been ill lately. Debbie explained she'd felt fine. She'd had a minor cold, she said, but otherwise had never felt better.

"That's what happened," Dr. Jacobson said. "The baby caught a virus and died." He said viruses were the most common cause of miscarriages. He calculated the baby had died around January 17, the last time Debbie had been bleeding. He recited some statistics about the frequency of miscarriages in early pregnancy, but Debbie wasn't listening. She was numb with shock. She heard the doctor talking, but his words weren't registering. She had just been dealt the worst news of her life, and she didn't care about statistics—she cared only about her baby.

She wondered if it had suffered. Although it was little more than a clump of rapidly changing cells, she had started to bond with it, like a living and breathing infant. It was as real to her as any child. She started to blame herself, as she thought of all the things she had done wrong. She should have taken better care of herself. She had been working too hard. She should have gotten more rest. She shouldn't have gone to California.

Dr. Jacobson tried to console her, saying she should start another cycle of treatments right away. "Your body is primed," he said. The best time to get pregnant, he said, was right after a miscarriage, when her body was still surging with hormones.

From her books she knew she would need a surgical procedure to extract the fetal tissue from her body. Between her tears she asked him to schedule a D and C. But Dr. Jacobson said it wouldn't be necessary. He hoped she would experience a "resorption," he said. The fetal tissue would absorb itself into her system. He told her to wait for a couple weeks to see what happened.

Debbie still wasn't focusing on what he was saying, but she *did* know that he wasn't making sense. "I've never heard of that," she said.

"Have you ever seen anyone who's been hit really hard on the arm?" he asked as he rolled up his shirtsleeve. "It leaves a large bruise, right? And what happens to the bruise? It just goes away, right? It just dissipates into the skin. That's what we're hoping for you." He said the baby would reabsorb into her system.

After resorption he said the chances were much better that she would get pregnant very quickly. In fact, she was probably so fertile at the moment that they could eliminate the Clomid from her treatments and use just the HCG.

When they got home, Debbie sat at the kitchen table and cried for the rest of the evening. Steven had to break the news to their parents—Debbie was incapable of phoning them herself.

In the following days friends sent them flowers and notes of condolence, giving their home the feel of a funeral parlor, except there was no memorial service, no casket, and no burial. The only tangible proof their child had ever existed was the set of sonogram pictures Debbie kept in her bedroom. She looked at them often in the days after the miscarriage, each time breaking into tears.

Steven had never seen her so upset, nor had he felt so despondent himself. He was thrust into the role of the stalwart husband, offering support and strength, even when he needed support himself. Together "they" had gotten pregnant, and now "they" had suffered the miscarriage.

A week later Debbie started bleeding again. It seemed like her normal period, but Dr. Jacobson said it was part of the miscarriage process—she might pass some fetal tissue, he explained, and he wanted her to collect a sample so he could analyze it. Later he said his tests confirmed that a virus had killed the baby, which only intensified Debbie's guilt.

Otherwise she had no obvious signs of a miscarriage. She had no heavy bleeding or cramping, and she certainly didn't pass the remains of an embryo. Just as Dr. Jacobson had predicted, she was experiencing a resorption.

When she told her mother and some of her friends, they said they had never heard of such a thing. Her mother asked if Dr. Jacobson knew what he was talking about. "Of course he does," Debbie said curtly. Dr. Jacobson was one of the top physicians in his field, she said. "Everybody knows him. He's even been written up in *Good Housekeeping* magazine."

Because they had told practically everyone they knew about the pregnancy, now when people asked about the baby, Debbie had to explain it was gone. The miscarriage was painful enough without constantly being interrogated about it. The worst questions were about the resorption. Some of her friends seemed rude with the way they gave her the third degree about her doctor's qualifications. She became defensive and withdrawn. And soon, rather than answer the questions, she started to avoid her friends altogether.

Debbie and Steven barely had time to mourn the loss of their child before they were back at the clinic trying to conceive another one. Debbie had been told on February 4 that she lost the baby—three weeks later, on February 27, she resumed the HCG shots.

After one month Debbie's period was late. Dr. Jacobson told her to bring in a urine sample. Just as he predicted, she was pregnant again. "I told you so," he said. He told Debbie she had conceived the first week after she resumed the treatments.

To the best of our estimate, this patient conceived on 3/5/87 and would be expected to deliver around Nov. 27, 87. We thank you for referring this pleasant couple and share their joy in this pregnancy.

Cecil B. Jacobson, M.D.

They didn't tell many people this time, just their families and a few close friends, in case something went wrong again. From the beginning the second pregnancy was more difficult than the first. Debbie felt sluggish and tired. Dr. Jacobson told her she should be thankful she didn't have morning sickness. Then, a week later, the real problems began. She started bleeding again. Dr. Jacobson prescribed some progesterone suppositories, and the bleeding stopped. He gave her a pregnancy test a few days later, "just to be sure the pregnancy is viable," he said, and the test was positive.

She lived in fear every time she went to the bathroom, frightened she would discover blood. She was concerned about what the constant stress was doing to the baby. She wouldn't forgive herself if she killed another one. One day, when she felt she couldn't take it anymore, she called Dr. Jacobson in tears.

He told her about the power of positive thinking. Relax and take it easy, he said. If he thought bed rest was the solution, then he would prescribe it, but otherwise, he counseled by way of a long-winded explanation, Debbie wouldn't miscarry just by working too hard. The conversation boosted her spirits and helped her get past the latest crisis. The next day she felt better again.

During the next few weeks she continued her regular HCG injections and progesterone suppositories and took a pregnancy test every week. At six weeks Dr. Jacobson said she was far enough along to start monitoring the pregnancy with sonograms again, and for the next three weeks she got a sonogram every week. He pointed out the sac each time and measured its growth. The sonograms were still as murky as ever, but Dr. Jacobson seemed pleased with the progress, so Steven and Debbie didn't question a good thing. They were gaining more trust in him all the time. His predictions about resorption had come true, and so had his prophecy about being primed to get pregnant right away.

By the time Debbie was ten weeks, she'd had twenty-two injections and three sonograms. Although she still felt tired all the time, she hadn't hemorrhaged in more than a month and was settling comfortably into an uneventful pregnancy. Then, on May 13, she went with Steven for her normal sonogram appointment. They went into the examination room where Dr. Jacobson prepped Debbie and turned on the machine. Right away the expression on his face told them the news was bad.

"The sac is down," he said. Debbie had miscarried again.

If Dr. Jacobson noticed their grief, he didn't react to it. "Don't be discouraged," he said. "Many women miscarry." One of his patients had lost seven babies, he said, and was getting HCG shots five days a week. Even his own wife had miscarried several times.

Debbie was too upset to talk, so Dr. Jacobson pulled Steven aside and told him not to allow Debbie to give up. He compared it to falling off a horse. Debbie had to pick herself up and get back into the saddle again.

When they got home, Debbie went to her bedroom and shut the door. She gathered up her keepsakes of the baby, then sat on her bed and tore up the sonogram photos, ripped the pages from her diary, and threw out the pregnancy tests. She told Steven she wanted to stop the treatments. She couldn't take any more. The emotional toll wasn't worth it. She hadn't even recovered from losing the first baby, and already she was grieving for another one.

Steven left her alone, but a few days later, when he thought the time was right, he told Debbie about his conversation with Dr. Jacobson. "He thinks we should try again," Steven said. "He says you're primed for pregnancy. This one just didn't take."

Obviously, Steven wasn't ready to give up. In time Debbie decided she wasn't either. The next one would be different, she told herself. The third time would be the charm.

Chapter Six

During the late 1960's and early 1970's, Cecil's star continued to rise at George Washington University. Although he was no longer one of "Barter's Boys"—Dr. Barter left and was replaced by a new department chairman—he was still the prima donna of the ob/gyn department. The new chairman, Dr. James Sites, was a softspoken gentleman whose style often clashed with his bombastic lab genius. People would remember Cecil's occasional temper tantrums as he tried to get more space for his lab and resources for his research. "Cecil drove Dr. Sites crazy," one resident would remember. Yet Dr. Sites tolerated Cecil's outbursts, believing he was working with a true prodigy. "As a geneticist he was tops in the city, if not in the country," Dr. Sites said.

Dr. Sites was a practicing ob/gyn who collaborated with Cecil on research into the causes of early miscarriages. He thought so highly of the young geneticist that, whenever he was stumped by a particularly vexing case, he sent the patient to Cecil for a genetic evaluation. As Dr. Sites later explained, "There are only three things you have to know in infertility. Are there eggs and sperm? Is there an incubator to grow them? And is the way to get them together normal? Most of us would find out if these three criteria were met." And if not, they would turn to Cecil for help. "Every practicing obstetrician has patients that Dr. Jacobson has worked up," Dr. Sites would say.

For more than a decade Cecil was the only geneticist in the Washington area. He instructed a full courseload of genetics classes at GWU and was often called upon to conduct special courses for obstetricians in training at several local hospitals. Most of the future obstetricians in the Washington area in those days received the extent of their genetics knowledge from Cecil, and practically every local ob/gyn learned to do amniocentesis from him, or from someone he had instructed.

He was constantly charging through the university corridors with a gaggle of students in tow. He became known as the Pied Piper of George Washington University. "It was like a duck and his ducklings," a former colleague remembered. He was generally one of the most popular professors on campus, who had a talent for injecting humor and vitality into boring and technical subjects. He took a keen interest in his students, both professionally and personally. If students needed money, he was good for a loan. If there was a personal problem, they could count on Cecil to help. He was quick to inquire about a student's family and was especially helpful to the incoming Mormon students, instructing them on the relationship between Mormon beliefs and science.

One student, John Lyles, who later became a Virginia obstetrician, learned so much from Cecil's course in beginning genetics that he signed up for two others. "He was an excellent teacher," Lyles would remember. "He brought genetics to life." Cecil taught his students how to draw amniotic fluid from the womb and study the chromosomes under the microscope. He taught students how a person's genes would affect future generations of ancestors and took them to a facility for the mentally retarded in Laurel, Maryland, to see firsthand how devastating birth defects could be. He even allowed his students to sit through his genetic-counseling sessions with patients, a practice that in later years would be ethically forbidden.

"He was just a regular, down-to-earth sort of guy," remembered one of his students, Doug Lord, who would become a Maryland obstetrician. "He wasn't one of these highfalutin guys who didn't want to talk to you. He liked to be one of the guys. Any peculiarities he seemed to have were chalked up to his being a devout Mormon."

But not all his students were so impressed. One of them was Dr. Richard Falk, who would later become director of the reproductive endocrinology department across the

street at the Columbia Hospital for Women. Dr. Falk was a
transplanted New Yorker who had worked at the National
Institutes of Health before attending George Washington
University. Before leaving New York, Falk had been told
by a geneticist at Mount Sinai Hospital about an "oddball"
type of doctor who was conducting "spectacular research"
in Washington, but whose studies couldn't always be veri-
fied. Falk had forgotten about the conversation until he
attended one of Dr. Jacobson's lectures on reproduction
and recognized Cecil's unusual name.

Even as a young resident Falk thought his instructor's
teachings were "way off base" and discarded his views
as a laboratory-bound geneticist who didn't have much
hands-on experience in treating patients. He and some of
the other residents would joke behind Cecil's back as he
counseled the students on the perils of tobacco, alcohol,
and caffeine and their link to birth defects. They called it
his "Mormon Agenda."

Falk couldn't understand how Cecil had become such a
respected figure at the university. He considered his professor a joke and thought that anyone who listened to
him closely would conclude he was more bluster than
substance.

He once took a tour of Cecil's lab and, like most other
visitors, was startled by the bizarre displays Cecil had
arranged, ostensibly to shock his guests. On the wall of his
office he'd hung a picture of a microcephalic infant—someone born with a small head. The photo was eye-catching,
to say the least, and those who saw it would never forget
it—an infant with a tiny head attached to a normal-sized
body, like something out of a freak show. Falk thought
it was bizarre that Cecil displayed it so prominently on
his wall.

Cecil also kept a collection of jars on a laboratory shelf
containing the mangled remains of fetal specimens that
didn't survive their horrible genetic defects. He enjoyed
startling his visitors with a tour of his grotesque display,
until one night someone broke in and destroyed it.

Years later Falk would look back and say: "Cecil sold
Robert Barter and Jim Sites a bill of goods that he was

a bloody genius. And basically that's all it took in those days. Medical schools were operated under a good-old-boy system. If the chairman wanted to hire someone, he got slapped on the back and was brought aboard."

Left to Cecil's own devices, his office would have been a disaster. When he got stuck in the lab, or holed up with a patient in his office, he had little concept of time. "He was like an absentminded professor," his secretary, Patty Drake, would recall. Like most of his employees, Patty would say she loved working for him. "He never got angry with any of the help."

Cecil worked long hours and rarely missed a day of work. Even when his appendix ruptured, he was out only a few days before he was back in the office, showing off the huge scar across his large belly.

Over the years he began to emerge from his lab to devote more time in the university hospital clinic, as he moved from a purely research role into working more directly with patients. As the GWU staff geneticist, he was often called in to consult on the difficult infertility cases, and he was still the man to see for amnio; but rather than just issuing a report to the referring physician, he was meeting with the patients himself.

His consultation sessions could be fascinating, or at the very least, entertaining; he spent as much time spinning whimsical stories about the mysteries of science and the future of genetics as he did discussing a patient's immediate problems. "He wasn't like other doctors," a patient from those days would recall. "He was always up. He was always cracking jokes."

During a typical workup he might suddenly veer from his discussion of infertility or genetics into a debate about politics, or religion, or the state of the economy, or the woeful morality of minorities, or the robber-baron attitude of insurance companies that he thought were pillaging the country. He counseled couples on the hereafter and advised them on their sex lives, sometimes going into such graphic detail about techniques and positions that he caused many a patient to blush. Some patients were mesmerized by his every word, viewing him as a true genius who could provide answers to more than just questions of infertility. Others were offended by his pompous attitude and bolted from his office after the initial consultation, never to be seen again.

The consultations were supposed to last thirty minutes, but he couldn't adhere to a tight schedule. He would get so wrapped up in lecturing his patients that he was constantly running late for his next appointment. His secretary learned to leave at least an hour's gap between appointments and ignored him whenever he checked his upcoming appointment book and told her to fill the void with more patients. She would nod and pretend to agree, but soon enough he was running late again and the patients were backed up in the waiting room.

He was just as lackadaisical about billing. "Money was not his concern," his secretary would say. "If I didn't send out billing notices, he didn't care. He never would have charged anyone." He often got months behind and was constantly in trouble with the university's billing department, especially after a change in hospital administration put more emphasis on physicians as income producers and money makers.

From a financial standpoint Cecil's practice was a disaster for the university hospital. The other ob/gyns could do a dozen pap smears in the time it took him to counsel one couple. He ignored attempts by superiors to make him more cost conscious, his counseling sessions didn't get any shorter, and the patients in the waiting room continued to wait.

By the early 1970's a new development was incorporated into Cecil's amnio work. Sonography, also known as ultrasound, was introduced. Like a battleship tracking a submarine, the sonogram relies on ultrasonic waves to locate a fetus in the womb. For Cecil's purposes it could locate the fetus and placenta to make sure he was sticking the needle into the proper place. He no longer had to feel a woman's abdomen, then blindly stick the needle into the sac.

The first machine in the Washington area was operated by Dr. William Cochrane at Columbia Hospital for Women. Cochrane, a native of Scotland, became known as the dean of ultrasound in the nation's capital, and Cecil would send him patients to confirm the date of the pregnancy or locate the placenta before an amnio.

Even the early, primitive machines could detect major abnormalities like anencephaly, a rare condition in which the brain is missing, or hydrocephalus, in which the skull is filled with liquid. But on several occasions Cecil used the new technology in an experiment to diagnose microcephaly, a fetus with an abnormally small head, like the one in the picture on the wall of his office. The condition was usually associated with mental retardation if the mother had been exposed to rubella or X rays during early pregnancy.

Cecil somehow got the notion he could diagnose microcephaly by charting the size of the fetal head. He referred several patients to Dr. Cochrane without informing the sonographer about his theory, but only asking for head measurements. Dr. Cochrane was alarmed when he looked at the patients' charts and realized what Cecil was doing.

For a pregnancy to qualify as a true microcephaly case, the slow rate of fetal head growth had to be dramatic, but that wasn't what Cochrane was seeing in Cecil's cases. There was only a slight growth discrepancy, which meant nothing in an early pregnancy. Cochrane would later say that in a quarter century of performing ultrasounds he saw less than a half-dozen microcephaly cases—and he didn't know of anyone who could diagnose the condition from an early sonogram. "Nobody else was doing it before, and no one else has done it since," he would say. But Cecil was diagnosing the cases almost routinely—or at least he thought he was.

After the first few cases Dr. Cochrane started writing on the charts, in bold letters, that it was *not* a case of microcephaly. He never knew whether Cecil advised his patients to abort after receiving the sonogram results, but rumors later circulated that Cecil shut down his experiment when a woman elected to terminate her pregnancy as a result of Cecil's microcephaly diagnosis, and an analysis of the fetus showed it did not have the disorder.

When George Washington University got its own ultrasound machine, Judy Alborelli was hired as the sonographer. She wasn't surprised when she later heard about Cecil's microcephaly studies.

"He would try almost anything. He worried about nothing," she recalled. "He had kind of a godlike attitude. He was very cavalier."

She worked with Cecil to scan the patient while he drew the amniotic fluid. Once they even performed a sonogram live on a morning TV talk show to demonstrate the new technique. Although she considered him an "ace" at performing amnios, she realized he was less than skilled at reading sonograms, even though she thought he was no worse than most doctors with whom she worked. Many of them, however, were astute enough to call her aside, out of the patient's earshot, and ask questions about the scan. But not Cecil. He purported to be an expert, even when he didn't have a clue what he was talking about.

One year he convinced Judy to go to South America with him to work at an indigent hospital that served the poorest barrios of Caracas. Cecil often spoke of the fascinating research he was conducting in Venezuela, where birth defects—caused by poverty, incest, and poor nutrition—were rampant. He avoided specifics, but he told some of his GWU colleagues that it was research that couldn't be performed in the United States, where rules governing medical ethics were more rigid.

When Judy agreed to be his radiologist for the trip, he assured her that he would pay for everything and arrange all the accommodations, but when it came time to leave, he got sick and couldn't make the trip. Judy went alone and soon discovered that none of the trip was paid for, and the accommodations consisted of a room at the home of a Venezuelan physician who had invited Cecil.

The hospital where Judy worked was more primitive than anything she had ever seen. The patients' livestock wandered the corridors, and fighting cocks squared off in the building as patients cheered them on.

Although Cecil hadn't visited the hospital in a couple of years, his legacy remained. They spoke of him in awe, like a living legend, the brilliant American doctor who bestowed so much knowledge on them. "He was like a god," Judy remembered.

She got an indication of the local physicians' high regard for American doctors when she was scanning a patient one day and made an offhand comment that she suspected the patient had a pelvic abscess. It was only a suspicion, but the surgeons acted on it immediately. They whisked the patient into the operating room and opened her up. Afterward Judy didn't mention her suspicions until she was sure of her diagnosis. She could only imagine what Cecil's shoot-from-the-hip style had done to patients.

In 1971 Cecil received what he considered to be one of his greatest honors. He was appointed by President Nixon to the first of two three-year terms on the President's Committee on Mental Retardation. He was one of the few physicians on the twenty-one-member committee— the rest were advocates for the mentally retarded, parents of retarded children, or political appointees, like the head of a New Jersey union who didn't know anything about mental retardation, but who had supported Nixon. Cecil would say his appointment was the result of his work on microcephaly.

Among the committee members he was one of the most active and popular appointees. At the presidential Christmas party each year at the White House, he dressed as Santa Claus and handed out candy canes to mentally retarded children, and he was instrumental in investigating ways to deinstitutionalize the mentally retarded and raise public awareness of the lack of legal rights for the handicapped. He often led group discussions and impressed the lay members with his medical and scientific knowledge. "He was a very good contributor," remembered committee member Michael Gartner, a Washington attorney. "His credentials were very good and his personality was very pleasing. He was an innovator." But that lofty opinion wasn't shared by most of the staff, and many of the medical experts who were hired as consultants.

Early in his tenure he bombarded the executive director, Fred Krause, with a list of topics he thought the committee should address. One of them was developing "fact sheets" on mental retardation that could be disseminated to the public. He set out to show how lead poisoning was a major contributor to mental retardation. Although his overall theory was correct, his details were so full of inaccuracies, misstatements, and generalizations that the executive director wouldn't allow Cecil's fact sheets to be released to the public under the committee's name.

From then on one of the staff members became the self-appointed "truth squad" to keep a wary eye on the outspoken new member. "I thought he was a real blowhard," remembered Mary Gray, the editor of the committee's annual report, who had been a White House speech writer during the Kennedy administration. "He would give out facts and figures on anything you could think of. In large part, he made them up." At first, when she tried to warn the other staff members about Cecil, she was told she was overreacting. They viewed him as a harmless eccentric who might pop off from time to time, but who came up with some brilliant ideas. In fact, some staff and committee members thought so highly of him, they sent their wives to him for amniocentesis and genetic counseling.

In time, however, the executive director came to agree with Mary—their new member needed watching. "Sometimes you didn't know where he was coming from," Fred Krause would say. "He was coming up with his own data, or something he had brought back from England. It would take a little time to understand who, or what, he was talking about." When Cecil was interrogated about the source of his facts, he often answered like a seasoned politician. "We couldn't nail him down," Krause said. "He wouldn't answer a question clearly. He'd give you so much information that you were lost in the sea of what he was saying. As a nonmedical person, I didn't know what he was talking about."

Especially critical of him were some of the medical experts who served as consultants to the committee. After many of Cecil's presentations, or "pronouncements," as they came to be known, the consultants often called Krause and warned him about the unreliability of Cecil's information. One consultant, Dr. Louis Cooper of New York, a nationwide expert in vaccines and rubella, assumed that Cecil was one of the political appointees. Once, in the midst of Cecil's discussion of some topic, Dr. Cooper tapped a staff member on the shoulder and asked if Cecil was a "real doctor." Another consultant was Dr. Felix De la Cruz, who still remembered Cecil from the fiasco over the amnio textbook. "He used to make pronouncements and outrageous statements that a person who was not a physician really couldn't challenge," Dr. De la Cruz would say. Despite Cecil's position on the GWU faculty, the executive director didn't consider him one of the committee's medical authorities, even on genetic issues. Official questions on genetic counseling were directed to a consultant from the University of Southern California.

Yet, personally, he was well liked. When his ideas were shot down, he wasn't combative. He accepted the rejection and moved on to his next project.

One issue that Cecil tried to champion was getting the committee to endorse amniocentesis to the public as the safest and most reliable method of genetic screening. He even presented a research paper for the committee to publish. Mary Gray, as the committee's chief writer and editor, was in charge of reviewing it.

"Facts that Cecil stated with great authority," she later said, "turned out to have a tremendous number of inaccuracies." For instance, he contradicted the accepted medical practice that amniocentesis should be performed between the fourteenth and sixteenth weeks of pregnancy, because he said it could cause an excessive number of miscarriages. He thought it should be performed much later in the pregnancy. Mary contacted several experts within the National Institutes of Health who dissected Cecil's paper line by line and pointed out the errors. She returned to the committee's executive director and said, "If I have anything to do with it, this paper will never be published." When the director read it, he agreed.

After it became apparent that the staff editor was responsible for holding up the paper, she started receiving calls from the offices of conservative congressmen on Capitol Hill. "They really leaned on me," she would remember. One call was from an aide to Congressman James Buckley of New York who demanded to know why the paper was being withheld and when it would be published. For her protection she circulated a memo to the staff and committee members listing the specific objections to the paper. The committee ultimately decided not to publish it.

After Cecil was named to a second three-year term and appointed the chairman of a subcommittee on the prevention of mental retardation, he used his new position once again to prompt the committee into actively promoting amniocentesis. It touched off another debate on the safety of the procedure and whether it was even the most effective diagnostic tool for the committee to advocate. Eventually, Cecil was voted down, and the presidential committee never placed its stamp of approval on Cecil's amnio work.

In later years Cecil would refer to his work on the presidential committee as a major highlight of his career. A photograph of him and other committee members posing with President Nixon was prominently displayed in his office, and he would often speak of his close association with Caspar Weinberger, who, as then secretary of Health, Education, and Welfare, presided over committee meetings. Cecil would refer to him on a first-name basis and later kept a picture of Weinberger over his desk. "I'm always under Cap's eye," he once told a visitor. But others on the committee wrote it off to Cecil's propensity for name-dropping and doubted that he ever spoke to Weinberger outside of a committee meeting. When asked years later about their relationship, Caspar Weinberger would say he had never heard of Cecil Jacobson.

In 1973 Cecil's standing at George Washington University abruptly changed. Dr. Sites left the university for a similar position at Fairfax Hospital in suburban Virginia and was replaced by Dr. Allen Weingold, from New York. Dr. Weingold didn't have the patience of his two predecessors toward Cecil, especially when Cecil pulled his prima donna routines. Others in the department thought it wasn't a coincidence that after one heated exchange with his new boss, Cecil's lab space shrunk rather than expanded.

Although Dr. Weingold was impressed by Cecil's early pioneering work in amnio, he was more concerned about Cecil's lack of credentials. On paper Cecil was nothing more than a licensed physician. He wasn't even a board-certified obstetrician, like every other doctor in the department. He had been traveling to England practically every summer to continue his studies at Cambridge, but he'd never completed his Ph.D. Basically, Cecil was a research scientist with questionable qualifications to be treating patients.

Dr. Weingold was concerned about how much time Cecil was spending with patients and away from the lab. One day he called Cecil to his office and advised him that if he continued to move from a strictly research position into the active handling of patients, he needed to upgrade his credentials. He suggested that Cecil go to England and complete the doctoral work on which he had already devoted years. But before Cecil could get started, his candor and outspokenness got him into trouble once again.

By the mid-1970's the science of genetics was growing by leaps and bounds. Only two decades earlier scientists could barely count the number of chromosomes within a cell. Now they were making babies in a test tube and talking about cloning humans. Already the cells of mice and humans had been fused to make a human/mouse hybrid, and lower forms of animals were being cloned. There was talk of young couples someday using computer cards to determine their genetic compatibility before marriage to make sure they wouldn't pass along a debilitating disease. Instead of proposing marriage the couple would match cards.

The future of genetic engineering seemed limitless, and there was genuine concern about possible abuses. Meetings were convened of the nation's top theologians, ethicists, lawyers, philosophers, and physicians. Some were calling for a "National Genetics Task Force" to coordinate research and set priorities for funding.

Not surprisingly, Cecil loudly joined the debate and helped fuel the controversies. At medical seminars and public forums he described his visions for the future of genetics, espousing his beliefs in the ability to use amniocentesis to create a master race through sex selection. He discussed his sperm studies and the possibility of using animals as surrogate mothers as if it were fact, not mere speculation.

Some of GWU's most generous benefactors began to take notice of his controversial proposals and complained to the university. As Dr. Weingold would explain, "I was getting a lot of commentary from people who had heard him at various meetings, that his jumps of logic were way beyond where we were scientifically." Dr. Weingold and the other department heads wondered what to do about their loose cannon. It was one thing to discuss these highly controversial topics in the setting of a think tank, where philosophers and scientists could debate the merits of his ideas; but Cecil insisted on ruminating in public forums, where the media could pick up his speeches and report them as fact.

Action was finally called for when the National Foundation / March of Dimes let it be known to Dr. Weingold that a university grant application was in jeopardy as long as Cecil continued to preach ideas inconsistent with the goals of the foundation. Dr. Weingold summoned Cecil to his office again. He explained the public wasn't ready for these "sensitive issues," and he urged Cecil to "reacquaint" himself with his laboratory research and genetic counseling rather than digressing into "flights of fancy."

At the very least, if Cecil was so intent on engaging in the scientific debates, Dr. Weingold thought he needed to upgrade his credentials and establish his credibility. He gave Cecil three "assignments."

First, he insisted that Cecil complete his Ph.D. He'd been working on his doctorate for years and had nothing to show for it.

Second, he said Cecil needed to validate his work into the causes of recurrent miscarriages by obtaining a research grant and documenting his findings in a peer-review publication. Unlike his early years, there wasn't much published research coming out of Cecil's lab these days. "You present widely at meetings," Dr. Weingold told him, "to lay persons, government panels, and scientific sessions, but I have not seen enough in print."

Third, Dr. Weingold wanted Cecil to publish the results of his amnio experiences. He pointed out that Cecil probably had performed more amnios than anyone in the world, yet he'd never summarized his work. "It needs to be documented in a peer-review publication showing your success rates, failures, and complications," Dr. Weingold said.

Cecil left for England on yet another sabbatical to complete his doctoral studies into the timing of ovulation and the causes of habitual miscarriages.

He even received a vindication of sorts for his pioneering amniocentesis work when the results of the government's long-awaited NIH study on the safety of amniocentesis were released in October 1975. After so many years of argument, debate, and controversy, Cecil was proved to be correct. Amniocentesis was safe and effective. The researchers determined that the miscarriage rate of women who had an amnio was "not statistically significant" from the women who didn't have an amnio. But the report did little to appease Dr. Weingold, who was becoming dissatisfied with the pace of Cecil's progress. Despite Cecil's trip to England, nothing was appearing in print, and he wasn't any closer to obtaining his Ph.D. "I don't know what he was doing with his time, but it was apparent it wasn't going anywhere," Dr. Weingold would say.

By mutual agreement Cecil resigned from George Washington University in 1976, ending a fifteen-year association with the university. But his account of the departure would be markedly different from Dr. Weingold's.

Cecil would say he resigned because the university had become so "saturated" that he couldn't obtain enough room for lab space, and he decided to split his lab "like an amoeba" and open his own clinic across the river in

Virginia. The new location was closer to home so he could spend more time with his family. He would claim that his new clinic was merely an extension of the university program—an assertion that the university would staunchly deny.

Despite the resignation Cecil never missed a beat. He moved the laboratory one day and started seeing patients the next. In 1976 the Reproductive Genetic Center opened for business in Vienna, Virginia.

Chapter Seven

All her life Chris Maimone's ambition was to be a mother. Having a career never interested her—she just wanted to have kids. As a girl, whenever she played with dolls or baby-sat for the neighbors' kids, she was dreaming what it would be like to have children of her own someday. Even during college, when her friends were plotting career moves and planning to enter the business world, Chris set her sights on being a housewife. She planned to get married, become pregnant, and stay home to raise a family. But she never planned on having an infertility problem.

Chris was a petite woman who resembled singer Paula Abdul. Her husband, Larry, was a burly Italian who worked for the government. They met while Larry was an amateur photographer shooting a wedding as a favor to a friend, and Chris was a bridesmaid in the wedding party. Even while they were dating, they talked about having kids. Chris wanted four. Larry wanted as many as they could afford.

At first their family planning had been right on schedule. Married less than a year, Chris was three months pregnant and starting to wear maternity clothes—when she suffered a miscarriage. There was no explanation for it. She just lost the baby. She walked into the bathroom one day and suddenly felt flushed. "A hot flash," she described it. When she rushed to the doctor's office, her obstetrician couldn't detect a fetal heartbeat. He told her the baby was gone.

She underwent a D and C, and when she awoke from the anesthesia, her physician, Dr. John Doppelheuer, was sitting at her side. "It's okay to cry," he said, patting her hand. He explained that Chris would need time to recover, not only physically, but emotionally, and he recommended some support groups for her to contact to help her cope with the difficult times ahead.

As he predicted, her body healed quickly, but the emotional scars were longer lasting. She became depressed and withdrawn. She couldn't sleep. She didn't eat. She cried every time she saw a baby at the grocery store or a pregnant woman at the mall. Even TV commercials featuring a mother and child were enough to draw tears. She blamed herself for the miscarriage, believing that a better diet or more sleep would have made a difference. She was angry that her body had betrayed her.

Larry worried about her. "It wasn't your fault," he said, assuring her she had done everything possible.

Her most difficult time was when she stood in as godmother for her nephew a few weeks after her miscarriage. Her sister had offered to find someone else, but Chris insisted she could go through with it. She stood on the altar, cradling her nephew in her arms, the tears streaming down her cheeks, praying that someday she would be able to hold one of her own.

In the weeks ahead she was amazed to discover how many of her friends and acquaintances had suffered miscarriages—even her own mother had suffered two of them before Chris was born. It was something her mother had never mentioned before, and she told Chris that no matter how much she loved her three daughters, she would always grieve for the two she lost.

In time Chris and Larry resumed their quest for a baby, determined not to let one setback stop them, no matter how devastating the loss. Each month was like watching a pot boil as Chris waited for her period, hoping it wouldn't come, then disappointment and heartache after another wasted cycle. When several months passed, she consulted her doctor and asked if something was wrong with her. Dr. Doppelheuer performed a series of tests and concluded Chris had an ovulation deficiency. He prescribed a fertility drug called Clomid to assist her in ovulating.

Larry didn't want her using fertility drugs. He was concerned about possible side effects. But Chris had resolved to do whatever was necessary, and if powerful drugs would help, then she would try them.

She took the drugs for three months, in increasing dosages, before Dr. Doppelheuer suggested they try another approach. He was an obstetrician and gynecologist, he said, not an infertility specialist, and it was becoming evident the Maimones needed more help than he could offer—so he referred them to an in-vitro fertilization institute that specialized in infertility problems.

The in-vitro procedure was to be used as a last resort, only if several cheaper and less radical options failed. They took special courses in the treatment of infertility, and Chris got a complete medical workup; then her new doctor prescribed a second drug, Pergonal, in conjunction with the Clomid. Larry was even more upset, but Chris overruled him again.

They had barely started the program when the bills came due. The treatments were costing between $1,500 and $1,800 a month, more than their mortgage and car payments combined. Chris was working as an administrative assistant at a medical laboratory, and Larry had just taken a new job with the U.S. Department of Housing and Urban Development. They discovered their insurance wouldn't cover infertility treatments. They considered delaying the treatments or putting them off all together, knowing they couldn't afford more than just a few months before they went broke, but having a child was so important to them they decided to take out a second mortgage on their house.

A few days later Chris was having lunch with a woman at work when the conversation turned to the cost of Chris's treatments. The woman said her sister had once gone to an infertility specialist. She hadn't gotten pregnant, but at least the doctor's fees were reasonable. "You only pay what he pays for the medication," she said. There were no expensive markups.

"What's his name?" Chris asked.

"Dr. Cecil Jacobson," the woman answered.

The first time Chris saw Dr. Jacobson, she instantly disliked him. "I wasn't one hundred percent comfortable,"

she would say. "I don't know why. It was just a feeling."
His weight bothered her and so did his appearance. She
thought he was dirty and unkempt. His clothes were wrin-
kled, as if he'd been wearing them for days.

And then there were the animals.

His office was decorated in early-American barnyard.
There were pig figurines on the table, and the wallpaper
was patterned with buffalo. (Or was it cattle? She wasn't
sure—some sort of bovine creature.) Even his explanation
about his early infertility work on animals didn't appease
her. She still thought his fascination with pigs and cows
was weird.

Under normal circumstances Chris would have walked
out of the place, but she was so dead set on becoming a
mother, she would have done anything to have a baby—
especially after she saw the hundreds of baby pictures on
his bulletin board. Suddenly she was willing to submit to
an examination by a man who physically repulsed her,
and to ignore the assorted livestock scattered around his
office—just on the chance he could help her.

After months of being poked and prodded, leaving
nothing to the imagination, Chris was relieved that Dr.
Jacobson wanted only to take a brief medical history
from her. No pelvic exam, no pap smear, no blood tests,
not even a reading of her blood pressure. He looked at
Chris's temperature chart and the pedigree form his office
had sent her.

He said he was confident Chris would conceive and
bring home a baby if she stayed with his program for
eighteen months. Chris told him about her miscarriage and
explained how traumatic it had been. He said he couldn't
guarantee she wouldn't have another one. Miscarriages
were much more frequent than people realized, he said,
especially in the early pregnancies that he was able to
diagnose. "If something happens, you have to pick yourself
up and start over again," he advised. He told her to keep
a positive attitude, and to keep her tears and emotions in
check. "I don't want any boo-hoos," he warned.

Chris told him about the drug therapy she had been
prescribed at the in-vitro institute. Dr. Jacobson called

it preposterous. He didn't believe in prescribing power-ful infertility drugs, he said. He preferred a more natural approach. All Chris needed, he concluded, was some HCG shots, lots of sex, and patience. That's exactly what Larry wanted to hear.

Dr. Jacobson told Chris she had a common ailment, one he had treated many times before. He diagnosed her as having a "major risk of fetal defect," for which he prescribed HCG three times a week. And to make sure the mucus in her vagina didn't interfere with the sperm's delicate mission to fertilize an egg, he said he wanted to try artificial insemination for a while.

Since they had no insurance, Chris asked if she could have her lab work performed at the medical lab where she worked in order to save themselves some money. Employees got their lab work for free, and the lab could do her hormone tests to determine when she was ovulating. But Dr. Jacobson said he didn't use outside labs—they were too slow and their results were unreliable. He performed all his own lab work on the premises. Besides, the best way to determine the time of ovulation, he explained, was by keeping daily temperature charts.

On the way out he walked them by the baby photos on the bulletin boards again. He promised that once the Maimones were successful, they could add a picture of their own baby to the others on the wall.

Dr. Jacobson didn't waste any time. He scheduled the first insemination two days later, on Wednesday, June 3, 1987. Chris left work early and rushed to the Metro station to pick up Larry for the four-thirty P.M. appointment, but on the way to the clinic they got caught in the rush-hour traffic and were running late.

Dr. Jacobson greeted them at the door. "Where's the semen specimen?" he asked. Larry said he'd just gotten off work and didn't have one. Dr. Jacobson handed him a small vial. "Fill it up," he said, and directed Larry to a bathroom in the hallway near the elevator.

Larry went into a stall and started to masturbate, but he was too nervous and embarrassed to produce. It didn't help matters when a man came in to use the bathroom. Larry waited for him to leave, then resumed masturbating until he ejaculated into the tiny jar. When he returned to the clinic, he tried to act nonchalant as he carefully cradled the bottle in his hand, hoping no one would realize where he'd been or what he'd been doing. Fortunately, no one was in the waiting room. Dr. Jacobson escorted them to the lab, where he poured some of the sperm onto a slide and examined it under the microscope. He said he was checking for its count and motility. In a moment he pronounced it a potent batch. "You've got enough here to impregnate the whole city of Washington," he told Larry.

As he motioned for Larry and Chris to look for themselves, his elbow knocked over the vial. Horrified, Larry watched as most of his sperm spilled onto the counter. The doctor scooped up the container before all the contents leaked out.

Larry was devastated. "I'm not doing it again, Doc," he said painfully. "I worked too hard."

"There's still plenty here," the doctor assured him.

As they went into the examination room, Chris was surprised that a nurse wasn't present. She thought it was the law. But since Larry was there, she didn't protest. Dr. Jacobson filled a syringe-type instrument with the semen, and as he got ready to insert it, he called Larry over to watch. He explained he was inserting the sperm above the vaginal mucus and hoped it wouldn't take long for the "good stuff," as he called it, to fertilize an egg.

The insemination took only a few moments, and when he was through, he instructed them to go home and make love. He told Larry it was imperative that Chris have an orgasm. She couldn't get pregnant without one, he said. And he told Larry it was his job to make sure that she did.

The sound of a ringing alarm clock was enough to give Larry Maimone an erection, or at least that's what he liked to tell people. Every morning, when the alarm went off at five o'clock, Chris and Larry woke up and made love. It didn't matter whether they felt amorous or not. They didn't dare miss a day. Otherwise Dr. Jacobson would scold them like naughty children for not drawing arrows on Chris's temperature chart, and he wouldn't give them a gold star at the end of the month. On the days surrounding Chris's ovulation, they were instructed to make love twice a day, once in the morning and again at night.

At first Larry looked forward to his morning trysts like a groom on his honeymoon, but before long the novelty wore off. Some mornings he and Chris would have preferred to sleep in rather than get up to make a baby. And that's exactly what sex was becoming—a mission performed on cue to make a baby. Gone was the romance, passion, or spontaneity. Chris once confided to a friend that the demands of prescription sex were grating on their nerves, but her friend didn't have much sympathy. "That would never happen to me and my husband," her friend replied. "My husband is ready any time." But Chris knew better. Let them try having sex on demand day after day, week after week, and see how well her macho husband performed.

On the days when Chris was inseminated, she would rush into the examination room and Larry would rush to the bathroom to masturbate, then return with the "good stuff," as Dr. Jacobson called it. Then Dr. Jacobson would inject Chris with HCG and send her home, with instructions to make love and have an orgasm.

The first month Chris had two inseminations and two HCG injections. The next month she had five inseminations and eleven injections. Although the doctor's prices were reasonable, it was still expensive. The inseminations cost only ten dollars—much less than what other doctors were charging—but with each insemination Dr. Jacobson did a twenty-five-dollar semen analysis and gave Chris a twenty-five-dollar HCG shot, so the total office visit cost at least sixty-five dollars. And they were going to the clinic three times a week. Larry was getting new insurance coverage, but it wouldn't kick in for another six months. Chris didn't want to wait that long. So they paid Dr. Jacobson out of the loan they had secured with the second mortgage on their house.

Besides the costs Chris had another problem. She was

having adverse reactions to the hormone injections. The HCG shots sometimes made her crazed, like Dr. Jekyll and Mrs. Hyde on an estrogen high. One day she would feel wonderful, on top of the world, anxious to make love with Larry and get about the business of conceiving a child. The next day she would bite his head off if he said good morning the wrong way.

She blamed herself for not being able to function like a normal woman. All her life she'd dreamed of having children; then, when she was old enough and had gotten married, she couldn't do it. "I'm a failure," she told Larry.

The second month of hormone injections continued well past Chris's time of ovulation—she was already at day thirty-two of her cycle, and her period still hadn't started—so the next day at work she had the lab run a pregnancy test. When she got the results that afternoon, the test was positive. She rushed to the phone to call Larry, but he was in a meeting. She told his secretary the call was important and asked her to barge in. When Larry came on the line, she told him in a choking voice, barely louder than a whisper, "You're going to be a daddy."

When Chris called Dr. Jacobson to tell him about the test results, he didn't seem very enthusiastic. He told Chris that if she didn't have her period by her next visit, she should bring in a urine sample and they would do another pregnancy test. She was disappointed by his reaction, but she suspected he had helped so many women get pregnant over the years that it had become routine. Even so, she had expected him to display a little more enthusiasm for her. When she and Larry went to celebrate that evening at their favorite Chinese restaurant, their waitress was more excited for them than Dr. Jacobson had been.

During Chris's next appointment she brought a urine sample to the clinic. They gathered around the doctor's desk in the room with the buffalo wallpaper, and Dr. Jacobson mixed the urine sample with the reagent from the pregnancy test. It took only a few moments for the plus sign to appear.

"Congratulations," Dr. Jacobson said, standing up to shake Larry's hand and hug Chris. Now he seemed genuinely thrilled. Chris suspected he'd only been disappointed that he couldn't break the news to them himself. He told them they were fortunate to have conceived so quickly. Most patients weren't so lucky after only a month or two of treatments, he said. Then he filled out the pregnancy report.

To the best of our estimate, this patient conceived on July 9 and would be expected to deliver around April 2. We thank you for referring this pleasant couple and share their joy in this pregnancy.

Cecil B. Jacobson, M.D.

For the time being Chris and Larry decided not to announce the news of their pregnancy until they were sure it was safe. Chris told her immediate family and Larry told his, but otherwise they kept the information to themselves. Dr. Jacobson informed Chris that there was a strong chance she could still lose the baby. She realized that at least one of every five pregnancies ended in miscarriage, and Dr. Jacobson said his statistics were even higher because he diagnosed the pregnancies so much earlier than other doctors.

He made a crude statistical chart, like a bookie figuring a point spread, and explained the weekly odds of carrying the pregnancy to term. Because Chris was three weeks pregnant, she had only a 50-50 chance, he said, but the odds would improve each week.

Week 3—50-50
Week 4—35-65
Week 5—25-75
Week 6—5-95

After the sixth week he said she should be out of danger and he would start monitoring the pregnancy with ultrasound exams. Until then he wanted her to continue on the

HCG shots, and he would give her a weekly pregnancy test to make sure the pregnancy was still viable.

A few days later Dr. Doppelheuer called Chris to see how she was doing. She hadn't spoken to him since he had referred her to the in-vitro institute, and he was interested in how her treatments were progressing.

She explained she wasn't at the institute anymore. She had started seeing Dr. Jacobson.

"How did you get the reference?" Dr. Doppelheuer asked.

She explained that a woman at work had told her about Dr. Jacobson's reasonable prices. "Guess what," she said, deciding to share her secret. "I'm pregnant." She told him about the artificial inseminations and the HCG injections. She expected him to congratulate her, but instead he asked if she was certain she was pregnant.

"Yes, I'm sure," she said, somewhat offended. "I passed a pregnancy test."

He wanted to know if she was still taking the HCG.

"He's got me on HCG every other day to support the pregnancy," she explained. She was becoming annoyed at what seemed like an inquisition.

"Are you aware you could be getting false positives from the HCG on your pregnancy test?" Dr. Doppelheuer asked.

"No, I wasn't aware of that," Chris said.

He gave her a brief physiological explanation, saying that a woman's body produced enormous amounts of HCG when she got pregnant, and the pregnancy tests were designed to detect the presence of HCG in a woman's system. "What would happen," Dr. Doppelheuer asked, "if you stopped the HCG for several days? Would your pregnancy test still come back positive?"

Chris said she assumed so, but she wouldn't dare. "I can't stop the injections," she said. "If I stop them, I'll lose the baby."

When she got home that evening, she told Larry about her conversation with Dr. Doppelheuer. At first she had suspected Dr. Doppelheuer was just jealous because another doctor had succeeded where he had failed, but now she thought there was something more to his questioning. "I got the feeling he thought something was wrong," Chris said. It wasn't what he said so much as how he'd said it.

Larry told her she was being ridiculous. Ever since her miscarriage any little twinge or question was cause for alarm and could send her into a panic. Dr. Jacobson had told them about the power of positive thinking and explained that stress was the worst thing for her. Larry was constantly trying to boost Chris's spirits. "Come on, Chris," he said. "Dr. Jacobson knows what he's doing. What do you think is wrong?"

Chris said she didn't know. She just had a feeling.

The next day at work Chris called the assay department and spoke with one of the lab techs. She explained she was calling on behalf of a customer and asked if injecting a woman with HCG could cause a false-positive pregnancy test.

"Sure," the technician answered. Most tests were HCG based, he said, meaning they searched for the existence of HCG in a woman's system to determine if she was pregnant. He explained there were two types of pregnancy tests— urinary tests and blood tests. The urinary, also known as beta tests, measured the amount of HCG in a woman's urine and reported the results as either positive or negative. A blood test, also called a serum test, measured the HCG in the bloodstream and could determine how long the woman had been pregnant. But with either test, he said, an excess of HCG could cause a false-positive result.

That evening she told Larry about her conversation with the lab tech. "What's your point?" he asked. "What are you trying to prove?" Again Chris said she wasn't sure. But the next time she went to the clinic, she raised her concerns with Dr. Jacobson.

He told her there was no way the hormone injections would affect his pregnancy tests. The HCG dilutes from a woman's body within twenty-four to forty-eight hours, he said, and could not cause a false-positive reading. He was so sure of himself that he left no doubt he knew what he was talking about.

Just to put her mind at ease, Chris decided to have herself tested at the lab again, this time with a blood/serum test. So far she had taken only urinary tests, the same as any home-pregnancy test she could buy over the counter, but the serum test was more sophisticated. She went to the phlebotomy department down the hall and had a blood sample drawn. A few hours later she checked the computer and saw her results were ready. Her HCG level was 355 units, which, according to a scale attached to the chart, meant she was three weeks pregnant—and right on target with Dr. Jacobson's calculations.

Dr. Jacobson performed a follow-up pregnancy test a few days later, and another one a week after that. Both were positive. Chris continued to get her HCG shots three times a week. In addition to the seventy-five dollars she was paying for the shots, she was paying another thirty dollars for the pregnancy test. She asked again if she could have her pregnancy tests performed at work, explaining that she could get the lab work for free, but Dr. Jacobson repeated that he didn't use outside labs. But as a compromise he allowed her to take home some vials of HCG and showed Larry how to inject her.

Chris was less than five weeks pregnant when, one day, she went into the bathroom at work and discovered she was bleeding. The same thing had happened just before her miscarriage. She panicked and called Dr. Jacobson right away. It was Thursday afternoon and he wasn't in, but the receptionist told her to call him at home. When she reached him, he didn't seem too concerned. He said many woman experienced bleeding during pregnancy. It was perfectly normal. Even so, if she lost the baby, she could get pregnant again. "If you're having a miscarriage, it's better to have it now rather than later," he said. This was nature's way of disposing of imperfect pregnancies. He advised her to relax, stay off her feet that weekend, and come see him first thing Monday morning.

She barely moved all weekend. By Monday morning the bleeding had practically stopped. Chris took a urine sample to the clinic, and Dr. Jacobson tested it. He said she was still pregnant.

"If I had miscarried," she asked, "would the test still come back positive even if the fetus wasn't there?"

"It could," he answered, "but it's unlikely." He said the only way his test would register positive was if the placenta was growing. He gave her a prescription for progesterone suppositories to control the bleeding and help maintain the pregnancy.

Despite the doctor's assurances Chris was still concerned about the bleeding. She knew it wasn't normal, no matter what he told her. Two days later she had the lab run another blood/serum test. She was still pregnant, the test indicated, but the results were startling. According to the test results she was still only three weeks pregnant and her HCG levels had actually dropped. The test registered 274 units, down from 355 units a week earlier. She asked one of the lab techs if that was normal. He said the levels should be doubling every two to four days, not going backward.

According to a chart attached to the test, her levels at five weeks should be in the thousands, not 274 units.

Weeks after Conception	HCG Range
1 week	0–50
2 weeks	40–1,000
3 weeks	100–4,000
4 weeks	800–10,000
5–6 weeks	5,000–100,000
7–8 weeks	20,000–200,000
9–12 weeks	10,000–200,000
2nd trimester	8,000–50,000
3rd trimester	6,000–50,000

During her next appointment she asked Dr. Jacobson why the levels were decreasing. He said the lab had obviously made a mistake. "That's why I don't use outside labs," he said. "They're prone to errors." That's also why he didn't use blood tests. The ranges were so varied, it made the tests unreliable and practically impossible to read. The urinary tests were much easier to understand, he had found—just a simple plus or a minus that Chris could see for herself.

The next week, when Chris went to see him again, he gave her another pregnancy test and said it also was positive. In fact, she appeared to be doing so well, that he said it was time to start doing sonograms. The Maimones would be able to see their baby for the first time for themselves.

Larry looked forward to the big event with great anticipation. Chris drank glass after glass of water to fill her bladder, as Dr. Jacobson instructed, but when she got to the clinic, she had to sit in the waiting room for so long that she thought she would wet her pants. When they were finally summoned to the examination room, Chris lay down on the table, and Dr. Jacobson spread the jelly on her stomach, then turned off the light and moved the transducer over her abdomen.

It took only a moment for Dr. Jacobson to find the baby. "There it is," he said. Larry moved closer to get a better look.

"There's the sac," Dr. Jacobson said. "See the sac?"

Larry squinted, trying to see what the doctor was talking about, but the screen was so murky he couldn't see anything.

Dr. Jacobson pointed to a dark area and outlined it with his tracer. "Can you see it now?" he asked.

Larry wasn't sure, but he thought he saw it.

Chris squirmed to get a better look, but Dr. Jacobson told her to lie still. "Don't worry," he said. "Larry's seen everything."

He manipulated the machine's knobs and dials until the perimeter of the shaded area was marked by cursors on the screen. "Okay," he said, "the sac is twenty-one by twenty-one by twenty-five." He checked the figures against a fetal-growth chart on the wall and said he was very pleased with the progress. He made a Polaroid print and handed it to Larry.

Larry said he couldn't make out the baby and asked the doctor to point it out again.

Dr. Jacobson pulled a felt-tip pen from his pocket.

"Here's the sac," he said, outlining a shaded area on the Polaroid. "And here's the fetus." He drew a circle around a darker area within the previous circle.

Larry handed it to Chris. The picture brought tears to her eyes. The first picture of her baby. Their little miracle of science. Their little miracle of God. Chris decided it was finally safe to tell her friends and the rest of her family that she was expecting.

Chapter Eight

When Cecil left George Washington University in 1976 and opened his own clinic in Virginia, he was practically the only game in town for amniocentesis. During his first few years in business for himself, he was performing more than five hundred amnios a year, sometimes as many as seven in a day. Most patients were referred to him by his former students or fellow faculty members who had gone into private practice. Even the university hospitals were sending him patients.

When an obstetrician treated a pregnant woman in her late thirties or forties who statistically had an elevated risk of Down's syndrome, she was usually sent to Cecil for a genetic assessment and amnio. Or when a doctor had an especially difficult case, like a woman who had her kidneys x-rayed before realizing she was pregnant, Cecil was asked to check for possible chromosomal damage.

He staffed his new clinic with a handful of Ph.D. candidates and medical students from GWU hired to work in the lab. Few people knew the real reason why he'd left the university. He simply told people he had outgrown his cramped quarters and decided to move on. He tried to coax his sonogram tech, Judy Alborelli, to follow him, but after the fiasco of her trip to South America she turned him down. She wanted a career of her own and realized that anyone working in Cecil's office would be subjugated to him. With Cecil around there wasn't enough room for two experts on anything.

Cecil decided to perform the ultrasounds himself and bought his own machine. Considering his past lack of expertise, Judy was surprised. He wasn't required to pass

a proficiency exam or demonstrate even a remote knowledge of how to operate the equipment. To become an
instant expert, all he had to do was buy the machine and
turn it on.

Soon after opening his clinic he recalled some of the lessons
he'd learned while working on the pigs in England and
applied them to his patients, though he downplayed the
link with his animal experiments, realizing that few women
would look kindly on the comparison.

Benita Weiner was an early patient who had gone to Cecil
at age forty-one after aborting a Down's syndrome baby in
midterm. She had heard about Dr. Jacobson through some
medical contacts of her husband, who was a psychiatrist.
Her obstetrician told her she would be wasting her time
seeking help from a geneticist. "They'll just prick your finger and tell you everything is chromosomally all right," the
doctor told her. But Benita decided to try him anyway.

"He seemed a little full of himself," she would remember
after their first meeting. She was accustomed to doctors
who were "reserved and very cautious," but there was
nothing circumspect about Cecil Jacobson. "He was a very
flamboyant kind of person," she would say.

All the plaques on his wall and his self-proclamations
about being a medical pioneer who had "developed amniocentesis" didn't jive with the bombastic, disheveled physician she met. When he prescribed a simple regimen of
HCG and told her she had nothing to worry about, she
wondered whether he was "for real, or psychotic." But
within a month she was a life-long convert. After just a
few HCG injections, she conceived twins. She carried one
baby to term, but the other didn't make it. Dr. Jacobson
told her it died and resorbed. Still, she gave birth to a baby
that other doctors told her she would never have.

The practice of treating infertility patients was an
emerging field during the late 1970's, much as genetics
had been when Cecil got involved more than a decade
earlier. There was as yet no such thing as an infertility
specialist. A woman who experienced difficulty conceiving
was treated by her ob/gyn, or her husband consulted a

urologist, but Cecil was having as much success as any of them. As word of his triumphs spread, he began picking up more referrals for infertility patients. Although other clinics, like the Columbia Hospital for Women, had a policy against treating women in their forties because of the slim chance of success, Cecil didn't turn any patients away. He wasn't afraid to treat anyone. He even treated women who were menopausal. He told one patient that other doctors were too timid to take chances and experiment. "They're not inventive enough," he said. "They're not willing to go forward."

He was a referring physician's dream. He didn't do pap smears. He didn't examine patients. He didn't treat gynecological problems. Most of all, he wasn't a threat to steal a patient. If a woman complained of a vaginal infection, most doctors would treat the condition themselves, but not Cecil. He would send her back to the referring physician, thus ensuring that the doctor would keep a paying patient—a fact that wasn't lost on more than one doctor who referred cases to him.

He was especially valuable when a woman was losing patience with her ob/gyn because she wasn't getting pregnant. The doctor could send her to Cecil and wash his hands of a troublesome patient. If Cecil succeeded, the doctor still got his patient back—because Cecil didn't deliver babies either.

His patients generally fell into two camps—either they raved about him, or they thought he was a kook.

He practiced medicine differently from practically any doctor in town. While other doctors urged women to abstain from alcohol during pregnancy, he routinely prescribed it to alleviate a patient's bleeding and cramps, despite his religious restrictions and his earlier studies linking alcohol and birth defects. He didn't examine patients or prescribe powerful infertility drugs, and he recommended surgery only as a last resort. He even measured the length of a pregnancy differently from everyone else. The standard practice was to calculate from the last menstrual period, but Cecil counted from the date of conception. So when an obstetrician would say the woman was ten weeks pregnant, by Cecil's calculations she was only eight.

But perhaps what distinguished Cecil most from other doctors was treating patients through prayer and the power of positive thinking. His treatments reminded one patient of a stop-smoking program. "He had a way of encouraging you and of making you feel that you really could do it. I think part of me kept saying it's hopeless. It's just hopeless, because so many doctors had told me it was. He'd keep saying, 'Don't give up. Try another month. Just a month at a time. It's kind of like quitting smoking. Just do it a week at a time, a month at a time.' "

He sometimes used his clinic as a pulpit to espouse his religious beliefs. He spoke to some people of his belief in reincarnation and lectured others against drinking alcohol and reading pornography, saying it would inhibit a healthy sex life and cause infertility.

"The power of prayer is as important as anything I can do here," he once told a patient. "I don't know how it works, but it works." He often prayed with patients to find the answers to difficult decisions or to ask for help in conception. He asked one woman if she ever dreamed of having a child. When she said she had, he told her, "Well, that means God wants you to have a baby."

Cecil often talked of his medical practice as doing the Lord's work. His religious affiliation was evident to whoever walked into his office. A large framed photograph of the Mormon Temple in Salt Lake City hung on the wall behind his desk, and Mormon promotional material often lay in his waiting room.

Mormonism was more than a religion for him—it was a way of life. He was a top official in the local Church. At one point he was appointed to the Council of Twelve Apostles, which decided policy for his stake, a group of between four thousand and six thousand Church members. He could spend days at a time without coming into contact with a non-Mormon. His best friends were Mormons, his neighbors were Mormons, many of his patients were Mormons. He lived down the street from the Mormon meeting house in a home built by his best friend, a Mormon.

He invested with Mormon business partners in Mormon business ventures, and he banked at a savings and loan that was primarily controlled by Mormons.

To most of Washington the Mormons were an exotic and misunderstood religion. The magnificent Mormon Temple—a white, imposing fortress that resembled the castle from the *Wizard of Oz*—was the most visible, and most mysterious, church in the area. Tens of thousands of motorists passed it each day on the Beltway just north of Washington, but only Church members in good standing were allowed inside. Non-Mormons had been excluded since shortly after the temple was completed and sanctified in 1974, when the last tourists were ushered out and the carpets where they'd walked were torn up and replaced.

Since then the temple had been the site of secret religious ceremonies, such as baptisms and marriages for the dead. Men and women stood waist-deep in a pool of holy water and were baptized as proxy for strangers who had been dead for centuries. Marriage "sealing" ceremonies were held for long-dead husbands and wives to bless their union for eternity. The names of the deceased were gleaned from the extensive genealogy files the Mormons had been collecting for decades from vital statistics around the world. The Mormons believed they were once spirits awaiting a humanly body to inhabit on earth. By virtue of helping women to give birth, Cecil could have believed he was actually assisting the spirit children of his ancestors to find a place on earth.

The daily activities of the Jacobson family revolved around the Church. Their large, rambling house, built by Cecil's best friend, Ellsworth Knudson, was in the shadow of the McLean stake's church steeple. The Jacobsons were some of the most active members of their ward. Cecil sang in the choir and taught Scripture study for high-school students. He was a Boy Scout leader for the Church troop and tithed his salary. His wife headed the children's religious-study group and made sure the church was decorated with fresh flowers from her garden. His children were active in youth groups, and when they were old enough, they went off to perform missionary work as their father had done in Germany.

Cecil's primary volunteer work for the Church was running its 181-acre farm near the Blue Ridge Mountains that raised food for the Mormon poor. For eight years, beginning in 1979, he spent almost every Saturday—and most Tuesdays and Thursdays, when he closed his clinic—toiling at the farm from dawn until late afternoon. He supervised armies of Church volunteers who planted and harvested corn, tomatoes, raspberries, and grapes that were shipped to a Church cannery near Andrews Air Force Base, then distributed to the needy of the Church.

He set aside a small patch of land for himself to conduct experiments on hybrid fruits and vegetables. The farm manager would call Cecil's hybrid corn "absolutely some of the best Silver Queen that you ever tasted," but Cecil didn't take kindly to the heckling he received when one batch turned out to be inedible, especially after he lectured his volunteers about the different strains of corn and the care with which they should be grown.

The Jacobson home was a bustling place. Cecil, a strict taskmaster with the children, tried to instill the work ethic in his sons. While the other neighborhood kids played baseball or soccer on weekend mornings, the Jacobson boys were required to do chores. "He thought Saturday mornings were his time to teach his children to work," a neighbor noticed. The boys played some football and were accomplished wrestlers, but otherwise they toiled around the house or helped at the Church farm or Cecil's farm near the mountains.

Joyce was the calming influence on the family. A gentle, soft-spoken woman, she was considered a "saint" for putting up with Cecil. She raised their seven children while Cecil tended to business. Joyce was an excellent cook, and Cecil was an appreciative consumer. Their home was known for huge feasts and frequent pool parties. Cecil found any excuse to entertain.

Every Monday night, considered Family Night within the Church, he organized a group of families to go to Fuddruckers for mounds of hamburgers and fries, or to

Long John Silver's for fried seafood. As the children played video games, Cecil would lead a discussion of politics, or religion, or history, or science. Normally he dominated the discussions and won the debates. "Cecil loved to pontificate," his longtime friend Carol Terry would say. "And he loved to pontificate about politics." Cecil was a staunch conservative who rarely lost an argument.

One of his best friends, Ellsworth Knudson, who lived a few houses away, was as large as Cecil, and the two were often mistaken for brothers. They went to church together, their wives were best friends, and their children would later become business partners. "A lot of Cecil's rhetoric was jive," Ells would say. "He couldn't resist looking at five apples and calling it a bushel. It doesn't mean they weren't apples, and it doesn't mean there weren't all the apples that could have been eaten that night. But to Cecil, that was a bushel."

Cecil was a master storyteller who usually played fast and loose with the facts. The Knudsons had a family code for when "Uncle Cecil" was warming up for another tall tale. They called it "*E before I*," meaning they would hear a lot of Entertainment before Information.

Ask him for the time, and he might start with a dissertation about ancient sundials. "He could talk on all sides of an issue," recalled his medical-school friend, Tom Jones. "He's opinionated, sometimes people think he's overopinionated. But that goes along with people who are doing things the way they think they should be done."

His group of Church friends included the upper echelon of Washington's business community, including top government officials, the pollster for President Reagan, realtors, doctors, a high-ranking officer in the Organization of American States, lawyers, builders, contractors, and the legislative assistant for Utah senator Orrin Hatch.

Even among Church members there were few neutral feelings toward Brother Cecil. "Either you were in his corner, or not in his corner," his friend Bob Walthius, a top State Department official, would say. Cecil's blustery personality grated on some fellow Mormons, just as with his fellow doctors. Even his best friends realized he had a way of turning people against him. "He is very much an 'I know best' kind of guy," Carol Terry would say. "You have to cut through to find the genuine, brilliant, caring man."

During male-only Scripture sessions he liked to spark debate with an outlandish comment, then sit back and enjoy the controversy he created. Afterward some of the Brothers would ask him if he'd really meant what he said. He would just laugh and say he'd enjoyed the show. Even his bishop would consider him a "gadfly," albeit an endearing one.

In his early years he shocked the Church elders with his iconoclastic views on Creation by announcing his belief that humans had descended from apes. "He marched to his own drummer," Walthius said. "He never minced words. He rubbed a lot of people the wrong way, but he didn't care. When I first met him, he had some definitive ideas about Creation. But as he got older, he pretty well toed the line on Church doctrine."

Yet he wasn't afraid to stand up to Church leaders when he thought they were wrong. He once bucked the elders when he supported a woman who was being chastised for getting pregnant out of wedlock. His GWU colleagues would remember how he performed an amnio on her and "was very much on her side" when the rest of the Church was against her.

But whenever his medical research was leading toward a potentially volatile issue within the Church, like amniocentesis or counseling women on abortion, he first consulted the Church leadership and got their permission. As he later would explain, "Before I would do any medical procedure, I made it a practice to discuss it with authorities in our Church. These aren't fellow members; these aren't occasional acquaintances; these are people who are authoritative in my belief—just to make sure that what I am contemplating doing is not going to go against their interpretation of the tenets of the Church and possibly cause problems for me or my children."

He also would say he checked with Church leaders before starting his artificial-insemination program. Officially the Church condoned artificial insemination only if a husband's semen was used, not the semen of an anonymous donor. But Cecil was known sometimes to ask his Mormon Brothers to donate a vial for the cause. "He was always trying to ask different men if they would be donors," recalled Caroline Stephenson, a neighbor and a good friend of the Jacobson family. "But in the Church a lot of people have very strong feelings about artificial insemination and wouldn't do it."

At various Church functions, she would sometimes overhear him soliciting donors, saying hundreds of families had been "blessed" as a result of his artificial-insemination program. But even with his impressive powers of persuasion, he got few takers. "They were being noncommittal because they were embarrassed," she said. "Cecil saw no reason there should be a hang-up. He looked on it as helping, not some dirty-old-man thing." But when Cecil approached her own husband, she was glad that he refused. "I don't think I would want my husband to be a donor for anybody else, but I understand the need for it." Still, she said she knew of a couple of Brothers who accepted Cecil's offer.

Chapter Nine

For the first few years after leaving George Washington University, Dr. Jacobson continued his affiliation with the school as thesis adviser to more than two dozen students seeking their advanced degrees. Unknown to the department chairman who banished him, Cecil was officially known as an "adjunct professor" who directed the research of Ph.D. students, even though he didn't have a doctorate himself. When the department chairman, Dr. Weingold, found out, he put a stop to it. Even so, for the next decade Cecil continued to portray himself on his résumé and in correspondence as an adjunct professor with George Washington University, as if he were still teaching and overseeing doctoral dissertations.

He also touted his affiliation with another medical school, the Eastern Virginia Medical School, in Norfolk, Virginia. At the time, Eastern Virginia was emerging as one of the leading institutions for reproductive medicine in America and in a few years would become famous when its doctors performed the first in-vitro fertilization in the United States.

Cecil was recruited by Mason Andrews, a former Virginia state legislator and Norfolk vice mayor, to establish a cytogenetics laboratory similar to his lab at the university. Over the years Andrews had been impressed with Cecil's presentations at the various obstetrical conferences. "Dr. Jacobson was widely known as a pioneer in his field. So we naturally felt privileged to be able to obtain his services." Despite the fact he wasn't an ob/gyn, Cecil also lectured in some courses as an associate professor of obstetrics and gynecology.

His new boss, Dr. Anibal Acosta, wasn't aware of Cecil's troubles at GWU either; he knew only of Cecil's reputation. "He was the person with the most qualifications in the Washington area," Dr. Acosta would explain, and for the next two years Cecil gave him no reason to think otherwise. "I certainly had a lot of respect for him," Dr. Acosta would say. "He was very knowledgeable." Cecil set up a genetics lab and drove several times a month to Norfolk, a three-to-four-hour trip from Vienna, to collect amniotic fluid from patients. Then he grew the cultures in his lab back home and analyzed the specimens. His fees were reasonable; in fact, some people thought he wasn't charging enough. Sometimes he didn't charge the Eastern Virginia patients at all.

In the late 1970's he was responsible for obtaining a grant to fund additional genetics work. The grant money led to an expansion of the medical school's research activities, which, ironically, later cost him his job.

As the medical school grew, it recruited Drs. Howard and Georgeanna Jones from Johns Hopkins University. Known as the First Couple of reproductive medicine in America, a few years later they would lead the first test-tube-baby team in the United States. They recruited their own geneticist from Johns Hopkins to work with them, and Cecil's part-time position was abolished. Although he had started the lab that made the revolutionary work possible, by the time the first in-vitro baby was born, Cecil had returned to his private clinic. He didn't even receive a footnote for participating.

But long after leaving Eastern Virginia, he continued to wear his affiliation with the medical school like a badge of honor. Although he was on the job for only a few years, he would make it sound like a lifetime association. More than ten years later he was still describing himself as a faculty member at Eastern Virginia, long after most people at the university had forgotten he'd ever worked there. And sometimes he would claim that the reason he wasn't on the staff at GWU anymore was because of his association with Eastern Virginia. "You cannot hold dual staff privileges," he claimed.

In later years Mason Andrews, who had recruited Cecil to Eastern Virginia, would call him one of the most brilliant men he had ever known, but he also considered Dr.

Jacobson to be a "constitutional psychopath." Andrews compared him to a man he'd known who had been in the military: every time the soldier returned home from an assignment, he promoted himself another rank. The man already was an officer. There was no reason to impress people, but he felt the need to inflate his importance. Dr. Andrews viewed Cecil as the same ilk.

In time Cecil was becoming so isolated at his clinic in the suburbs that he began to lose touch with most of his genetics colleagues. His clinic was the only facility that treated infertility patients in the Washington area that wasn't affiliated with a university hospital, and therefore not subject to peer review or oversight. He dropped his memberships in the professional associations. He would say it was to save money, but others suspected it was at least partly due to the earlier rejection of his research papers.

By 1980 he stopped publishing research altogether, although he remained a popular after-dinner speaker who was often invited to address medical groups. Once he was asked to participate in a series of panel discussions, sponsored by Abbott Laboratories, on the medical/legal aspects of a physician's practice. Five doctors engaged in a debate that the company taped for distribution to its medical customers, but once Cecil started talking, he dominated the discussion. "He spoke for ninety percent of the time," recalled one participant. The company assembled another panel, without inviting Cecil, and taped the session using a replacement.

Another time he was asked to deliver the keynote address at the annual convention of the South Atlantic Association of Obstetricians and Gynecologists. The invitation was a great honor, bestowed upon him by the department chairmen of medical schools throughout the southeastern United States. It was even more impressive considering that Cecil wasn't an obstetrician. He was made an honorary member of the group, one of the few nonobstetricians to be so honored.

He spoke to a packed meeting room of obstetricians and gynecologists at the Homestead resort in West Virginia about his old eggs theory and his work in creating trouble-free pregnancies by timing ovulation. One of the few geneticists in the crowd that day was Faye Redwine, Cecil's former lab assistant, who by then was running her own genetics lab at the Virginia College of Medicine in Richmond. She was seated between two obstetricians and was surprised at how superficial Cecil's presentation sounded. "It was based on no data," she would remember. "He showed a bunch of slides of degenerating eggs and made a whole bunch of conclusions."

Faye had always suspected this day would come. Cecil's lack of preparation was catching up with him, and Faye thought he was crashing and burning in front of his distinguished audience. She actually felt sorry for him. She was seated between two obstetricians, and near the conclusion of Cecil's rambling presentation, one obstetrician leaned over and commented to the other on Cecil's research. "Isn't this the most fascinating stuff?" he asked.

Faye was dumbfounded. She thought Cecil's presentation lacked any substance at all. "He hadn't said anything," she would remember. Yet the obstetricians gave him a thunderous round of applause. As usual, he'd dazzled them once again, but Faye wasn't fooled. "He was the geneticist in and among obstetricians who knew nothing about genetics," she would say. "So he had this natural professional barrier, a cushion, where the obstetricians didn't have a clue what he was talking about. So he was safe."

As the field of genetics went through rapid advances, Cecil wasn't keeping up with the new developments. For years he had been eyeballing the shape of chromosomes and setting them in pairs, but now his colleagues were using new and improved methods of diagnosing abnormalities. One method was called chorionic villi sampling, in which a small sample of tissue was taken from the placenta and analyzed in the laboratory, providing earlier results than amniocentesis.

In later years, when one of his amnio cases went awry and the patient intended to sue, an outside expert from the

University of Virginia was called in to examine the quality of Cecil's chromosome analysis. The expert discovered that Cecil was a decade behind the current practices of preparing cells for interpretation. In the mid-eighties, he was practicing mid-seventies cytogenetics, as if time had stopped in his laboratory the day he branched out on his own.

By the early 1980's, Cecil's infertility work was constituting a larger part of his practice, and he was treating more patients with HCG. Cloistered at his clinic, he was working without oversight or controls. There were no department chairmen to rein him in.

Soon obstetricians started having problems with some of the patients they sent to him. From time to time a patient would return from his clinic with a bizarre condition. Her medical records showed she had passed a pregnancy test, and the measurements Cecil had taken from the sonogram indicated normal growth of the fetus. But when the obstetrician examined her, he discovered the woman wasn't pregnant. Cecil would explain to the doctor that the woman had obviously miscarried and the fetus must have resorbed. These resorptions didn't happen very often, at least not enough to overshadow the cases in which he was successful, and most obstetricians accepted Cecil's explanation. After all, he was supposed to be the expert, but occasionally someone disputed his diagnosis.

The first person to do so was Dr. Edward Gahres in 1979. A tall, thin man who usually wore a bow tie, Ed Gahres had known Cecil for more than fifteen years. They had attended the university together, with Gahres a couple years ahead of Cecil, and over the years they had collaborated on prenatal research projects. Their spina bifida studies led to Cecil's questionable LSD research, and Dr. Gahres sometimes performed abortions based on Cecil's genetic counseling, because Cecil couldn't do the abortions himself. He had also assisted Cecil's in-vitro fertilization studies. Gahres had performed some of the hysterectomies from which Cecil obtained the eggs he tried to fertilize.

After leaving GWU, Dr. Gahres opened a private office not far from Cecil's clinic. He referred his amnio patients to Cecil and some of his difficult infertility cases and patients who required artificial insemination. For the first few years most of the patients he sent to Cecil came back happy and pregnant. But then there was a problem.

Gahres had been been treating a woman for quite a while, and she still hadn't gotten pregnant. Frustrated, she went to Dr. Jacobson on the recommendation of her neighbor. The next time Gahres saw her, she said she was pregnant. When he gave her a routine blood test to establish the date of the pregnancy, her HCG levels were alarmingly low. The level corresponded with a very early pregnancy, or one that was dying, despite the woman's assertion that she was entering her second trimester.

Dr. Gahres sought a second opinion and referred her for a sonogram. The radiologist reported he couldn't detect a viable pregnancy either, although he thought he observed echoes that he believed to be the remnants of pregnancy tissue. But when Dr. Gahres performed a D and C, he found no evidence of pregnancy whatsoever. In fact, the pathology report showed the woman's uterine lining was coated with "luxurious secretory endometrium," which indicated the woman hadn't been pregnant anytime in the recent past. Otherwise the thick lining would have washed away if the woman had miscarried.

Dr. Gahres questioned his patient about the obvious conflict. When she explained she had been treated by Dr. Jacobson with injections of HCG, Dr. Gahres understood the discrepancy right away. The injections could cause the woman to pass a pregnancy test, and he suspected Cecil had misinterpreted the response from the injection as a positive pregnancy.

When Dr. Gahres called Cecil to inform him of the mistake, he related his findings that the woman wasn't pregnant. He told Cecil the HCG injections had probably tripped the pregnancy test, but Cecil disagreed.

"Eddie," he said gruffly, "you're wrong." By the time Cecil administered the test, he said, the hormone was so diluted in the woman's system that it wouldn't have any affect.

Dr. Gahres persisted. He said he'd found no evidence that the woman was pregnant. It must have been the HCG, he said.

Of course the woman was pregnant, Cecil responded, but by the time Dr. Gahres saw her, she had already miscarried and resorbed.

Dr. Gahres had engaged in enough debates with Cecil over the years to know he couldn't win. He ended the conversation before it got heated. He hadn't called Cecil in anger, but only as a friend who was trying to warn a colleague that he was making a mistake; but Cecil's obstinacy surprised him. They had known each other a long time and had followed similar career paths. The only difference between them was that Ed Gahres was a board-certified ob/gyn, and Cecil wasn't.

Dr. Gahres was also chairman of the ob/gyn Department at Alexandria Hospital. One of the hospital's staff members was in trouble, and while Gahres was discussing the allegations with the Virginia State Board of Medicine, he mentioned the problem he'd encountered with Cecil's patient. He told the board's secretary, that Cecil was apparently making mistakes in diagnosing pregnancies and was refusing to listen to reason, but the medical-board official said there was nothing his agency could do. The board could act only on a patient's complaint—not a complaint from another doctor—and he told Dr. Gahres he would be wise to drop the matter. "You're going to wind up getting sued," the board official said.

Dr. Gahres went back to his patient and explained that she hadn't been pregnant. He said her pregnancy had been caused by the HCG injections, and he asked if she would file a complaint against Dr. Jacobson.

The woman got upset. Of course she was pregnant, she said, just as Dr. Jacobson had told her, and she scolded Dr. Gahres for doubting Cecil. A few days later Dr. Gahres got a call from the woman's attorney. He warned Gahres to stop interfering. Otherwise, the attorney said, he would file suit to stop him.

Gahres finally dropped the matter, but from then on he stopped sending his infertility patients to Cecil. However, he still thought enough of Cecil's amniocentesis work and genetic workups that he continued referring genetic patients to him. And from time to time he sent him a couple who wanted artificial insemination. Cecil was still having the best success rates of anyone around.

Another doctor who saw some of Cecil's dubious pregnancies in those days was Dr. William Cochrane, the dean of Washington ultrasound. He hadn't had much contact with Cecil since the days when Dr. Jacobson was experimenting with using ultrasound to diagnose microcephaly, or small-head disease. But now obstetricians were coming to Dr. Cochrane and asking for a second opinion on some of the women who Cecil was claiming were pregnant.

After seeing two or three patients Dr. Cochrane tried to warn the women to question what Cecil was telling them, but he didn't succeed. "I don't think I ever got through to a Cecil Jacobson patient," Dr. Cochrane would say. "His patients were the most loyal patients you would ever meet. If you even raised a doubt about how they were being treated, or about any of his findings, they would get quite irate and accuse you of not knowing what you were talking about. After getting berated I decided to just keep my mouth shut and keep my opinions to myself."

Yet another doctor who butted heads with Cecil was Dr. Douglas Lord, who operated an ob/gyn practice with his partner in Silver Spring, Maryland. He had been one of Cecil's students during the mid-1960s and later referred about forty or fifty patients to Cecil when Dr. Jacobson was first starting his clinic. "Everybody came back happy with Cecil," Dr. Lord would remember. "It was rare that anyone would have anything negative to say."

Dr. Lord was first impressed when Cecil had succeeded in getting a woman pregnant when even the most respected experts had failed. One patient, a veterinarian who was a personal friend of Dr. Lord, had sought help from Drs. Howard and Georgeanna Jones, the famous husband-and-wife infertility team, who at the time were still practicing at Johns Hopkins University. The Joneses were considered among the preeminent infertility experts in the country, but they were unable to help Dr. Lord's friend. Then the veterinarian and his wife went to Dr. Jacobson, and before long the woman was pregnant. "When you have someone who was a failure at Johns Hopkins and they went to Cecil and he got them pregnant, that's pretty impressive."

From then on Dr. Lord referred all his semen-analysis cases, and his most difficult infertility patients, to Cecil. One of those patients was Sharon Heyward.

Sharon first went to Dr. Jacobson in 1977, a year after Cecil opened his clinic. By then she'd had twelve miscarriages. Cecil analyzed the semen of Sharon's husband and concluded that the seminal fluid was too thick and the sperm itself was "elongated-headed." He said the semen was the cause of the miscarriages, and he prescribed vitamin C to cure it. The next time Sharon got pregnant, she carried the baby to term. "After all the letdowns I'd had, this man was God," Sharon would later recall. "I had gone to all these regular ob/gyns and never had any success, and here he gave me this baby."

When Sharon wanted to get pregnant again a year and a half later, she returned to Dr. Jacobson rather than Dr. Lord. But this time Cecil's program was different. The first time he'd given her Provera, but now he was prescribing HCG. The first time he'd sent her to a nearby hospital to get a sonogram, but this time he was doing sonograms in his office.

She got pregnant again and carried the baby for two months before she miscarried. However, this miscarriage wasn't even remotely similar to her dozen previous ones—no pain, no blood, no passing of tissue. Dr. Jacobson told her she had resorbed. Although she'd never heard of such a thing, she accepted his explanation.

Three months later she got pregnant again with Dr. Jacobson's help. This time he told her she was carrying twins. Within weeks the first one died. Dr. Jacobson told her it had resorbed. The second fetus lasted two months before it also resorbed.

Believing that something was wrong with her, Sharon started to blame herself for killing the babies. "I would see TV programs about babies, and I couldn't take it," she would remember. Around the house she was constantly on the verge of tears. Her temper was short. She would start screaming for no reason.

When she got pregnant that summer for a third time, Dr. Jacobson diagnosed twins again—but said one was conceived in August and the other in September. Soon one of them died. Dr. Jacobson said it wasn't strong enough and was "taken over" by the other one. The second fetus continued doing well, by his account, until Sharon reached her fourth month, when Cecil referred her to Dr. Lord to continue her care until delivery.

When Dr. Lord examined her, he knew right away that something was wrong. There was no conceivable way that Sharon was four months pregnant. Sharon suggested she might be resorbing another baby and told him about the previous miscarriages and resorptions.

Dr. Lord said her story was ridiculous. "That doesn't make any sense," he said.

He sent her to a nearby hospital to have some blood drawn. The next day, after the results were in, he called her at work and said he wanted her to have a sonogram.

"Why?" Sharon asked.

"The pregnancy test came back negative," he said. "I want to see if something might have happened."

After the scan Dr. Lord called Sharon into his office and said the results were conclusive. He said she wasn't pregnant.

"Could I have resorbed?" Sharon asked.

Dr. Lord said it wasn't likely. "Something's not right," he cautioned, "and I don't want you going back to him."

Sharon consulted an attorney and planned to sue Dr. Jacobson for negligence in using his sonogram machine. The lawyer, Julie Brasfield, from a large Washington-area firm that specialized in malpractice and personal-injury cases, said Sharon didn't have a case. There was no law in Virginia that a doctor, nurse, or even a licensed sonographer had to be certified to operate a machine. Anyone could open an office and start performing sonograms. In the end it would be Sharon's word against a well-respected doctor who could produce a host of medical experts to support him. Sharon realized she didn't have a chance. "I would be the little girl crying wolf because I didn't get a baby," she said.

Sharon's husband tolerated her guilt and outbursts for a while longer, until it became clear she wasn't getting any better. She had to pull herself together, he finally told her. She already had a husband and a baby who needed her. She couldn't grieve forever over children she had never had. She sought psychiatric counseling and learned to deal with her grief, but her maternal urges were still unfulfilled. She became a foster mother for stray children, trying to help runaways and juvenile delinquents as much as she was trying to help herself. In time she got pregnant again. Through sheer force of will she carried the baby to term— without help from Dr. Jacobson or any other specialist— and delivered a baby girl.

Dr. Lord wasn't sure what had gone wrong in Sharon's case. He believed a physician was entitled to an occasional mistake, and though Cecil had obviously blundered, Dr. Lord gave his former professor the benefit of the doubt. But then another patient came to him a few months later with the same story.

He wasn't sure what to do. He'd never confronted another physician about a patient. But when he examined a third nonpregnant woman a short time later, he decided to call Cecil and find out what was going on.

"You and I have been friends for a long time, but we've got some problems here," Dr. Lord told him. "You've done a lot of good for my patients, but this is bizarre. It makes no sense."

Cecil's response was cold, nothing like the kindly and approachable professor Dr. Lord had known. Was Cecil's family okay? Was he having financial problems? Dr. Lord offered to help. "If there's something I can do, I'll come down and have lunch and maybe we can figure out what's wrong."

But Cecil didn't want any help. "You don't know what you're talking about," he said icily. There was nothing wrong with his medical diagnosis. He'd always been out front of other doctors. "I know what I'm doing," he insisted. "You're wrong."

Dr. Lord told Cecil that what he was telling these women about resorption was a "bunch of crap." And if Cecil refused to listen, then he was ending their relationship. He wouldn't be sending Cecil any more patients. "If one of them has a serious problem and they decide to sue you, I'll testify against you," Dr. Lord warned. "I'm really upset with what you're doing."

Chapter Ten

Summer 1987

When Debbie Gregory was pronounced pregnant for a third time, her elation was tempered by doubt. It had been barely a month since her second miscarriage. "I haven't even had my period yet," she told the doctor. "How can I be pregnant?"

Dr. Jacobson checked her temperature chart and said there was no doubt. Although there wasn't much of a temperature rise, he said she obviously had ovulated. The proof was in the positive pregnancy test on his desk.

Debbie was determined to carry this pregnancy to term. Applying Dr. Jacobson's program of positive thinking, she became a consummate optimist. "Nothing can happen this time," she told Steven. "It's just got to work out. At least the odds have to be in our favor."

Steven was relieved to see her spirits improving. Since starting their infertility treatments, she had become a changed woman, often morose and withdrawn—avoiding their friends and crying in her bedroom—until he'd started to worry about her mental health. But with the news of the latest pregnancy, she was back to her old self and determined not to fail again. Even so, she suspected that something in her anatomy was killing off the babies—maybe it was just a simple problem that could be easily corrected. But even if it was something serious, she needed to know.

Since her teens she had religiously consulted her gynecologist for twice-a-year checkups, but after going to Dr. Jacobson for more than a year, she hadn't even had a pap smear. He'd never examined her, except for the time when he'd briefly checked for swelling of her ovaries and prescribed the fertility drug Clomid. Since she wasn't seeing her regular gynecologist, Dr. Barter, anymore, she asked Dr. Jacobson for a referral to another doctor whom he trusted.

This wasn't her first request, but he'd never followed through. "I'll refer you as soon as you get pregnant," he'd told her. Then, when she was pregnant, he advised her to wait until after the first trimester, when her ob/gyn would follow her progress until delivery. But even though both pregnancies had progressed into the second trimester, he'd never referred her, and now she was insistent.

"If there is something wrong with me, it's not going to do any good to be pregnant," she told him, and explained her suspicions about an inherent problem that was making her destroy babies.

He told her to wait until she was a little further along so the obstetrician could examine the fetus and give her a pap smear at the same time, but Debbie was adamant. "If something is wrong, I want to know about it." If he didn't give her a referral, then she would look through the yellow pages and find a doctor herself.

Dr. Jacobson finally relented and selected a group of four ob/gyns that he'd known for years. "Gray-hairs," he called them with respect. On July 3 Debbie went to see Dr. Leonard Eppard of Annandale, Virginia, who had gone to medical school with Cecil. One of Dr. Eppard's partners was Dr. John Doppelheuer, who also was Chris Maimone's doctor and who would later play a significant role in Debbie's and Chris's cases.

Dr. Eppard had been referring patients to Cecil for years, either for amniocentesis, artificial insemination, or a bit of reassurance that other physicians weren't comfortable in rendering. A typical referral might be a highly educated woman in her late thirties who was panicked that her child might be born genetically deformed. Before learning she was pregnant, she had attended a party where she had downed a glass of wine or walked through a cloud of cigar smoke, and was worried about the effect on the baby. Dr. Eppard knew the risk was insignificant, but there was no way to assuage the woman. So he would send her to Cecil.

Dr. Jacobson would do a pregnancy test and a sonogram and tell the woman that everything was all right. "You have a great baby there," he would say. "It's a wonderful, healthy baby." The woman would leave his office feeling better. The alternative would be to send the patient to a high-tech infertility institute, where she would spend thousands of dollars on a medical workup and a battery of expensive tests that couldn't reassure her any more than Cecil would.

Dr. Eppard realized he was resorting to a form of "quackery," as he called it, but as long as Cecil's prices were reasonable, he didn't have a problem. The patient needed absolute reassurance when there wasn't any. "But Cecil didn't seem to mind that too much," Dr. Eppard would say. "He would tell these women everything was fine, but he didn't know any better than I did. I have difficulty doing that. And I was glad I knew somebody who could do it."

Dr. Eppard elicited a medical history from Debbie, and she explained the problems she'd been having with miscarriages. Because the pregnancy was so early—only four weeks by Dr. Jacobson's calculations—Dr. Eppard didn't hold out much hope of being able to detect a heartbeat. A standard stethoscope wouldn't pick up a heartbeat for another month or two, but an instrument known as a Dop-Tone meter—an amplified stethoscope that operated like radar—might be able to pick up something. He put on the headphones and listened for a short while before conceding it was too soon. He told Debbie he wanted to see her again in three weeks, and she made an appointment.

Two days later Debbie started to hemorrhage again—just as her guests were arriving for a weekend Fourth of July cookout in her backyard. She'd been such a recluse lately that she felt it would be therapeutic to invite some friends over. She'd told only a few people about her second pregnancy, and even fewer about her third, and when she started bleeding, she kept up the façade of cheerful hostess rather than go through the entire explanation about her miscarriages.

As soon as her guests left, she called Dr. Jacobson at home. "Relax," he said, and told her to drink some vodka or beer to ease the cramping. "Bring a urine sample with you tomorrow morning."

At the clinic he gave her a pregnancy test, and it was positive; then he gave her an injection and two bottles of HCG so she could inject herself at home. He said he wanted to do another pregnancy test later in the week "just to be sure" and told her to continue with the HCG and the progesterone suppositories he prescribed.

The cost for the day was $110. On the way out she settled her account at the front desk. During her last visit she had paid him $185, but she still owed him more than $300. Normally he was tolerant about letting her run a tab, but once, when the account got too large, he mentioned that Debbie needed to pay up. "My accountant will get all over me," he told her. Lately the bills were starting to mount again. Each visit could cost more than $100 once the HCG shots, pregnancy tests, and sonograms were added. And she was seeing him so often. So far she'd had more than sixty HCG shots, thirteen pregnancy tests, and nine sonograms and had paid him $3,170. The money wasn't important. She figured it was a small price to pay for getting pregnant, especially since her insurance company was paying for most of it, anyway.

Debbie's sonograms started at week seven, on July 13, 1987. Dr. Jacobson drew two concentric circles on the photo to outline the tiny embryo and the sac around it.

Week eight—July 20. He measured the size of the sac as twenty-four by twenty-three by forty centimeters and said Debbie was doing well.

Four days later she kept her next appointment with Dr. Eppard. Again he was unable to detect the heartbeat. Not wanting to alarm her, he explained the baby was probably lying in an unusual position, obscured behind the bladder or another internal organ.

Week nine—July 27. Dr. Jacobson detected embryo movement and said the sac was growing, measuring twenty-three by forty-two by twenty-eight centimeters. On their Polaroid he outlined it with a felt-tip pen.

Week ten—August 3. The sac was now forty-six by forty-six centimeters, he said, considerably larger than the week before. He saw "Junior" moving again, and for the first time he measured the crown-rump, the distance from its rump to the crown of its head, at thirty centimeters.

Week eleven—August 10. A new development. Dr. Jacobson measured the fetal head for the first time. The head circumference, known as the biparietal diameter, or BPD, was 1.7—exactly what he said it should have been. He started keeping a chart of the fetal head growth. The crown-rump measurement was thirty-eight centimeters, and the sac was up to fifty by fifty centimeters.

Week twelve—August 18. Debbie had another appointment with Dr. Eppard. He listened for a heartbeat but didn't hear it. This time his concern was evident. He told Debbie he wanted to do a pelvic exam, and afterwards he explained that Debbie's uterus was undersized for a woman who was supposed to be three months pregnant. He wanted to refer her for an independent ultrasound exam.

"Why, what's wrong?" she asked. "Dr. Jacobson has been doing them every week, and everything is fine."

Dr. Eppard explained that he should have located the heartbeat by now, and he wanted a second opinion from an expert.

She told him about Dr. Jacobson's sonograms, and how he had seen the heartbeat and pointed out the movement of the baby.

Dr. Eppard tried to be diplomatic as he explained that some sonography equipment was more sophisticated than others. He suggested that, just to be safe, she get a second opinion. There was no risk involved, he said. "It's painless. It won't hurt you or the baby." He set up an appointment for her with the Washington Ultrasound Associates.

When Debbie got home, she told Steven that something was wrong—she could sense it from the doctor's demeanor.

"Wait a minute," Steven said. One doctor said everything was fine—a doctor they had been seeing for nearly a year and a half—and the other doctor, whom Debbie had just met, was putting vague notions in her mind that something was wrong. "Who are we going to believe?" he asked. "You're going to trust this new doctor above Dr. Jacobson?"

Debbie was confused. Despite her doubts she had to admit Steven's argument made sense. Debbie didn't know anything about Dr. Eppard. He seemed nice enough, but she thought he certainly didn't have Dr. Jacobson's credentials. "We talked about it," Debbie would later remember, "and once I got calmed down, I agreed with my husband." When she kept her appointment with Dr. Jacobson the next day, she told him about Dr. Eppard's concerns, and his reaction surprised her.

"He has no right upsetting you," Dr. Jacobson said sternly. Debbie was *his* patient, not Dr. Eppard's, and he shouldn't be interfering. He scolded her, saying she should not have allowed him to do a pelvic exam. Considering the bleeding she'd been experiencing, the procedure was dangerous and potentially life threatening to the baby. "If the cervix is open enough to bleed, then it is open enough for bacteria to get up inside and kill the baby," he said.

Debbie had never seen him so upset. His face turned red and he was breathing heavily. Debbie tried to calm him down. "Dr. Eppard said that maybe the equipment at Washington Ultrasound was more sophisticated," she said.

"There's nothing wrong with my equipment," he replied curtly. His machine might not be as modern as some of the latest models on the market, he admitted, but it was in perfect working order. "I do amniocentesis with it all the time." She didn't need another ultrasound, he said, it was just a waste of time and money. He led her to the sonogram room and quickly scanned her. "See, the baby is fine," he repeated after a few moments of hovering the transducer over her abdomen. From where Debbie was lying she couldn't see anything. He measured the sac as sixty-two by sixty centimeters, about 20 percent larger than the previous ultrasound. He pointed out the heartbeat and said he didn't know why Dr. Eppard couldn't locate it. "Sometimes you can't find it easily," he said. "Particularly early in a pregnancy."

After listening to Dr. Jacobson, Debbie felt guilty for having questioned him. As she prepared to leave, he gave her another pep talk, assuring her that everything was all right. "I have been taking care of you," he said. "I have been doing ultrasounds. You're on hormonal support. Everything is fine." He repeated there was no need for another sonogram. "I'll call Dr. Eppard and I'll tell him so."

As usual she felt reassured and decided to follow his advice. Why waste her money on another sonogram? she thought. She was spending enough already. So she canceled her appointment with Washington Ultrasound Associates and continued her course of treatments with Dr. Jacobson.

Chapter Eleven

Pregnancy agreed with Chris Maimone, and she was wearing it well. She was gaining weight, her stomach was "pooching out," as she called it, and her breasts were swelling. During one visit Dr. Jacobson examined her breasts for tenderness and showed Larry how well her milk ducts were forming. He said it demonstrated that the pregnancy was progressing normally.

Before long Chris was growing out of her clothes. She still had some maternity outfits left over from her last pregnancy, the one that ended in a true miscarriage, but she didn't feel comfortable wearing them, so one Saturday afternoon she dragged Larry to the mall. Normally she couldn't bribe him to go shopping, but he didn't mind this time. He browsed through the baby toys and infant clothes while Chris bought two new outfits. She proudly wore one out of the store, as if it were a neon sign proclaiming she was pregnant.

They stopped to eat lunch, and as Chris got up from the table to go to the bathroom, a woman at the next table remarked loud enough for Chris and Larry to hear that Chris wasn't big enough to be wearing maternity clothes. When Chris came back from the rest room, she was crying. Larry tried to comfort her. "She doesn't know what she's talking about," he said, and told Chris that if she felt more comfortable in maternity clothes, then she should wear them.

Chris refused to wear the outfits at work. For the time being she didn't want the people at the lab to know she was pregnant, at least until she was sure this one was safe. After her miscarriage she was fed up with people who offered condolences, or told her horror stories about someone's sister or cousin who had suffered a miscarriage, so she bought some larger pants and let people think she was gaining weight.

At the clinic Dr. Jacobson was starting Chris on weekly sonograms. No matter how many times Larry sat through a sonogram exam, he still couldn't see the image of the baby—until Dr. Jacobson pointed it out to him. Dr. Jacobson always gave them the Polaroid, and they showed it off like the proud parents they hoped to be.

One weekend they went to visit Chris's mother and father in northern Maryland and showed them the ultrasound pictures of their future grandchild. Chris's mother studied it closely, but said she couldn't make out a baby. When she saw how her comment affected Chris, she quickly pointed out that sonogram pictures were always difficult to read. "I never saw anything with your sisters' either," she told Chris.

Larry got the same reaction when he showed the people at work and no one could see what he was talking about. Larry figured they weren't as excited as he was.

In late August, when Chris was seven weeks pregnant, she had another blood/pregnancy test at work. Again the HCG levels were consistent with a three-week pregnancy. The levels should have been between 20,000 and 200,000 units, but they were only 341. Dr. Jacobson blamed shoddy lab work again, but this time Chris had her doubts. She was getting an uneasy feeling that things weren't going right, and to ease her mind, she considered visiting her own obstetrician, Dr. Doppelheuer.

By the end of her second month Chris started bleeding again. "It's just like my first miscarriage," she told Larry, terrified that she was losing another baby.

Dr. Jacobson told her to lie flat on her back for the next twenty-four to forty-eight hours, and to double up on the progesterone suppositories, taking one in the morning and another at night. If the bleeding subsided, she could return to work part-time on Thursday, he said, but no matter what happened, he wanted to see her again on Friday.

Chris took the rest of the week off. She stayed in bed with her feet inclined above her head. Initially her boss had been understanding when she called in sick or left early to go to the clinic, but she was missing so much work that he was losing patience. Chris didn't care. She would quit in a heartbeat if it meant carrying the pregnancy to term.

On Friday Dr. Jacobson performed another sonogram and put Chris's fears to rest. The pregnancy was still viable, he said, and he detected fetal movement and a heartbeat. He told Chris he wasn't concerned about the bleeding as much as the possibility of a genetically damaged child. He said he wanted to perform an amniocentesis to eliminate any doubts.

Chris said she didn't think an amnio was necessary. There was no history of genetic problems in her family, or Larry's either, and her age wasn't a factor—she was only twenty-eight. She also thought it was too risky to stick a needle into the sac and risk another miscarriage. She considered the pregnancy a gift from God, and even if the genetic tests showed her child had Down's syndrome or some other genetic defect, she would never abort it. Genetic deformities or not, this was her baby and she was keeping it.

Dr. Jacobson, however, was insistent. The risk of genetic problems was too high, he said, and he couldn't rest easy until he was certain. The decision didn't have to be made right away, he said. They could discuss it again later.

Although Chris wasn't scheduled to consult her obstetrician for another month or so at the end of her first trimester, there were too many questions nagging at her—the bleeding, the questionable lab tests, and now Dr. Jacobson's insistence about an amniocentesis. She decided not to wait any longer.

"I want to go see Dr. Doppelheuer," she told Larry.

Dr. John Doppelheuer was a graduate of the George Washington University School of Medicine who practiced with three of the "gray-hairs" that Cecil often talked about—Dr. Leonard Eppard, Dr. Harry Beavers, and Dr. Eric Kolvareid. Although Dr. Doppelheuer had been a medical student at GWU while Cecil was on the faculty, the only contact he would remember was having attended one of Cecil's lectures on infertility—and that it was at "total variance" with all the other lectures he'd heard on the subject.

On September 8, 1987, Chris went to see Dr. Doppelheuer. By coincidence Debbie Gregory was already in the office that day for her scheduled appointment with Dr. Eppard. Debbie was apprehensive about facing Dr. Eppard after Cecil had threatened to tell him off for doing the pelvic exam. She was relieved that Dr. Eppard wasn't available, and she was shuffled off to his partner, Dr. Doppelheuer.

Dr. Doppelheuer reviewed Debbie's chart and noticed that his partner hadn't been able to hear a heartbeat during Debbie's last two visits. He examined her abdomen to feel for "uterine expansion," but didn't find the enlargement he would have expected in a woman nearly three months pregnant. He listened with a Dop-Tone but still didn't hear a heartbeat. With some patients, even when he didn't hear the fetal heart, he still got a sense of "something there," but this time he heard only soft, squishing sounds indicating Debbie's uterus was empty.

Debbie sensed his concern. "What's wrong?" she asked. "You can tell me if something's wrong with my baby."

He said he wanted to examine her further. He wanted to perform a pelvic exam, but after the way Dr. Jacobson had reacted to the last pelvic, she told him it was out of the question. She explained that Dr. Jacobson had seen the heartbeat during a sonogram, and she couldn't understand why Dr. Eppard couldn't find it.

Dr. Doppelheuer had to admit an ultrasound machine was more reliable than a Dop-Tone. "Don't worry," he said, not wanting to frighten her. "I'm sure we'll hear it the next time."

As Debbie was leaving, Chris and Larry were in the waiting room. The two women had never met. Like most of Dr. Jacobson's patients, they usually rushed in and out of the clinic to get their shots and rarely met the other women. As Debbie was settling her bill and scheduling her next appointment, she remarked to the receptionist that she was a patient of Dr. Jacobson. Chris overheard her and tapped Larry on the shoulder. "She goes to Jacobson too," Chris whispered, pointing to the woman at the front desk wearing maternity clothes.

When it was their turn, the Maimones went in to see the doctor. Chris brought him up-to-date about her pregnancy and told him about Dr. Jacobson's insistence that she have an amnio. Dr. Doppelheuer said he didn't want to second-guess another physician, but he didn't think an amnio was necessary. He generally didn't recommend the procedure unless there was a history of birth defects, or if the woman was older than thirty-five.

His examination of Chris was a carbon copy of the examination he'd just performed on Debbie—there was no uterine expansion and he couldn't hear a heartbeat.

"I don't understand," Chris said. "How come you can't hear the heartbeat when Dr. Jacobson is seeing it?" She told him that Dr. Jacobson had shown Larry the pulsating blip on the screen. She even pulled the photo out of her purse to show him.

The coincidence was too great for two women from the same doctor to have identical symptoms of false pregnancy. Their dates of conception were only eleven days apart. Although he had a vague recollection that someone had told him about Dr. Jacobson's problems with false pregnancies, he gave Cecil the benefit of the doubt. Maybe his sonogram machine wasn't calibrated properly. Or maybe Dr. Jacobson was sloppy. He decided not to tell Chris and Larry about Debbie Gregory, and suggested that during their next appointment they should ask Dr. Jacobson to count the baby's heartbeats. A fetal heartbeat was much more rapid than the mother's and should be easy to distinguish, he said.

When Chris returned to Dr. Jacobson's four days later, she didn't mention her visit to Dr. Doppelheuer. He performed his routine sonogram. Once again he said he saw the baby moving and pointed out its heartbeat. Larry asked him to count the beats.

Dr. Jacobson intently studied the screen and told Larry to count off ten seconds on his watch, then quickly figured the math in his head. The heartbeat was 120 beats a minute, he said, exactly what it should be.

Chris Maimone's second visit with Dr. Doppelheuer took place on September 30, three weeks after the first one. She was more anxious than ever to hear the baby's heartbeat. She was supposedly fourteen weeks pregnant now, and Dr. Doppelheuer knew if he didn't hear it, something was seriously wrong. He applied the gel to Chris's stomach and listened through his headset. The womb was silent. He stopped, cleaned off his equipment, and listened again. Again he heard nothing.

Chris didn't need to be told the gravity of the situation. Dr. Doppelheuer said he wanted to send her for an independent sonogram. It was nearly six P.M. and too late to arrange an appointment for that afternoon, but Dr. Doppelheuer said he would call the sonographers and set up a meeting for the next day.

"Please make it for first thing in the morning," Chris said. She would be too anxious to wait all day.

Washington Ultrasound Associates was the oldest and largest radiology group in the Washington area, with offices in Virginia, Maryland, and Washington, D.C. Founded by Dr. William Cochrane, the Scottish radiologist who had once cautioned Cecil about trying to make microcephaly diagnoses from sonograms, the group included at least a dozen of the top radiologists in the area.

When a technician took Chris to one of the examination rooms, Chris explained she was fourteen weeks pregnant and her doctor couldn't detect a heartbeat. As the technician performed a brief scan, Larry noticed the striking difference between this machine and Dr. Jacobson's. It was like the difference between an ancient black-and-white television and a new state-of-the-art color model. This picture was so sharp and clear, they could easily make out the image of Chris's uterus. It looked like a hollow football. But Larry realized that if Chris was fourteen weeks pregnant, it shouldn't be hollow at all. They should be seeing a baby in it.

Chris had seen a similar picture once before—during her miscarriage.

"Why are you here?" the technician asked, sounding puzzled.

Chris repeated that her doctor hadn't been able to hear the heartbeat.

"I'll be right back," the technician said, and went to get the doctor. Larry followed her out the door.

"What's the matter?" he asked. The technician didn't answer and started to turn away.

"The baby's dead isn't it?" he asked. The nurse grabbed his arm. "You've got to be strong for her," she said, then went to get the doctor.

Chris was crying when Larry went back inside. In a few moments the radiologist, Dr. Peter Dunner, came in. A short, stocky man with a thick mustache, he was moving quickly, as if he had an office full of patients backed up and he was late for his next appointment. He went directly to the machine and scanned Chris for a moment, then, without looking up, asked why she was there. He seemed annoyed that they were wasting his time.

Larry answered. "My wife is three months pregnant," he said.

Dr. Dunner turned to glance at Chris, then looked back at the screen, continuing to run the probe over Chris's stomach. "No, she's not," he said. "She's not pregnant."

"What do you mean?" Larry shot back. They were braced to hear the baby had miscarried, but that's not what Dr. Dunner was saying.

"Look," Dr. Dunner said, pointing to the screen. "Look at the uterus. It's empty." If Chris was three months pregnant, her uterus would be extended to at least twice that size. Again he seemed annoyed they were wasting his time.

"Hold on, Doc," Larry said, becoming indignant. Of course she was pregnant. How could the doctor make such a stupid mistake? "I've seen the baby," Larry said. "We've counted the heartbeats. What are you trying to pull?" Chris thought that Larry was going to hit him.

But Dr. Dunner wasn't backing down. He wanted to

know where they had seen this phantom fetus and its imaginary heartbeat.

"Dr. Cecil Jacobson," Larry said, and explained that Dr. Jacobson had been treating them for several months now.

"Calm down," Dr. Dunner told Larry. He told Chris to get dressed. "I want to see you in my office."

They were too confused to make much sense of what the radiologist was trying to tell them. Chris was crying hysterically. Larry felt powerless to help. He had cooled off and was trying to rationalize the situation. "I can understand a miscarriage like she had the last time," he told the radiologist. "But I can't understand how there is nothing there at all." He said Dr. Dunner must have made a mistake. "You're not reading it right. I saw the sonogram. And I saw the heartbeat for myself."

But Dr. Dunner said he was absolutely certain of his diagnosis. "There's nothing there," he said flatly. "I'm really sorry that I had to be the one to tell you this, but Mrs. Maimone is not pregnant."

They left the radiologist's office and went back to Dr. Doppelheuer's. He apologized as if it were his fault. But he concurred with Dr. Dunner's diagnosis. "Chris is not pregnant," he concluded.

They couldn't believe what was happening. If Drs. Dunner and Doppelheuer were right, that meant Dr. Jacobson had been deceiving them. He had to have known there was no baby. But why would he lead them on? They didn't have a rational explanation. Chris had an appointment with Dr. Jacobson the next afternoon. They asked Dr. Doppelheuer what they should do.

Dr. Doppelheuer said they had two choices. Chris and Larry could either skip the appointment and get on with their lives, or they could confront Dr. Jacobson and demand an explanation. But then Dr. Doppelheuer smiled wryly as he suggested a third option. What would happen, he wondered aloud, if they kept their appointment and pretended nothing had happened? Wouldn't it be interesting to hear what Dr. Jacobson had to say? Would he still see the baby? Or would he say it was gone?

"This could be a mistake," Dr. Doppelheuer said. "Let's give him the benefit of the doubt. But don't indicate you saw me or went to get an ultrasound, and see what he says."

The Maimones didn't sleep well that night, lying on the couch in each other's arms, the television tuned to a late-night movie they didn't watch. Chris fought to stay awake, knowing she would be haunted by nightmares if she slept. They recounted their visits to Dr. Jacobson, looking for the warning signs they must have missed, and studied the sonogram photos, trying to find a baby. They felt so foolish. They couldn't believe anyone could be so cruel as to deliberately mislead them. They talked long into the night, trying to decide whether Dr. Jacobson had lied to them or had made a mistake. And together, through the wee hours of the morning, they formulated a plan to find out.

Chris called the clinic as soon as it opened and spoke to the doctor's wife. Her appointment was scheduled for late that afternoon, but she couldn't wait that long, so she explained that Larry had a conflict at work and asked to reschedule her visit for that morning. Mrs. Jacobson said there were several patients ahead of Chris, but she was certain they could squeeze her in.

When they got to the clinic, two pregnant women were waiting to get amnios. Chris's eyes were red and puffy from crying most of the night. Her nerves were shot. Even in the waiting room she was on the verge of tears whenever she looked at Larry. When they were finally summoned into the examination room, Dr. Jacobson asked if everything was okay. "No more bleeding?"

Chris couldn't answer, so Larry mumbled that everything was fine.

As Chris climbed onto the examination table, she was so nervous she couldn't control herself. She was shaking and trembling so violently, she was sure the doctor would notice. Larry stood against the wall near the light switch, watching Dr. Jacobson's every move. In the dim light from the screen he watched Dr. Jacobson apply the jelly to Chris's stomach and operate the probe, crouching on his stool like a huge catcher awaiting a fastball. In a moment Dr. Jacobson announced, "There's Junior."

Chris had hoped the doctor would have an explanation. She would have believed almost anything he told her, but when he claimed he saw the baby, she was disappointed— she felt betrayed.

Larry remained against the wall, forcing himself to wait. "Is everything fine, Doc?" he asked.

Dr. Jacobson said everything appeared to be normal. He pointed out the baby's head and said he saw its arms moving. He referred to his chart on the wall and made his measurements. Then he printed the sonogram photo.

Larry asked again if everything was all right.

The doctor repeated that everything was fine.

Larry flipped on the light. "Doc, we need to talk." He told Dr. Jacobson what the other doctors had found. "They said there's no baby, Doc. What's going on here?"

Dr. Jacobson's face turned red. Larry thought he was going to have a stroke.

"Don't bullshit me, Doc," Larry said, becoming agitated. "What's happening here?"

Dr. Jacobson said he didn't know what Larry was talking about. Of course Chris was pregnant. Of course there was a baby. Larry had seen it himself, hadn't he?

"Then why are two other doctors telling us differently?" Larry asked.

Dr. Jacobson said he would scan Chris again to dispel any doubts. He asked Larry to extinguish the light and turned to face the machine. He examined Chris again, but this time his diagnosis was different. A moment earlier he had seen a baby moving, now he said he saw only "fetal matter." He wasn't certain if the pregnancy was viable or not.

"What's going on here, Doc?" Larry asked accusingly. How could he see "Junior" one minute and only "fetal matter" the next?

Dr. Jacobson didn't have much to say. He explained he was pressed for time. His amnio patients were waiting in the lobby, and he needed to tend to them. When he had more time, he wanted to examine Chris more thoroughly. He told them to come back after lunch and he would do a pelvic.

"I'll think about it," Chris said, then left with her husband.

They went to the nearest pay phone and called Dr. Doppelheuer. They held the phone between them so they both could hear. "He sees a baby," Chris said, sobbing into the phone. "I'm so confused. I don't understand. Yesterday there was no baby, and today Dr. Jacobson is saying there is a baby."

"I'm sorry," Dr. Doppelheuer said, and insisted there was no doubt. "You are not pregnant," he maintained. "You have to realize that."

Chris explained that Dr. Jacobson wanted to examine her again and do a pelvic. "What should I do?" she asked.

Dr. Doppelheuer said he couldn't advise her. "It's your body," he said. "You have to make your own decision." But he emphasized again that she wasn't pregnant, no matter what Dr. Jacobson told her. If she still had doubts, he suggested she talk to Dr. Dunner again.

They called Dr. Dunner's office and asked if he was absolutely certain. He said there was no mistake. He offered to scan her again, at no charge, and said he would get his boss to render a second opinion.

Chris and Larry went to a McDonald's restaurant down the street to get a drink and try to make some sense of the dizzying events. They considered going home, but wondered what Dr. Jacobson would see at the afternoon appointment. Would he see Junior? Or just pieces of a baby? Would the baby be there, or nothing at all?

When they returned two hours later, Dr. Jacobson had composed himself. With Chris's permission he examined her and said her uterus was enlarged to twice its normal size, which indicated pregnancy, no matter what the other doctors were telling her. Then he performed a sonogram and said the sac appeared to be collapsed, but he wasn't sure.

"You're still pregnant," he said, but he couldn't guarantee that she would carry the pregnancy to term. Then he took them to his office and closed the door.

Larry demanded an explanation. Why were the other doctors claiming Chris wasn't pregnant? They had nothing to gain.

Dr. Jacobson said he didn't know. He insisted again that Chris was pregnant. How could they think otherwise? Hadn't they seen the positive pregnancy tests for themselves? Hadn't they seen the baby on the sonogram screen? They had even measured the heartbeat. There was no doubt Chris was pregnant. "You see what I see," he said.

The office intercom buzzed several times, but he ignored it. His wife came to the door, saying a patient was on the phone and urgently needed to speak to him. He snapped at her, saying that he was in the midst of a conference and couldn't be interrupted. He told her to take a message. Returning to the Maimones, he handed Chris a small specimen bottle and told her to collect any tissue she passed so he could analyze it for chromosomal abnormalities. But he said it probably wouldn't be necessary—he hoped Chris would experience a resorption.

He rolled up his shirtsleeve and explained the phenomenon of resorption. "Have you ever seen a bruise?" he asked.

They decided to call Dr. Doppelheuer from Jacobson's office. The two doctors conferred on the phone; then Dr. Jacobson handed the phone to Chris. Dr. Doppelheuer told her that under no circumstances was she to allow anyone to perform a D and C on her, and he ordered her to stop all injections of HCG and progesterone suppositories.

No pronouncement was necessary, but it was clear that Chris was no longer Dr. Jacobson's patient. The mantle of primary physician had passed to Dr. Doppelheuer. And for the first time in days Chris felt a sense of comfort.

As they were leaving, Dr. Jacobson reminded Chris to collect the tissue in the specimen bottle. In any event, he said, the office visit and sonogram were on the house. "I don't charge for bad news," he said.

Chapter Twelve

When Chris left Dr. Jacobson's office, she rushed to the nearest department store to buy some new clothes. Her maternity outfit was suffocating her—she felt dirty and violated—and had to get out of it right away. She bought a pair of blue jeans and a new blouse, then went back to Washington Ultrasound Associates.

She was shaking and felt sick to her stomach. A nurse brought her a blanket; then Dr. Dunner came in and scanned her again. His diagnosis didn't change.

His boss, Dr. Cochrane, came in. He'd seen enough of Dr. Jacobson's cases over the years to know what to expect. He briefly looked at the screen and said he didn't see a pregnancy, then walked out without another word. The Maimones got the impression he'd rather be anywhere than in that examination room.

Dr. Dunner asked them what they planned to do next. Larry said they weren't sure, but were considering a lawsuit. The doctor warned them that suing a respected member of the medical community could take a lot of time and cost a lot of money. Even so, he offered to testify if they needed him. "Don't get mad," he said. "Get even."

The next morning, October 3, 1987, Debbie Gregory had an appointment with Dr. Doppelheuer. It was supposed to be a routine visit. She convinced Steven to go with her so he could meet the doctor who would deliver their baby. Steven had never been to a gynecologist's office before, and he was curious to see what it was like.

Debbie was supposedly eighteen weeks pregnant, nearly halfway through her pregnancy. Even before Dr. Doppelheuer examined her, he knew he wouldn't hear a heartbeat. When Debbie wouldn't permit him to do a pelvic exam, he was gentle but insistent. And afterward, for the second time within two days, he had to tell a patient there was no baby.

"The baby has died?" Debbie asked, thinking she had suffered a third miscarriage.

"No," Dr. Doppelheuer answered. "You're not pregnant. There is no baby."

Like the Maimones, she didn't believe him at first. It was his word—the word of a doctor she had seen only twice—against the physician she had come to trust as a friend. He told her about Chris and sent her for a sonogram. The diagnosis came back: "No evidence of pregnancy."

Early the next week Dr. Doppelheuer referred Debbie to Fairfax Hospital. The head of the ob/gyn department, Dr. James Sites, had once been Cecil's boss at George Washington University and considered him a brilliant geneticist, but for the past few years he had been hearing troubling stories about his once-prized staff member. Doctors were complaining about Dr. Jacobson's phantom pregnancies. The complaints had become so numerous—at least five doctors affiliated with Fairfax Hospital had complained to him—that he finally confronted Cecil about the problem.

As Dr. Sites would later explain, "I told Dr. Jacobson that I thought there were many reports coming out of patients who supposedly were pregnant when another doctor said they were not." Dr. Sites even suggested that Cecil get out of the infertility business and confine himself to genetic counseling, but Dr. Jacobson didn't listen. He claimed he was right and the other doctors were wrong. He predicted he would eventually be exonerated, just as he'd silenced his critics over amniocentesis. "My success rate is as good as anyone else's," Cecil told him, and said there was no reason to reevaluate the way he was treating his infertility patients.

When Dr. Sites examined Debbie, he didn't mention any of this. He confirmed the other findings. "You're not pregnant," he told her.

"You're absolutely positive?" Debbie asked.

To demonstrate while doing an internal exam, he placed Debbie's hand on her stomach and pushed against it with his own from the inside. If Debbie was pregnant, there was no way he could do that.

"How can Dr. Jacobson make a mistake like this?" Debbie asked.

Dr. Sites explained that Cecil was a geneticist, not an infertility specialist. "He shouldn't be practicing fertility," the doctor said. He suggested that Debbie take a break, then seek treatments from a competent fertility expert. He said he would be glad to make a referral.

A few days later Dr. Sites wrote a letter to Dr. Doppelheuer to relate the findings of his examination. "It was indeed a pleasure to see this interesting and nice lady, and I do thank you for having referred her to me," he wrote. He sent a copy of the letter to Dr. Jacobson and also called Cecil to discuss Debbie's case personally. Cecil was out of town, so he left a message, but the once-rising star of his department never returned the call.

He never called Debbie and Steven either. Although he had treated her for more than a year, and she was supposedly four months pregnant when she last saw him, he never contacted her to find out what had gone wrong. She never heard from him again.

On November 25, 1987, Dr. Doppelheuer wrote a formal letter of complaint to the Virginia State Board of Medicine. He was violating an unwritten rule of medicine. Doctors didn't complain about other doctors.

"It is with considerable regret and great reluctance that I write this letter," he stated, and described Dr. Jacobson's treatment of Chris and Debbie. "I would appreciate your investigation of this matter."

Dr. Doppelheuer told the Maimones that there was no assurance the medical board would take action. If they were serious about seeing that Dr. Jacobson was stopped, he suggested they file a lawsuit.

Finding a lawyer to take their case was as difficult as finding a good infertility doctor. They considered thumbing through the yellow pages or calling one of the personal injury lawyers who advertised on TV, but this wasn't a simple traffic-accident injury. The facts were complicated and the case would be tough to prove. They needed an expert.

Larry called some lawyers he knew at HUD, but they weren't able to help. Chris called the attorneys who represented the medical lab; they didn't handle medical malpractice cases, but they gave Chris the names of three lawyers who did.

When Chris spoke with the first one, he suggested she file in small claims court to get her money back. Chris was furious. When she called the second attorney, she snapped, "Don't put me off like the other guy did."

The attorney, Robert Hall, a prominent Fairfax, Virginia, lawyer, wasn't sure Chris had a case either. He knew of physicians who had misdiagnosed a pregnancy before. It wasn't a crime, or even a case of malpractice. His quick assessment was they could never convince a jury that the doctor had done anything more than make a simple misdiagnosis. Then Chris said there was another case and explained what Dr. Doppelheuer had told her about Debbie Gregory.

"That kind of mistake ought not to happen twice," he said. "Why don't I set up an appointment, and you and your husband can come in and we'll talk about this."

Bob Hall had been suing Virginia physicians for twenty years, but he'd never heard of Cecil Jacobson. He checked with his contacts in the medical community and got an evaluation of Dr. Jacobson. Some people spoke in awe of his reputation as a genetics pioneer. Others considered him a joke.

Someone from the obstetrical unit at Fairfax Hospital said Dr. Jacobson's amnios were considered so unreliable that his predictions of a baby's gender were no more accurate than a coin flip. An obstetrician Hall sometimes hired to examine medical records said he'd attended some of Cecil's genetics lectures and had once walked out because Cecil was so full of himself. A few days later, while questioning an obstetrician about a case against another local doctor, Hall asked the doctor if he'd ever heard about Cecil's patients being told they were pregnant when they were not. The doctor obviously knew something, but he wasn't talking. The physician had been obliging and cooperative until Hall asked him about Cecil, then abruptly changed the subject. Hall wasn't surprised. He had witnessed the circle-the-wagons mentality of the medical community before. But the doctor's attitude was another confirmation that Hall was onto something.

Meanwhile Debbie and Steven Gregory had decided to retain a lawyer of their own. They went to Richard Boone, who operated a small legal practice defending doctors in Arlington, Virginia. His clients included a large HMO chain and most of the podiatrists in the Washington area. As he listened to the Gregorys' story, he would later admit he didn't believe much of what they were telling him. "In my business you get to the point where you think you've heard it all," he would say, "and then a case like this comes along."

At first he declined to take their case. He told them he didn't sue doctors, he defended them, and lawyers generally didn't cross the line. He gave them the names of several other attorneys, but in a few weeks the Gregorys were back, insisting that he take their case.

By then Boone made some inquiries about Dr. Jacobson. Two clients—a reproductive endocrinologist at one hospital, and a radiologist at another—told him that questions about Dr. Jacobson's treatments had been circulating for years.

Boone also contacted a doctor who had studied under Cecil at the university, and she said Dr. Jacobson had required his medical students to perform questionable experiments on aborted second-trimester fetuses until she complained to university officials.

Another university doctor told Boone that Cecil used to interfere with the patients of other physicians and perform unauthorized amniocentesis. The practice stopped after one woman elected to have an abortion based upon Cecil's recommendation. When the attending physician discovered what he'd done, he went ballistic and complained to the head of the department.

The more Boone heard about Dr. Jacobson, the more he became convinced he wouldn't lose much business by suing him, so when Steven and Debbie returned a third time, he agreed to represent them. He told them up front that he didn't expect to win much money, but he would assist them in going after Jacobson's medical license, which was really what the Gregorys wanted anyway.

Bob Hall and Richard Boone had known each other for years, more often as adversaries than allies. When Debbie and Chris got their respective attorneys in touch with each other, they realized they had a potential medical scandal on their hands. They were picking up enough rumors and hospital gossip to indicate that Debbie and Chris weren't isolated examples. The problem was locating the other cases. They briefly considered putting an ad in the paper or contacting the media; then the solution to their problem called Bob Hall's office.

A Washington television station was conducting an investigation into errors made by medical laboratories. The station's investigative producer had discovered a case that Hall was representing involving a fourteen-year-old girl who had been erroneously diagnosed as having gonorrhea. The producer asked if he could interview the girl or her parents. Hall arranged an interview with the girl's mother, who appeared in silhouette, and explained how her daughter had undergone a series of painful and embarrassing treatments before the laboratory error was discovered.

After the interview Hall mentioned that he had another story that might interest the TV station. He said it involved a local infertility doctor who was preying on the vulnerability of his patients.

Chapter Thirteen

In the years leading up to Chris Maimone's and Debbie Gregory's bogus pregnancies, Dr. Jacobson's patients were experiencing a spate of disappearing fetuses that would be described as "unheard of" in the annals of medicine.

Some women had supposedly lost fetuses that were so advanced they could practically survive outside the womb, but Dr. Jacobson's persuasive explanations about resorption were usually accepted with little question. The patients believed in him and trusted him. He cried with them and prayed with them. They considered him a friend. Even as other doctors insisted that what Cecil was telling his patients was nonsense, he ignored them or told them to mind their own business. And the number of resorptions soared, like no other medical practice in the world.

Vickie Eckhardt started her infertility treatments with Dr. Jacobson in 1981, a year after she married her second husband, Bill. She suffered from blocked tubes caused by a defective Dalkon shield. After she had a laparoscopy, Dr. Jacobson wanted her to try HCG, a new and controversial treatment he was using. "He said he was on the cutting edge," Vickie would recall. "He had a lot of success with it, but there were a lot of doctors who did not agree with what he was doing."

She set up appointments for HCG injections every Monday, Wednesday, and Friday between nine and ten-thirty A.M. or four and five P.M., and Dr. Jacobson told her to have daily intercourse from the tenth day of her cycle until the second day after ovulation. If she followed his instructions, he guaranteed, she would have a baby.

She got "pregnant" three times, but the pregnancies never progressed far enough for her to see her obstetrician. It seemed that whenever it was time for a referral, she had a miscarriage and resorption.

The fourth time Vickie advanced to twelve weeks. Then, in the sonogram room one day, Dr. Jacobson showed Vickie and her husband the bleak image of what he described as the dead fetus flopping over inside her. "See, there's your baby," he told them.

As Vickie and Bill cried, Dr. Jacobson told them to sit with him a moment. "Let's all join hands and say a prayer," he said, and together they prayed for the latest of the four dead babies.

During her previous three miscarriages Vickie had heeded his warning about a D and C, but this time she scheduled an operation to remove the three-month-old fetus that was supposedly inside her. When she told him about the appointment, he got "very upset" and told her to wait a couple of weeks. Maybe the baby wasn't dead after all, he said. He told her to delay the D and C for two weeks, then come back in for another sonogram.

Vickie waited for two weeks, then got the D and C anyway. As she was lying in the recovery room, the doctor, Harry Beavers, explained he hadn't found anything. "Are you sure you were pregnant?" he asked.

Vickie said that's what Dr. Jacobson had been telling her. The doctor said he knew Cecil very well. They had gone to George Washington University together. "Dr. Jacobson wouldn't tell you that if it weren't so," he said.

When Vickie kept her appointment with Dr. Jacobson and told him about the D and C results, he said he wasn't surprised. The pregnancy obviously resorbed during the two weeks Vickie waited for the D and C, just as he predicted it would.

Vickie went on to have a total of seven resorptions. "We kept doing the same treatment over and over," she would say, "and I kept getting the same results over and over. I couldn't—I just couldn't take it anymore." During five years of treatments she spent more than $4,500.

*   *   *

Curiously, the number of resorptions increased as Dr. Jacobson's amnio business was shrinking. During the early years of his clinic he was treating more than 500 amnio patients a year. During his best year, in 1983, he performed 519 procedures, an average of more than three a day. But the next year his business began a steady decline. His amnio and genetics practice had been financially rewarding—at one point he claimed a net worth of $3.6 million—but he was losing his monopoly on amniocentesis as more hospitals offered the procedure to patients. Doctors could perform amnios in their office and send the amniotic fluid to mail-order companies for analysis. Furthermore, new advances in genetic screening, like chorionic villi sampling and chromosome banding, were replacing amniocentesis as the preferred method to detect birth defects. But Cecil wasn't keeping up with the latest advances. He was becoming a medical dinosaur and lagging behind the market.

When a nearby hospital formed a joint venture to offer amniocentesis with one of Cecil's main competitors, it stole away much of his business. One obstetrical group, which had been referring their amnio patients to him for nearly twenty years, suddenly switched.

In 1984 the center actually lost money for the first time. Cecil slashed his own salary by forty thousand dollars and cut his payroll in half, but it didn't help. The next year the clinic grossed even less. The signs of financial deterioration were everywhere. Elizabeth Vosbeck, who had been in charge of the amniocentesis lab, was cut back to only a few days a week. His lab supervisor was logging so few hours that she was forced to find another job. He stopped funding his employee retirement plan. When the receptionist-secretary left, he didn't replace her, and his wife did the books and worked the front desk. Cecil's daughters worked in the lab, culturing specimens and reading slides. Meanwhile he had several outside business interests that were going sour. A furniture-manufacturing company and a computer-leasing venture were in financial trouble.

Investigators would later claim that it was no coincidence that the number of fake pregnancies began to soar just as Cecil's business was hitting rock bottom. They would point to a key decision in 1986 as the catalyst in what they would call a scheme to defraud patients—about the same time Debbie Gregory and Chris Maimone were beginning their treatments.

Dr. Jacobson switched brands of pregnancy tests. For years he had been using a test made by Organon. But in 1986 he switched to a test made by Abbott Laboratories of Chicago. The Abbott test was at least ten times more sensitive than the Organon test. The Organon test required an HCG blood level of five hundred units to register positive, but the Abbott test needed only fifty units. This meant that any woman who got injections of HCG three times a week was virtually assured of registering positive on the Abbott test.

The Abbott test was also a huge money maker. Despite Dr. Jacobson's claims of having the most reasonable prices in town, he had a tremendous markup on the pregnancy tests and bottles of HCG he sold to patients. The Organon brand had cost him more than $10 wholesale. But he could buy the Abbott tests in bulk for $2.75 each. Since he charged patients $30 to $35 for each test, he could make a profit of more than 1,200 percent.

The bottles of HCG were a profit center, too. He could buy the hormone for about $9 a bottle and sell it to patients for $25. Since each patient was getting three bottles a week, he was making $75 a week on a $27 investment. He was using so much of the hormone by the mid-1980's that, at one point, his supplier couldn't even fill his orders. He became one of the largest purchasers of HCG in the country.

The number of resorptions soared in 1986 and 1987. One of his patients during that time was Marilyn Lewis, a registered nurse who wanted a baby "more than anything in the world." He told her that he'd never failed to get a woman pregnant provided she explicitly followed his instructions, and he explained there was more to having a baby than just matching the eggs and sperm. The power of prayer and positive thinking were just as important. "If you believe hard enough that you want to be a mother, you'll be one," he said.

He pronounced her pregnant after one month of treatments. "It blew me away," she would say. "I was so excited I couldn't stand it. It was like a miracle. And I attributed it mostly to Cecil."

Although she supposedly miscarried, she accepted his explanation of resorption, even though as a nurse she knew it didn't make medical sense. She believed what he told her. She had no reason to doubt him. During the two years she would see him, he became one of her closest friends. "We got incredibly close," she remembered. "I relied on him heavily." When she had personal problems, she called him at home. She came to know his wife and two daughters, who worked at the clinic. She felt like a member of their family. "I thought he was a very good friend," she would say. "I loved this man."

During her second pregnancy she made it to eighteen weeks, the time when she normally would have an amniocentesis, but Dr. Jacobson told her it wasn't time yet. He wanted to wait, but by her next visit the baby was gone.

When she supposedly conceived a third time, she decided not to take any chances and called in the "heavy hitters," as she dubbed them, a practice of parentologists who specialized in high-risk pregnancies. Dr. Jacobson told her it was foolish and unnecessary, but she went to them anyway.

She was supposedly more than two months pregnant, but they discovered an empty uterus. Dr. Jacobson offered an explanation. He claimed the baby had resorbed since Marilyn's last visit when they had seen it on his sonogram machine. He encouraged her to try again, but Marilyn decided to give her body a rest. Before she resumed her treatments, however, she saw a TV broadcast that would forever change her mind about her good friend the doctor.

Mary Sutphin had three suspect pregnancies and resorptions. The last time she was supposedly ten and a half

weeks when she went to see her obstetrician, Dr. Michael
Hotchkiss. He examined her and found "nothing there."
He did a blood test and sent her for an ultrasound. Both
tests confirmed she wasn't pregnant. Yet when he called
Dr. Jacobson to discuss the discrepancy, Cecil didn't try to
sort out the disagreement. Instead he ordered Dr. Hotchkiss
not to examine the patient. Dr. Hotchkiss said it was
too late.

When Mrs. Sutphin went to see Dr. Jacobson, he agreed
there had been a mistake but claimed it wasn't his error.
He blamed the mistakes on everyone else. He said the lab,
Dr. Hotchkiss, and the radiologist who had scanned her
were all wrong. The reason they didn't find the baby, he
said, was because it was sleeping. He was more adept at
diagnosing early pregnancies than any of them, he maintained. "Go home and get a good night's sleep. Everything
is fine."

But everything wasn't fine. During her next visit he said
the baby had died and blamed it on a "virus" that was
"going around." He tried to persuade her that a D and C
wasn't necessary, but she got one anyway.

Her obstetrician's partner, Dr. Ronald Zielinsky, performed the operation. Normally, he would have expected
to remove fifty grams of tissue from the uterus of a woman
who was nearing the end of her first trimester, but he
retrieved only about one cubic centimeter. He stated on
his operative report that he tried to find more tissue, but
there wasn't any. In all his years of practice he would say
that this was the first time he'd ever performed a D and C
on a woman who wasn't pregnant.

Two of Cecil's patients came from rural Virginia, where
they worked at a hospital near the West Virginia border.
Barbara Mull was a registered nurse. Dawn Graham was
a sonography technician. They had known each other for
years, but didn't realize they were both patients of Dr.
Jacobson until they saw each other at the clinic.

Barbara had two "pregnancies" and a resorption. Dawn
had three. But what made Barbara's case so unusual was the
fact she was menopausal. Before she went to Dr. Jacobson,

two doctors had diagnosed her as prematurely menopausal. One doctor considered her situation so hopeless, he wouldn't give her fertility drugs. The other said there was nothing he could do and referred her to specialists at the University of Virginia. But Barbara wouldn't give up. When she heard about Dr. Jacobson from a patient at the hospital, she rushed off to see him.

He said he could help, and—true to his word—he pronounced her pregnant within a matter of weeks. She asked him why her other doctors were so inept. His program was so simple, why couldn't they figure it out? Just a few hormone shots and she was pregnant. He said the other doctors were "pussies" who were afraid to take chances.

Although she would become intensely devoted to him, she thought some of the things he did were strange. During one visit she brought her ten-year-old daughter with her, who was thrilled to be having a younger brother or sister.

"Your mother is going to have a baby," Dr. Jacobson told the girl, but warned her not to get too excited. Sometimes "things didn't always go right," he said.

"I thought it was a strange way to put it," Barbara would say. "I didn't expect to have any trouble." She hadn't experienced problems with her daughter's birth, "and I didn't expect that I would this time." But Dr. Jacobson seemed to be expecting something to go wrong.

When Barbara got to fifteen weeks, she booked an appointment with an obstetrician in her hometown. Dr. Jacobson got upset and told her it wasn't time yet. But Barbara knew that her obstetrician was so busy that if she canceled this appointment, she might not get another one—so she kept the appointment over Dr. Jacobson's objections.

Dr. James Stafford examined her and gave her a urine test. He said she wasn't pregnant. She got hysterical and had Dr. Stafford call Dr. Jacobson, who told her to come in right away. She drove directly to his office and he was waiting for her. "He did an ultrasound and he said that I had not miscarried as of yet," she recalled. The fetus was there, he told her, but the sac was a little low. He told her to come back the following week.

When she returned, he said the fetus had died and was resorbing. Meanwhile her obstetrician, who worked in the same hospital as Barbara, was trying to get her to schedule a D and C to surgically remove the supposedly fifteen-week fetus. But her loyalty was with Cecil. She believed his explanation about resorption, even though, as a nurse, she'd never heard of it. For days she tried to avoid the obstetrician, once even running down a hospital corridor to get away from him.

"I was really angry with Dr. Stafford. I don't know why, but I blamed him," she would say. "Dr. Jacobson had told me everything was all right, and Dr. Stafford had told me it wasn't."

Dawn Graham was having the same problem as her friend Barbara Mull. She had also learned of Dr. Jacobson while working at the hospital. For years her cancer unit had been sending him patients for genetic counseling.

On her first visit he said her problem wasn't serious and guaranteed she would be pregnant within a year. "God doesn't give you babies," he told her. "I do." He pronounced her pregnant almost right away.

Of all his patients Dawn was the most skilled at reading ultrasounds. Part of her job at the hospital was to locate tumors in cancer patients (she had even passed a special training course), but during her first sonogram on April 15, 1987, he tried to tell her he saw the sac and a heartbeat, and she told him she didn't see anything. As she later recounted, "I tried to move the screen over just a little so I could see, but he moved it back. He asked me several times if I saw anything, but I did not clearly see anything."

He measured the circumference of the sac and marked it with his cursor, then made a print and drew a green circle around the sac. It didn't look like any scan she had seen before. She asked if it was a sagittal view or a longitudinal view, meaning was it head-to-toe, or sideways. He didn't bother to answer. When she continued to ask questions, he got annoyed with her. "Do you want the picture or not?" he snapped.

Although he routinely gave patients multiple sonograms week after week, Dawn would never get another one. Through three pregnancies and two resorptions, he never scanned her again. Of all his resorption patients, the one woman who knew what she was talking about was kept out of the sonogram room for the rest of her treatments.

Susan Dippel had been trying to conceive for two and a half years before her husband's urologist referred them to Dr. Jacobson. He came with such high recommendations that they drove all the way from their home near Annapolis, Maryland, to his clinic in Virginia, at least an hour away.

Dr. Jacobson said he could help, but only if they followed his program for eighteen months and gave it enough time to succeed. Susan showed him her previous medical records, including the details of a prior laparoscopy, but Dr. Jacobson wasn't interested. He handed them back without a glance, then prescribed HCG.

She got "pregnant" twice. He told them the first was killed by an "infection" and resorbed. The second one progressed to nearly three months. She was aware that HCG could cause a positive pregnancy test, but she believed him when he said it had no effect. "I questioned him quite frequently," she would say. "He repeatedly told me that there was no way that the injections would trigger a false positive." He had been using HCG for so many years, he told her that he certainly would know if it caused false-positive tests.

He convinced her that she needed the injections for the baby's survival. It wasn't a fluke, she thought, that she started bleeding and lost the first one as soon as she stopped taking the hormone. When he wanted to stop the injections for the second pregnancy, she consulted an ob/gyn for a second opinion. She wanted to know if she should stay on the HCG for a while longer, or discontinue it as Dr. Jacobson wanted. Dr. James Haddock was surprised she was taking the hormone at all.

He did a sonogram, and when he couldn't find a heartbeat, or a fetus, or any sign of a pregnancy, he performed a second one. The results weren't any better. He told her not to inject herself for a few days, then took a sample of blood and sent it to the lab for analysis. As soon as the blood was drawn, Susan sneaked into the next room and fixed herself like an HCG junkie, hoping it wasn't too late.

The blood test showed her HCG levels of 228 were well below the threshhold for a viable pregnancy. Dr. Haddock would call it one of the "lowest moments" of his life when he had to inform Susan that her baby was dead. During all this time, however, Dr. Jacobson was telling her the pregnancy was normal and progressing quite well.

During her final appointment with Cecil, she didn't mention her visit to Dr. Haddock. When he did a sonogram, he pointed out a heartbeat. He said it was so "distinctive" there was no mistaking it. Susan said she was "quite confused" by the conflicting diagnoses. Cecil said the other doctor was obviously wrong.

She never went back to Dr. Jacobson. She started treatments with another doctor and, within a few months, got pregnant and gave birth to a son she named Matthew. She later wrote a nasty letter to the urologist who had referred them to Dr. Jacobson and warned him never to send anyone to Dr. Jacobson again.

Cecil's former student, Dr. Richard Falk, had never been impressed with his professor. But after becoming director of the Reproductive Endocrinology and Infertility Division at Columbia Hospital for Women in Washington, he was even more convinced that Cecil was incompetent—or even worse. Over the years he'd seen eight or ten of Cecil's vanishing-pregnancy cases. He'd gotten to the point where he could predict what would happen to a woman as soon as she said she was a patient of Dr. Jacobson.

The most bizarre case was that of a forty-nine-year-old woman who was menopausal. She hadn't been able to bear children for several years, and tests revealed she had no eggs left in her ovaries. Yet Dr. Jacobson claimed she conceived and later resorbed her fetus. When Falk tried to convince her it was impossible, she became indignant and refused to listen. She accused him of jealousy because Dr. Jacobson had gotten her pregnant when Falk had failed. Out of curiosity he later checked the hospital's statistics and discovered that if Cecil's diagnosis was accurate, the woman would have been a medical miracle. Out of 260,000 births at the hospital none had been by a woman aged forty-nine or older, especially a postmenopausal one. And not one woman had ever resorbed a fetus.

Jean Blair and her husband, Jim, suspected Dr. Jacobson was a white supremacist from the way he talked to her about his ability to create "top-of-the-line kids." Her husband, Jim, was a District of Columbia firefighter, whose buddies at the firehouse would tease him about his failure to get his wife pregnant. "I can do it if you can't," one of his friends said. Yet those same guys privately sought his advice when they discovered he was seeing an infertility doctor. Some of them had the same problem but didn't want anyone to know it.

Jean was pronounced pregnant six times, including once with twins, but miscarried and resorbed them all. "When we thought we were pregnant, we were on top of the world," she would say, "and when we lost it, it was completely the opposite."

Dr. Jacobson told her a virus must be killing off the babies, so she curtailed her visits with friends and family for fear of germs. She became so despondent that her husband sought Dr. Jacobson's advice. Cecil said not to worry. Depression was a side effect of the hormone shots.

One time, after being told she had lost another one, Dr. Jacobson walked her into the waiting room and shook her husband's hand. "Congratulations," Cecil said for the benefit of the other patients, as if the Blairs just learned they were pregnant.

Judith Dowd was a forty-five-year-old attorney, who would soon become an administrative-law judge for the Social Security Administration. She had about given up hope of having a child. A series of infertility specialists and even surgery couldn't cure a blockage of her tubes, and she finally conceded that time had passed her by. Then, at her health club, she met another woman in her forties who said Dr. Jacobson was one of the few doctors in the area who would still treat women their age.

Judy's pregnancy would advance further than any of the other resorption patients. When she got to the end of her fourth month, the time when Cecil would normally perform an amniocentesis, she began pestering him. If any patient was a high-risk candidate for a Down's syndrome baby, it should have been Judy because of her advanced age, yet he told her to wait. He showed her statistics that indicated even his oldest patients delivered normal children.

When she was nearing the end of her fifth month, it was getting too late, and she urged him to do the amnio right away. He said he needed to do an ultrasound first. When he checked the screen, he said the picture was "blurred," which meant there was bleeding in the sac. He listened for the baby's heartbeat and let her listen, too, but all she could hear was a regular, steady beat, not the rapid patter of a baby's heartbeat. Yet he claimed it was the sound of her baby.

He wanted to delay the amnio because the picture wasn't clear enough for him to see where to stick the needle. By the next appointment she was nearly twenty-three weeks pregnant, and past the time for a safe amnio.

On the ultrasound that day he said he couldn't see anything, indicating the baby must have died. He blamed it on "some sort of virus." He convinced her that the twenty-three-week-old fetus would resorb and persuaded her to start another round of treatments. She had gotten only a single HCG shot before she went away for the weekend with her husband. When she returned to town, her friends told her she'd missed a television program about her doctor. She watched the rest of the series eagerly. She was shocked by what she saw.

Chapter Fourteen

WRC-TV had a longtime tradition of investigative reporting, though the tradition ran hot and cold depending on the philosophy of the station management at the time. In 1987 the market research indicated viewers craved investigative stories, and the station, owned by the NBC network, had installed a full-time investigative unit that was sweeping the national journalism awards.

The on-air correspondent was Lea Thompson, a nationally known consumer/investigative reporter whose exposés over the years had led to legislative reforms and product recalls. Millions of hair dryers were taken off the market following her revelations that they emitted dangerous asbestos fibers. And her stories about the dangers of the DPT vaccine prompted Congress to establish a multimillion dollar fund for infant victims and their families.

Her years of standing, success, and awards had given her a unique setup in local television news. She commanded a staff that was considered huge in local television news. The consumer/investigative unit consisted of an investigative producer, Rick Nelson, who produced in-depth investigative series; a consumer producer, Elizabeth Crenshaw, who produced daily consumer reports; an office manager/researcher, Sheila Duffy; and a staff of college interns, who did the grunt work every semester for college credit.

After the tip about Dr. Jacobson from Chris Maimone's attorney, there was considerable skepticism in the newsroom. How could a woman not know if she was pregnant? Were these women dumb, or just naive? Several people had heard of Dr. Jacobson before. One reporter's wife had gone to him for amniocentesis, and the producer in charge of the special-projects division had consulted Dr. Jacobson briefly for infertility treatments. His wife didn't get HCG, but they didn't get a baby either.

Because the Reproductive Genetic Center was not affiliated with a hospital or university, Dr. Jacobson's office was sacrosanct—he was a small fiefdom unto himself—responsible only to the state board of medicine, which made sure he promptly renewed his medical license. Not even his laboratory was inspected for accuracy or quality control. Negotiations were under way in the U.S. Congress at the time to require periodic inspections of laboratories in physicians' offices, but the powerful medical lobby was staunchly opposing the measure and ultimately would defeat it.

As a result there were no inspection reports to alert the public about problems within the clinic. A computer search for news items didn't turn up much either. Dr. Jacobson had been written up in several *Washington Post* articles and was frequently quoted as an authority on everything from genetic damage caused by chemicals to amniocentesis as a means of foretelling the gender of a child. Even the Channel 4 medical reporter had once included him prominently in a series of stories about infertility and childbirth.

The only available public records were lawsuits filed by patients. Lea's producer canvassed the seven courthouses in the Washington area, looking for lawsuits to indicate any dissatisfaction with Dr. Jacobson's work. He didn't find any accusations of improper infertility treatments, but there were several malpractice suits over the years regarding his amnio and genetics work, all settled out of court by his insurance company with no admission of liability.

While the lawsuits raised questions about the quality of Dr. Jacobson's genetics practice, they didn't confirm the allegations about his infertility treatments or help to locate other patients.

When the Maimones learned of the station's investigation into Cecil's practice, Chris and Larry protested that they had no desire to go on TV. Their attorney, Bob Hall, tried to convince them that it was in their best interest to tell their story publicly, and possibly flush out other victims to bolster their case, but the Maimones felt this was a private tragedy that shouldn't be shared with the world. They also didn't want to publicize the fact that they intended to sue a doctor. Chris worked at a medical laboratory that relied on referral business from doctors, and she worried about possible repercussions from her boss. She also worried what her new infertility doctor would think. They were going to the in-vitro fertilization clinic again, just as Dr. Doppelheuer had recommended in the first place. They suspected their new doctor wouldn't take kindly to finding out they were suing their old one.

Hall finally convinced them to at least talk with the producer off the record, and to provide background information, on the condition they wouldn't be identified.

In early December 1987, about two months after leaving Dr. Jacobson, they met with producer Rick Nelson at their attorney's office. Larry did most of the talking and made it clear he didn't trust TV reporters, but in time he was revealing some of the most intimate and painful moments of their marriage. He and Chris gave the producer their medical records and authorized him to speak with the doctors who had determined Chris wasn't pregnant, then lent him their once-precious sonograms—just to make sure Dr. Jacobson didn't take advantage of somebody else.

Meanwhile the attorney representing Steven and Debbie Gregory was trying to convince them to speak with the media. Unless there was some publicity, Richard Boone told Debbie, they might never locate other patients. Debbie could file suit, win a judgment, even cause Dr. Jacobson's medical license to be revoked, but unless the press learned of it, no one might ever know. "You can't stop him unless people know what he's doing," the attorney said. But Debbie's wounds were still too fresh, and she needed more time to think about it.

Dr. John Doppelheuer wouldn't speak with the reporters either. When the TV producer called him, he said that television wasn't the proper forum to air his complaints—he'd already taken the appropriate action—and he made it clear there was no need for the producer to call back.

Dr. Dunner was more amenable. He was so offended by what Dr. Jacobson had done, calling it "reprehensible," that he didn't hesitate to talk. His only prerequisite was that Chris Maimone not be identified by name. The interview was hurriedly arranged for early the next morning, before Dr. Dunner could change his mind.

The photographer assigned to the story was Chester Panzer, one of the most talented cameramen at the station, who ironically had consulted Dr. Jacobson a decade ago when Chester and his wife, Mindy, suspected they had an infertility problem. Chester had seen Dr. Jacobson only briefly for an initial consultation and thought Cecil was so strange that he never went back. Since then he and his wife had two children without help from any specialists.

When he and the producer arrived at Washington Ultrasound Associates, Chester set up the camera in Dr. Dunner's office, and the producer asked Dr. Dunner to describe his examination of Chris Maimone.

"I scanned the patient," the doctor said, "and there was a completely normal-looking uterus and ovaries, with no evidence of a pregnancy whatsoever."

"You had no doubt she was not pregnant?" Nelson asked.

"None whatsoever," he said. "I'm very confident of my results."

"And she had not been pregnant recently?"

"The only mistake could have been that a pregnancy was so young that it couldn't be seen, meaning a pregnancy of a week perhaps. But for a fourteen-week pregnancy, there was not the slightest doubt of my findings."

He described how a fourteen-week pregnancy should appear on a sonogram screen. "At fourteen weeks details of the uterus are quite visible. You can make out the head, body, heart, spine, and bladder. With superb equipment you can even see structures inside the head and kidneys."

But Dr. Jacobson's sonograms didn't have any of those characteristics, he said.

The doctor was being direct and unequivocal, without pulling any punches.

"How do you feel about this?" Nelson asked him. "What's going on here?"

"I feel at the very least there has been an error in the interpretation of an ultrasound. At the *very least*," he stressed.

"And at the very most?" Nelson asked.

Dunner started to answer, then hesitated. He didn't want to speculate. "I don't know all the facts," he said. "I'm not prepared to comment."

Dr. Dunner used the sonogram of a fourteen-week fetus to demonstrate on a view box how it would have been virtually impossible to miss Chris's baby—if it were actually there. As they concluded, Dr. Dunner's boss, Dr. William Cochrane, walked in. He'd been out of the office and was startled to see the TV gear strewn about. He called Dunner into an adjoining room as the TV crew packed up to leave.

Dr. Dunner was visibly shaken when he returned. He told the producer that the interview would have to be canceled, and he asked for the tape.

"That's ridiculous," Nelson said. There was no way he was turning over the tape.

Dr. Dunner said he hadn't consulted Dr. Cochrane before the interview, and his boss had chewed him out. Their medical practice was based on referrals, he said, and his boss didn't want him publicly commenting on cases referred to them by other physicians.

The producer said he would check with his own boss, then quickly retreated, taking the videotape with him. The interview had gone so well he didn't want to lose it, but by the time they got back to the station, Dr. Dunner was already calling. He was pleading as he made another appeal to rescind the interview. He gave Nelson the names of two sonography experts who could review Dr. Jacobson's scans on camera. One was from Johns Hopkins University Hospital in Baltimore, and the other was from

Cecil's alma mater, George Washington University. The producer said he would think about it and hung up without making a commitment.

As a mother of three, Lea Thompson knew a thing or two about human reproduction. These resorptions that the doctor was talking about made no sense to her, and when she asked her own ob/gyn about Dr. Jacobson, he said the HCG treatments would certainly cause positive pregnancy tests. However, he didn't feel qualified to publicly criticize another physician's practice and wouldn't appear on camera.

She contacted a group of infertility patients, known as Resolve, and asked about Dr. Jacobson. Although the leaders of the group had heard of him and some of his problem pregnancies, they were reluctant to cause problems for any doctor who could possibly help them. They invited Lea to attend one of their meetings, but they wouldn't introduce her to any of Cecil's former patients.

She was surprised about their uninhibited discussion of sex, as the couples shared explicit information about techniques and methods that would best get the sperm to fertilize the egg. They held passionate discussions about their common problem, which seemed to be the most overriding concern in their lives.

Meanwhile Lea's producer was contacting some of the local infertility experts, beginning with the National Institutes of Health, where a leading infertility researcher confirmed that treating patients with repeated HCG injections was "not accepted practice." Other local infertility experts didn't want to get involved at all.

One of the few who agreed to talk about Cecil's practice was Dr. Saffa Rifka, an Iranian-born specialist at the Columbia Hospital for Women. The local fraternity of infertility specialists was small enough that Dr. Rifka had known of Cecil for years. He had even seen several of Cecil's patients, including one woman whose tubes were so severely blocked that it would have been virtually impossible for her to become pregnant, despite what Dr. Jacobson had told her.

Dr. Rifka said he wasn't the only local doctor who had treated Cecil's nonpregnant women. "There's six or seven of us here in Washington. It's a club. We know each other, and each one has had plenty of cases."

"Why doesn't anybody turn him in?" Lea's producer asked.

"How can you turn him in?" he asked. A doctor couldn't sue another doctor for malpractice. "A patient sues a doctor," he said. "We just enlighten the patient." Since Dr. Jacobson wasn't doing surgery, his mistakes weren't considered serious enough to be life threatening. "It's not like he cuts on people and the patient has a bowel perforation and she's severely sick and everybody goes bananas. In office medicine if you don't cut, your blunders are limited and contained." By the same criteria, a heart surgeon's mistakes would instantly attract attention.

"Could this just be bad medicine?" the producer asked. "Or would you have to make these mistakes on purpose?"

"It's very hard to differentiate between intentional and unintentional ignorance," he said.

When Dr. Rifka was asked if he would publicly criticize Cecil on television, the doctor declined. "I don't think it's a good idea," he said. "I don't want to get into a legal battle with him. It's not that I'm afraid, but it's not good ethics. If you put me in a medical-society forum, I'll talk. I don't think I can go on TV and put myself against him. What if he sues? Would you send lawyers to defend me, to protect me in court?"

Without patients to appear on camera, or doctors to blast Cecil's practices, the TV investigation was headed nowhere. The reporters needed to find some way to infiltrate the clinic to see for themselves how it operated. They considered staking out the office and talking to patients as they left, or trying to get hired for a job. Then someone suggested they pose as patients and record their consultation session with a hidden camera.

Rick, Lea's producer, volunteered to pose as the husband, but Lea was too well-known to go undercover herself. Normally, their researcher was used in undercover situations, but Lea was concerned about sending her and

Rick in together. The doctor might ask sensitive questions about their sex lives, and any indecision or conflicting answers could betray them. Rather than having someone pose as his wife, they decided to use his real wife.

Joyce Nelson, mother of two sons, was so angry when she heard how the patients had been treated that she volunteered to help. She made an appointment and, in a few days, received the standard package of pedigree forms and temperature charts. For their cover story they would explain that Rick had two children from a previous marriage, but Joyce was childless. And to make sure he wouldn't examine her, she would say she was starting her period.

The appointment was set for mid-December. Joyce was nervous. She had never been involved in an undercover investigation. Her husband assured her she would be fine— just answer the questions and let the doctor do the talking. He was carrying a black-and-white eight-millimeter camera mounted inside a large leather duffel bag, more suitable for a gym than for a doctor's office. As they walked into the office building, WRC-TV cameraman Ron Minor discreetly photographed them from an unmarked car in the parking lot.

Inside, the waiting room was empty. Mrs. Jacobson, who was working at the front counter, told them to have a seat and summoned the doctor. In a moment he ambled out and greeted them warmly. They followed him to his office and sat across the desk from him. The producer adjusted the camera on a chair beside him, trying to act nonchalant as he focused Dr. Jacobson in frame.

As rehearsed, they said Rick had two children from a previous marriage, but Joyce couldn't get pregnant. "You were smart to marry a proven sire," Dr. Jacobson told her. "If you were in the dairy business, you'd understand what I mean."

He asked how long they had been married, if Joyce's periods were regular, and whether she had ever had pelvic surgery, cramping, or unusual bleeding. He didn't bother to jot down the answers but just nodded at each response.

"What kind of work do you do?" he asked her.

"I work at the Armed Forces Institute of Pathology," she said. "In the veterinary services."

The doctor perked up. Over the years he'd known a lot of AFIP employees, he said, and he recalled some of his work there on baboons and chimpanzees. The human race could learn a lot from the animal kingdom, he said. Animals that fail to reproduce are "culled from the herd," which might be a good lesson for humans to learn.

"Do you do laboratory work? Secretarial work? Or gal Friday?" he asked.

"Sort of all that," she said, trying to be vague.

He inspected her hands. She obviously didn't work around the lab bench, he said. "The acid really chews you up. You can tell the bench person from the administrative person." He asked if either of them worked around radiation or radioisotopes. They said they didn't.

"You've never been exposed to dangerous chemicals that you know of?" Again they each said no.

"Okay," he said, finishing with the preliminaries; then he got down to business. "There are three ways to handle infertility," he said. "The first way is to pat you on the head, say, 'Don't worry,' point you toward bed, and let nature take care of itself. That's good for one or two years.

"The second thing is to hit you with the kitchen sink, which is what most doctors do. I think that's wrong." He turned to Joyce. "A person like you, with no scars on your belly and no pelvic problems that we know of—why get a couple-hundred-dollar procedure which is not that helpful?" He said 80 percent of infertility doctors recommended surgery, but he didn't. "It's not that I don't realize those procedures are available, it's that in a person such as you, with no real reason to push it, you've got lots of time to have a child. Your age is very modest. You're not going to be leaving the area. I see no reason to accelerate it beyond what's needed."

He said he felt the same way about artificial insemination. Why start with insemination, he asked, which is "more expensive and more traumatic," until they'd had six to nine good cycles of intercourse coverage? "I'm a little more amenable to move early toward insemination if you have to have something done."

Thus far his presentation seemed very reasonable, as he rambled on about the secret of his success, explaining his theories about old eggs and timed intercourse. From his years of research and clinical studies, he'd discovered that the key to treating infertility was simply timing ovulation to mate the egg and sperm at precisely the right moment. "People just don't understand that," he said. "Sperm live for a couple of days. The egg is good for only six hours. New data shows it might be as short as two to four hours." The trick was to have the sperm ready to impregnate the egg as soon as ovulation occurred, and to succeed, he wanted them to have intercourse every day.

They thought it was odd that he made constant comparisons between humans and animals. "Man is much different from the rest of the mammals," he said. "You don't put your tail up in the air and moo when it's time to ovulate. Or you don't ovulate with orgasm like the rabbits. Man will make love at any time during the cycle."

Another barrier to conception was the female anatomy. "The vagina is a horrible place. It's like a pickle jar. It's very acid, so it doesn't ever get infected." And a woman's cervical mucus, he said, wreaks havoc on invading sperm. "Only about one percent of the poor little buggers ever make it up into here where they're safe. The rest of the time they get chewed up." The cure would be to bypass the cervical mucus through artificial insemination.

The Nelsons weren't saying much; Dr. Jacobson was doing all the talking. Even when he asked a question, he didn't wait for an answer before he meandered from one subject to another. He spent a lot of time bragging about the success of his insemination program. "We use only the finest semen we can purchase," he explained, and said he needed to analyze Rick's sperm before deciding if insemination would be the best course of treatment.

"The first thing we want to do today is decide—do we go with your husband, or with Brand X?" Turning to Rick, he asked, "Did you bring your semen sample?"

Nelson said he had.

"Why don't we go look at the semen together, and that will satisfy that question."

On the way to the laboratory he said this was one of his favorite "gimmicks." Couples got a kick out of viewing the husband's sperm under a microscope, he explained. Peering into the eyepiece, he hemmed and hawed a moment, then announced that Rick didn't have a fertility problem. "He has enough sperm for the whole neighborhood," he declared, and invited the Nelsons to take a look.

When they returned to his office, Cecil said the question was resolved. "We know we're going with you," he said to Rick, "not Brand X. And we're going to go with the bedroom, not insemination. So if it's all right with you, we're committed for a half-year, or a year, program."

Rick and Joyce hadn't committed to anything, but he didn't seem to notice and continued on, sounding like a salesman trying to close a deal. He told Joyce he wouldn't tolerate any emotional outbursts if the program took longer than expected. "I lose my patience with emotions," he said. "None of this 'Boo-hoo, I can't get pregnant.' " He said one of every six couples can't get pregnant, and another one out of six can't have a second child. "After three kids then you start breeding like rabbits."

He also said he didn't want Joyce gaining a lot of weight when she got pregnant. He wanted her to follow a strict regimen of exercise and a high-protein diet. He advised them to get some Jane Fonda exercise tapes. "Exercise is the most erotic thing there is before you go to bed at night," he said. "Do you like to dance?"

"Not really," Rick said.

The doctor ignored him. "The finest exercise in Washington is nude dancing in the privacy of your bedroom. Except that the husband doesn't last long. He loses his center of gravity and is afraid he'll fall and break something." He laughed at his joke.

He asked Rick what kind of exercise he preferred. Rick said he played a lot of softball.

"Softball is great for him," he said excitedly. "It's combative. It's competitive. It's the hunt. The gathering of the men. The burning of the fire. The whole primitive thing."

Furthermore, it was safer than football or basketball. "You don't seem like the health-club-type people, thank God. I'd stay away from the hot tubs. It's what we call the sewer traps with VD. I'd really stay away from that."

Turning to Joyce again, he told her it was important that she drink a lot of liquids. "The number-one cause of life shortening in women is the fact that they underconsume liquids," he said. If women drank enough water, they'd never get constipated. Lack of liquids causes recurrent bladder infections and eventually kidney infections he asserted. Then comes high blood pressure and strokes. He said he sees it happen "all the time."

He told her to keep a two-quart bottle of water in the refrigerator and drink from it often, even if she constantly had to urinate. "I know that's a problem when you're at work and have to use a dirty toilet." He said men are able to consume a much greater quantity of liquids than women. "I don't worry about him," he said of her husband. "He can throw down three beers, a quart of water, and a bottle of Gatorade. But I've never seen a woman drink two glasses of anything. Mainly because she gets teased every time she tittles." He told Rick that he shouldn't tease his wife or daughters whenever they had to tittle.

Rick didn't respond—he didn't know what to say. The doctor moved quickly to the next subject.

He told them that he wanted to work on the sexuality of their marriage. Fantasize and be communicative, he suggested. "Most couples have intercourse a couple of times a week. But we might have to go four or five times a week." He told Rick to abstain from alcohol—"antierection medicine," he called it. "It's almost as bad as saltpeter." And he told them to refrain from pornography.

"Stay away from the dirty books and all the crap people tell you. Just be experimental. The worst thing that's happened to American marriages are all those people like damn Joyce Brothers and Donahue—these idiots who try to tell people what's good in bed. It used to be you could try all different things and it was neat. Now some dirty bugger makes a porn movie about it, and it's negative and it's dirty. If you have to listen to any of the therapists, I think probably that old lady Ruth—whatever her name is—is probably closest to the truth. She tells people to leave the doctoring alone and go on vacation. Everything either works out or you kill each other."

He told them to go to bed early. "Develop a bad back. Bathe together like you used to." He asked if they had pets. Rick said they had cats and dogs.

"You don't have pets in the bedroom, do you?" He didn't wait for a reply. "It's not good when you kids are getting started and one jumps into bed with you and goes—" He began howling like a hound dog. "Or it's underneath the bed." He started howling again. "The pets know what's going on. They're worse than kids. They'll get in between you if they can.

"When's the last time you kids bathed together? It's been a while, hasn't it?" He sat back, looking pleased with himself. "You'd think I was peeking in your window, wouldn't you?"

He prattled on for more than half an hour, commenting on everything from the politics of Jimmy Carter's presidency—"Mr. Carter was a funny President. I don't think he really knew his address. But he was a nice guy."

To minorities—"They're out there breeding like bloody rabbits," he said. "Indigent people don't follow good nutrition in the belief that the bigger they get, the healthier the baby." Yet only black babies were available for adoption. "You don't have white babies put up for adoption," he said.

To taxes—"The government takes your money in selective taxation and pours it down the rathole" to support the indigents and minorities who are having one baby after another.

Finally he started talking about HCG. He explained that the hormone was produced by the developing embryo. "It's what we test for in pregnancy," he said. "So we'll give you this shot every other day at the time we're having you have intercourse. And of course, when we go to insemination, we always use a shot to keep the cost of repeated injections down." They thought he had eliminated the insemination option after analyzing the sperm, but now he was pushing it again.

He asked to see the couple's pedigree chart. "We want to make sure you're not breeding idiots," he said as he surveyed the Nelsons' family tree. He noted that none of their relatives had died of intestinal cancer. "That's good," he said. "Intestinal cancer is the only cancer that's hereditary." Satisfied there was no history of genetic defects, he asked Joyce when her period would be starting. As rehearsed, she said the next day. He pulled out a calendar and started to calculate.

"The time to get you pregnant is right through Christmas," he said, and figured they should start the HCG injections on the twenty-fifth of the month. Since that was Christmas Day, he said they would have to wait a month, because he'd be away for the holidays.

"We still want you to start your intercourse on Christmas Eve or Christmas Day, and continue until your temperature comes up and stays up." He told Joyce to make an appointment for the following month. They still hadn't committed to anything, yet Cecil was already rushing them out the door.

"I just have a few questions," Nelson said, concerned they didn't have enough on tape. "I want to know a little more about human chorionic . . ." He paused, pretending he couldn't pronounce the name of the hormone. "What is that exactly?"

Dr. Jacobson launched into a technical and exhaustive description of HCG, explaining how it was supposed to stimulate the ovaries and time the release of the egg. "Do you understand that?" he asked.

Nelson didn't say anything, but once again Dr. Jacobson didn't seem to notice.

"Without HCG there wouldn't be a test-tube baby in the world, and very few dairies would be in operation. We use it on sheep and cattle. It's used much more extensively in the animal population than on humans."

He explained he would monitor the pregnancy with temperature charts and said he wanted Joyce to start charting her temperature. "We'll watch the baby's growth with ultrasound," he said, "and we'll offer you amniocentesis."

"For the last twenty-five years, I've personally done amnios on over sixty-five hundred patients. We've never lost or compromised a pregnancy," he said. "I'm very careful. I've got a little lady who does all the laboratory work."

Nelson thought of the lawsuits he'd found, but he didn't say anything. Instead he asked how much the treatments would cost. Dr. Jacobson seemed uncomfortable with the question—even defensive. He said his clinic was much cheaper than the competition. "The majority of the cost I put in the first consultation," he answered. "The shots cost twenty-five dollars. If we go to insemination, I only charge sixty dollars, and that includes the HCG shot. A lot of places charge $125 or $150 for the insemination alone."

"How about insurance?" Rick asked.

Dr. Jacobson explained that insurance would cover most elective procedures, but not infertility treatments. "If you want to have an abortion, or if you want to get your breasts taken off or put on—then insurance will cover it." He asked which company insured them.

Rick said they belonged to a health maintenance organization. Dr. Jacobson said the HMO wouldn't reimburse them.

"We also have Blue Cross–Blue Shield," Rick said, scrambling to keep the doctor talking about insurance.

"Why do you have two different plans?"

Trapped, Rick said he was switching from one plan to another.

"Which one are you switching to?" the doctor asked.

He said they were picking up Blue Cross.

The doctor looked pleased. "Blue Cross–Blue Shield will cover it," he said. He went on to explain his disdain for the insurance industry. "Insurance companies run this country," he said. He was paying $520 a month in premiums and had never filed a claim during the past twenty-five years. "So you can imagine how much money they've made off me. They give my wife hell every time she gets the kids shots. We've got a two-hundred or three-hundred-dollar deductible. Per kid."

He said the profits the insurance company were making off him were being used to subsidize treatments for alcoholics, diabetics, drug addicts, and AIDS patients. "It costs a quarter of a million dollars for some freak to die of AIDS. He doesn't die any slower, or any better. You can imagine how many people have to pay five hundred bucks a month to pay for that."

But he said he'd discovered a way to bypass the arbitrary rules of the insurance companies. "I'm not treating you for infertility," he said to Joyce. "I'm treating you for a major ovulatory defect. Which sounds horrible, and for which we may have to use gonadotropin, which is a fancy name for HCG. So we'll write it so that it's not infertility. My bill is coded so that everything can be filed with insurance." Rick thought that, basically, he was advocating insurance fraud.

When the hour was up, Dr. Jacobson escorted them toward the door. As they got into the elevator, Joyce said he'd seemed like a nice man, nothing like the horrible person she had expected to meet. Her reaction was no different from most of his other patients over the years. The Pied Piper of infertility could always draw a following.

When Nelson got back to the office, Lea was waiting to hear what had happened. The consultation had been so bizarre, he said it would take some time to sort through it. He told Lea how the doctor had been howling like a dog and discussing everything from Dr. Joyce Brothers to nude dancing, but he hadn't mentioned resorption at all, and his explanation of HCG sounded plausible.

The most unusual part was Dr. Jacobson's phantom diagnosis. "He must be clairvoyant," Rick said. Without even examining Joyce or checking her medical records, he had diagnosed her as having a major ovulatory defect. His diagnosis would have been impossible. Joyce had gotten a tubal ligation several years earlier after the birth of her second son.

Overall, the meeting hadn't done much to advance the story. But then they got a break. They located another patient. The woman was willing to be interviewed on camera—and she and her husband had plenty to say.

Chapter Fifteen

Renea Jennings knows when her infertility problems began—the day she quarelled with her husband and fell down the stairs and she lost her baby. She was only seventeen at the time. The marriage had been a mistake, and so was the decision to have a baby. Even after she remarried, she waited several years to be sure her marriage was solid before deciding to start a family.

Her decision wasn't made hastily. As the youngest of five children, she watched enviously as her older sisters "got pregnant easily" while she tried month after month to conceive, waiting for her period, hoping it wouldn't come, then disappointment and heartache as another month was squandered. The months turned into years and time was becoming precious.

Her husband, Louis, was just as anxious for a family. He was an automobile dealer, the son of Kay Jennings, one of the most powerful women in the Washington-area car business.

Renea sought help from a succession of doctors and underwent a series of surgeries. One surgeon discovered her ovaries were so encased in scar tissue that her situation was hopeless. She consulted another doctor, who peeled away the tissue with laser surgery, but found her fallopian tubes were severely damaged. She tried artificial insemination, but that didn't work either. They applied to the county adoption agency even though there was a five-year wait. Renea investigated the possibility of a private adoption, but discovered a Caucasian baby was too expensive, even if they could get one. She was beginning to resign herself to a life without children, hoping only for her turn on the adoption lists, when a friend told her about Dr. Jacobson—the doctor who didn't give up on anybody.

She visited the clinic in September 1986, a month before Debbie Gregory resumed her infertility treatments. Without examining Renea, or even consulting her voluminous medical records, Dr. Jacobson assured her that he could help. "Biologically speaking, there's not a woman in the world who can't get pregnant," he said. As long as Renea and Louis had "the right parts," he guaranteed them he could help them conceive. "If you follow what I tell you to do—to the letter—you will get pregnant," he said. The key, he said, was positive thinking.

He told Renea that her problem wasn't scar tissue or blocked fallopian tubes, but the stress of daily living. Louis was working too hard at the car dealership, and Renea was too tense. "You young people don't realize you have to relax when you have sex." He told them to buy a hot tub and fool around. Pour themselves a couple of glasses of wine or vodka, then "have a good time" in the hot tub.

He instructed Louis about foreplay and different ways to excite a woman, going into such detail that Renea got embarrassed. He told Louis to stop spending so much time at the office and pointed to the family portrait on his desk. "I didn't get these seven kids by being gone all the time."

He started Renea on HCG injections and within seven days, according to his calculations, she was pregnant. After so many years of disappointments their prayers had been answered. "We had given up," Louis Jennings would later say. "And now this miracle worker had performed a miracle. I had gotten Renea pregnant."

Renea's treatments were identical to those of Debbie and Chris. She got HCG shots three times a week, even after conception. At six weeks she began weekly sonograms that were too murky to see. And when she started bleeding, he told her to drink some vodka and prescribed progesterone suppositories. He answered her questions about HCG by saying the amount he was giving her was too small to affect a pregnancy test and would be flushed from her system in a day or two.

Through the first two months Renea had never been happier—and she'd never felt better; her only complication was an allergic reaction that she blamed on the hormone injections. Sometimes after an injection she had trouble breathing, as if she had asthma. Dr. Jacobson insisted it wasn't the HCG. He blamed it on her pets, the three cats and two dogs that she pampered like children, and told her to get rid of them. Normally, she followed his advice, but not this time. Her pets were part of the family, and there was no way she was getting rid of them.

They started making plans for the baby—Renea bought toys, clothes, and books on prenatal care. They knocked out a wall between two upstairs bedrooms and started building a nursery. And she notified the county adoption agency that she was pregnant. She was required to report her pregnancy so her name would be scratched from the rolls. After four years they were almost to the top of the list.

When she passed her second month, she told Dr. Jacobson that she wanted to see an obstetrician. He said it wasn't time yet. There was no need to waste her money, and he explained that he would refer her when she was ready. She became persistent during her next visit when she saw a woman bolt from the clinic in tears. Renea knew her name was Carol; they had spoken to each other several times in the waiting room. Renea caught up with her at the elevator to see if she could help. Carol said she'd just been told her baby was dead, then started crying as she got onto the elevator.

When Renea went in for her injection, she insisted on a referral to an obstetrician. Again Cecil said it wasn't time yet, so the next day she made an appointment on her own and didn't tell him.

She was supposed to be ten weeks pregnant, but the doctor couldn't hear a heartbeat and said her uterus was too small for a ten-week pregnancy. When Renea told Dr. Jacobson, he got upset. He asked why Renea had disobeyed him. "I don't know why you want to waste your money," he said. He took her to the sonogram room, laid her down on the table, and made some hurried measurements. For the first time he wasn't optimistic about the prognosis. He said the baby was no longer growing at a normal rate and he wanted to discontinue her HCG injections. He scheduled the next appointment in two weeks. The date would have been Christmas Eve.

Within days of stopping the injections Renea started bleeding again. She called Dr. Jacobson at home, and he said it didn't sound good. He told her to bring a urine sample to her next appointment. The pregnancy test was negative. He performed a sonogram, and as soon as he saw the screen, he started shaking his head. "I hate to tell you kids," he said. "I have some bad news. Your baby is dead." He said Renea must have contracted the flu.

Renea said it was impossible. She hadn't been sick. "I've never felt better in my life," she said. But Dr. Jacobson said there was no mistake. "Sometimes you can get the flu and not even know it," he said.

This miscarriage was vastly different from Renea's last one. No pain. No cramping. No bleeding. Dr. Jacobson explained that she most likely would experience a resorption. He rolled up his shirtsleeve. "Have you ever seen anyone who's been hit really hard on the arm?"

Renea was gradually becoming hysterical. Dr. Jacobson told Louis to watch her closely. "Sometimes women who receive news like this get suicidal," he said. He told Louis to give her some vodka and put her to bed. Once the resorption was complete, Renea could start the next cycle of treatments. On the way out he told Louis there would be no charge that day. "I don't charge for bad news," he said.

At home reminders of the baby were everywhere. The unfinished nursery. Baby toys. Tiny booties hanging from the Christmas tree. "I don't know what to do," Renea told Louis. "I've got this baby inside of me. It's dead. And it's not coming out."

She had been charting the growth of the fetus and knew from her baby books that a three-month fetus was supposed to be the size of a grapefruit. Dr. Jacobson's explanation of resorption didn't make sense to her. "It's too big," she said. "How could it resorb itself?"

Louis called the obstetrician who had examined Renea. The doctor said resorption was possible, but not probable. Then Louis called Dr. Jacobson at home. He seemed annoyed and told Louis to give Renea something to drink and put her to bed. Everything would be fine, he said.

Renea spent the night sobbing and clutching the tiny pajamas her child would have worn. In the morning she told Louis she couldn't cope with the idea of carrying the dead baby inside her. It had to come out.

Louis checked the yellow pages and started calling doctors. Because it was Saturday, he got only answering machines. He called the emergency rooms at the local hospitals, asking anyone he could find about the likelihood of resorbing a three-month-old fetus. Each time he was told it was possible, but not probable. He finally found an office that was open in Woodbridge, Virginia, and made an appointment for that afternoon.

The doctor wasn't in, but his assistant examined Renea. She took a sample of Renea's blood, sent it off to the lab, and tested a sample of Renea's urine in the office. The pregnancy test registered negative.

Next, they went into the sonogram room. Unlike Dr. Jacobson's machine, Louis and Renea could clearly see the images on the screen. When the physician's assistant pointed out Renea's ovaries, they could actually see what she was talking about. Renea's uterus was normal-sized, not expanded as it should have been if she was three months pregnant. She explained her doubts that Renea was pregnant, but since she wasn't a doctor, she wanted a second opinion, so she set up an appointment with a radiologist.

On Monday morning Renea was examined at an ultrasound diagnostic center in Woodbridge. The radiologist reported he found no "definable pregnancy" and told Renea that if she recently had miscarried, there would be signs of fetal tissue in her uterus. He asked the name of Renea's doctor. She told him Dr. Jacobson.

"Oh, no," he said. He'd been hearing stories about Dr. Jacobson for years.

*   *   *

Dr. Jacobson's office called after Christmas to set up Renea's next appointment for hormone shots. Rather than confront the doctor, Louis only said that Renea wasn't emotionally ready to start the treatments again. "It would have been putting Renea through a lot," he later explained. "It wasn't worth it."

As the months went by, and their grief subsided, their emotions slowly turned to anger. In retrospect, too many of Dr. Jacobson's explanations failed to add up. Renea had seen enough women leave the clinic in tears to suspect that others were having phantom pregnancies too. Suspecting they'd been duped, the Jennings started shopping for an attorney. They were more interested in revenge and seeing the doctor was punished than winning a malpractice suit. They contacted several attorneys who declined to take their case, until they finally arrived at the law firm of Ashcraft and Gerrell, a high-volume legal practice that specialized in personal-injury cases.

They spoke with an attorney named Bob Adams. While Adams was discussing the case in the lunchroom the next day, he was overheard by another attorney, Julie Brasfield. For years Julie had been waiting for a case like this. In 1981 Julie was the lawyer who had spoken with Sharon Heyward, whose resorbing pregnancy had prompted Dr. Douglas Lord to confront Cecil. At the time, Sharon's complaint was considered to be the result of a negligent sonogram, and the matter wasn't pursued because Sharon was an isolated patient. But when Julie heard the other attorney discussing the case in the lunchroom, "Everything just clicked," Julie would say.

She retrieved Sharon Heyward's file from storage and told Renea and Louis Jennings that she would help them go after Dr. Jacobson.

For nearly a year Renea had been too embarrassed to discuss her ordeal outside the close company of her mother and sisters. But with time she was finding it cathartic to discuss openly what had happened to her. One day while house hunting she told her real-estate broker about Dr.

Jacobson. The woman said Renea's story sounded familiar. Her son had recently told her about another woman who had a similar miscarriage after contracting the flu. The realtor said she didn't know the woman's name, or even the name of the doctor, but when she called her son, she was told the woman's name was Debbie Gregory.

On December 17, 1987, the Jennings were interviewed on camera at their attorney's office. Renea and Louis sat next to each other in a conference room, nervous and holding hands.

Renea believed Dr. Jacobson had intentionally misled her. "I think he was in it for the profit. I hate to say anything about somebody else, but I feel the guy is preying on the desperation of women who can't get pregnant. Maybe every now and then he lucks out and somebody gets pregnant from the HCG."

She was upset about the many warning signs she had missed, but was especially upset that so many doctors apparently knew of his phantom pregnancies and had not reported him. "It just really angers me that a person like him can sit back in his seat and collect money for doing the things that he's doing."

Louis agreed with Renea. "I think Dr. Jacobson has found a hole in the market—desperate women who want to have children—and he's filling it. He's giving them the promise of a child. I don't think it is hatred—I think it is just greed for money. There are a lot of desperate women out there who want to have children—and they'll pay for it."

He called Dr. Jacobson "one heck of a salesman" and suspected the doctor had intended to string them along from the beginning. "He sold me in ten or fifteen minutes. Looking back on it, I think the guy would have strung us out a whole lot longer if we hadn't gone to get a second opinion.

"If this was back in the Old Testament days, we'd take him out to the edge of town and stone him. Moses would have said, 'Take him to the edge of town and stone him. Stone the whole family and wipe out his seed.' "

Chapter Sixteen

Known as the "expert's expert," radiologist Roger Sanders of Johns Hopkins University in Baltimore was consulted by sonographers from all over the eastern seaboard when they were stumped by a complicated ultrasound case. One of Sanders's admirers was Dr. Peter Dunner, the radiologist who had examined Chris Maimone. Dunner suggested the reporters interview Dr. Sanders so he could abrogate his TV interview.

Dr. Sanders, a small man with a crisp British accent, was chief of radiology at Johns Hopkins. A graduate of the Oxford Medical School, he had written extensively on the use of ultrasound in obstetrics and gynecology and was the coauthor of a top textbook in the field.

In early January, Lea Thompson, her producer, and cameraman Chester Panzer drove to Baltimore in a driving snowstorm to meet the radiologist at his private office. They brought the sonograms of Chris Maimone and Renea Jennings for Dr. Sanders to analyze. They were conducting a blind study, the doctor unaware of the patients' names or even the identity of the physician who took the photos.

Lea gave him the first set of sonograms, and he laid them on his desk in chronological order.

The first one was Chris Maimone's sonogram taken at five weeks. Dr. Jacobson had circled in green ink what he said was the sac. Dr. Sanders took a long look before answering. "This first one," he said, "shows a picture of the bladder—and behind it is an extremely vague picture of the uterus." He looked confused. "Unfortunately, someone has drawn a little circle on this image."

"Do you see a baby there?" Lea asked him.

He continued to study the Polaroid. "I do not see a baby—or even a convincing gestational sac."

He placed it back on the table and picked up the next one—Chris Maimone at seven weeks. The quality was much better, he said, but he still couldn't see much. "It certainly does not look like a pregnancy, or for that matter, even a uterus. I don't know what it is. It could be bowel. But it's probably an ovary."

The third one was Chris at nine weeks. "It's a very indifferent image," he said. "There could be a sac here, but I think probably not. I think it's just bowel. There's no convincing evidence of pregnancy on this view." With his pinkie he pointed to the crown-rump measurements Dr. Jacobson had made. "The measurements your doctor are giving are appropriate for a nine- or ten-week pregnancy. They correlate exactly. But they are measurements of nothing. I don't know what he's measuring. There's no crown-rump. No biparietal diameter. He's taking measurements of nothing at all."

He didn't see a baby in the next two photos either. According to Dr. Jacobson's measurements, the fetus had actually shrunk from the previous week. "That's a little surprising," Dr. Sanders said.

Next, he picked up the sonogram Dr. Jacobson had taken shortly before Chris had gone to Dr. Doppelheuer for a second opinion. "This one shows what I think most likely is bowel," he said. "It's not even a good view of the uterus." Again he said there was no baby.

The final one was taken on October 2, the day the Maimones had confronted Dr. Jacobson. Dr. Sanders said the quality of this one was good. "This time we can easily see the bladder," he said. "And we can see the uterus." He pointed to the Polaroid with his finger. "It's clear the uterus is empty. There's no suggestion of pregnancy here."

"There's no baby there?" Lea asked for emphasis.

"There's no baby," Dr. Sanders replied.

He pointed out the measurements. "I'm not quite sure what they are. It's not quite clear where the caliper was placed. At least it wasn't placed in any sensible fashion."

He got his own calipers out of the desk drawer and tried to figure out what Dr. Jacobson had been measuring. "They are measurements of nothing at all," he said.

Lea interrupted him. "Doctor, what if I told you this is supposed to be the picture of a fetus that is at least twelve weeks old, maybe more?"

Dr. Sanders was startled. He looked down at the sonogram again. "This is a good-quality image, and there's no evidence of anything inside that uterus."

"And you don't have any question about that?"

"On this view I'm confident there's nothing going on."

The second set of sonograms were those of Renea Jennings at six and a half weeks, eight weeks, and fourteen weeks. Her attorney retained Renea's three other sonograms for safekeeping.

Dr. Sanders said the first one was "not a very good study," but he thought he saw the bladder and vagina. He said the doctor had circled the vagina in green ink and had called it a pregnancy.

"What about this one?" Lea asked as she handed him Renea's second sonogram. "This one is at eight weeks. Do you see a baby there?"

"He's outlined what's supposed to be the sac," Dr. Sanders said. "But you can see it doesn't correspond with any real structures. There's no echogenic outline."

The third one was no exception. "There's no baby on this study," he said firmly. "There are measurements being made, but they are not measurements of any real structures." He reviewed all three again. "On these first two images I'm confident there's no baby. On the third image"—he paused—"it's just such a technically poor sonogram, it's hard to say for certain there's nothing there."

"Judging from what you've seen," Lea asked, "you don't think there ever was a baby in this woman?"

"I don't think there was a baby there at any time."

"Do you see any way in the world a doctor who is a fertility specialist, and who does amniocentesis and sonograms for a living, could say there was a baby there?"

The camera zoomed in for a tight shot of Dr. Sanders's reaction. "No," he replied. "No, I really don't see how that could be said."

"What do you think about this doctor?"

"It sounds like malpractice to me."

When Dr. Sanders was finished, Lea told him that a doctor named Cecil Jacobson from Vienna, Virginia, had taken the sonograms. Dr. Sanders had never heard of him.

She explained that Dr. Jacobson normally took multiple sonograms during a pregnancy, about every week or two. Dr. Sanders said that normally only two sonograms were taken, one early in the pregnancy and another late.

Could the repetitive sonograms be harmful? she asked.

"Not that we know of," he said. "But on the other hand, it is not standard practice to take sonograms at weekly intervals. That would be fee gouging, I believe."

The camera angle was changed, and Lea asked many of the same questions again. Dr. Sanders examined the ultrasounds once more, commenting on what he saw. He was becoming more at ease with the camera, even to the point of hamming it up a bit. He looked at several sonograms again and repeated that he didn't see a baby.

"Then, what is it?" Lea asked.

"It's probably bowel. It's hard to say because the quality of the sonogram is so indifferent. There is a suggestion of a sac—but I think it's fecal material."

"Wait a minute," Lea interrupted. "Fecal material? What do you mean?"

Dr. Sanders pointed to one of the sonograms on which Dr. Jacobson had measured the length of Renea Jennings's baby. "This is a measurement of a small structure which I believe to be bowel contents." Throughout the interview he had been referring to bowel, but Lea thought he had meant bowel as in a body organ, not as in human waste. "What you're saying is—he's measuring fecal matter and calling that a baby?"

"That's correct," Dr. Sanders said. That's exactly what he'd been saying the whole time. He picked up another sonogram, one with numbers and drawings all over it. "See these measurements? It looks like he's measured some fecal material as the fetal head."

"Is that right?" Lea asked in astonishment.

Dr. Sanders explained it more bluntly. "He's measuring a lump of shit and calling it a baby."

"What do you think of that?" she asked.

"I guess it's fraudulent practice."

"I'm astonished," she said.

The doctor agreed. "I'm horrified."

Although Dr. Sanders was an expert in ultrasound, he conceded he didn't know much about HCG or resorption, even though he thought the total resorption of a fully formed fetus would be impossible. If the reporters wanted a definitive answer, he suggested they talk to his colleague at Johns Hopkins, Dr. Edward Wallach.

There was no question about Dr. Wallach's credentials. Considered one of the top infertility doctors in the country, he not only was chairman of the obstetrics and gynecology department at Johns Hopkins, he also was the immediate past president of the American Fertility Society. Over the years he had delivered more than twenty-five hundred babies and had written more than two hundred medical publications, including the leading textbook in the field.

When the TV crew arrived, Dr. Wallach was pressed to attend another meeting, but he set aside some time for the interview. He wasn't informed of the subject matter beforehand, only that it involved infertility treatments.

Lea began by asking a few general questions about the success rates and costs of various infertility treatments. They discussed the expense and limited chances of success for in-vitro fertilization, and the rising concerns over the screening of donors for artificial insemination, because new diseases like AIDS were being discovered all the time.

"One of the things that strikes us," Lea said, "after having talked to a lot of these infertile couples, is that they can reach a desperation stage when they believe almost anything that anyone tells them. Do you sometimes feel that way about couples that you see?"

"Sure," Dr. Wallach said. "They're grasping for help. They'll do most anything." Very often, he added, they're looking for creative, far-out ways of getting pregnant, because the routine approaches haven't succeeded.

"Let me ask you about one treatment we have come across," Lea said. "Is it an accepted practice to give HCG to bring about pregnancy?"

The doctor said the hormone was used under certain circumstances to aid in ovulation.

"Would it be accepted practice to give three injections a week—for twelve weeks?"

Dr. Wallach seemed puzzled. "It's unusual to give it for that long," he said. "It's usually given just before somebody would ovulate to provoke ovulation and release of the egg. It's occasionally given to stimulate the ovary in women who have a certain condition called gluteal phase defect, or corpus luteum defect, to keep the ovary producing progesterone." He said HCG was routinely used during in-vitro fertilization procedures, although using it during twelve weeks of pregnancy was very unusual.

"Would it work?" Lea asked.

"Would it work to do what?"

"If you gave a woman three injections a week, five thousand to ten thousand units each time, through twelve weeks, would that help a woman get pregnant and retain the pregnancy?"

Wallach paused a moment. "It might help a woman get pregnant the first week, but to give it for twelve consecutive weeks, I don't think it would help the pregnancy at all."

"Do you see any reason why somebody would use that much HCG?"

"The reason for using HCG in someone who is pregnant would only be to supplement what the placenta is producing in the way of HCG—and I don't think that would necessarily help the pregnancy at all. If the placenta wasn't capable of producing enough HCG through the first twelve weeks of pregnancy, it would suggest there was something abnormal about the pregnancy itself."

"So let me make sure I understand this," Lea said. "You give HCG to a woman to help her get pregnant. But there's no reason to give HCG after she's pregnant?"

"There's one reason. For a woman who has an inadequate functioning corpus luteum." The HCG would help stimulate the corpus luteum into producing sufficient amounts of progesterone, he said. "But there are other ways of handling the problem, and one is to give her progesterone itself. It's simply a more direct method."

"Have you ever heard of someone using a treatment like this?"

"I'm not aware of it," he said. "I'm not aware that people would give it for twelve weeks during pregnancy."

"Would it hurt you to use that much?"

"I don't think it would necessarily hurt. It's much easier to take progesterone by a suppository form than to take injections. But I doubt very much it would be hazardous. HCG is a very safe substance. It's produced in great quantities during pregnancy, and women tolerate it quite well."

"If you gave somebody ten thousand units of HCG, would it set off a pregnancy test?"

Dr. Wallach thought for a moment. "It would be absorbed into the blood and excreted in the urine," he said. "Certainly, it could give a false-positive pregnancy test if it's in high-enough concentration in the urine."

"How long does HCG stay in the system?" Lea asked.

"The half-life of HCG is probably about a week to ten days, meaning it would still have perhaps fifty percent of its effect within a week to ten days. And it would take another week or so to disappear completely."

"If you were given three shots of HCG a week, would it be easy to trip a pregnancy test?"

"Yes," he said without hesitation. "I think you'd get a positive blood pregnancy test with that."

Dr. Wallach glanced at his watch. He was nearing the time for his next appointment, and the interview was showing no signs of wrapping up.

"What would the HCG do to a woman?" Lea asked. "Would she feel like she's pregnant? Would her breasts grow? Would her hips grow?"

"HCG would produce many of the manifestations of pregnancy," he said. "It would stimulate the ovary to produce significant amounts of progesterone and some estrogen. And those hormones are to some extent responsible for symptoms of pregnancy."

"What would it do with her menstrual cycle?"

Dr. Wallach said it would interrupt the cycle, but eventually the patient would experience bleeding.

"The reason HCG works is—it stimulates the ovary. The job of the corpus luteum is to produce progesterone for the first twelve weeks of pregnancy in large quantities. If the woman is not pregnant, the corpus luteum in a normal cycle will last two weeks, and then a woman will have a period and she will start a new cycle." The amount of HCG produced by the placenta increases at an almost logarithmic rate during the first twelve weeks of pregnancy, he said. "So it reaches astronomical levels by twelve weeks. It virtually doubles every forty-eight hours."

"Let me ask you this," Lea continued. "How big is a fetus at three months?"

"It's probably five centimeters long."

"Can you show us how big that would be?" she asked.

He cupped his hands together. "It's probably about the size of a small grapefruit," he said, demonstrating for the camera.

"I would think that's large enough so that if you were to miscarry, you would know it," she said.

"Oh, absolutely."

"Have you ever heard of a woman who was three months pregnant who miscarried and didn't know it?"

"At twelve weeks I think she would know—and the doctor would know."

"This situation that we're talking about," Lea said, "in every case the baby was resorbed at up to twelve weeks of pregnancy. Have you heard of that happening?"

"No," he said. "That's very unusual." But, he added, it wasn't impossible. There is a rare phenomenon called "missed abortion" in which the embryo dies and remains in the uterus until it is resorbed. But that occurs in early pregnancy, he said, not at three months.

"Would it be almost impossible?"

Dr. Wallach smiled. "In my field you see remarkable

things. We're told there's such a thing as 'immaculate conception.' So nothing is impossible. There are things that are highly unlikely, but not impossible. And I think this would be highly unlikely."

"Do you think we've got a problem?" Lea asked.

Dr. Wallach wasn't sure. He would need a lot more information. "If this is something that is happening on a consistent basis, I think it would be unusual. If it's happened once, or maybe twice, maybe it's coincidence."

"How about four times?" Lea asked.

"Four times?" he repeated, looking surprised. "If this same pattern repeated itself four times, I'd be concerned." In his entire career he'd never seen four cases of a resorbing early pregnancy, much less a resorbing three-month pregnancy.

Lea told him about the four patients she knew of and said two of them had experienced three resorptions each.

"So you're talking about six or eight resorptions?" he asked, looking more concerned.

"Six or eight that we know about. We believe there are others out there."

Dr. Wallach wasn't in such a rush anymore. His interest was piqued. But before he condemned anyone, he would still need more information. What were the HCG levels for each woman? Were the levels increasing or decreasing? They should have been doubling every forty-eight hours, he said.

Lea's producer dug into his briefcase and pulled out the copies of Chris Maimone's three blood/pregnancy tests that were performed at her medical lab. Dr. Wallach put on his glasses and studied them carefully. He said the levels, between three hundred and four hundred units of HCG, indicated a woman who was three weeks pregnant.

The producer explained the tests were taken at various intervals when the patient was supposedly three weeks, seven weeks, and twelve weeks pregnant.

Dr. Wallach seemed shocked. "There's no way," he said.

"How do you know that?" Lea asked.

"If she's twelve weeks pregnant, her levels should be in the hundreds of thousands of units."

"Maybe it's what you could get from a couple of shots of HCG?" Lea asked.

Dr. Wallach concurred. He said that's exactly what it could mean.

As the interview began to wrap up, Lea thanked Dr. Wallach for his time. "One of the reasons we've come to Baltimore is—"

Dr. Wallach finished the sentence for her. "It's better to go out of your area."

"That's right. Everybody knows him in Washington. And I'm afraid there are a large number of very respected doctors who send their patients to him." She finally told him the name of the doctor.

Dr. Wallach said he'd heard of him.

She explained that Dr. Jacobson was a genetics pioneer and a professor at George Washington University and the Eastern Virginia Medical School in Norfolk.

"Are you sure?" Dr. Wallach asked. "I don't think so." He was familiar with the personnel at Eastern Virginia, and Dr. Jacobson's name had never come up.

They showed him a copy of Dr. Jacobson's résumé, which listed him as a professor of obstetrics and gynecology at the school. Then Lea showed him Dr. Jacobson's diagnosis of Joyce Nelson. She explained that Dr. Jacobson had diagnosed her as having a "major ovulatory defect" without examining her or any of her medical records.

"What did he do?" Dr. Wallach asked. "Just take her history?"

"That's right."

"That's crazy," he said.

"What do you think of this diagnosis?" Lea asked.

Dr. Wallach started laughing. "I can't say this on television." He cupped his hand over his mouth and whispered. "Bullshit."

Lea said she needed a response that she could use on television.

" 'Ovulatory defect' means that somebody isn't ovulating, or ovulating normally. There's no way of determining that from simply a history alone."

"Does it surprise you that he wouldn't do an examination?"

"Sure. An examination is part of the routine approach any physician uses in trying to arrive at a diagnosis."

"Could you arrive at that diagnosis without examining a patient?"

"Under only one circumstance. If she was absolutely not having any menstrual periods. If she had what we call amenorrhea. She is not ovulating. But then I wouldn't use this terminology. I'd say the patient has amenorrhea."

"But you would probably examine her anyway, would you not?"

"Not probably. I would definitely examine her."

Lea said she was confused as to why a doctor would do this to his patients. "Is there a lot of money to be made in treating infertility?" she asked.

"There could be tremendous amounts of money, because as you point out, people are desperate. They'll try anything, or do anything, when they're at the end of the road."

"So this is an area that could be ripe for greed?"

"I'm sure there are entrepreneurs all over the world who are taking advantage of people who are frustrated."

"It's got to be disappointing," Lea said.

"We spend a good part of our time teaching medical students, residents, our colleagues, our patients, the right way to do things. And when somebody comes along and totally ignores what is appropriate, or what is expected, it does damage to all of us."

Chapter Seventeen

When Lea Thompson called Dr. Jacobson to request an interview, he couldn't have been more accommodating. She explained that she was doing a story on infertility and wanted to speak with him about his controversial new treatment. "You obviously feel it works," she said. "I wonder if you'll do an interview with us about what you do."

"What should I wear?" he shot back, leaving no doubt he was primed to go on TV. "I don't own a white coat," he said. "I'm not the white-coat type."

Without any prompting he gave Lea a brief history of his credentials and accomplishments, telling her about his amniocentesis work, his appointment to the President's Committee on Mental Retardation and his affiliation with the medical schools in Washington and Norfolk. She wondered whether he was putting her on, or whether he really didn't have a clue about why she was calling. She finally interrupted him and arranged a time. She wanted to come over right away, before he had time to change his mind, but he was busy with patients, so they agreed to meet the following Monday afternoon.

Dr. Jacobson rushed out to greet Lea and her cameraman Chester like long-lost relatives and offered them a tour of his clinic. Lea's producer was waiting in the van. They were worried Dr. Jacobson would recognize him from his undercover visit as a patient, so he listened via a wireless microphone that Lea was wearing.

This was obviously a big day for the doctor and a rare opportunity to bask in the spotlight again. He certainly wasn't acting like a man with something to hide. He played the gracious host as he led Lea past his baby-picture wall of fame. She was suitably impressed.

"All of these are your babies?" she asked in astonishment.

"We try to encourage people to send birth announcements and pictures of the babies," he explained. Each baby was the product of a high-risk pregnancy. "I don't see normal ones. I just see people who have difficulty getting pregnant, or keeping pregnant, or have major problems during pregnancy."

He pointed to the picture of a woman propped up in a hospital bed with a baby leaning against her, and he told Lea how he had saved the paralyzed woman's child when other doctors said it couldn't be done.

He took Lea to the laboratory where his daughter Pam was hunched over a microscope and offered to do a "voice-over" for the TV audience to explain how his daughter was photographing amnio slides and cutting out karyotypes.

Lea thought the lab seemed stuck in time, more like a musty high-school chemistry lab than a modern doctor's office. The vials and beakers on the shelves were dusty, certainly not the pristine and sterile environment she would have expected. His amnio equipment seemed antiquated and out-of-date, not like the new equipment her own doctor had used when she had had an amnio during her last pregnancy.

He led her to the file room and proudly showed her the results of a quarter century of work. He said he'd treated fifteen thousand patients over the years, equally divided among amniocentesis, genetics counseling, and infertility.

"This is what sixty-five hundred amnioceteses look like," he said, pointing to thousands of slim files jammed into filing cabinets against the wall. "Each of these is an abnormal baby," he said, referring to pink-coded files. In these cases he'd counseled the woman to have an abortion.

He took her to another bank of file cabinets. "That's fifteen or twenty years of infertility," he said with a sweeping motion toward the files. "Each chart tells a story," he explained almost whimsically as he ran his hand across the files.

"See these ones? These are artificial-insemination cases. You can tell by the code on the top." He pulled one out.

"This patient has had three babies with us." Like many of his insemination patients, the woman had come to him from South America. "I made a mistake down there once. I trained female physicians. And for some reason South Americans don't go to female physicians. They'd rather go to a male one, which is a shame. I think, really, they just like to come up here and shop at Tyson's Corner."

He pulled out another insemination file. "This girl thinks I'm great. She's been inseminated twice and has three babies. She had a set of triplets." Another woman had gotten pregnant after one insemination, went eighteen months before she managed to conceive again, then had a second baby. "Same patient, same doctor, same donor," he said.

He explained that artificial insemination had become a risky business since the onslaught of AIDS. Even his insurance company didn't know he was operating an insemination program. "If they knew," he said, "they would probably shut me down." But now he was taking extra precautions in screening his donor. She noticed he said "donor," not "donors," as if he used only one. "I know the person," he said. "I know his wife. They've been married for a number of years."

He told Lea about the story he'd heard of an AIDS patient who intentionally sold contaminated semen to a sperm bank and infected four babies. "He knew he had AIDS, and he purposely lied so he could spread the disease," the doctor said.

"Is that right?" Lea asked skeptically. She had reported several AIDS-related stories but hadn't heard of that one. She was certain the case would have made national headlines.

"Look at Rock Hudson," the doctor continued. "He gave AIDS to two of his lovers. Look at Liberace. He gave it to two."

Again Lea was skeptical. "Is that true?"

Dr. Jacobson assured her the story was accurate. He'd gotten it from an authoritative source. "It was in *People* magazine," he said.

Lea doubted the magazine reported any such thing.

*   *   *

If Cecil was the least bit wary of the investigative reporter in his office, he didn't show it. He took Lea to his private office, where she was startled by the bizarre animal wallpaper. In the corner he'd set up an American flag that was blowing in the breeze of a small fan.

He showed Lea the portrait of his family.

"They're good-looking kids," Lea said. "There's definitely a family resemblance."

"My older kids grew up not knowing who I was or what I did," he admitted. "I was always in the lab, or down at the university. I did a lot of traveling." One child was now a special-education teacher, another was in geology, and a third was entering business. His daughter in the other room wanted to teach music, but none of them were interested in following their father's career. "I might be able to con the younger ones into going after my mistress of medicine," he said.

As Chester set up the lights and camera for the interview, Dr. Jacobson made sure that Lea was aware of his accomplishments. He claimed he had a doctorate degree from Cambridge University and was a board-certified ob/gyn. She had done enough research on him already to know that neither statement was true. "As I told you on the phone," she said, getting to the point of the visit, "some of your colleagues consider your treatments controversial."

Dr. Jacobson said he'd heard those concerns before. "I don't mind being controversial. I was very controversial on amniocentesis. The first five years people said it couldn't be done." Now he was hearing the same concerns about his HCG treatments. "HCG is new. It's successful in some people and it's unsuccessful in others. That's the frustration. But that's the history of infertility. If you got everyone pregnant the first time, then you'd have magic."

"And this works?" Lea asked.

"This works. We'll see five years from now how many of the people the HCG worked on."

"How many people have you used HCG on?"

"Probably fifty. It's only been in the last year. The people who are easy to get pregnant, get pregnant and leave.

You're left with the people that the conventional therapy doesn't work with."

"One expert we talked to says after the first few weeks the HCG would be useless. It wouldn't do anything."

He didn't respond directly and instead got sidetracked in discussing the ovulation of farm animals. Lea didn't follow what he was talking about and moved on. She asked about his use of repeated sonograms. "Many doctors say one sonogram, maybe two, are the most that are needed."

"That's the way I practice medicine," he said. "I've performed sonograms during 6,592 amnios to date, and I've never lost a baby from it. I've never had damage to the baby. A woman has never miscarried as a result of it."

But Lea said she was talking about his infertility patients. "Do you need to do them every week?"

"If the patient is bleeding, yes. As soon as we see an embryo heart, we stop giving the sonograms unless they have complications. When you see the embryo heart, in the vast majority of cases the woman is not going to abort beyond that stage."

"As you know," Lea said, "we've been working on this story for some time. We've run across some unhappy customers who tell us that after repeated sonograms and shots of HCG, you told them they were pregnant, and then their ob/gyns told them they weren't pregnant."

Dr. Jacobson insisted the other doctors were wrong. The women were pregnant, he said, but had suffered a "missed abortion," and the attending physicians had missed it while performing a D and C. He disputed concerns that HCG would cause a pregnancy test to register positive and claimed he had conducted in-depth studies by injecting nonpregnant women with HCG, and none of the tests came back positive. He also denied the hormone would cause the physical changes his patients experienced, like enlargement of the breasts or uterus.

"Let's talk about two unhappy customers who have come to our attention," Lea said. "One of them is Chris Maimone. She went to see her doctor after you told her she was three months pregnant. Her doctor sent her to a radiologist to get a sonogram. He told her she was not pregnant. She came back to you. You told her she was pregnant."

Dr. Jacobson answered quickly, "She called and wanted to see me that day because she was having a problem. She came in between two amniocentesis patients and wanted to be seen right away. I turned on the machine and I said it looks all right. And her husband says, 'You're wrong. You're wrong. You're wrong.'"

Cecil said he wasn't the only doctor who had made a mistake in Chris's case. "She had a pregnancy test earlier in the same pregnancy done somewhere else," he said, obviously referring to the blood test at Chris's lab. "And the doctor who runs Fairfax Hospital examined her earlier in her pregnancy and found that her uterus was enlarged." He obviously was referring to Dr. Sites, his former department chairman at GWU. But Dr. Sites had determined she wasn't pregnant. "I'm sorry Chris feels that way," he continued. "But you can't practice complicated medicine without ocassionally having misunderstandings. If I could have seen her later in the day when I had more time—"

"You're saying you may have made a misdiagnosis?" Lea asked.

"There's no question I made a misdiagnosis. She was sandwiched between two patients. If she could have come in later in the afternoon when I had time set aside, there never would have been that misunderstanding. That's what happens in medicine."

"And in the meantime she lost that baby?"

"Absolutely. I did a pelvic exam and her uterus was down. I do not routinely do pelvic exams with infertilty patients, because women mistakenly think that pelvics cause miscarriages. I don't know of any evidence that a pelvic exam carefully done can cause a miscarriage. But if you do a pelvic and the woman miscarries, she thinks the doctor caused it."

"Let me make sure I understand about Chris Maimone's situation. You're saying she must have lost that baby in between the times you saw her?"

"The baby died. It doesn't have to pass." He started to explain about the phenomenon of resorption.

"I've never heard of that before. Explain that to me," Lea said. "A baby can resorb?"

"It's a thing we've seen for a long time in twins, where you deliver one baby and you look at the placenta and say, 'Geez, this was twins.' "

"Even up to fourteen weeks, a baby can absorb?"

"That's right. You can have missed abortions even up to fourteen weeks."

"And it's gone," Lea asked with disbelief.

"Sometimes it's in the process of resorbing," he replied. "Most of it is fluid that doesn't have to go anywhere. It can leak and you won't even know it." He asked if she'd ever had a bad bruise. "Where does the blood go? It's resorbed in, isn't it? And it's the same thing when you have bones break. Your body can reabsorb bone. The only thing your body can't reabsorb is enamel."

Lea asked how a fetus like Chris Maimone's, which was supposedly twelve or fourteen weeks and the size of a grapefruit, could resorb.

"No. No," he said. "A twelve-week embryo is not much bigger than a cherry tomato." He indicated the size with his thumb and index finger.

"How far along could a pregnancy resorb?" Lea asked.

"Probably sixteen to eighteen weeks, at the extreme. Probably eight to ten weeks is when most of it would cease." He said the progesterone suppositories he prescribed promoted resorption.

"Is resorption rare?" Lea asked.

"I think resorption is very common," he claimed. He didn't understand why Chris was so upset.

"She feels you defrauded her," Lea said. "She feels you told her she was pregnant when she really wasn't pregnant."

"Why would I try to defraud a patient?" he asked. "That's just stupid. You know me. You see the way I work. You know what I've done for years."

Lea didn't mention that she'd never heard of him before his resorption problems came to light, and he wasn't as famous as he considered himself to be. Instead she said she knew of another disgruntled patient who had the same complaints. "It's Renea Jennings," she said.

Dr. Jacobson said he couldn't discuss Renea's case because it was apparently headed for a lawsuit, but then began discussing it anyway. He said Renea and Chris collaborated in hiring an attorney to sue him. "You've got to be very careful that you don't name her on television. Her lawyer would get upset."

He said it troubled him that any of his patients were unhappy. "I spend a lot of time with them," he said. "You can look at my appointment book. I bill by the unit service, not by my time. I feel horrible when people aren't happy." He said his work had been inflaming emotions for years. "People said I was fraudulent about amniocentesis. People would say, 'Jacobson cooks the results with a Ouija board.' That's bullshit. How can you tell whether a baby's normal or abnormal, or what sex it's going to be, with a Ouija board? That's stupid."

"As it so happens," Lea said, moving on to the next topic, "our producer and his wife came to see you. This is Joyce Nelson I'm talking about. And you diagnosed her as having a major ovulatory defect."

"She must have had irregular ovulation," he said, then turned to the cameraman. "Turn off the camera a second." Chester ignored him and let the camera roll.

"Insurance will not cover infertility," the doctor said. "So you can't use a categorical diagnosis like infertility. You have to say something specifically is wrong. If you put 'major' in front of it, the insurance company doesn't give people as much static." He had done the same thing with amniocentesis, until someone sued him.

"But you never did an exam on her," Lea said. "Don't you have to do an exam in order to say it's a major ovulatory defect?"

Dr. Jacobson said he'd checked Joyce's temperature chart and reviewed the medical records from her previous doctor.

"I don't think so," Lea said. "You didn't get her records or her temperature charts."

"Then why did we see her so soon?"

Lea didn't know. "You're saying that you could make that diagnosis without a physical exam?"

"You can't make it *with* a physical exam," he argued. "You can't feel the eggs. You can't feel what her past problems were." Because her previous doctors had already examined her, he didn't want to add unnecessary costs by repeating another doctor's workup. "Needless studies and needless surgeries, that's where the abuse of infertility is," he said.

Lea realized the doctor wouldn't agree to sit still much longer. They had been talking for nearly an hour already. "Just a couple more questions," she said, "then we'll get out of your hair."

She told the doctor about her visit to Dr. Roger Sanders, the Johns Hopkins sonography expert. "He told us that what you had circled on those sonograms was fecal material—human waste—and was not a baby."

Dr. Jacobson never flinched. "You can't make that statement from a Polaroid," he said. A snapshot wouldn't accurately reflect embryonic movement or indicate what he'd seen on the screen.

"So you're saying he made a mistake?" Lea asked.

"No. I'm just saying you can't make that statement from a Polaroid."

When Lea finished her list of questions, she was doubtful she had scored many points. Dr. Jacobson had lived up to his advance billing. He had an answer for everything, whether it made sense or not. Lea's producer, who had been listening in the van, called the clinic and reminded Lea about Sharon Heyward's case. "Dr. Jacobson said he'd been using HCG on patients for only a year," Nelson said. "Sharon's case is almost ten years old."

Lea went back to the doctor and apologized, saying she had a few more questions. Despite the grilling he'd just received, he agreed to resume the interview. The lights were quickly rearranged, and Lea asked him about Sharon Heyward. He remembered her case instantly.

He said Sharon was a good example of the inexact science of HCG therapy. "She had a lot of miscarriages before I saw her, I think twelve or thirteen." Then she had two children as a result of his work. "The first pregnancy went well, then she had one or two resorptions, then had her second child." He said he was upset that she never came by to say thank you.

Lea corrected him. The second baby was born after Sharon had left him. "You told her that she was pregnant, and then she went to see her doctor, who told her she wasn't pregnant." That diagnosis had led to the heated exchange between Cecil and Sharon's doctor, Douglas Lord. "It's just incredible to me how one doctor can say she was pregnant, and another doctor can say she was not pregnant in a period of one or two days."

"It's very rare," he said. "It doesn't happen frequently. And when it does happen, it's very disturbing." He had used the same methodology on the disgruntled patients that he'd used successfully on many other patients, he said. "That's why Sharon's a good example. If you stick with it, you'll have your baby."

Lea gave him a brief rundown of the disgruntled patients. "We have the Jennings case, we have the Heyward case, we have the Maimone case. In every one of these cases the baby resorbed. There was never a miscarriage. Never a tissue to show for this."

"But there were pregnancy tests, there was enlargement of the uterus. There were repeated sonograms. People are sold when everything turns out well and the baby is normal. But miscarriages are so frequent that when they happen, people have to have a reason for it." He claimed again that he'd been using HCG on patients only during the past eight to ten months and all the results weren't in yet.

"Didn't Sharon Heyward have HCG?"

"No, Heyward definitely did not have HCG," he said.

"And you're convinced it works," she asked.

"Ask Mrs. Heyward," he said.

"But you said she didn't use HCG."

"She used progesterone suppositories. It's the same thing. It's the same process without HCG. The HCG does not make any big difference. Do you understand? It's just another way to get the body to make progesterone."

Lea didn't understand, but it was impossible to debate

him. "Do you think down the road that your colleagues are going to regard HCG as an accepted practice?" she asked.

"Remember, I helped pioneer HCG for the induction of ovulation for genetic reasons. That's well accepted now. Do you understand? We were using it when it was used only in animals."

Lea said that's not what she meant. Would his colleagues someday accept his theory of using HCG to support a pregnancy?

"We're just now getting information from large numbers of patients," he said. Only time would tell.

Chapter Eighteen

After spending more than two hours with Dr. Jacobson, Lea could understand how his patients, and even her producer's wife, had fallen under his spell. He seemed so charming, sincere, and believable that even Lea had her doubts. But once she dissected the interview, she realized how blatantly he'd lied. Among his statements that she could prove false were

1. He said he was an ob/gyn.

2. He said he'd gotten a doctorate degree from Cambridge University.

3. He said he'd been using HCG on patients for only the past year; then he said it had been only eight months.

4. In Chris Maimone's case he said another doctor had given her a positive pregnancy test.

5. Also in Chris's case he claimed another doctor had misdiagnosed her. This was an apparent reference to Dr. Sites, his former department chairman, who actually had determined she wasn't pregnant.

6. He claimed he stopped using HCG when he detected an embryo heart during a sonogram.

7. He said he'd examined Joyce Nelson's temperature charts and previous medical records.

8. He misrepresented his teaching affiliations with George Washington University and the Eastern Virginia School of Medicine.

He told so many half truths and outright lies that it was difficult to separate truth from fiction. How could they believe him when he claimed resorption was common, or HCG wouldn't trip a pregnancy test?

They could show that his sonograms weren't pictures of babies, but images of bowel contents. And one of the top infertility experts in the country said his treatments and theories on resorption didn't make sense, but they still hadn't proved that his HCG injections would trip a pregnancy test. If they gave the injection to Lea or one of the women in the office, they would have to wait a month to prove she wasn't pregnant, but several experts they contacted claimed HCG would cause anyone to pass a pregnancy test. What would happen, they wondered, if they injected a man? If he passed the test, it would conclusively prove that Dr. Jacobson was wrong about the injections too.

Lea's producer volunteered to be the guinea pig. They checked with several doctors and were told there was no danger if a man took the hormone. It was sometimes prescribed for weight loss or used in body building as an alternative to steroids.

They bought some home-pregnancy tests and the next morning tested his urine as a control test. It was negative. Then they arranged for a registered nurse to administer the shot. Her name was Sharon Shockley, wife of Milton Shockley, the manager of the news desk. When she came down to the station that evening after feeding her kids, Lea noticed her producer seemed nervous. She asked if he wanted to cancel the experiment. He gave her some macho-sounding answer about the camera crew being on overtime and said he wanted to get on with it, but Lea knew him well enough to realize he was having second thoughts.

Even if the experiment worked, Lea was concerned it would be perceived as trite and sensational. She considered calling it off herself, but figured if it didn't work, they just wouldn't use it.

They set up in a third-floor ladies' rest room. It was larger than the men's room and didn't have urinals in the background. As they were ready to proceed, Lea was suddenly struck by the foolishness of the situation. Her producer was standing in the ladies' room and was preparing to drop his pants and get injected with a hormone made from women's urine. She almost started laughing. "You can't drop your pants all the way," she told him. "You have to make it tasteful." Nelson unbuckled his belt and lowered his slacks until a portion of his hip was exposed.

When the needle punctured his skin, she discovered her producer wasn't so macho after all. He flinched and complained that it hurt.

What a baby, she thought. They couldn't use the audio portion without making him sound like a sissy.

The next morning Lea was getting her daughters ready for school when the phone rang. It was Rick.

"I think congratulations are in order," he said.

Lea was still drowsy. "What are you talking about?"

"The test is positive," he said. "I'm pregnant."

Rick passed the home-pregnancy tests each morning for the next three days; then Lea called her gynecologist and arranged for him to take a blood test. When he showed up at the gynecologist's office, the receptionist ushered him into the back room before the other patients saw him. The doctor took a sample of blood and said the results would be ready in a few days.

Nelson continued to pass the home-pregnancy tests for the rest of the week. When the results of the blood test were ready, it showed his HCG levels were 433 units, indicating he was three weeks pregnant, just like Chris Maimone's tests.

That afternoon he called the company that manufactured the pregnancy test used by Dr. Jacobson to see if his HCG levels were high enough to trip the test. Dr. Jacobson had claimed during his interview with Lea that a level of more than 3,000 units was necessary to affect the test, but a spokesman for the company, Abbott Laboratories in Chicago, said that wasn't true. The test could pick up HCG levels as low as 25 units and certainly a level of 433 units.

The producer called Dr. Jacobson for a reaction, and to inform him about the station's experiment. Cecil said he doubted that either the manufacturer or the experiment was correct. "That's something that goes against the established literature," he said, and claimed he had once tried a similar experiment using three men as test subjects—and none of them tested positive. According to his research, an injection of 15,000 units in a 140-pound person would have no bearing on the test. "We've never had a false-positive test," he said, and claimed that he never tested a woman for pregnancy until a week after he injected her.

On February 15, 1988, WRC-TV broadcast the beginning of a week-long series of reports about Dr. Cecil Jacobson. Less than a week before the series was scheduled to air, Debbie and Steven Gregory finally relented to tell their story on camera, giving the station four victims—the Gregorys, the Maimones, Sharon Heyward, and Renea and Louis Jennings. The reports were titled, "Conception or Deception?" Anchorman Dave Marash introduced the series that evening on the six o'clock news. "Tonight we begin a shocking series of special reports on infertility. One in every five couples cannot conceive children without help, and that means there are a lot of desperate people out there—people who would do almost anything to have a child—people who would believe anything."

During her lead-in Lea Thompson described Dr. Jacobson as a "well-known fertility specialist who served on a presidential commission. He is a medical pioneer who performed the first amniocentesis in the United States. He is a man who calls himself a baby maker. But some of his patients call him a fraud. They say they were led to believe they were pregnant only to find out later they were not. Is it conception or deception?"

The first story, which detailed the case of Renea and Louis Jennings, lasted almost ten minutes, an extraordinarily long time for a local newscast, and was wrapped around a commercial break.

"I feel like the guy is preying on the desperation of woman who can't get pregnant," Renea said.

Chris Maimone's case was also included, though she was identified only as "a twenty-nine-year-old Fairfax County woman."

Dr. Roger Sanders was shown as he examined Chris's and Renea's sonograms and explained Dr. Jacobson had set the measurements of the fetus in midair, and they were actually measurements of nothing. And the object that Dr. Jacobson claimed was the fetus, he said, was actually bowel contents.

The second broadcast detailed the case of Debbie and Steven Gregory and explained the uses and misuses of HCG.

"We truly believed in the man and everything he told us," Debbie said.

"I've never seen my wife pregnant before," Steven explained. "Then it's all taken away from you. As far as I was concerned, we lost our first child that day. I can't believe he didn't know."

Dr. Wallach explained that prolonged use of HCG was worthless, except that it would make a woman look and feel pregnant. And they included the footage of their HCG experiment, as Lea's producer got injected and passed pregnancy tests for a week.

They showed the undercover visit to Dr. Jacobson's clinic, and how he diagnosed the producer's wife as having a major ovulatory defect, without conducting a single test.

And Sharon Heyward explained, "I used to have miscarriages where my body would abort the fetus, and once I started going to Dr. Jacobson, my body would absorb them."

Both stories included Dr. Jacobson's denials that he had done anything wrong. "Why would I defraud a patient?" he asked. He said he was considered controversial when he'd pioneered amniocentesis, and his infertility treatments were no different. He predicted he would be exonerated again in time.

The third story took the medical community to task for not exposing Dr. Jacobson.

"In the process of doing this story," Lea said, "we learned of more than two dozen fertility specialists and obstetricians, gynecologists and radiologists, in the Washington area who know about Dr. Jacobson and what he is doing. Some even joke about him. But not one doctor would talk about him openly on camera.

"Doctors at Fairfax Hospital, George Washington, Sibley Hospital, and Georgetown Hospital have all seen cases of what they call Jacobson's nonpregnancies—yet never reported them.

"Several doctors from Washington Ultrasound Associates did their own sonograms on three of the four Jacobson patients highlighted in this series and confirmed they were not pregnant—yet none of those radiologists ever went to anybody in authority."

Bob Hall was interviewed and blasted the medical community's practice of protecting its own. "The doctors in the field knew this was going on and tolerated it. That's wrong. There ought to be somebody in the system who can come out and protect these patients."

A spokesman for the Virginia State Board of Medicine acknowledged that medicine historically was run by a "good old boy system" of doctors who looked out for one another. But the spokesman vowed that the accusations would be fully investigated.

The story concluded with brief excerpts from Debbie's and Renea's interviews.

Debbie: "I may be naive for believing in this man for so long, but when you are wanting a baby and you are trying to get pregnant and you have got a doctor who you believe is a well-respected member of the medical community, you believe him. He becomes your friend, your confidant. You trust him."

Renea: "I don't know how he goes to sleep at night, knowing what he has done, and what he continues to do."

Before the first story was off the air, the WRC switchboard was besieged with calls. Dozens of patients with similar stories described their desperate attempts to have children and said they had consulted Dr. Jacobson as a last resort. They were led to believe they were pregnant, many of them multiple times, only to be told they were miscarrying and would resorb. For years they had suffered in silence—each woman believed her problem was unique to herself—but now, after seeing other women with identical stories, they wanted to talk. The memories came flooding back. Some reacted with tears; others with rage. Some accused him of fraud. Others described stunning incompetence.

One woman said Dr. Jacobson told her the problem was "all in my head." Later another doctor discovered she had fibroids and required surgery to get pregnant. Dr. Jacobson might have found the problem, she said, if he had bothered to examine her.

A man from Hagerstown, Maryland, said Dr. Jacobson didn't examine his wife either. If he had, he might have discovered her ovarian cancer, which was detected two years later.

One woman, a teacher, said she had suffered a legitimate miscarriage but refused a D and C based on Dr. Jacobson's advice. When she went to another doctor, he hospitalized her immediately. She had been carrying the remains of a dead fetus for weeks. "You're a mad man," she quoted her doctor as telling Dr. Jacobson. "I will never send another patient to you."

One woman's problems dated back to Cecil's days at GWU, where she had been a patient from 1971 to 1976. Each time she got pregnant and passed a blood clot, he told her she had miscarried and analyzed the tissue. And each time the results indicated the tissue was that of a genetically normal female. Only later another doctor discovered she had endometriosis and couldn't have been pregnant. She said Dr. Jacobson must have been culturing her own tissue and telling her it was a miscarriage.

Some callers had stories about Dr. Jacobson's amnios. One woman said she waited six weeks for amnio results, then received a form letter stating she was expecting a daughter with the normal amount of chromosomes. "He waited so long, it would have been too late for an abortion," she said.

Another woman said Dr. Jacobson had told her that if he detected an abnormality, he would notify her and set up an abortion. On the day the results were due Dr.

Jacobson told her the culture had gotten contaminated and he wanted to draw more fluid. "I got hysterical," she recalled. Nevertheless, she had fluid drawn a second time, but that sample was also ruined. "Needless to say, I never went back a third time," she said. By then it would have been too late for a safe abortion. Fortunately, she gave birth to a healthy son.

One call was from a registered nurse who worked for an endocrinologist. After seeing "too many" of his nonpregnant patients, she said she wrote an anonymous letter to the Fairfax County Medical Society but no action was taken. Later she said she tried to coax a group of infertility patients who belonged to the organization called Resolve to get involved, but the Resolve members were "too distressed" about their own situations and "too frightened to offend doctors." She wouldn't identify herself because she couldn't afford to be known as a nurse who complained about doctors.

Most of the calls, however, were about resorptions. Dozens of them came in from Maryland, Virginia, and the District of Columbia, some from as far away as Baltimore, Richmond, and West Virginia. One woman said she had been told she had triplets and resorbed one each month until they were all gone. She felt like a mother eating her young.

Another lady said the constant stress and pressure had overwhelmed her. "He told me to have sex every day and take Tylenol. It got to be too much for me, and I quit."

Jean Blair described her seven resorptions. Vickie Eckhardt had also suffered seven. Two callers were still patients of Dr. Jacobson and had been pronounced pregnant that week.

The most emotionally fragile of all the callers had received a positive pregnancy test that morning and now was near hysteria on the phone. Already she had gone through two resorptions and said she had spent about $5,000. Now she didn't know whether or not to return.

Another woman said she had been seeing Dr. Jacobson for five years and had suffered eleven resorptions. She was supposedly pregnant when she called the switchboard, or at least that's what Dr. Jacobson had been telling her for the past two weeks, ever since she was artificially inseminated. But her period had started that morning, an indication that she was resorbing another one. When she saw the series on TV, she was stunned. "It's a nightmare," she said. She had called Dr. Jacobson that morning and asked him about the allegations. "He said nothing like this had happened to him before, and he would continue to treat patients as if nothing had happened. I can't believe he is maliciously doing this. Maybe he's sick."

These weren't illiterate women. They were teachers and realtors and professionals—intelligent, middle-aged women who were nearing the end of their childbearing years. One was an attorney, and a couple were nurses. One woman who worked for a rival TV station applauded Lea's story, even if her station had to get scooped for her to learn she'd been tricked.

Besides their tales of tragedy, many of Dr. Jacobson's patients also had bizarre stories about their dealings with the eccentric infertility doctor.

Ellen Pierce said that when she was being artificially inseminated, Dr. Jacobson handed her husband a vial of the anonymous donor's sperm and told him to hold it. "This makes it yours," Cecil told him.

When Amanda Sturgeon was having a miscarriage, Dr. Jacobson looked at the sonogram screen and described her baby as it disintegrated into little pieces. "There's a piece. There's a piece," he said. Amanda's husband promptly passed out on the floor.

Despite the frequent miscarriages in his clinic, Dr. Jacobson didn't provide psychological counseling for his patients. Most hospitals and infertility clinics supplied therapy programs to aid the victims of pregnancy failure, but from what the women said, Dr. Jacobson seemed oblivious to their needs. Sometimes he warned a husband to watch the wife closely in the

Dr. Cecil Jacobson while he was a professor at George Washington University Medical Center in Washington, D.C., during the early 1970s.

Jacobson (*standing*, *far right*) at a meeting of the President's Committee on Mental Retardation. He often touted his membership and his friendship with former cabinet official Caspar Weinberger (*seated*, *center*), who later said he'd never heard of Cecil.

Dr. Jacobson told Debbie Gregory that this was a view of her three-month-old fetus. He circled the image and said the baby was sucking its thumb in the womb. A week later, Debbie learned there was no baby.

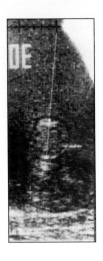

The hormone that Dr. Jacobson prescribed made patients look and feel pregnant. Debbie Gregory posed for this photo when she was supposedly three months pregnant, around the same time that the above sonogram was taken.

Chris Maimone's sonogram at twelve weeks. Cecil claimed that the pregnancy was progressing on schedule, but a sonography expert from Johns Hopkins studied the photo and concluded that Jacobson had circled bowel contents and called them a baby.

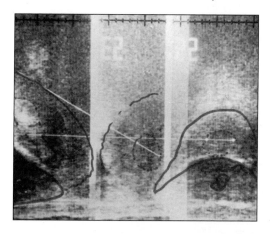

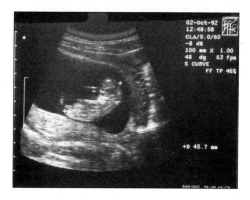

A three-month-old fetus is readily apparent in the womb, as evidenced by this sonogram.

Dr. Cecil Jacobson and his father, Cecil, Sr., outside the federal courthouse in Alexandria, Virginia. Dr. Jacobson's mother died shortly before the start of the trial. AP/Wide World Photos

Dr. Jacobson and his wife, Joyce. She told *People* magazine, "Anyone who got his sperm is lucky." © Manny Rocca/*The Washington Times*

The prosecution team: Assistant U.S. Attorney Randy Bellows (*center*) with Postal Inspector Randy Willetts (*left*) and paralegal Jane Nelson.   © Deanna Dimuro

Flanked by his father (*left*) and attorney James Tate (*right*), Jacobson fields questions from a group of reporters. © Walter Oates/*The Washington Times*

Berry's World

OH YEH?
WELL, **YOU** LOOK LIKE
DOCTOR CECIL JACOBSON,
TOO!

Dr. Jacobson's case attracted worldwide attention as he became grist for cartoonists, late-night TV monologues, and even a *Saturday Night Live* skit featuring actor John Goodman. But while the public poked fun at Cecil, the jokes and insults weren't funny for the parents of Dr. Jacobson's donor children. © Jim Berry, 1992 by NEA, Inc.

© Garner '92/*The Washington Times*

Artist's rendition of Randy Bellows cross-examining Dr. Jacobson. Despite the overwhelming evidence of paternity tests, Jacobson admitted fathering only one patient's child. Ironically, the child had Down's syndrome.   © William Hennessey

first days after a miscarriage. Women could become suicidal, he cautioned, but otherwise his only counseling was to tell women he didn't want to hear any "boo-hoos" if they should lose a child. Miscarriages were nature's way of disposing of imperfect conceptions, he said. The ensuing psychological problems weren't his concern.

For many women the most vivid memories of their years with Dr. Jacobson were how hard they cried for their lost babies, and how much they blamed themselves for causing the deaths.

But not all callers were protesting against Dr. Jacobson. A handful of viewers called to support him and blasted the station for broadcasting the series. One of them was Bo Walters, who owned a farm in the mountains next to Cecil. "I'm opposed to what was said about Dr. Jacobson," Bo said, and credited Dr. Jacobson for helping him have two children. "Dr. Jacobson is the forerunner in a lot of different programs. We look at him as if he's godlike. He's only guilty of trying too hard." He said the doctor's explanation about resorption makes sense. "Horses and calves absorb babies," he said.

"I have only good things to say about him," a woman named Fran said angrily. She had two children because of Dr. Jacobson's HCG treatments. "I think it's silly that you gave the pregnancy test to a man immediately after the HCG shots. When I had the treatment, the pregnancy test would never be given until about three weeks after the injections." For every failure she said there were probably twenty-five to fifty successes. Why didn't the station report those?

And a Virginia realtor named Kathryn seemed ready for a fight when she called the station. Her child wouldn't be here today if it wasn't for Dr. Jacobson.

By the end of the week forty-one women had called the station to report questionable pregnancies. Together they experienced more than seventy resorptions. Arrangements were made to have them bring their sonograms to the station so their Polaroids could be viewed by sonography experts.

One of the last calls would prove to be the most significant of all. It wasn't from a patient. It was from one of Cecil's former employees. Her name was Donna Kessler, and she had worked at the clinic as a laboratory technician during the early 1980's. She said she was shocked by what she'd seen on TV, but she wasn't calling about the resorptions. She had information on what would prove to be an even more explosive topic. She wanted to talk about Dr. Jacobson's sperm bank.

Chapter Nineteen

Cecil had begun experimenting with artificial insemination while at George Washington University during the late 1960s, following one of his sabbaticals to Cambridge. His first patients were animals, primarily pigs, but in time he began working on humans.

For years doctors had bought their sperm from a place known as Dr. Kelso's sperm bank in downtown Washington. Dr. Kelso, a pathologist, had the largest registry of sperm donors in the area and sometimes would even have the semen delivered to a doctor's door. Most of his donors were young medical students who picked up spending money by masturbating into a jar and selling their semen. Cecil would admit that while he was in medical school he had volunteered on occasion to be a donor for other doctors. Dr. Kelso normally paid five dollars for a jar of sperm and sold it for ten, but when he died, his sperm bank died with him, leaving most of the Washington area without a ready source of fresh semen. Cecil stepped in to fill the void.

He'd gotten some nitrogen tanks and experimented with freezing sperm. By the time he opened his own clinic, his insemination techniques were as advanced as any physician in the area, and soon some of his former university colleagues were referring their male patients to him for treatment of semen problems.

He was constantly sounding the alarm on how continued exposure to chemicals and pollutants were drastically reducing sperm counts in America. When he'd first started in the genetics field, a man's normal sperm count was 120 million, but even in Washington, D.C., with its lack of major industries or large sources of pollution, a

189

normal sperm count, he would claim, had dropped to 50 million. By prescribing an antibiotic and vitamin C, he was altering the viscosity and the acidity of the semen, and doctors who referred the men to him were pleased with the results. Couples were coming back pregnant.

The primary attractions for Cecil's insemination program were its anonymity and the large selection of donors. Most couples were embarrassed by having to resort to artificial insemination. In most instances it was such a private matter that they didn't tell even their family or closest friends. The husband was especially embarrassed, having to carry the stigma of being unable to impregnate his wife.

Cecil promised his patients that the inseminations would be held in the strictest confidence. All his files were coded, he said, so it would be impossible to determine which patients got the husband's semen and who got the sperm from an anonymous donor. Only Cecil knew the secret code, and he vowed to "take it to my grave."

He assured his patients that each donor was carefully screened. They were medical students of high intelligence, or seminary students of the highest moral caliber. To be included on his registry, each man had to meet a list of qualifications. The donor had to be married, free of sexually transmitted diseases, a proved sire of healthy sons and daughters, and have no history of hereditary disease. He didn't use students who sold their semen for a profit, and he strongly preferred men who were making a conscious effort to be a donor.

Going through Dr. Jacobson's insemination program was like shopping at a mall for sperm donors. He offered to provide tall men, short men, dark men, or thin men. He said he could match eye color and hair color. It seemed no request was too difficult. Usually a couple wanted a donor who closely matched the husband's physical characteristics so they could avoid embarrassing questions about why the child didn't look like the father. When a Jewish couple wanted a Jewish donor, Cecil claimed he found them one. When a six foot, nine inch husband requested someone his size, Cecil came up with a tall donor.

An early patient, "John Stone," had such a low sperm count, he couldn't get his wife pregnant. Like most couples, he and his wife were uncomfortable about the process and had a lot of questions. Cecil told them about his screening process and the high quality of his donors. If they stayed with him for six to nine months, he said, the chances for success were 85 percent.

Even though Mr. Stone had a low sperm count, Cecil told him to masturbate into a small jar, then mixed his sperm with that of an anonymous donor. Dr. Jacobson said it was a psychological ploy so the Stones would never know whether the donor or the husband was the biological father.

Mrs. Stone got pregnant after three inseminations and delivered a healthy child. When the Stones wanted another baby, they asked for the same donor. Cecil checked his coding system and said they were fortunate. The donor still lived in the area and was available.

Mrs. Stone got pregnant again after just two inseminations, but this time there were problems. The child was born with a "health problem." When they decided to have a third child a few years later, they asked to use a different donor in case the problem was hereditary. Dr. Jacobson said he would find another one.

Over the course of eleven years the Stones had three children, and after each one they sent him an announcement of the birth and a baby picture for his bulletin board.

Each success seemed to bring in new patients. For Carol Franda, Cecil was the first doctor to offer encouragement in the twenty years since her ovaries had been irradiated during an X-ray treatment. Other doctors had told her she was sterile and advised her to undergo a hysterectomy, but Cecil encouraged her not to give up. He said one egg might have been spared and she owed it to herself to try. "He was an incredible optimist," she would say. "To finally have a doctor say, 'Here's a little bit of hope. Go ahead and try'—that was really amazing." He inseminated her with her husband's semen and she got pregnant. After giving birth to a son she would become one of his most vocal supporters.

He told another couple, "John and Mary Ruby," who were trying to have a child through artificial insemination, that he would never give up on them. If the couple wanted to stop the treatments, they would have to leave him, because he would never quit on them. When they got behind in their payments, he sent them a Christmas card and wrote off their $345 bill as a present. They eventually had a healthy daughter.

But not all his cases had happy endings.

"John and Mary Green" were referred to Cecil in the late 1970's. Mr. Green had his vasectomy reversed but still couldn't produce fertile sperm. Treatments by a urologist were unsuccessful, and as a last resort their doctor sent them to Cecil.

The Greens were concerned about using an anonymous donor. They didn't want their child to have the same father as a neighbor down the street, but Dr. Jacobson assured them he had a large pool of donors from which to choose. He said he had about fifty of them, each one a celibate seminary student or an intelligent future doctor.

When Mrs. Green was inseminated, Cecil instructed her and her husband to go home and make love. "Make sure your wife has an orgasm," he told Mr. Green. "It will help her get pregnant." They were perplexed by the instructions, especially since Mr. Green wasn't producing fertile sperm, but they followed the doctor's orders anyway.

Normally, the husband was present during each insemination, but once, when he was out of town on business, Dr. Jacobson told Mrs. Green that he still wanted her to have an orgasm. He told her to go directly home and masturbate. Or, if she preferred, she could use his office. "It's your choice," he said.

As she later recalled, "I flew out of there. I couldn't get out fast enough."

Mrs. Green eventually conceived, just as Cecil assured her she would. When it came time for her to have an amniocentesis, he advised against it. Because her age wasn't a factor and the donor's genetics were perfect, he told her the chances of something being wrong with the baby were no greater than something going wrong with the amnio. "You've waited so long for a baby," he said, "you wouldn't want anything to go wrong now." But when the baby was born, it had a serious genetic problem. It had Down's syndrome. Despite his years of research, Cecil hadn't detected the disorder.

Mrs. Green and her husband underwent genetic testing, and it was determined that neither of them was the carrier. They suspected the problem was with the donor. Mrs. Green wrote a letter to Dr. Jacobson to inform him of the disorder and suggest he get his donor tested. Perhaps Dr. Jacobson had neglected to screen one of the donors, and if so, he should drop the donor from the program.

Dr. Jacobson sent an immediate reply. "My heart is saddened by the condition," he wrote, but he was convinced the problem was not due to his donor. "In your case this is not possible," he said. The parents are rarely a carrier in the type of birth defect that afflicted the girl, known as a translocation type of Down's, and he cited statistics to prove the chances were minuscule. Even so, his donors were carefully screened. "Chromosome tests are a routine part of my donor-selection criteria," he said. "You should definitely use amniocentesis in subsequent pregnancies. Please keep me informed."

The tone of the letter angered Mrs. Green. She felt Dr. Jacobson was talking down to her. Since the masturbation episode, she hadn't felt comfortable with him anyway, and now she had no assurances he had thoroughly tested all his donors. Maybe he'd been too busy that day trying to get one of his patients to masturbate in his office.

She had promised to send Cecil a birth announcement and a photo of the baby, but when the pictures were developed, she and her husband were shocked by what they saw.

The baby didn't resemble either one of them.

"Who does she look like?" she asked her husband.

The baby was round-faced and chubby, not like either one of the Greens. They attributed the difference to the Down's, but as she would later explain, she and her husband had another suspicion. "We both had the same feeling that she looked a lot like Dr. Jacobson."

                          *   *   *

"John and Patricia James" never had those suspicions. They
were different from most of Dr. Jacobson's infertility
patients. They weren't desperate. They weren't at the end
of the line. In fact, they weren't even considered infertile.
They were diagnosed as "subfertile," meaning John had a
low sperm count.

They were both highly educated professionals who had
met in college, before graduate school, and were accustomed to finding logical solutions to their difficult problems. They approached their fertility problem the same
way.

After several years of unsuccessful attempts to conceive,
they sought help from specialists. From the beginning they
placed parameters on how far they would go. They were
both deeply involved in their respective careers and were
secure in their marriage, and it wouldn't be the end of
the world if they never had children. At the time they
felt they would rather remain childless than raise someone
else's baby.

One specialist prescribed hormones, and another treated
John's sperm by spinning it, freezing it, and trying to
concentrate it, but nothing seemed to work. They eventually ended up at the offices of Planned Parenthood. A
counselor gave them the names of two doctors who were
considered specialists in artificial insemination. One was
Cecil Jacobson, who, the counselor said, was enjoying
"phenomenal success."

"He was a very loud, large, overwhelming presence," Mrs.
James would remember from their first meeting. "He was
very enthusiastic and exuberant." Cecil diagnosed them as
having a pH incompatibility. He examined John's semen
and said it was potent enough, but just needed a "boost,"
which he could fix with a treatment he'd developed. He
told them to try his insemination techniques for six to nine
months, and if that didn't work, they would try something
else. He virtually guaranteed they would leave his clinic
with a baby, one way or another. "If you want a baby,
we'll see that you get a baby," he said.

When Patricia was ovulating, she went in for the insemination. Dr. Jacobson sent John to the bathroom to masturbate, and he returned with a vial of semen. Dr. Jacobson inserted it deep into Patricia's cervix, then told them to go home and make love. He explained that intercourse would aid the movement of the egg down the fallopian tube, and they wouldn't know whether the insemination or the intercourse was responsible.

"We did it, not necessarily because it made sense," Patricia would say, "but because this was his program, so we followed it. If he had said turn around three times and kiss the floor, we would have done it."

The first insemination didn't work, so they tried again the next month. Patricia was inseminated twice on successive days. Each time John went into the bathroom to masturbate and handed his vial of sperm to the doctor. Once, to relieve the anxiety, John jokingly asked him, "Are you sure you've got the right sperm?" He didn't hear the doctor's response, or if he did, he couldn't remember it.

Patricia's period was normally so regular that she knew right away when she was pregnant. She had the pregnancy confirmed with a test at her HMO. She didn't see Dr. Jacobson again until he contacted her several weeks later and urged her to get an amnio. Even though Patricia wasn't considered a high-risk pregnancy—she was less than thirty-five years old with no history of genetic defects—Dr. Jacobson said it was necessary because there had been "manipulation" of the conception. "This is a safe procedure," he told her, "and you ought to have it done."

Prior to the amnio they scheduled a sonogram. When he scanned her, he pointed out one fetus, then another. "We've got twins in here," he bellowed, loud enough for the patients in the waiting room to hear. He told her that carrying twins increased the risk of premature birth and mental retardation, and he reiterated his insistence that she get an amnio.

Patricia resisted. She didn't believe an amnio was justified. She contacted her obstetrician and a couple of specialists she knew and asked their opinions. One was a geneticist who obviously didn't think much of Jacobson.

An "odd character," he described him, and told her to consider the source when considering his advice. If she wasn't willing to accept the normal genetic risks of bearing a child, the geneticist said, then she shouldn't have gotten pregnant in the first place.

In the end she decided not to have an amnio—and she never set foot in his clinic again. Years later she would marvel at how little time she actually spent with the man who would forever alter her life.

When her twins were born, they were not premature as Dr. Jacobson had predicted but were well past their due date. Soon people noticed there was something different about the children. They didn't resemble either John or Patricia. The parents were small and dark. The children were large and fair.

People made stale jokes about the mailman and the milkman, but John and Patricia didn't think much about it. At one point John briefly researched his ancestral tree in search of an ancestor with a light complexion, but he didn't find anything—although he didn't look too hard, either. "It must be in the genes somewhere," he said. They never suspected what had really happened.

Chapter Twenty

The day after the first installment of the television exposé about Cecil's clinic, he was sitting in the office of his ward bishop, discussing church business and the problems of a Mormon Brother. As he got up to leave, he told the bishop that he had a few problems of his own to sort out. The bishop hadn't seen the broadcast, but Cecil told him about it. "I'm really upset that people would look at me in that light," he said.

The bishop, Frank Matson, was a long-time assistant to Utah senator Orrin Hatch and general counsel to the Senate Committee on Labor and Human Resources. Cecil told him that he'd always viewed his medical practice as a public service, not as a way to make money, and he'd been fortunate to have been blessed with a special knowledge that most physicians didn't have. "That doesn't make me immune from mistakes or failure," he said, but hundreds of people wouldn't have children without his help.

Cecil poured out his heart, saying he was being vilified for trying to help people. He was concerned about where allegations might lead—patients were already calling to cancel appointments—and he worried that it would threaten his practice so he couldn't continue to help people.

As Bishop Matson watched the rest of the series, he didn't recognize the man who was being portrayed on television. "Whether the allegations are true or not," he would say, "it's beside the point. It's not the man I know." He was convinced that whatever blunders Cecil had made were "mistakes of the head, not of the heart."

A few of the other Church members weren't so charitable. They had expected that sooner or later Cecil's big mouth would get him into trouble. They didn't believe he was evil, but he'd sometimes been too impressed with himself for his own good.

The Monday-night gatherings at Fuddruckers were dominated by discussions of Cecil's situation. His friends couldn't believe what was being said about him on television. The reports seemed mean-spirited and vindictive. Cecil's best friend, Ells Knudson, felt as if he'd been personally attacked. "He does his best to help women have babies, and this is the thanks he gets," Ells said. He thought the allegations didn't make any sense. Of all his patients, how did he pick these few women as pigeons? "What pigeon profile did they fit to fall under this demonic scheme?" Ells asked.

Cecil said he'd done the interview only because he expected to get some free publicity and claimed his words were taken out of context. His friends weren't surprised. They had seen that TV woman in action before. Carol Terry claimed the reporter spliced tape to change the meaning of stories and told outright lies on the air. Ells said he'd seen her night after night going for the jugular, which was typical of the one-side investigative reporting he saw on television. He and the others thought the use of the hidden camera in Cecil's clinic was despicable.

The finger-pointing went full circle as they blamed reporter Lea Thompson, attorney Bob Hall, and each of the vindictive patients for Cecil's woes. Basically, it was everyone's fault but Cecil's. Someone claimed the reporter had an ulterior motive for attacking Cecil. Her husband, Durke, was a Maryland attorney who hoped to pick up some business from the patients who were planning to sue Cecil. In reality Durke Thompson would have nothing to do with any of the patients, but some of Cecil's friends were spreading the story as fact.

In the weeks ahead Cecil became less active in Church functions and avoided people he'd known for years. "He was so embarrassed, he didn't know which way to turn," his friend Duayne Stephenson would remember. "He'd been a hero, and suddenly he was a villain."

Worst of all was the effect on his family. Their friends noticed that his wife went into a state of "denial," trying to carry on as if nothing had happened, even as her husband was being made into a public spectacle. She couldn't understand how his patients could be saying these terrible things about him. She had worked in the office and had known most of the patients. She knew what was going on there and had never seen an attempt to deceive anyone.

Their children were catching the brunt of the abuse. The oldest ones were away at college or were starting families of their own, but the youngest kids were still in grade school, where other children could be especially cruel. They were being teased and ridiculed by classmates. One of Cecil's friends would remember that garbage was dumped on the Jacobsons' front lawn, and another friend would claim a cross was burned in the yard, although the cross burning was never confirmed.

Cecil's business continued its downward spiral, only now at an accelerated pace. Some patients still went to him for amnios and genetic counseling, but his infertility business practically shut down overnight. Patients who had been going to him for years suddenly stopped calling.

Cecil became mired in a deep depression. The doctor who once had been so proud to run into former patients at the supermarket now was too ashamed to be seen in public. He had been talking for a while about moving back to Utah, to be near Joyce's family and his aging parents, and now the prospect of shedding his shattered reputation and starting over seemed more appealing than ever. But before he had a chance to move, there would be a host of new charges to answer. The TV story would become the least of his problems.

In April the patients who had called the television station after "Conception or Deception?" were invited to gather at WRC-TV to discuss their former doctor. More than twenty of them showed up, each bringing, for a medical expert's examination, the sonogram photos she had kept as a reminder of the baby she supposedly had lost. Rows of folding chairs were arranged in a large semicircle, and cold cuts and soft drinks were spread out on a table in Studio A, where Meet the Press and other NBC shows were taped. Lea welcomed the patients and their husbands and thanked them for attending. Two camera crews moved among them. Lea explained that the purpose of the meeting wasn't to cause more pain or embarrassment and told anyone who didn't want to be photographed to move to the back of the room. Two women changed seats.

Meanwhile Lea's producer went into an adjoining room with one camera crew to interview Bill and Susan Dippel, the couple from the Annapolis area, whose doctor determined she was not pregnant within hours of Dr. Jacobson telling her the baby was fine. Since then Susan had sought help from another physician and gotten pregnant right away. She brought her son, Matthew, with her. Some of the other infertility patients would later admit to feeling resentment because a baby was at the meeting.

Lea's job was to placate the crowd and get them talking with each other, then select the couples with the most interesting stories to be interviewed in the next room. "I hope you all will mingle and get to know one another," she told them. "Do any of you have any questions?" she asked, not realizing the floodgate she was opening.

Karen Pascal, a rehabilitation counselor at the National Institutes for Health, and her husband, Christopher, were sitting near the front. She told Lea that when she started with Dr. Jacobson, she had researched his papers at the NIH library but didn't find anything about his HCG research. When she'd asked him about it, Dr. Jacobson handed her a brown envelope containing a manuscript. He'd told her it was the results of his latest study, which he said would be published soon. "These things take a while to get into the journals," he told her.

Karen said she had noticed that the postmark was a year old. Apparently the paper had been submitted for publication and rejected. Turning to face the rest of the crowd, she said, "What he told us seems to me to be fraudulent. Did he present himself in this manner to anyone else?"

Several people answered at once.

"He told us he could get anyone pregnant," Louis Jennings said above the rest.

"I believe he was using us as guinea pigs," blurted out one man sitting in the back of the room.

"I truly believed I was an isolated case," said a woman sitting off to the side with her husband.

"What do you think now?" Lea asked her.

"I think he's a fraud," she said.

For the next two hours the horror stories poured forth. They told of believing the doctor's improbable explanations about HCG, tiny heartbeats on sonograms, and babies that dissolved. They were frustrated and angry at Dr. Jacobson's colleagues who looked the other way rather than trying to stop him.

The couples reminded Lea of the people she'd met a few months earlier at the Resolve meeting. She saw the same pain, heartbreak, even desperation—only this time they had the added indignity of being traumatized by a doctor they had trusted.

One woman believed her HCG injections had caused the cancer of her uterus that was diagnosed three years later. Three women discovered they were referred to Dr. Jacobson by the same physician, leading to suspicions that the doctors might have been in collusion.

Jim Blair, a Washington, D.C., fireman, explained that he and his wife, Jean, were getting ready to leave Dr. Jacobson after more than a year, when Dr. Jacobson tried to convince them to stay, saying he was doing a research paper and coming up with these "really great results."

"We were getting tired of the resorptions," Jim said. His wife, sitting quietly beside him, explained that she had had seven resorptions within thirteen months.

Jean said she had 105 injections during her treatments. Another woman said she got injections for a year and a half, while another woman had them for two years. Bill Eckhardt said he recently read the warning label on the package insert and saw that the manufacturer warned against extended use of the hormone. Now he was worried for his wife, Vickie, because she had gotten injections for nearly five years.

Ellen Pierce said she had been fighting a weight problem

ever since taking the hormone for two and a half years. "I gained forty pounds," she said.

Renea Jennings said she couldn't lose weight either. "I've been on every diet in the world," she said, "and the weight doesn't come off."

Another woman said she had ballooned to 175 pounds. "You think you're pregnant because you're gaining weight, but it's all water."

One woman said she hadn't received an HCG shot in years but was still feeling the effects. "I have two days out of my period when I can't even move. I have headaches so bad, and nausea so bad, that I can't even get up out of bed." She remembered how she tried to tell Dr. Jacobson that the shots were adversely affecting her, but she said he wouldn't listen. "I kept telling him, 'These shots are making me depressed. They're making me tired. I'm having fuller periods than I've ever had before. I'm completely, totally exhausted.' And he kept telling me, 'No. It's just your imagination. It's just a weird feeling that you're having.' "

Lea suggested the women might qualify for the first scientific study on the long-term effects of HCG. She asked if Dr. Jacobson had ever told anyone that the HCG injections would not trip a pregnancy test. Nearly every woman raised her hand.

"For people whose pregnancies went on for several months," Lea asked, "did he continue the HCG injections after he announced you were pregnant?"

Again there was near unanimous agreement.

Ellen Pierce said that as soon as she stopped taking the HCG, she started bleeding, but Dr. Jacobson told her it was nothing to worry about. "He told me that a lot of women spot and bleed through the whole pregnancy." But after four resorptions she went to several gynecologists and explained she was a former patient of Dr. Jacobson. "They all just kind of winced," she said.

For many women a catharsis was taking place. Some were laughing, some were crying, some were getting so angry they couldn't wait to tell the group what Dr. Jacobson had done. Only a handful of people were participating. Lea asked the others to get involved.

A woman named Barbara tried to bring a focus to the discussion. "We're talking about the physical trauma we all experienced—ranging from one woman's uterine cancer all the way down to the weight gains we all had." But what bothered her the most, she said, was the "absolute emotional trauma" she had been through. "In my mind when that man told me I was pregnant, and I was losing that baby, I was ready to jump off the bridge."

One woman who hadn't spoken before meekly raised her hand. In a quivering voice she said she had lost nearly a dozen fetuses and had been undergoing counseling for the past several years to deal with the emotional crisis. She had tried to kill herself several times, she confessed. Her husband grabbed her hand and held it as a hush fell over the crowd.

Several other women admitted they had undergone psychological counseling. One woman said it took repeated visits to a psychiatrist before she was finally convinced that she wasn't subconsciously killing her babies.

Lea asked if anyone had ever confronted Dr. Jacobson.

The woman named Barbara spoke again. She said she had tried to confront him during almost every visit. "And he kept giving me different answers." Whenever she asked him about the HCG, the sonograms, and the resorptions, he kept assuring her that everything was normal.

"Did anyone else confront Jacobson?" Lea asked.

Charlotte Gooch raised her hand. She had written him a letter in 1982 after learning she wasn't pregnant. "And he sent me a letter back saying he was sorry about the death of my baby."

"And you never saw him again?"

"No."

Lea asked why she hadn't complained to the medical authorities.

"Because I thought I was an isolated case," she said. She didn't suspect the same thing had happened to anyone else, until she saw the story on the news.

"What do you think is his motive?" Lea asked.

Money and ego, she said. "He wouldn't have given that

interview to you if he didn't have a terrific ego. That was very obvious. It was incredible he did that interview."

The woman who had tried to commit suicide also had a theory. "I think he really believes he was placed on this earth to help people have children," she said.

"I don't think he meant to deceive," said Carol. She had first gone to Dr. Jacobson while he was still at George Washington University. "I don't think he is evil. I think he is so caught up with his own success, and his own personal life, and himself." She recalled one example of his being so self-centered that he had insisted on giving her HCG even though she told him her temperature chart indicated she wasn't ovulating. "I said, 'Don't you see my chart?' And he said, 'Oh, it doesn't really matter.' He wasn't listening to me," she said. "He was much more involved in himself."

Ellen Pierce wasn't so charitable. "I have to believe he knew what he was doing. But I also believe he developed some kind of rationalization. I think he wanted to believe he is on the edge of some kind of discovery; I think he was using us to get there."

Another man named Chris stood up. "He feels if you believe you are going to get pregnant, and he believes you're going to get pregnant, he can make it happen. It's a feeling of power, and of influence, and believing that positive thinking makes a difference."

That's what Barbara thought, too. "He honestly believes that if you think you are pregnant, you are going to get pregnant. I think in many ways he has some kind of real superiority complex. But I don't think he's criminal. I think he just has a very big ego problem. I think he still does."

"It's like a placebo," another woman interjected.

Another woman thought he was "nuts."

"I don't know if anyone realizes this," Ellen Pierce interjected, "but Dr. Jacobson is a Mormon. And Mormons believe that women are put on the face of this earth to become pregnant. I really believe that has something to do with it—just because of the way he was raised."

A woman from the back of the room who had yet to speak raised her hand and sat quietly until Lea recognized her. "He really needs to be stopped," she said firmly. "I don't say that lightly, because I know it's his livelihood. But he's got to be brought to the realization that he has to take responsibility for what he's doing to us and to our families."

The meeting had lasted more than two hours, and several couples had to leave. Others were so engrossed in the discussion that they would have stayed all night.

Louis Jennings asked the others if Dr. Jacobson had discussed explicit sexual techniques with them. "Did he make any suggestions about how you should have sex?" he asked.

Several couples said Dr. Jacobson had discussed techniques and positions with them.

"I just want to know," Ellen Pierce broke in, "did anyone go through artificial insemination with him?"

Several couples raised their hands. Ellen said she had been inseminated and wanted to compare her situation with the others.

Lea and her producer looked at each other from across the room. They had been waiting to speak with an insemination patient since the call from Dr. Jacobson's former lab tech.

"Did the insemination work?" Lea asked. She moved closer, and the cameraman followed.

"No. We didn't have children. It never worked. But I was just curious." She said that before every insemination Dr. Jacobson asked for an additional fee for the donor. The fee was separate from what the insurance would cover. "We paid him under the table," she explained. "He said the money was for the donor."

Lea stopped her. "Wait a minute. Let me get this straight. You went to him for artificial insemination? And he told you there would be another fee?"

"He said the fee for the donor was twenty dollars. But on our insurance bill he wrote INS, which is insemination. Our insurance company paid for the procedure, but not for the donor. So we paid him twenty dollars in cash every time we saw him."

"And how many times did you have artificial insemination?" Lea asked.

"I had inseminations maybe twice a month. Whenever the temperature on my chart went up."

"Let me ask you—what did he say about the donor?"

"He said the donor matched my husband and me. Our coloring and our genetics. And that he was about average intelligence. In essence, there were no specifics. We never saw him, of course."

"Do you know what he told me?" Lea asked.

"What?"

"He only had one donor."

"God," the woman said in shock, hiding her face in her hands. "It was probably him." It was said more as a joke than an accusation, and the other patients started laughing.

Charlotte Gooch spoke up and said she also had gone to Dr. Jacobson for artificial insemination. "He told us he had just one person," she said. "He said he was healthy and he was a Caucasian. And that was it." Charlotte said she later discovered there was a good reason why the inseminations didn't work. Her uterus was tilted and her fallopian tubes were overlapping, so she couldn't have become pregnant without surgery.

Another woman raised her hand across the room and said she too had been artificially inseminated. Lea and the cameras moved toward her.

"How many times did you have artificial insemination?" Lea asked her.

"It depended on how well I was ovulating. Sometimes once a month. Sometimes three times a month. He'd tell me I had four hours to get home and have sex immediately when I got there. Hopefully there wasn't a traffic jam or they weren't working on the bridge."

"Did he ever tell you who the donor was?" Lea asked.

"No, he didn't. He only said he would match my husband's olive-toned skin."

"Did you get the idea that he just had a multitude of donors?" Lea asked.

"He told me he had people who came to him on a regular basis. People who were qualified because they already had healthy children. He wouldn't use anyone else. But he said if I knew someone who was willing to be the donor, he would gladly pay him the twenty dollars to come in and do it."

The woman said Dr. Jacobson had told her there was no sperm bank at the clinic. "Supposedly this guy came in at the same time I did. But I never saw a guy there. I was beginning to wonder when he went into the bathroom, if he wasn't coming back with his own. It's terrible to say, but we didn't see anybody."

The woman's husband, who had been sitting quietly next to her, finally joined in. "We didn't see anybody at all," he said.

Chapter Twenty-One

During all her insemination treatments the woman who would become known as "Mary Johnson" never saw her anonymous donor either. She was so desperate for a child that she literally risked her life to have one. Her doctor told her that a pregnancy was tantamount to a death sentence. Married as a teenager, she'd suffered two miscarriages. Her reproductive organs were too small to carry a baby, and she was warned that if she tried again, it could kill her. But Mary was a feisty soul who didn't take crap from anyone. If she wanted a baby, she would have one.

For all her spit and vinegar, her husband, Bill, was a pussycat. Once when a construction company tried to beat him out of a paycheck, he was content to sit back and let it happen, but Mary went after his boss with a vengeance. "Don't you fuck with me," she told him. "I'll make your life miserable." And she went home with the cash.

Another time, when a customer wouldn't pay Bill for a job, Mary called the deadbeat herself. "You better give him the money, or I'm going to pay you a visit."

After marrying Bill she used various birth-control methods but had a problem with each one. Finally Bill got a vasectomy. "I really didn't want to have kids anyway," he said. "I don't get into babies."

Soon afterward she started a day-care service in her home and began having second thoughts about motherhood. Despite the risk she told Bill she wanted to try again. "That's what women are put here for," she said.

She read an article in *Time* magazine about a clinic in Virginia that specialized in artificial insemination. She told Bill about it one night, but as he later recalled, he wasn't too keen on the subject. He'd gotten a vasectomy, in effect, to save her life, and now she was changing her mind. "We don't need any kids," he told her. Yet he realized how inflexible Mary could be when she set her mind to something.

"I'm not going to fight you if you want to go," he said. "If this is what makes you happy, then okay."

They went to see Dr. Jacobson in the mid-1980s. Despite years of warnings from other physicians, he gave her hope. "There's no reason why you can't get pregnant," he told her.

"He made me feel real comfortable," she would say. She wanted the donor to resemble Bill. It was important because they weren't telling their families about the insemination, and they wanted to avoid embarrassing questions about why the baby didn't resemble him. Dr. Jacobson assured them he had a "perfect match." She was surprised he was able to find someone so quickly, but people were always telling Bill he looked "familiar," so she thought it really didn't seem so strange.

When she went in for the insemination, she was concerned about accidentally running into the donor. Anonymity was so important to her that it bordered on paranoia. She imagined the donor standing outside the doorway, watching as she left the clinic and following her home. When their child was born, he would park down the street and watch the youngster playing in the front yard. "The way the world is now you never know if somebody's going to blackmail you," she would say.

Dr. Jacobson assured her that the donor wasn't there. He described him as a medical student at George Washington University.

"How do we know he's able to produce kids?" Mary asked.

"He has children of his own."

"How do we know he's disease free?"

He was a "religious man" who was "happily married," Dr. Jacobson said. Although he couldn't guarantee the baby would have the donor's eyes or hair—"Genetics don't work that way," he said—he could assure her the donor was musically inclined and very good in math, and the child could acquire those traits.

The fee was fifty dollars for the insemination and twenty dollars for the donor. He asked for the donor's fee in cash. A check could be traced and leave a paper trail, he explained, so Mary handed him twenty dollars, and he put it in his pocket.

She thought it was weird that he never examined her. He just guided her toward the stirrups and told her to get undressed. When she was in position, he told her to relax. He explained that most women didn't become pregnant after the first insemination. It usually took two or three. He left her in the dark, after telling her again to relax, and returned about fifteen or twenty minutes later with a syringe-type instrument filled with semen. He inserted it, padded her with a tampon-type sponge, and told her to go home and have sex with her husband. If they didn't have intercourse, then he wanted her to masturbate herself to an orgasm. The conversation made her uncomfortable.

He told her to keep a detailed temperature chart and keep track of the occasions when she and Bill had sex. She didn't know why he cared—maybe he'd forgotten that Bill had a vasectomy, or maybe, as she would say, "It was just something that got his rocks off."

Mary got pregnant by the second month. She went to Dr. Jacobson for only two pregnancy tests, then began seeing her obstetrician. When she was nearly four months pregnant, Dr. Jacobson called and said he wanted her to have an amnio.

She told him that she didn't like needles. "You're not sticking a needle in my belly button," she said.

But Dr. Jacobson was insistent. "You're a high-risk pregnancy," he said. "You've got to have it. You've got to make sure the baby's okay."

"If there's something wrong with my baby," she said, "I don't want to know about it when I'm four months pregnant. I'll find out when it's born. I'll deal with it then."

But Dr. Jacobson didn't give up. He even offered her a discount. "I'll give you a hundred dollars off," he said, then phoned her at home a few days later. He told her again that an amnio was important. She could sense he was getting angry with her. Nevertheless, she decided against it.

Bill was relieved that he didn't have to go back to the clinic. He didn't like the doctor anyway. He thought Dr. Jacobson was a blowhard who was "laying too much bullshit" on them. "There's something wrong with him," he told Mary. He didn't like the way Dr. Jacobson tried to impress them with his long-winded medical terms. "He was talking all this garbage that was way over the top of your head. Anybody who wasn't in the medical field wouldn't understand it," Bill said. There was also something else about the doctor that gave Bill a "sneaky suspicion." He couldn't put his finger on it, but it bothered him.

Mary didn't put much stock in her husband's suspicions. "You feel like that about everybody," she said.

A few nights later, as they were going for a drive and discussing the doctor, Bill said, out of the blue, that he suspected Dr. Jacobson had used his own sperm for the insemination. "I bet that son of a bitch used his own shit," he said.

"That's disgusting," Mary said. "That's not even funny."

Bill realized he'd struck a nerve and quickly dropped the subject. "I was just joking," he said, and didn't mention it again, but it was something he always wondered about.

Mary's delivery was extremely difficult. She gave her doctor implicit instructions on how to handle a life-threatening emergency. "If it comes down to me or the baby, then you save the baby," she said.

She had to have a cesarean section and elected to remain awake so Bill could stay in the room with her. They gave her an epidural, then a second one. When Bill walked into the operating room, he saw his wife lying on the table with a sheet propped over her like a tent. In the midst of all the activity and confusion and high-tech equipment, he found a bit of solace in the fact that the medical instruments were kept in a Crossman toolbox, just like the ones used by some of the guys at work.

The rest of the scene was surreal. On one side of the tent lay his wife, pumped full of painkilling drugs and wanting to know what was happening, and on the other side were the doctors, discussing real estate and the value of their homes as if they were sitting down to dinner. Then they were slicing into his wife, "just like they were cutting a cake."

"What's going on?" Mary asked.

"Not too much," was all Bill could manage.

Then one of the doctors reached in and pulled out the baby by the shoulders, wiped it off, and handed it to Bill. It was a boy. They called him Jesse.

No one knew about the insemination, not even Mary's family, and especially not her in-laws. She knew Bill's family wouldn't approve. The only person she told was a neighbor. When Bill found out, he couldn't believe it. "What are you telling her for anyway?"

Mary said it had just slipped out over a cup of coffee.

"When a couple of women get together," he said disgustedly, "they just talk about everything. The carpet comes up."

Within days of the birth they suspected a problem. One of the baby's eyes drifted off to the side. Their pediatrician said the problem would correct itself as Jesse got older.

When the baby was seven weeks old, Mary took him to show Dr. Jacobson. She hadn't seen him since the day he'd tried to pressure her into getting an amnio. She wouldn't have made a special trip to his clinic, but since she was in the neighborhood, she decided to drop in. He wasn't aware the baby had been born—she had never sent him a birth announcement or a picture to put on his bulletin board, as he'd asked. He held Jesse and showed him around the office and said how happy he was that everything had turned out all right. Jesse was sleeping most of the time, and Mary didn't mention the problem with his eye, but every time she went to her pediatrician, she asked about the disorder. "He'll outgrow it by the time he's a year old," the pediatrician said. "All babies have muscle problems with their eyes." But the problem didn't correct itself.

The pediatrician continued to insist Jesse would grow out of it, but one day, when the baby had pneumonia, Mary took him to the emergency room. The doctor who examined him took one look at his eye and said he had strabismus, a wandering-eye disease. "Have you ever thought about getting his eyes checked?" he asked.

Jesse was a big rough-and-tumble boy—which pleased Bill. At first he resented the tiny intruder in his home, who spilled milk all over the kitchen and soiled his diapers, but once Jesse got older and developed a personality, Bill thoroughly enjoyed him. Jesse acquired an interest in the Teenage Mutant Ninja Turtles and took karate, and even when he kicked his dad in the groin a few times, Bill didn't get angry with him.

The addition of a child to the family was turning out better than Mary had expected. It seemed to solidify the marriage. Mary even forgot about her displeasure with Dr. Jacobson and came to thank him for helping with the baby she never would have had.

Even when she saw the story about him on television in 1988, she almost called the TV station to complain. He had helped her conceive when everyone else had given up on her. She felt like cursing out those whimpering women who couldn't have babies—and trashing the reporter who was maligning him.

Chapter Twenty-Two

Four months had passed since Dr. John Doppelheuer had complained to the Virginia State Board of Medicine about Dr. Jacobson. The board's sluggish response was typical. At any given time there was a backlog of more than one thousand complaints against Virginia doctors, and only a handful of trained investigators to sort through them. The board was often accused over the years of being more concerned with protecting doctors than protecting the public. Investigations by newspapers and a state task force had uncovered serious flaws in the system. But lately the board was thought to be doing a better job, though there was still much room for improvement.

State officials blamed much of the problem on the doctors themselves. Bernard L. Henderson, Jr., who was director of the Virginia Department of Health Regulatory Boards, answered critics by saying, "One of the biggest frustrations we have is that a code of silence still exists among professionals."

When Bill Eckhardt and his wife, Vickie, contacted the board, they were interviewed by an investigator who was a retired FBI agent. Vickie thought it strange that he didn't ask many questions. Then, when they offered him copies of her medical records, he declined to take them, saying he would obtain them from Dr. Jacobson. But what upset them most was his habit of glancing at his watch. He was late for another appointment, he explained. He seemed to have better things to do than interview the Eckhardts about their doctor.

Chris and Larry Maimone got the same impression of him. Chris offered to give him a copy of her papers and records, including a day-by-day description of her treatments, but the investigator told her it wouldn't be necessary. Instead he took notes as she described her visits to the clinic. When she later read her statement, it was full of errors.

When Sharon Heyward filed a complaint, she was totally ignored. She didn't hear from anyone at the medical board until the TV station did an update about the slow progress of the medical board's investigation.

Meanwhile months went by without the patients receiving any feedback from the board, leaving them to wonder whether their complaints would be pursued. Bill and Vickie Eckhardt received a letter nearly three months after their complaint, explaining that the board had determined there was merit to the allegations, but saying nothing of what the board planned to do, or how long it would take. Bill called the agency's headquarters in Richmond to find out when a disciplinary hearing would be scheduled, but he was told that the board was too busy to furnish that information. He would have to call the agency each month to find out for himself. Otherwise he wouldn't hear from anyone unless more information was required of him.

"It seems the doctor is getting more protection than the patients he's treating," Bill complained. Vickie was skeptical, too. "I don't know how interested they are in really doing something about it," she said. "I feel like it's a joke."

While the state medical board's investigation seemed to be going nowhere another agency, the Federal Trade Commission, was taking an interest in the case.

When Michael Katz, an investigator for the Federal Trade Commission, saw "Conception or Deception?" he knew it was his kind of case. Katz had been an investigator for nearly twenty years and was considered a throwback to the days when the FTC was an aggressive advocate for consumer protection, before the agency was down-throttled during the Reagan-Bush administrations. He specialized in cases that affected consumers—elderly citizens who lost their homes to unscrupulous home-equity thieves, or adoption-fraud schemes in which desperate couples paid up to ten thousand dollars for Mexican children who were never delivered. From what he'd seen on television, Dr. Jacobson's patients were the kind of victims he thought the agency should help.

Katz was a long-haired artist and accomplished sculptor whose work was displayed at some of the finest galleries in Washington, D.C., and sometimes his politics didn't mesh with the bureaucrats running the agency. He'd been the original creator of the FTC's used-car rule, which would have required mandatory inspection of used cars and disclosure of defects, but when the rule was watered down by the agency after months of compromise, he refused to rewrite it. That kind of attitude earned him a reputation as a renegade by FTC standards.

After seeing the Jacobson story on television, he wrote a preliminary report and submitted it to his superiors, but rather than being assigned to the case, he received a reprimand. The commission didn't want any more "bleeding-heart cases," he was told. The agency's new priority was to investigative deceptive telephone solicitors. He wasn't sure whether the rebuke was the result of the Jacobson case, or of his long-running feud with his bosses. Either way, he wasn't ready to give up. "When someone tells me I can't do something," he would say, "it makes me want to figure out a way to do it."

A few months later, after he was transferred to another division, he submitted his proposal again. This time his new bosses were interested. He was teamed up with an FTC lawyer, Mark Brown, a tall, lanky former pitcher for the University of Michigan, who was a newcomer to the agency.

They began by rounding up the victims who had called the station, to determine who would be interested in cooperating. By then many of the couples were anxious for some agency to initiate disciplinary action against Dr. Jacobson. Still, Katz and Brown ran headlong into the patients' backlash toward the medical board.

Larry Maimone flatly refused to meet with FTC attorney Mark Brown. He was so disillusioned with the medical board, he wanted nothing to do with the FTC. What good could the FTC do? The agency didn't have the power to put Dr. Jacobson in jail; it was empowered only to intervene in cases of deceptive advertising. It could levy a civil fine and get an injunction to stop the doctor from continuing to engage in deceptive advertising. Why bother? He could still be practicing medicine and nothing would change.

Brown and Katz eventually interviewed more than twenty couples who agreed to cooperate with the FTC and who described the broken promises, the squandered years, and the lost opportunities to get reliable medical help elsewhere.

The investigation took more than three months and was based on allegations that Dr. Jacobson had used false advertising and misrepresentations to dupe patients into believing they were pregnant.

The FTC alleged Dr. Jacobson had devised a "pattern of fraudulent behavior" that affected up to five thousand women. The estimate was based on Dr. Jacobson's own statements during his TV interview, when he'd claimed he'd treated fifteen thousand patients during his career, of which one third were infertility patients. Since each couple had spent between one thousand and six thousand dollars for treatments, the FTC estimated Dr. Jacobson generated approximately $2.5 million through his infertility program.

According to the charges, Dr. Jacobson's fraudulent activity started the moment his patients walked in the door. During the initial consultation he portrayed himself as an infertility specialist, although he was not board certified in any medical specialty. He told patients that his treatment was responsible for bringing thousands of babies into the world and misrepresented to some that he had an 85 percent success rate. To others he claimed he was responsible for twenty thousand births.

"His only concern appears to be convincing his patients at the outset that they will become pregnant so they will commence treatment," the staff maintained in its charges. Calling Dr. Jacobson's actions "a carefully orchestrated scheme to defraud consumers who are desperately attempting to have children," the staff requested that the commission seek a permanent injunction to stop Dr. Jacobson from fraudulently treating patients, and to reimburse his patients for the money they'd spent.

In support of the allegations the agency contacted the same medical experts from Johns Hopkins University that the TV station had relied upon—Dr. Roger Sanders and Dr. Edward Wallach—and also arranged an experiment with Dr. Marian Damewood, head of the Johns Hopkins in-vitro fertilization program. Dr. Damewood agreed to test the urine of women who had been injected with HCG as part of the IVF program, but who had yet to be implanted with fertilized eggs. She would later admit to being more than a little embarrassed at conducting such a simple-minded experiment. Any first-year medical student would know the pregnancy tests would be positive, and she was concerned her colleagues would ridicule her because the results were so obvious. Her only question was how long the hormone would continue to affect the tests.

The FTC bought a batch of Abbott pregnancy tests, like the ones Dr. Jacobson had used, and Dr. Damewood tested the urine of twenty-six in-vitro patients at intervals of twenty-four and forty-eight hours after the injections. To no one's surprise each test was positive.

The heart of the FTC's case was based on the sworn affidavits of six former patients—Debbie Gregory, Susan Dippel, Nina McClain, Jean Blair, Vickie Eckhardt and Sharon Heyward. Among them they had twenty-three pregnancies and resorptions. Although many other patients could have been included in the suit, the FTC selected the six strongest ones—women who had consulted a doctor soon after a resorption and were told there was no evidence of a pregnancy.

Jean Blair and Vickie Eckhardt each told of having seven resorptions. Nina McClain said Dr. Jacobson told her she had come to the right place because he was the "only game in town" for treating infertility, and guaranteed that she wouldn't leave without a baby. Sharon Heyward explained how the doctor's treatments changed from the first time she saw him, shortly after he opened his clinic, until she consulted him for help in conceiving another child several years later. By then he was performing his own sonograms and giving women multiple HCG injections.

Susan Dippel told of being led to believe her pregnancy was progressing satisfactorily, then confronting Dr. Jacobson after her own obstetrician determined she wasn't pregnant. She said Dr. Jacobson told her it was "possible I was about to miscarry and that only time would tell." She and her husband spent $2,735 with Dr. Jacobson, then conceived a child almost immediately after leaving him.

Debbie Gregory's affidavit was the most emotional. "I was thirty-four years old when I first went to Dr. Jacobson," Debbie wrote. "I am now thirty-eight years old. I still have not had a baby. I understand that my chances for a successful pregnancy are less than when I was thirty-four. Had I not been led to believe that I had an 85 percent chance of getting pregnant under Dr. Jacobson's care, and had he not repeatedly told me I was pregnant, I would have sought competent treatment elsewhere. I believe my chances of having a baby would be much greater had I not gone to Dr. Jacobson."

As the FTC investigation was getting under way, another branch of the federal government, the United States Congress, was also involving itself in infertility-fraud allegations.

The Congressional Office of Technology Assessment was nearing the end of a two-year study of the nation's infertility industry and had discovered a system that was ripe for fraud and abuse.

An estimated 2.4 million married couples, 15 percent of married Americans, were considered infertile, yet no one was monitoring the quality of their care. The American Fertility Society had voluntary guidelines, but there were no assurances that doctors were following them or even knew about them. No federal or state requirements existed to ensure that the doctor doing the procedures was trained or qualified in treating infertility.

Patients could not get reliable information about the success rates of their clinic—beyond what the doctor told them. Some clinics were making outrageous claims about their achievements, despite the fact that half of the 169 IVF and GIFT clinics had never produced a birth. Many of them were citing national statistics and claiming them as their own.

There was a time when Cecil might have served on the OTA advisory panel as the resident genetics expert, but he wasn't even considered. Instead the members were some of his genetics contemporaries from the old days, including the doctor who replaced him at the Eastern Virginia School of Medicine in Norfolk. The OTA study cited thousands of research papers on the causes and effects of infertility, but none of Cecil's sixty-six publications was mentioned. His work had long been supplanted by new research.

One of the scientists who headed the OTA study was Gary Ellis, who presented some of the data at a seminar on biomedical ethics at the University of Minnesota. One of those in attendance was Congressman Ron Wyden, an aggressive young Democrat from Oregon who used his position as chairman of the obscure Subcommittee on Regulation, Business Opportunities, and Energy to champion a number of high-profile causes. His hearings on medical-lab errors, the cosmetics industry, and the pricing of prescription drugs would generate national headlines and earn him a reputation as a fierce consumer advocate. As always, Rep. Wyden was seeking another issue to explore when he heard Gary Ellis's presentation on the sorry state of the nation's infertility clinics.

By chance they returned to Washington on the same flight. When Wyden got back to his office, he handed his staff an outline that looked as if it had been written on the back of an airsick bag, and it detailed the parameters of their next investigation. It was called "Sex Sells" and was another high-profile issue that Wyden could sink his teeth into.

Just as the congressional investigation was getting underway, the WRC-TV story broke. The subcommittee had a perfect villain in Cecil Jacobson to headline its congressional hearings, and had its choice of sympathetic victims to show how an unchecked medical system allowed abuses to continue. Staff investigator D'Ann Murphy, a fast-talking, high-energy woman, was assigned to lead the project, and she contacted the TV station for help in finding patients.

From experience Murphy anticipated resistance from the medical establishment, which historically had fought any governmental attempts to regulate medicine, but she didn't expect the "religious zeal," as she called it, from the people who were supposed to be the good guys.

As she contacted the leading infertility societies to which most practitioners belonged, no one disputed that some clinics were inflating their success rates and that regulations were needed, but the societies wanted the industry to police itself. They argued that a full-scale congressional investigation of a few egregious examples would defame the whole industry and would scare away couples who were seeking professional help. While acknowledging some isolated problems in the field, they argued that the treatment of infertility was an emerging specialty, and that the problems would correct themselves in time.

As the subcommittee staff was gathering information, they discovered another problem. Most of the clinics had in-house laboratories that were unregulated and had never been inspected. Clinics were operated by doctors who had no laboratory experience, resulting in tremendous variations in lab practices. Many clinics were nothing more than a glorified doctor's office. No standard lab controls were in place, nor were there quality-control assurances. In fact, the labs were exempt from any regulation at all.

The subcommittee planned to send a detailed questionnaire to infertility clinics nationwide to gauge the success rates of each one, but just developing the proper questions to include in the survey took months to complete, as each special-interest group wanted input and fought over wording. Disagreements developed into screaming matches. When it became clear that D'Ann Murphy was proceeding anyway, four of the most respected leaders of the infertility industry headed to Washington for a face-to-face meeting with the congressman himself. Physicians from Yale University, Johns Hopkins, the Cleveland Clinic, and the

American Fertility Society, met with Congressman Wyden and his staff, trying to head off the investigation before it got much further. They expressed their concerns that whatever results were obtained through the survey wouldn't be an accurate measure of a clinic's success. Facilities that treated high-risk patients would naturally have lower success rates than institutions that treated easy cases.

The congressman said he would take every precaution to develop a questionnaire that would reflect their concerns, but he made it implicitly clear that the survey was going to happen whether the infertility societies were involved or not. American couples were entitled to the facts, he said, and should be protected from the hype of the infertility business.

Once they were dragged kicking and screaming into the congressional investigation, the attitude of the fertility societies changed from outright hostility to passive resistance.

In the end a survey of twenty-eight questions was developed and sent to 224 IVF clinics throughout the country. A little more than half of them responded. As the returns were tabulated, it became clear that most clinics didn't come close to meeting their lofty claims of success. And the horror stories began to mount.

A doctor in Torrance, California, was accused of tricking patients into believing he was performing in-vitro fertilization when he wasn't even collecting eggs.

A twenty-nine-year-old Dallas woman spent seventeen thousand dollars on IVF treatments but was never told her doctor's success rate had dropped from 25 percent to 5 percent, or that the clinic's new embryo specialist had never produced a birth.

An advertisement for a huge chain of infertility clinics called IVF Australia was published in *The Boston Globe* and claimed the clinic had produced "236 babies born to date, with an additional 115 patients now pregnant." But in response to the congressional survey, the huge clinic admitted much different results. The company's Boston affiliate conceded its program had never produced a baby. "Our IVF program only recently began full operation," the institute's medical director wrote to Congressman Wyden, and the clinic had just retrieved its first egg for fertilization. The numbers cited in the ad were representative of the conglomerate's worldwide operations, but anyone reading the Boston newspaper would assume the local clinic had produced all those infants.

On June 1, 1988, Congressman Wyden convened his subcommittee's first hearing on infertility. Addressing a hearing room packed with TV cameras, patients, and representatives of the infertility industry, Wyden quickly set the tone for the hearing.

"Ten years ago, the world marveled at the birth of Louise Brown, the first 'test tube' baby," he said. "In the past decade the infertility industry has mushroomed: this year alone an estimated one billion dollars will be spent on treatments in the United States."

He quoted statistics from the OTA report—more than half of the 169 in-vitro clinics in 1987 had never produced a baby, and despite what the clinics claimed, the actual success rate was about 10 percent. Many in-vitro clinics had never experienced a birth but were using national statistics as representative of their own success rates.

The star witness was Vickie Eckhardt, who looked fragile and nervous under the glare of TV cameras. Her husband, Bill, sat beside her, holding her hand. D'Ann Murphy had selected Vickie and Bill after interviewing most of the victims who contacted the TV station. For the subcommittee's purposes Vickie was perfect. She was articulate, attractive, and obviously aggrieved. She hadn't been overexposed on TV—she contacted the station after the series aired and was included briefly in an abbreviated version that was broadcast on the *Today* show. Testifying in a shaky voice, and sometimes unable to hold back tears, Vickie told the subcommittee about her years of treatments with Dr. Jacobson.

"Being unable to have a baby is a very sad thing to try to live with," she said, "but finding out that someone has lied to you and given you false hope is in some ways even worse. I am a very private person, and it has never been easy for me to talk about my problem. But my husband

and I are both afraid that unless we, and other people like us, speak up, other infertile couples will be hurt the way we have."

Vickie told the committee how she became "pregnant" seven times and "resorbed" seven babies. "I always had the symptoms of being pregnant, but I continued to bleed," she said. "I told him I wanted to check with my gynecologist, but he always discouraged that. He just kept saying that there were lots of things we don't know about the causes of miscarriages and that we would just have to be patient and keep trying."

Through it all she did whatever Dr. Jacobson asked of her. "It is hard to explain to other people," she said, "but when you want a baby so badly and you are afraid you may never be able to have one, it is all you can think about. It affects the way you see the whole world."

She said she finally realized she'd been misled when she saw Lea Thompson's series on television. "Everything began to gel, and we realized that Dr. Jacobson had lied to us," she said. "We felt very, very foolish. We have always thought that we were relatively intelligent, but we must have been really stupid to let ourselves be duped like that.

"He out-and-out lied to me. He told me he could get me pregnant and this treatment is what I needed." But Vickie said her problem was blocked tubes, which Dr. Jacobson's hormones never could have cured. "He is the worst kind of fraud," Vickie charged. "He should have been a used-car salesman—at least then he could have applied his talents without really hurting anyone."

Chapter Twenty-Three

After the WRC exposé aired, the first batch of lawsuits was filed by Debbie Gregory, Chris Maimone, and Renea Jennings, three of the four women who went public with their complaints in "Conception or Deception?" The fourth woman, Sharon Heyward, was told her case was too old and the statute of limitations had expired.

The suits accused Dr. Jacobson of negligence, fraud, battery, breach of contract, and negligent infliction of emotional distress. Each woman, along with her husband, asked for two million dollars in damages, and another two million dollars in punitive damages.

Dr. Jacobson's insurance company, St. Paul's Fire and Marine, one of the largest insurers of physicians in the country, hired the law firm of Slenker, Brandt, Jennings, and Johnston. Cecil didn't retain a lawyer for himself but relied on the counsel provided by his insurance company. He'd been paying the premiums on malpractice insurance for so long, he told his friends, he thought the insurance company owed him free legal representation.

The primary attorney for Cecil's defense was Tara McCarthy. She had crossed swords with Richard Boone and Bob Hall before, and they wondered how she would react at defending a doctor who was accused of such heinous acts against women. She quickly left no doubt she would present an aggressive defense. She let Boone and Hall know she thought they were lower than slime for having the audacity to file suit against the kindly doctor. Boone wasn't sure whether she was merely posturing or whether she really believed so strongly in her client. She and Boone were from the fraternity of lawyers that defended doctors and didn't sue them, and he had used similar acts of gamesmanship before.

One of her first actions was to file a motion to get the cases separated. Virginia law didn't recognize class-action lawsuits—even husbands and wives couldn't sue together—so the Gregorys, Maimones, and Jennings had to dismiss their suits and file six separate ones. It was an important victory for Cecil and meant the defense could portray each case as an inadvertent mistake, rather than as part of a pattern.

Cecil, meanwhile, searched the medical literature for any authoritative sources who could support his use of HCG and his views on resorption. He located experiments that had been performed on animals, but nothing on humans. He even discovered a few references to resorbing pregnancies, but those were special cases of ectopic pregnancies fertilized outside the womb. He couldn't find a single citation, study, or research project that supported his position on HCG.

An analysis of his infertility cases revealed he had treated far fewer infertility patients than he had stated. Rather than having thousands of infertile patients, as he often claimed, he had treated only 380 women for infertility during the previous five years. He claimed 140 of them had gotten pregnant, an enviable 37 percent success rate, but much less than the 85 percent he sometimes quoted. But the rate of success got even smaller once other factors were considered. Of the 140 pregnancies at least half miscarried, bringing his success rate down to 18 percent.

The most startling statistic of all, however, was the number of resorptions. In court papers Dr. Jacobson claimed 75 percent of all his miscarriages resorbed, meaning more than fifty women had miscarried without passing the fetus or products of conception.

According to his statistics, he encountered more resorptions than probably any doctor in the world.

Dr. Jacobson faced his accusers for the first time in a conference room at his attorney's office, as he was questioned under oath at a pretrial deposition by the attorneys representing the patients who were suing him. Each side, armed with boxes of medical records and legal documents, huddled at opposite ends of a large conference table. Dr. Jacobson, although polite and courteous, at times seemed annoyed to be defending himself against what he seemed to consider nuisance suits.

Chris and Larry Maimone were the only patients to attend. They hadn't seen Dr. Jacobson in more than a year, since the day they had confronted him at the clinic. The moment Chris saw him, she started trembling, just like that last day in his office.

Her attorney, Bob Hall, questioned Dr. Jacobson, and from the beginning it was clear the attorney would have a difficult time pinning him down. Dr. Jacobson employed what Hall termed a "classic medical defense," designed to dazzle a layman with medical esoterica that only a physician could understand. Hall had seen it used many times before. Ask a doctor about aspirin, and he'll supply a dissertation about acetylsalicylic acid—and never answer the original question.

Dr. Jacobson offered no apologies for his treatment of Chris and insisted that she had been pregnant, no matter what the other doctors contended. He denied that she ever showed him the results of her blood tests in which the HCG levels were dropping. Even so, he said the test results would not have been a "totally ominous sign."

Hall showed him the five sonogram photos he'd taken of Chris, the same ones that some of the most respected sonographers in the country had said did not contain the image of a pregnancy. Hall asked him to describe the first one. Dr. Jacobson said it was a reflection of what he'd seen on the screen that day. He had circled the uterus with a felt-tip pen and outlined the sac.

The second sonogram, of Chris at seven weeks, was of better quality. Dr. Roger Sanders of Johns Hopkins University had said it was the view of an ovary or bowel contents, not a pregnancy, but Dr. Jacobson pointed out a "dot" which he said was the "cavity of the embryo." He remembered he'd seen the flicker of the heartbeat that day. "It's hard to describe," he said, "but if you see it, you'll never forget it."

He insisted he saw a pregnancy in each of the photographs, even though Dr. Sanders had said they were views of bowel contents or measurements of nothing at all. Cecil pointed out a fetal head in one sonogram and the baby's extremities in another. When Hall showed him the last one, taken moments before Chris and Larry had told him that other doctors said there was no baby, Dr. Jacobson said he could see the bladder and uterus very clearly, but it was difficult to see a "discernible" fetus. "When I initially did this, I thought I saw movement," he said.

Hall asked Dr. Jacobson to look at the photo again and explain what he saw this time. Was it a fetus, as Dr. Jacobson had initially told the Maimones, or was it was fetal material as he later claimed?

"It's definitely fetal material," he said.

"What should have been the size of that fetus at week fourteen?" Hall asked.

Dr. Jacobson said it was about "two or three inches." He disputed the characterization of most doctors that the fetus at fourteen weeks would be about the size of a grapefruit. He said it was closer to "a radish, with a cherry for a head."

"What happened to this fetus, Doctor?" Hall asked accusingly.

"The fetus obviously died and resorbed," he replied.

"Do you know why?"

"No, I don't."

Cecil's attorneys were scrambling to find a doctor, a scientist, or anyone who could support his medicine, or at least say he wasn't totally depraved. The number of lawsuits against him continued to mount. He gave them a list of doctors he'd known over the years who would review the medical records for the patients who were suing him and analyze the quality of their care. One of them was Cecil's longtime colleague, Dr. Edward Gahres. He was a peculiar choice to be consulted for help. He was the ob/gyn who had warned Cecil in the late 1970's that he was making mistakes and had alerted the medical board after Cecil told him to mind his own business. Dr. Gahres was astonished when he was asked to testify for Cecil and was designated as his expert medical witness. It was an indication of how desperate Cecil had become.

By then more disgruntled patients had filed lawsuits—eventually a total of twenty-three would sue him. The first case scheduled for trial was filed by Susan and Bill Dippel. Unlike the other patients who retained generally small law firms from the Virginia suburbs, the Dippels hired the powerful Washington firm of Williams and Connolly. The superfirm brought a new dimension to the case by virtue of the huge resources it could throw into the lawsuit.

The Williams and Connolly lawyers scheduled a deposition with Dr. Gahres to hear what Cecil's main witness would say when he got into court. At first it appeared as if he'd bought into Cecil's theories, saying that Dr. Jacobson's use of HCG was no worse for women than giving them injections of B-12. "The bottom line is, the use of HCG did no permanent harm to these women," he said.

He also agreed with several other aspects of Dr. Jacobson's practice. He believed Cecil was justified in using fresh sperm for artificial insemination rather than frozen semen. And he also thought Cecil used sound judgment in relying on temperature charts to monitor ovulation and pedigree charts to diagnose hereditary disease. Also, he thought Cecil's theories on resorption weren't too far off base either. More research was needed on the phenomenon of resorption, he said, and predicted that medical textbooks would be rewritten someday to support Cecil's assumptions.

When the Dippels's attorney, William Layman, questioned Dr. Gahres about Cecil's use of HCG, Dr. Jacobson's attorney, Tara McCarthy, objected. She said she was offering Dr. Gahres only as an expert witness on the issues of using HCG to stimulate ovulation and using fresh sperm in artificial insemination. She didn't intend to offer him as a witness on the prolonged use of HCG.

Layman wanted to know why not. Before Cecil's attorney

could stop him, Dr. Gahres explained that it was "inappropriate" to use HCG longer than two weeks after ovulation, as Cecil had been doing, then proceeded to explain that Dr. Jacobson's practice was so "unacceptable" that he had complained about him to the Virginia Board of Medicine. Tara McCarthy sat by helplessly as her expert witness proceeded to destroy her defense. Dr. Gahres continued to shoot holes in most of Cecil's theories, acknowledging that HCG would cause false-positive pregnancy tests and mimic the physiological effects of pregnancy—and any doctor who regularly treated infertility patients should have known it.

"Do you know of any other doctors besides yourself who confronted Dr. Jacobson?" the Williams and Connolly attorney asked.

"I know quite a few," he said. "But I don't think I'm in a position to tell you who they are." He said some of them had already been questioned by other lawyers and had refused to testify—either for or against Dr. Jacobson. But Cecil's work had been a frequent topic of discussion among local infertility specialists since the mid-1980's. Several doctors had tried to tell him that he was wrong, but Cecil ignored them. "Cecil honestly believed that what he was doing was right, and it was impossible to get him to change."

By the time the deposition concluded, it was obvious that if Dr. Edward Gahres was the best witness the defense could find, then Cecil was in serious trouble.

The Williams and Connolly attorneys also conducted a financial investigation of Dr. Jacobson to determine the extent of his assets, which was relevant to the issue of damages. They were shocked to uncover a series of questionable financial transactions.

After the TV broadcast, as patients were preparing to sue him, Cecil had conducted a virtual fire sale of his property. He transferred more than $1.7 million worth of holdings out of his name and into a limited partnership formed by his children and Ells Knudson's children a decade earlier. They called the partnership Jacobson-Ziff, named for a word derived from the Book of Mormon to describe a precious metal, and bought property and built houses to fund college and missionary work.

Cecil would claim that his children controlled the partnership and he had no direction over it, but according to the partnership's financial records, he personally guaranteed loans and freely moved money in and out of the company. One investigator would say that Dr. Jacobson used Jacobson-Ziff like a "personal piggy bank," but when Cecil was asked under oath by a Williams and Connolly attorney, he denied he had any affiliation with the partnership.

Cecil sold his farm to Jacobson-Ziff for $150,000, a substantial giveaway considering the property would be sold two years later for $600,000. Then he sold two valuable tracts of real estate, held in the name of the Reproductive Genetic Center, to Jacobson-Ziff. In one transaction the papers were backdated to make it appear the sale had occurred nine years earlier.

He signed checks on behalf of the partnership and made loans to himself from the company's account. One loan during the mid-1980s, while his clinic was facing financial difficulties, was for $250,000, yet when he presented a financial statement to secure a loan from the Mormon-operated Sailor's and Merchant's Bank, he reported the money as an asset and made no mention of the quarter of a million dollars he owed Jacobson-Ziff.

"I have no role in that at all, and haven't since it was set up by the lawyers," Cecil testified during the sworn deposition. He said his wife was the general partner and his children ran the business. "I don't do Ziff's work. I have no signature responsibilities or authority on Ziff."

Even with the opposing attorney holding a stack of certified documents showing that Dr. Jacobson wrote checks on the partnership's account, and guaranteed loans on the partnership's behalf, he denied under oath that he wrote any checks or guaranteed any loans. Although his name was affixed to a signature card at Sailor's and Merchant's Bank, he denied he had signature authority over the account.

The lies would prove costly in the years ahead. His friends would say he merely misunderstood the questions. He was a "vocal dyslexic," they claimed, who said one thing when he really meant another. But others would notice that, even faced with documented proof, he didn't hesitate to lie and rationalize to get himself out of trouble.

Chapter Twenty-Four

D r. Doppelheuer had complained to the Virginia State
Board of Medicine in November 1987, more than a
year earlier, and still no action had been taken. When Lea
Thompson prepared an update of her original broadcast,
her producer called the medical board but was told no date
had been set for a disciplinary hearing. He explained the
patients believed they were being ignored, but the board
spokesman, George Wilbur, said that wasn't the case. "We
tend to move ponderously," Wilbur said. "It's no longer
a good-old-boy network. Every complaint will be acted
upon. This won't be swept under the rug." He expected
a date for a hearing in the very near future, and it would
be open to the public.

That evening the producer called one of the board members from the northern Virginia area, Dr. Franklin J. Peper,
to see if he could shed some light on the board's next move.
Dr. Peper was perplexed at the call. He wasn't aware of
any complaints against Dr. Jacobson. "I have no information on this at all." He hadn't seen the TV station's
investigation, he said, nor had he heard of any criticism
of Cecil through the medical grapevine. What made Dr.
Peper's lack of knowledge about the case even more surprising was that he personally knew Cecil Jacobson. Cecil's
wife was one of his patients.

On December 8, 1988, the station broadcast its update.
"Since our story," Lea Thompson said, "at least nine couples have filed complaints with the Virginia State Board
of Medicine. Yet after all this time, the board hasn't even
called in Dr. Jacobson for a hearing. And since the board
meets only four times a year, there might not be a hearing
on this case until at least next spring."

Bill and Vickie Eckhardt were featured. Bill had been calling the medical board every month, trying to pressure the board into taking action. "I'm very skeptical," Bill said. "It seems he's getting more protection from the medical board than the patients."

"It's just taken too long," Vickie seconded. "Something should have been done a long time ago."

Although insisting there was no connection, the medical board filed charges against Dr. Jacobson within two weeks of the follow-up broadcast and sent a strong message that it meant business. The board didn't just accuse him of negligently mistreating his patients but charged that he had intentionally defrauded them.

"Under the guise of legitimate medical treatment," the charges read, "you fraudulently prescribed and administered" a succession of HCG injections, urinary pregnancy tests, and sonograms, then "fraudulently reported" that gestational sacs were developing. Later he "fraudulently informed" the patients the embryos were being reabsorbed, often after other doctors determined there was no pregnancy. "Such treatment was without accepted therapeutic purpose, contrary to sound medical judgment, and with the intent to defraud your patient," the board stated.

The disciplinary hearing was scheduled at the board's headquarters in Richmond on January 27, 1989. Since the full sixteen-member board met only four times a year, cases were considered in the interim by smaller groups, called informal conference committees. Dr. Jacobson's case fell to a committee whose members were Dr. Gerald Bechamps, a surgeon from Winchester, Virginia; Dr. Charles Van Horn, the president of the full board; and Dr. Thomas A. Wash, an obstetrician. The board also retained an expert in obstetrics and gynecology to advise them on technical matters. Dr. Anibal A. Acosta, a professor and ob/gyn who was in charge of the in-vitro fertilization program at the Eastern Virginia School of Medicine, had been Cecil's boss at the university ten years earlier.

Normally, the public was barred from the disciplinary hearings, fueling criticism that justice was too often meted out in secret, back-room deals. Cases were usually settled with such little fanfare that doctors could be brought up on charges and disciplined without their patients ever realizing a complaint had been filed. It became obvious as soon as a TV satellite truck pulled into the parking lot and pointed its antenna dish toward Washington that Dr. Jacobson's case wouldn't be settled quietly. This was the first time TV cameras would be allowed into a hearing room, but only after an exchange of phone calls between the attorneys for the TV station and representatives of the medical board.

Most of the complaining patients were present. For many of them this was the first time they had seen the doctor since he'd told them their baby was dead. Chris and Larry Maimone nearly didn't show up. They had moved to Richmond recently but were still undergoing treatments at the in-vitro clinic near Washington. Two months earlier Chris had learned she was pregnant. She informed her attorney, but she swore him to secrecy. She wasn't showing yet, and she didn't want the other women to know. Most of them still hadn't conceived, and she didn't want to hurt their feelings. She remembered how jealous she'd felt whenever she saw a pregnant woman or a mother pushing a stroller. She finally decided to attend the hearing and show the board she was serious about making sure Dr. Jacobson was punished.

Fighting for his professional life, Dr. Jacobson entered the hearing room, grim-faced and nervous. He was perspiring heavily as he sat down next to his two attorneys— Tara McCarthy, representing his insurance company, and Jim Tate, making his first appearance as Cecil's personal adviser. With so many investigations snowballing against him, he had taken a friend's advice and retained an attorney to put his own interests first. Jim Tate was a former federal prosecutor and Mormon bishop whom Church members often hired to handle real-estate transactions and prepare wills.

The board members were seated at a table facing Dr. Jacobson and his attorneys. When the hearing was called to order, Cecil was clearly in enemy territory. Surrounded by hostile patients and their attorneys, he avoided eye contact with the women sitting behind him and busied himself with a stack of papers. He presented the board members with a notebook he had prepared of his accomplishments, listing his awards, fellowships, and more than sixty publications. His tone was conciliatory and humble, as he explained he was just a simple doctor practicing complex medicine.

With Dr. Acosta sitting across the room from him, he was uncustomarily accurate in describing his academic affiliations, no longer portraying himself as an obstetrician or a professor at Eastern Virginia. Now he admitted that he'd been a faculty member only until 1984, and that he left GWU in 1976, despite what he'd been listing on his correspondence.

To ensure the privacy of the patients, each case was identified by a letter of the alphabet, from *A* to *G*. The board went through each one, asking about sonograms, HCG, and resorptions as they applied to each patient. Dr. Jacobson continued to defend his practices, maintaining that his diagnoses and methods were correct. During the questioning the board would turn on occasion to Dr. Acosta for his opinion. He made it clear that Cecil was not practicing standard medicine.

Patient C was Debbie Gregory. Dr. Jacobson told the board that Debbie had come to the clinic seeking an alternative to the "extensive pelvic surgery" that her own doctor was recommending, and that she had decided to try the HCG treatments of her own accord. At age thirty-four she'd been concerned she was too old to have a child safely, Cecil said, but she successfully conceived and carried the pregnancy for about two months until it terminated. He blamed it on a "severe virus" but wasn't able to confirm the diagnosis because "no tissue was recovered for chromosomal analysis."

Debbie conceived her second pregnancy a month later, he said, and continued the HCG injections for more than two months before she eventually lost that fetus too. Dr. Acosta was consulted about the benefits of using HCG for two months after conception. He said he didn't know of any.

The board was most interested in Debbie's third pregnancy, when Dr. Doppelheuer determined that she wasn't pregnant. The board chairman wanted to know how Dr. Jacobson could detect an advanced pregnancy one day, and then suddenly it could be gone.

Cecil didn't provide an exact explanation. "I treated this patient the same way I do other patients, many of whom go on to have babies."

Dr. Bechamps wasn't satisfied with the answer and asked again. How could he detect an advanced pregnancy on October 2, when the next day a gynecologist was unable to find it? Dr. Jacobson said he didn't know. He'd done the ultrasound himself and had observed the fetus. "That's what I saw, and that's what I wrote down," he said. "And that's what I communicated to the patient."

"Do you think you interpreted your ultrasound incorrectly?"

"No, I do not," he replied. He'd used ultrasounds on more than forty-five hundred amnio patients and obviously knew what he was doing.

"But you're telling this patient she's twelve to sixteen weeks pregnant," Dr. Bechamps persisted, "and the next day somebody tells her she's not pregnant. That's a tremendous emotional stress for a patient. You've been coaxing her along for three or four months, and she isn't pregnant."

"I wasn't coaxing her," Dr. Jacobson said. He was only describing what he saw. "This patient was pregnant," he said sternly, and he had believed the pregnancy was progessing normally. "That's why I continued her on HCG and sent her to her obstetrician."

In the back of the room Debbie couldn't believe what she was hearing. He'd never referred her to an obstetrician. In fact, she had battled with him about consulting another doctor. She couldn't believe he was lying so blatantly.

The board's questioning continued throughout the morning. Cecil and his attorneys had arranged for some of his satisfied patients to appear on his behalf and show the board members some of the babies his clinic had produced.

His supporters arrived throughout the day with their children in tow, until they had enough women to counteract the number of disgruntled patients.

During the lunch break Dr. Jacobson's defenders were outspoken in their animosity toward the women who had filed complaints. They openly accused Debbie, Chris, and the others of whining because they couldn't have children and said their failure to function as a woman wasn't Dr. Jacobson's fault.

After lunch Rose Hazel, one of the complaining patients who had called WRC-TV after its broadcast, was standing in the lobby waiting for the hearing to resume. Rose was a tiny, frail woman who had been seeing Dr. Jacobson until the day "Conception or Deception?" aired. When she had seen the promos about Dr. Jacobson, she had been excited that her doctor was going to be on television; but when she heard what they were saying about him, she was devastated. "He was like family to me," she later said. "Part of me was saying he couldn't possibly do this to me."

When she called the station, she was so distraught that she sounded suicidal. She was home alone, and the producer later called to check on her. She had an appointment with Dr. Jacobson for the following day, but she canceled it. "I just couldn't look at him again," she would say. "It just upset me that much."

Later she attended the meeting of patients at the TV station but was one of the women who asked not to be photographed and moved to the back of the room. She felt so betrayed by Dr. Jacobson that she started seeing a psychiatrist. After several months of counseling her psychiatrist suggested it was time for Rose to deal with her grief and suggested she contact a lawyer or file a complaint with the medical board. Only now was she beginning to emerge from her depression and return to normal.

That morning she had shared a ride with another patient. "It's amazing how similar we were in a lot of ways," Rose would say. "We talked mostly about our experience with him, but also about what we had gone through emotionally. I really thought of him as family. I think he thought he was God. Maybe his ego was just so big he thought women could get pregnant because he said they could."

While Rose was waiting for the hearing to resume, she overheard one of Dr. Jacobson's friends in the lobby explaining that Cecil was a saint. Cecil's supporter, a short, stocky woman was chastising the women who were complaining against him.

Rose interrupted and tried to explain what the empty promises and false pregnancy had done to her. "He told me I was pregnant when I never was pregnant," Rose said. "This wasn't my imagination. This really happened."

Cecil's friend wouldn't listen and started yelling at Rose, saying it wasn't Dr. Jacobson's fault the women couldn't get pregnant. She continued her harangue until Rose started crying.

From across the lobby Vickie Eckhardt saw Rose crying and walked over and told the woman to leave Rose alone.

The woman wheeled on Vickie and told her to mind her own business. She accused Vickie and the others of making unfounded complaints against Cecil. "Some people should never have babies," Cecil's friend told Vickie, "because they don't deserve them."

It was the most searing insult Vickie had ever heard. She felt as if she'd been slapped in the face. Barely one hundred pounds herself, she balled up her fists and was ready to throw a punch when some of the husbands and attorneys stepped in and separated the women. Tempers flared on both sides, and the argument threatened to develop into a fistfight. Finally Bob Hall yelled to Cecil's attorneys, "You keep your people on your side, and I'll keep my people on my side."

The hearing continued under an uneasy truce. Patients from both sides testified one at a time behind closed doors about their experiences with the doctor. In the hallway outside, the two factions kept their distance from each other.

The children of Cecil's supporters played in the hallway and ran through the lobby. Many of them bore a remarkable resemblance to one another, as if they were brothers and sisters. The resemblance was so obvious that practically everyone at the hearing noticed it. Even the board's executive director remarked to the staff attorney about the similarities.

The testimony lasted until late in the afternoon; then the board deliberated in private before Dr. Bechamps called the hearing back to order and announced the panel had reached a unanimous decision. The case against Dr. Jacobson was being forwarded to the full board with a recommendation that his medical license be revoked. It was the most severe action the committee could take. If the sixteen-member board agreed with the panel's decision, Dr. Jacobson's medical career in Virginia would be over.

The former patients cheered the decision and congratulated each other like the winning team at a football game. Dr. Bechamps banged his gavel on the table and tried to restore order. Dr. Jacobson and his entourage fled the boardroom and rushed from the building—with a TV crew in hot pursuit. One of Dr. Jacobson's supporters was mowed down as a cameraman tried to intercept the doctor.

"Would you kindly get out of Dr. Jacobson's way?" the doctor's attorney, Jim Tate, said sternly. "Would you kindly not be rude to him?"

The camera crew caught up with the doctor as he was reaching the sanctuary of Tate's car. "Excuse me, Dr. Jacobson," a TV producer said. "What is your reaction to the hearing?"

The doctor never looked up as he slid into the front passenger seat and shut the door without a word.

"I have a reaction to it," Tate said, drawing attention away from his client. "Why is the press not as interested in finding out how many women had babies as a result of this man's efforts? And why do they spend so much time trying to persecute him because a few women have complained?"

The producer reminded him that more than forty women had complained.

Yes, Tate said, but "a number" of Dr. Jacobson's success stories had called the TV station and were treated rudely.

"You people would not report their story," he said. "And I think that's unfair."

"What are the success rates?" the producer asked.

"What are the unsuccess rates?" Tate fired back.

"I know of at least forty."

"We know of at least three hundred."

"These women who resorbed," the producer asked, "where did the babies go?"

"When this proceeding is all over," Tate said, "I suspect we're going to have some babies that you all can interview. Good day, sir," he said, and closed the car door.

Just then Dr. Jacobson's other attorney was leaving the building. Tara McCarthy told the press she had nothing to say, but still managed to sting the opposition. "I'm sure you realize Dr. Jacobson is involved in other litigation. For that reason I don't subscribe to Bob Hall's approach of trying cases in the media."

Soon the triumphant patients filed out of the board-room. Some were savoring the victory, but for others the outcome was bittersweet. Debbie and Steven Gregory said they felt "satisfied" by the board's decision, but neither one was celebrating. The hearing was emotionally draining. "It's very difficult every time you go through it," Debbie said. "It's very difficult emotionally. You live it all over again. It's real hard."

Steven admitted he "teared up" during the hearing as Dr. Jacobson was talking about their baby, the one he called "Junior." "This brings it all back," Steven said. "Every painful experience." Obviously the other couples had been feeling the same way, he said. "I looked around the room and saw other people in the audience were crying too."

Bill and Vickie Eckhardt were more jubilant about the decision. They had pushed harder than anyone to get the medical board to act. "I have a lot more confidence now in the board," Bill said. "Before, I wasn't sure how this was going to be handled. But I think they did listen to it fairly, and they looked at all the information that had been presented to them on both sides. They had a unanimous decision in our favor that Dr. Jacobson had done things wrong and should not be allowed to practice medicine. I think that's what we all wanted."

Vickie couldn't believe how Dr. Jacobson had told such glaring lies. "There were a lot of discrepancies between what really happened and what he was saying happened," she said.

Reminded that the board's decision might mean that Dr. Jacobson would never practice again, Vickie said, "That was what I wanted when I first started all this—to see him out of medicine."

She and Bill vowed to attend the full board hearing to make sure their voices would be heard. "We want to make sure they hear both sides, not only the doctor's side," Bill said.

He conceded again that maybe he'd been wrong about the medical board. It had taken a while, he said, but in the end they were doing the right thing. He went home that day believing that justice had prevailed. But before the proceedings would be over, his confidence in the system would be shattered again.

Chapter Twenty-Five

Trouble was brewing within Dr. Jacobson's legal-defense camp, and the signs were everywhere. After a new law firm, Steptoe and Johnson, signed on to represent Cecil's insurance company in the Federal Trade Commission case, FTC lawyer Mark Brown heard through the legal grapevine that the firm's decision to represent Dr. Jacobson was a controversial one. There had been considerable acrimony during the partners' meeting, Brown was told, as some women resented the firm taking on the notorious infertility doctor as a client.

Then Cecil's insurance company put him on notice that it might bail out of the malpractice cases. He was given a "Reservation of Rights" letter in which the insurance company indicated it might not be liable to pay the doctor's possible damages. Then St. Paul's insurance company balked at providing an attorney for him during a federal-court hearing on the charges brought by the FTC. The agency was seeking a preliminary injunction to freeze Dr. Jacobson's assets after learning about his selling his property to the Jacobson-Ziff partnership, and to stop him from misrepresenting his success rates to patients. The insurance company relented shortly before the hearing and agreed to provide an attorney, leaving Cecil's lawyers little time to craft an appropriate response.

They claimed the FTC's case was based on the "largely unsupported allegations" of only six women who made up less than 2 percent of the doctor's infertility patients. The suit was "piling on" and was needless since Dr. Jacobson had already closed his medical practice. "The glare of extensive, ongoing national and local publicity during the past year has made it virtually impossible for him to conduct his practice" and has "created a poisoned atmosphere" that already forced him out of business. As examples, the lawyers cited two documentaries by Channel 4, a *60 Minutes* report, and several *Washington Post* articles.

Dr. Jacobson did not intend to reopen his medical office, as the FTC contended, but was devoting all his time to defending himself against the "maze of complex" malpractice lawsuits and the investigation by the Virginia medical board. Even so, the FTC had not shown that Dr. Jacobson engaged in a "pervasive pattern of deception" and the doctor could provide at least as many women who were totally satisfied with his services and did not claim fraud. In conclusion Cecil's lawyers argued that Dr. Jacobson was a medical pioneer whose work on amniocentesis had helped more than six thousand expectant mothers in the past twenty-five years. His contributions were "undisputed by even his most vocal critics.

"Dr. Jacobson's services have benefited many patients and physically harmed no one. It would be much more equitable for him to be able to dedicate himself to defending his conduct in other proceedings and dedicate his skills to research, instead of having his energies and resources drained in this unnecessary and ill-timed action."

Five of Dr. Jacobson's patients produced sworn affidavits stating that they owed their children to him.

A Virginia realtor stated her doctor had referred her to Dr. Jacobson in 1977 when she suffered a miscarriage at eight to twelve weeks. She followed Dr. Jacobson's advice not to have a D and C, she said, and never passed any fetal tissue. "I have every reason to believe that the fetus resorbed into my system, just as Dr. Jacobson suggested might happen," she maintained. Afterward she consulted Dr. Jacobson for infertility and got pregnant after just two HCG injections. She enclosed a photo of her daughter taken one hour after birth.

The affidavit of another woman, stated she resorbed her baby—a twin—in 1985. "I have every reason to believe that the second twin was resorbed into my body as Dr. Jacobson suggested might happen." She also delivered a baby, she said, after being treated by Dr. Jacobson with forty-three HCG injections.

The sworn statements of several other women were attached, including a woman who gave birth after being artificially inseminated by Dr. Jacobson. "I have every reason to believe that my two children are the result of Dr. Jacobson's treatment," the woman said. Another woman said she passed a pregnancy test fifty-four days after receiving her last HCG shot, then had a resorption.

One woman said she had suffered three miscarriages before consulting Dr. Jacobson, then "after just one injection of HCG, I became pregnant." She got progesterone suppositories and carried the baby to term. Two years later she got pregnant without Dr. Jacobson's help but lost the baby at eight weeks. She returned to Dr. Jacobson, had four HCG injections, and got pregnant again. Her daughter was born in 1984.

Dr. Jacobson also submitted a sworn affidavit to refute the charges against him. He said he honestly believed that each of the six women complaining against him had been pregnant and had subsequently resorbed her fetus. He acknowledged that resorption occurs in only a "small number of patients," but he said it was not "extremely rare" as the FTC contended. "In my practice I have seen many cases of fetal resorption where no significant tissue has been expelled and where no D and C had been required or performed."

He also said he had encountered no cases of false-positive pregnancy tests caused by HCG injections and that he'd never made a "guarantee" to a patient she would become pregnant or deliver a healthy child.

He disputed the FTC's claims that his infertility business had generated $2.5 million. He said 80 percent of his practice during the previous ten years had been amniocentesis, and only 20 percent was infertility. "My gross income from my medical practice has averaged about $250,000 per year. Only about $50,000 per year has been generated from my fertility practice."

In the previous five years he had treated 380 patients for infertility. "Of those 380 patients approximately 120 live, healthy babies were born as a result of treatments prescribed by me."

Lastly, he had closed his office and had no intention of reopening it until after his legal problems were finished. "Due to the widespread adverse publicity in this matter, I closed my medical practice to new patients in June 1988. Due to continued adverse publicity, I saw my last patient in September 1988 and closed my practice in its entirety in order to devote full efforts to my defense."

Dr. Jacobson didn't attend the hearing on the FTC's motion to obtain an injunction against him, but four attorneys showed up on his behalf. Two were his personal lawyers, Jim Tate and Diane Mahshie, and two others, Alan Schlaiser and Morgan Hodgson, represented the insurance company.

Because Cecil's lawyers didn't give the judge their formal response to the FTC charges until that morning, FTC attorney Russell Damtoft asked that it be stricken. Judge James Cacheris never entertained the request. Instead he went to the heart of the matter, asking why the FTC was pursuing the case if Dr. Jacobson was not practicing medicine anymore.

Damtoft explained that Dr. Jacobson still had a valid medical license, and though he was out of business for the moment, there were no assurances he wouldn't open another clinic and mislead patients again. "It appears that his behavior was at least recklessly indifferent, if not intentional. His misrepresentations were consistent, repeated, and sustained," Damtoft said. "From the declaration he submitted to the court this morning, it's clear that there's no recognition of his own culpability. He still maintains that these sonograms showed the presence of a baby. He claims there were no false positives in the administration of HCG, and he claims that there was resorption in all of those cases. If he was to open his practice tomorrow, presumably the practices would be exactly the same."

He said the government was not making a "draconian" request for an injunction. "We don't ask to prohibit him from practicing medicine." The FTC only wanted to stop him from making false representations to his patients and to freeze his assets so funds would be available for restitution.

"Dr. Jacobson's practices inflicted calculable emotional damage on a particularly vulnerable group—couples who were desperately trying to have children," the FTC lawyer said. "Moreover, he induced childless couples, many of whom are nearing the end of their childbearing years, to forgo legitimate treatment as they cling to the false hopes held out by Dr. Jacobson. It's hard to imagine a case in which the public equities could be any stronger."

One of Cecil's personal lawyers, Diane Mahshie, spoke on his behalf. She apologized to the court for the confusion caused when the insurance company "waffled back and forth."

"We did the best we could on very short notice," she said. "We are kind of here on a collaborative effort to do the best representation that we can for Dr. Jacobson today."

Again Judge Cacheris short-circuited legal maneuverings. If Dr. Jacobson didn't intend to practice medicine until all his legal problems were resolved, why didn't he just agree to a consent order that he wouldn't make false representations to his patients?

Mahshie said there were several reasons. Any agreement entered into by the doctor could be used against him in the other cases, she noted; furthermore, only six patients were complaining, and the defense had matched them "affidavit for affidavit" with satisfied patients. It was hardly a pervasive pattern, as the FTC contended.

"They had a year to find their six patients. We had a week to find our five." She told the judge that if he read the affidavits carefully, he would find that some of the women who were complaining against Dr. Jacobson actually had babies.

Judge Cacheris obviously had done his homework, and he corrected her. One woman had a baby *before* seeing

Dr. Jacobson, he said, and another delivered her child *afterward*.

Still, she argued, the number of unhappy patients constituted only one half of 1 percent of Dr. Jacobson's practice, a percentage that was wholly inadequate to warrant an injunction. In addition, there was no need to freeze Dr. Jacobson's assets. He had up to $4 million worth of insurance, more than enough to cover the claims of these women. "None of these women have alleged physical harm," she said. "They have alleged emotional distress and out-of-pocket expenses. These are not million-dollar cases."

Besides, Dr. Jacobson wasn't likely to take his money and run. "He's been around a year since the publicity started. He hasn't gone anyplace yet." The public's interest would be best served by allowing Dr. Jacobson to continue writing and doing medical research. An injunction would damage the doctor's reputation and credibility, she said, making it impossible for him to earn a living. "His ability to earn an income from research and writing is basically all that's left to him at this point."

The FTC presented a rebuttal. "Your Honor," the FTC attorney, Russell Damtoft, began, "Ms. Mahshie's argument misses the point." The FTC could have presented many more than six patients, but it didn't want to burden the court. This wasn't a numbers game. "Of course it didn't take Dr. Jacobson much time to come up with five patients." He had access to his files and knew which couples had delivered babies.

Even so, no one was saying that he didn't succeed in helping some patients. The real point was to stop him from claiming an 85 percent success rate, or making promises that he could guarantee a baby.

Once both sides concluded, the judge announced he was ready to make his ruling.

After listening to the evidence and reading the briefs, he said it was clear that Dr. Jacobson had maintained a "continuing practice of misrepresentations" and there were no assurances that it had "ceased or that it won't take place in the future."

He ruled in favor of the FTC and granted a preliminary injunction to halt the doctor from making misrepresentations to his patients. He stopped short, however, of freezing Cecil's assets.

Before the judge could rule on the request for a permanent injunction, Dr. Jacobson and his insurance company agreed to settle the charges. The terms of the agreement were for "settlement purposes only" and didn't constitute "an admission of any violation of law." Nor did it affect the malpractice suits.

The FTC obtained a copy of his patient files and sent notices to each of his infertility patients. Anyone who had been treated with HCG and who had a resorbing pregnancy was eligible for reimbursement for wrongful treatment. A $250,000 fund was established. More than one hundred of his patients were found to fit the category.

If Judge Cacheris thought he'd seen the last of Dr. Cecil Jacobson as he recessed the case, he was mistaken. The next time the doctor would stand before his court, the case would become the most sensational over which the judge had ever presided.

Chapter Twenty-Six

On June 1, 1989, nearly six months after the first disciplinary hearing, and more than a year and a half after the first complaint was filed against Dr. Jacobson, the Virginia State Board of Medicine scheduled the case for a final disposition. After the previous emotionally charged hearing in Richmond, which resulted in a near fistfight, this one promised to be fiery as well.

Women on each side—Cecil's accusers and defenders—were gearing up for the confrontation. The woman who nearly came to blows with Vickie Eckhardt told *The Washington Times* that she would definitely attend the hearing. "If he were still in business and I wanted to have a baby, I would not hesitate to go back to him," she said. "He is no fraud."

Joan Stallings, who suffered five resorptions and blamed the breakup of her marriage on the stress, told the newspaper that she planned to be there, too. "I look back and wonder how I could have been so stupid with that man and let him take advantage of me. I don't care about the money, but I just want to make sure that he doesn't practice medicine again. The emotional and psychological scars will always be there."

The board notified Dr. Jacobson that he had only two choices—either surrender his license or have it revoked by the board. Either way, he was out of medicine. But unknown to everyone involved, his attorney, Jim Tate, was working behind the scenes to negotiate a deal.

Dr. Jacobson was moving to Utah, Tate told an attorney for the board. He planned to teach at the University of Utah and conduct some "privately funded research" for the Mormon Church. But in order for Dr. Jacobson to obtain a college faculty position, he needed a medical license, so his attorney proposed a compromise.

Dr. Jacobson would agree to leave the state and never treat patients in Virginia again if the board allowed him to retain his license. The doctor had made some mistakes and was sorry, Tate said, but his actions certainly weren't intentional. He would promise to cease treating patients so no one would be hurt again.

At face value the proposal seemed entirely in Dr. Jacobson's favor, but the board's staff members saw some benefits in it, too. Since the board's jurisdiction extended only through Virginia, there was nothing to stop Dr. Jacobson from obtaining a medical license in Utah and opening another clinic. And even if the board revoked his license, he could appeal the decision and delay the final outcome for years.

On the eve of the disciplinary hearing the board postponed Dr. Jacobson's case to consider his offer. His initial proposition was rejected, but the board made a counter offer. In lieu of revoking his medical license, Dr. Jacobson had to agree that he wouldn't practice medicine or treat patients for at least five years, not only in Utah, but anywhere in the United States. He also would have to pay a seven-thousand-dollar fine.

The board was fulfilling its obligation to protect the citizens of Virginia from a dangerous doctor, and Cecil would be leaving the state without a blemish on his medical license. The agreement seemed to placate everyone—except the patients.

The patients weren't privy to the negotiations. Many of them were suspicious of the board already and feared their interests would be ignored if a back-room deal was cut. When details of the agreement leaked out a few days before the final disciplinary hearing was scheduled, some of the patients were livid. They thought it was an outrage that Dr. Jacobson would be permitted to keep his medical license. The board reacted defensively. A press release was issued under the name of Bernard Henderson, director of the Virginia Department of Health Regulatory Boards, stating that Dr. Jacobson had until four o'clock on the following Monday afternoon to accept or reject the board's offer. Otherwise he would have to submit to a formal administrative hearing before the entire board.

"It is not my general practice to issue a specific comment on disciplinary actions," Henderson said later that day, but because of the "potential misunderstandings," he thought it was important to justify the board's action. He called the consent order "the strongest and most decisive action possible" to prevent Dr. Jacobson from practicing medicine and would stop him "quicker and for a longer period of time" than if the board followed normal channels.

The board and the patients waited through the weekend for Dr. Jacobson's response. Finally, on Monday afternoon minutes before the deadline, his attorney notified the board that he had decided to accept the offer.

The patients seemed placated, at least until the details of the final agreement were made public, and Bob Hall noticed there was a serious omission in the wording. The board's charges contained no mention of fraud. While Dr. Jacobson previously had been accused of fraudulently treating patients, now he was accused only of negligent treatment.

When a special hearing was convened to ratify the agreement, the board members were accused of ignoring the results of the public hearing just to appease the doctor. "If you're going to do the public's business, then do it in public," Hall said to the board chairman. "What's the use of a public hearing when after we're gone, you get behind closed doors and work out something else?"

But the board members weren't talking. Their position was clear. The sanctions against Dr. Jacobson were the most serious that could be levied. Beyond that the board would have no comment.

There would be considerable disagreement on why, and how, all references of fraud were removed from the board's petition. Some would say the board had been swayed by the testimony of Cecil's patients who had successfully conceived children. But one person involved in the negotiations would acknowledge that Dr. Jacobson only agreed to the board's counteroffer provided that all charges of fraud were dropped.

Although Cecil was effectively barred from practicing medicine, the manner in which the outcome was handled further riled his patients, who viewed the board's performance as another form of betrayal, and another cover-up by the medical community intent on protecting its own.

Once the FTC case was settled and the charges from the medical board disposed of, only the twenty-three civil lawsuits remained. The cases could drag on for years and could cost his insurance company millions in attorney's fees, much less what the juries seemed sure to award the patients. St. Paul's insurance company moved swiftly to clear its books of its troublesome client and offered the patients a lump-sum multimillion dollar settlement of all the lawsuits.

Most of the patients didn't need any prodding to accept the offer. Steven and Debbie Gregory were so exhausted after three years of dealing with Dr. Jacobson, they were anxious to settle their case. So were Larry and Chris Maimone. Chris's baby was nearing delivery, and she didn't want anything to interfere with the birth. The less stress the better. Only Bill and Vickie Eckhardt were intent on taking Dr. Jacobson to court. They wanted to see him squirm on the witness stand, although Bill wouldn't have been satisfied with much less than a public hanging in the town square.

The insurance company's first offer was rejected by the attorneys representing the twenty-three patients. The next offer of $4 million was accepted. As part of the deal, Dr. Jacobson insisted on settling the cases without an admission of guilt, as in the settlements of the FTC charges and medical-board accusations.

Bob Hall devised a formula to divide the money based on how long each woman had been treated, how much money she had spent, how many HCG shots she received, and how many "resorptions" she suffered. Until the money could be divided, the funds were deposited in Richard Boone's trust account, making him for a short while the largest depositor at Virginia Commerce Bank. The bank vice president took him to lunch and sent him a potted plant.

Then there was a glitch.

Williams and Connolly attorney David Povich didn't think the settlement formula was fair. His clients, Bill and Susan Dippel, were entitled to a larger share because Williams and Connolly had done more work than the other firms. Furthermore, his case was the first set for trial, which prompted the negotiations to come to a head.

The other attorneys cried foul. The formula was set and everyone else had agreed—no one deserved more money than anyone else—but neither side would budge. The St. Paul's insurance company was offering to settle all the cases, or none. One holdout would cancel the agreement. Povich called everyone's bluff and went sailing, leaving them to finalize a settlement that favored his clients.

Boone bet Hall a case of bourbon that he could get Povich to change his mind. Povich had mentioned during the settlement talks that he'd cleared his calendar for two weeks for the Jacobson trial, but once an agreement seemed imminent, he planned a Caribbean sailing vacation with his wife.

Boone called the federal courthouse and discovered the case was still on the docket. No one had canceled it yet. With the permission of the other attorneys, Boone called Povich's office and said the patients had decided not to accept the settlement if Povich's clients got more than their agreed upon share. The money would be returned, he said, and the case was set for trial. Povich was due in court Monday morning.

Boone waited by the phone for the rest of the day, taking delight in knowing the influential arm of Williams and Connolly was reaching out via ham radios and ship-to-shore telephones to locate its vacationing partner. Around eight o'clock that evening an overseas operator called Boone's office and announced that David Povich was on the line.

Povich cursed Boone up one side and down the other. "He didn't repeat himself once," Boone would say. The settlement was finalized and Bob Hall paid off the wager with a case of Wild Turkey bourbon.

Chapter Twenty-Seven

The consensus was that justice had not been served. Some of Cecil's patients weren't satisfied when he fled to Utah in the summer of 1989 with what they thought was little more than a slap on the wrist. His insurance company had paid all his fines and settled the malpractice cases. He still had his medical license and could start seeing patients in five years. Presumably, the patients thought, he would open another clinic and start all over again once his past was wiped clean.

One of the people who was most outraged was an assistant U.S. Attorney named Barbara Ward. She was an experienced courtroom litigator who had been assigned to assist the FTC lawyers in federal court. As a woman, she felt personally violated. Several of her friends had delayed childbearing while concentrating on a career, then had trouble conceiving when they decided to start a family. A doctor who would take advantage of vulnerable women like that was despicable. From what she'd heard during the FTC proceedings, she believed that Dr. Jacobson was guilty of more than false advertising. She believed he'd been intentionally deceiving his patients and was guilty of a crime.

She went to her boss and got authorization to pursue the case further, then contacted Justin Williams, the head of the U.S. attorney's criminal division. She explained she was a civil prosecutor who didn't know enough about criminal law to prepare a case by herself, but if she was teamed up with a criminal prosecutor, she could certainly help build a case. She was assigned to work with Randy Bellows, a new lawyer who was joining the office from a silk-stocking Washington law firm at a substantial cut in pay.

With a degree from Harvard Law School, and a slate of big cases under his belt, Randy Bellows could have made a fortune in private practice. He'd tried his hand as a defense attorney and dabbled in corporate law, but sitting at the prosecutor's table was the job that fascinated him.

He'd taken a circuitous route from his days at Harvard Law to his latest stint as a federal prosecutor. Starting out as a public defender in Washington, he'd discovered he lacked empathy for the rapists, robbers, and murderers he was supposed to represent. He envied the prosecutors on the other side of the courtroom who he believed sought out the truth instead of finding ways to keep guilty clients out of jail.

He got a job at the U.S. Justice Department and was assigned to the criminal division's fraud section. From the first day he knew he'd found his niche. His forte was prosecuting white-collar crime and complex frauds. He prosecuted the largest maritime fraud case in history—a $45 million scam that involved selling stolen shipments of oil to South Africa and scuttling an oil tanker off the African coast. Then he went to work for Judge Lawrence Walsh, investigating the Iran-contra case. "I spent a year of my life doing something I can never talk about," he would say. Afterward he gave the world of corporate law a try, but representing people who sued other people over money didn't appeal to him, and within a year he went searching for another prosecutor's job at the U.S. attorney's office in Alexandria, Virginia.

He was immediately assigned two cases—looking into allegations that a network of military contractors were trafficking in classified Pentagon documents, and investigating allegations of fraud against a local infertility doctor.

Bellows was intrigued when he read the affidavits from patients in the FTC case and spoke with the attorneys who represented the women in the malpractice suits. He wasn't sure if he was dealing with a doctor who was out of touch, negligent, or had been intentionally defrauding his patients. Everyone seemed to have a different theory, and usually more than one. The attorneys told him about women who had been robbed of valuable time, women who thought Dr. Jacobson was their friend, women who went through divorce and psychiatric counseling and women who would forever carry the emotional scars of feeling betrayed.

Bob Hall, the attorney who had represented Chris and Larry Maimone, was convinced that Dr. Jacobson's conduct was intentional, the cruelest form of emotional torture he'd ever seen. He represented a total of sixteen former patients and offered to help by urging his clients to cooperate with Bellows. He also told the prosecutor about another aspect of the case—he passed along the secret of Dr. Jacobson's artificial-insemination program.

Randy Bellows's first order of business was to collect the mountains of medical records and legal documents that were already available from the investigations conducted to date. He requested that a seasoned investigator be assigned to help him, someone with experience in unraveling complex fraud cases. He was given Randy Willetts, an eighteen-year veteran U.S. postal inspector, with extensive experience in intricate mail-fraud cases. For the past year Willetts had been assigned to a task force investigating political extremist Lyndon LaRouche.

Willetts's job was to compile the information from the malpractice cases, and from the FTC and medical-board hearings, and make some sense out of it.

Although the cases of more than two dozen patients had been investigated so far, Bellows wanted to examine every one of Dr. Jacobson's patient files—all eight thousand of them. Unless he could examine the entire medical practice, he wouldn't know if the resorbing pregnancies were treated differently from the women who actually gave birth. He drew up a subpoena for all of Dr. Jacobson's medical records, dating back to Cecil's work at the university, then waited for the response. It was like firing the first shot across Dr. Jacobson's bow; it alerted him to the battle that was about to commence.

*   *   *

Cecil told his attorney he wanted to fight the subpoena. His records were confidential, he said, and contained sensitive information about the private lives of influential Washingtonians. The wives of congressmen, White House officials, and other powerful politicians had come to him for genetic counseling and infertility treatments. Some had undergone abortions. Others had revealed details of their sex lives. In the wrong hands the information could be politically explosive. Abortion-rights advocates could use it for propaganda purposes, even blackmail.

Jim Tate, Cecil's attorney, met with prosecutors Randy Bellows and Barbara Ward and tried to head off the investigation. He explained that Dr. Jacobson was already a ruined man. He had been banished from the area and was no longer treating patients. His medical practice was closed. Why was the government hounding him? There was no evidence of criminal intent. The agency with the proper authority, the Virginia State Board of Medicine, had already investigated the case, he said, and had found no evidence of fraud. Dr. Jacobson had been disciplined for negligence and barred from treating patients. The finding of fraud was excluded. He'd only made some honest mistakes for which he'd dearly paid already.

Bellows didn't say much. Barbara Ward did most of the talking for both of them. She angrily responded that Dr. Jacobson hadn't paid for anything. Telling a woman she was twenty-three weeks pregnant, then claiming she resorbed her baby, was not an honest mistake that a doctor should make. She made it clear the investigation was proceeding.

When Dr. Jacobson's records, filling fifty-two boxes and covering a quarter century of work, were delivered to Randy Willetts' office at the sprawling post office facility at Merrifield, Virginia, they presented an intimidating sight as they were stacked against the wall. Bellows and Willetts considered bringing in nurses from the Army or the National Institutes of Health to help them decipher the technical medical jargon, but once they examined a few of the files, they were surprised at the simplicity. For most patients the file contained little more than a billing record, a semen-analysis chart, and a report on pregnancy. Willetts suggested that before they pulled the files apart, they should number each page so the sonograms of one woman wouldn't get mixed up with the medical records of another patient. The task was larger than they expected. It took two secretaries more than two months to number every page. By the end they counted tens of thousands of documents.

The investigation remained stagnant for practically a year. Bellows was assigned to another case—known as Operation Uncover—that involved some of the nation's largest defense contractors illegally obtaining classified documents from the government. Barbara Ward left the prosecutor's office and went into private practice. Randy Willetts was assigned to investigate a savings-and-loan fraud in Baltimore. He continued to gather records and create a detailed indexing system on the Jacobson case. Finally, in February 1991, Bellows cleared his caseload. That afternoon he called Randy Willetts. "Let's get started," he said.

The two Randys were a contrast in styles and appearance. Willetts was a tall, handsome, athletic man who had an easygoing, laid-back manner.

Bellows was intense—a self-described "nerd"—who once was presented a pocket protector by his office colleagues when they designated him a member of "Nerd's Row," a group of offices occupied by some of the less stylish prosecutors. His office resembled a locker room, with suits hanging from the back of his door, and shirts stuffed into shelves.

Normally, when Willetts brought a case to an assistant United States attorney, it was practically gift wrapped and ready for trial. He interviewed the witnesses and suggested which ones should testify; but Bellows didn't operate that way. In essence, he wanted to act as an investigator himself, to collect evidence and conduct interviews. Willetts wasn't sure how he liked the arrangement, but he didn't have much choice. Bellows was in charge of the investigation, and in a battle of wills the prosecutor had the last word.

Bellows explained it wasn't for lack of confidence in Willetts. He wanted them both to be present during the interviews. He knew the interviews would be emotionally draining, and he didn't want them to have to explain things twice.

A paralegal, Jane Nelson, was also assigned to work with them. Jane was a mother of four and a grandmother of five. She had recently moved to the area from Colorado Springs, where she worked for the district attorney's office and had extensive experience working with the victims of street crimes.

The first couple the team interviewed was Bill and Vickie Eckhardt. The Eckhardts were still bitter from what they perceived as their mistreatment by the medical board and had given up hope that Dr. Jacobson would be adequately punished. They considered the case closed—and thought Cecil had won. He'd kept his medical license. His insurance company had paid all his fines. No one was sure what he was doing. The last information known about him was that he was conducting "privately funded research" for the Church.

Vickie, meanwhile, had started treatments at a nearby in-vitro fertilization clinic, but so far her efforts were unsuccessful. After spending thousands of dollars they still had no baby. Now they were trying to put some time and distance between themselves and their infertility nightmare. Bill had sold an office-cleaning business he owned, and they were planning to move to Maine where he would be a guide for bear hunters. He was leasing 234,000 acres from a timber company and getting permits to hunt. But then Bob Hall called and said the U.S. attorney's office wanted to speak with them.

Bill and Vickie were reluctant to get involved again. So far their cooperation had been a waste of time, but they were so resentful of what Dr. Jacobson had done, and so anxious to see him punished, that they decided to hear what the prosecutor had to say.

On first impression Bill and Vickie weren't taken with Bellows. His glasses were dirty and his clothes were rumpled. His office was messy.

"If this is going to be another song and dance," Bill told him, "then I'm not interested."

Bellows assured them he was sincere. "I'm not going to waste the taxpayers' money," he said. "If we don't have a case we can win, I won't take it to trial."

They spent hours scrutinizing the scant information contained in Vickie's medical records, trying to verify the dates of her appointments and determine what Dr. Jacobson had told her during each visit. After more than four hours Bill and Vickie still weren't sure they would cooperate. They needed some time to decide.

As they were leaving, Bill pulled the paralegal, Jane Nelson, aside as she walked them to the elevator. He wanted to know a little more about Randy Bellows. "Who's in charge of dressing him and getting him to court?" Bill asked. "It's lucky he can find his way out of the elevator."

Jane just laughed. "Don't worry," she told them. Randy Bellows was meticulous to a fault, she said, one of the top prosecutors in the office. They would just have to find out for themselves.

During the next few weeks more patients were brought in for interviews. They told of referrals to obstetricians that were never made and described how the doctor saw sacs and heartbeats that weren't there. He measured crown-rumps and head sizes and described scenes of "Junior" sleeping or sucking his thumb. He even told one woman he could see her baby's penis, an impossible accomplishment considering the quality of his sonogram machine and the supposed age of the pregnancy.

When it was Debbie Gregory's turn, Bellows carefully took her through each appointment and each sonogram, wanting to know precisely what the doctor had told her. The interview brought back painful memories that Debbie was trying to forget. Each time she told her story, it was like losing her babies all over again. "It defined heartbreaking," Willetts would remember. Jane got chills when Debbie described how Dr. Doppelheuer had told her there was no baby. Bellows felt guilty for making her relive her nightmare, but he needed to hear everything.

They had planned to spend two hours with her, beginning at two-thirty in the afternoon; then she was supposed to meet her husband for dinner, but the interview lasted well into the night. Debbie kept calling Steven to explain she'd be late, but it was nine o'clock before they finally finished.

With each patient Bellows made a list of what he called the "badges of fraud." These were signposts that would determine whether the doctor's mistakes had been random or intentional. Soon a disturbing pattern was emerging from the patients' stories.

As soon as a patient walked in the door, Cecil lied about his success rates, as demonstrated by the Federal Trade Commission. When doctors tried to warn him that he was making mistakes, he got angry and told them to mind their own business. Whenever another doctor discovered that a patient wasn't pregnant, he didn't try to resolve the conflict. Instead he got angry that the woman had consulted another doctor. He did everything possible to keep his patients from consulting their obstetricians.

It seemed he'd been telling patients in an almost evangelical manner not to trouble him with their problems, that he could guarantee them a baby; yet at the same time he was impervious to the mental and emotional needs of his patients.

For each woman there was some aspect of her treatment that couldn't be explained away as a logical mistake. Bellows had started the investigation with an open mind, but the more he heard, the more he was convinced the doctor had intentionally deceived his patients. Yet there was no greater evidence of deception than what Dr. Jacobson had done to his artificial-insemination patients.

The information about the doctor's sperm-donor program reached the prosecutor's office by a circuitous route. The TV producer, who had received the call two years earlier from Dr. Jacobson's lab tech, Donna Kessler, had told Bob Hall and some of the other attorneys about it. Since then it had become common knowledge among the people involved in the case. At the medical-board hearings almost everyone had noticed the striking physical similarity of the children of Cecil's supporters.

Hall had even asked Dr. Jacobson about his anonymous-donor program while questioning him during a deposition in one of the malpractice cases. Cecil had flatly denied under oath that he was his own donor. He admitted that he'd occasionally donated sperm when asked by other doctors but denied he was a donor for his own patients.

When Bellows heard about the allegations, he didn't believe them at first. During his meeting with Dr. Jacobson's attorney, he and Barbara Ward hadn't mentioned the doctor's donor program. They still weren't sure what they were going to do with the information, even if it was true. Barbara Ward had said she doubted the case would ever progress far enough for the information to become public. She believed Dr. Jacobson would settle this case, like all the others, once he realized the government knew his secret. "I'm sure if we confront him with this information, he'll just plead guilty," she said. "He'd be too ashamed to go to trial on something like this."

With the exception of the former lab tech who had called the TV station, none of Dr. Jacobson's former employees had ever been questioned about the donor program. Bellows assigned Randy Willetts to find the women who had worked for Dr. Jacobson over the years and bring them to the U.S. attorney's office for questioning.

The first one he located was a former receptionist who had worked for Dr. Jacobson in the mid-1980's. They met in a conference room on the fifth floor. Bellows asked some general questions about the clinic before finally directing the conversation toward the key question. "Do you know about Dr. Jacobson's donor insemination program?" he asked.

The woman said she'd never discussed the inseminations with Dr. Jacobson and didn't know much about the program. She only knew that she never saw any donors at the clinic.

A few days later they contacted another employee, a German-born lab technician who had worked for Dr. Jacobson for nearly a decade. She had been doing the clinic's chromosome analysis since 1979 and had worked at the clinic longer than anyone, with the exception of his chief assistant. The woman said business had been brisk at the clinic in the early days, but by the mid-1980's the volume had slacked off until she was working only part-time and finally had to find a more stable job.

They talked awhile longer, until Bellows asked if she had ever discussed the doctor's donor insemination program with him. She said she never had. Then he sprung the big question.

"Was there anything in the donor insemination program that you considered to be improper?" he asked

The woman paused before answering. She shifted uncomfortably in her seat. Her silence seemed to confirm that something had happened at the clinic that she was reluctant to discuss. A full minute passed before she answered.

They could see she understood the significance of what she was being asked and was trying to decide whether to tell them.

Finally, just when they thought they'd lost her, she said, "He was the donor."

Nearly every woman working in the office had realized that Dr. Jacobson was using his own sperm on his patients. It had been an uncomfortable joke among them. It had gotten to the point where they could predict his routine—whenever an insemination patient was scheduled for late in the day, they could anticipate one of Dr. Jacobson's extended visits to the rest room. Shortly afterward a sperm cup would appear on the table in the lab. He was the only man in the office. No one else had come in and Dr. Jacobson hadn't gone out. There was no doubt who had produced it.

The employees said the practice had been going on for years. No one could recall ever seeing a donor at the office. And no one had considered making a complaint against him. They didn't know what he'd been telling his patients. For all they knew, the patients realized what he was doing and approved. But Bellows and Willetts suspected that wasn't the situation.

A receptionist told them that Dr. Jacobson sometimes gave her the twenty-dollar donor fee to deposit in that day's receipts. And some of the employees talked about how the clinic's business was steadily dropping over the years, until they were forced to find other jobs.

Many of the employees were still loyal to Dr. Jacobson and felt guilty about getting him into trouble. Their loyalty was commendable. One woman even tried to rescind her story. After her meeting at the U.S. attorney's office, her husband called Randy Willetts and said his wife had misspoken—she didn't know for sure that Dr. Jacobson was the donor—she had only meant to say that it was her conclusion. Willetts said he understood. Of course she hadn't been in the bathroom with Dr. Jacobson. No one expected she had. But they could infer from the sperm cup suddenly appearing in the laboratory that Dr. Jacobson must have been the source.

Still, the man didn't want his wife to get involved. Dr. Jacobson had always treated them well, he said, and he was concerned the government would twist her words to say she definitely knew Dr. Jacobson was the donor.

The implications were enormous. There could be dozens, even hundreds, of Dr. Jacobson's children in the metropolitan area, oblivious to the fact they were related. The only way to determine the exact numbers was to search through his medical records and locate the donor insemination patients.

For years Dr. Jacobson claimed he kept a code—a foolproof method known only to him—to protect the anonymity of the donor and the patient. On each woman's pregnancy report he circled one of four letters—*N, H, A,* or *F*—to signify whether the woman had gotten pregnant through intercourse or artificial insemination.

Although no one affiliated with the case would discuss how the code was broken, it wasn't difficult to figure out.

Several of the resorption patients, who had been interviewed already, had been artificially inseminated, some with their husbands' semen and others with a donor's semen. By comparing the women who had used natural intercourse *(N)*, with the ones inseminated with the husband's semen *(H)* and the ones who had received an anonymous donor's sperm *(A)*, the code was incredibly easy to break. For all of Dr. Jacobson's boasts about having a foolproof code that he would take to his grave, the prosecutors deciphered it within a matter of minutes.

Paralegal Jane Nelson was assigned to search through Dr. Jacobson's files and find the donor patients. From the fifty-two boxes of records, still secured in a vault at the post office, Willetts had already isolated the infertility patients, about one thousand of them.

Jane spent days going through each one, looking for signs of a donor patient. In some files the husband had a semen problem, as indicated by medical records showing he had consulted a urologist before seeing Dr. Jacobson. In other files the man had a low sperm count, or no sperm at all, and the billing record indicated his wife had been charged for artificial insemination. But the most telling marker was the anonymous code.

Sometimes it seemed he had been trying to disguise the fact a woman had been inseminated by an artificial donor. Even though he had circled the *A* on the chart, he noted elsewhere on the record that he had inseminated the woman with "Husband Semen Concentrate."

It wasn't difficult to determine if the insemination had been successful. A birth announcement was usually included, often along with a thank-you note from the mother and a picture of the baby.

Although the U.S. attorney's office would not reveal exact numbers, it would become known through court documents that seventy-eight children were identified as possible offspring of Dr. Jacobson.

Now they had to decide what to do with the information.

Identifying the patients was the first step in what turned out to be a major debate within the U.S. attorney's office. Dr. Jacobson had told his patients that his donors were medical students or seminary students who were disease free and had fathered only a few children, but if he secretly used his own sperm on scores of patients without permission, then Bellows thought it was a clear-cut case of fraud. He wanted to prosecute—but Randy Willetts wasn't so sure.

The stronger cases were the bogus pregnancies, he argued. The sperm issue was getting off the track. Even more important, he worried about the impact on the families. He had no doubt the parents had been defrauded, but he was concerned about how they would react upon learning that Dr. Jacobson was the biological father of their child.

"In this case ignorance may be bliss," he argued. Presumably the parents were contentedly living in suburbia, satisfied with the baby they had brought into the world and ignorant of Dr. Jacobson's role. Willetts believed if only one family was destroyed, the case wasn't worth pursuing.

Bellows agreed. He had no intention of causing unnecessary pain or embarrassment, but his sympathy was tempered by outrage. He considered Dr. Jacobson's conduct the most egregious he'd ever heard of. The betrayal of trust was unforgivable, Bellows said, and the doctor needed to be prosecuted.

The debate raged on for days. "We think we're pretty smart and we're doing the right thing," Willetts said at one point, "but these are sensitive issues. Our involvement in this case will be over in a short while. These people will have to live with our decision forever."

As parents themselves, each of them tried to predict how they would react. Would they want to know? Or, as Willetts said, was ignorance bliss?

Jane Nelson sided with Bellows. She viewed the doctor's actions as a crime against women. It wasn't any different from a sexual assault, she said. "It's vicious and it needs to be prosecuted."

Her opinion intrigued Willetts, and he wondered how other women would react. When he went back to his office, he asked another postal inspector, Denise Cann, what she thought.

"So what?" Denise said. She wasn't offended by what the doctor had done. The couples had gotten their babies.

They had nothing to be upset about. Who cared whose sperm was used?

Her attitude was another confirmation for Willetts that maybe the government shouldn't get involved, but a few days later he ran into Denise again. She said she had been thinking a lot about what Randy had told her and had changed her mind. She thought the doctor's actions were inexcusable—a serious breach of trust. Yet she wasn't sure if she would want to know about it. Willetts wasn't sure either.

"You can make one thousand mistakes in an investigation," he told the others, "but we better not make a mistake with this one."

They were about to make a decision that a prosecutor, a criminal investigator, and a paralegal were not qualified to make. There were no courses available to prepare them for such Solomon-like judgments, and they all felt they needed the advice of a higher counsel.

Without telling Willetts and Nelson, Bellows contacted the Kennedy Institute of Ethics at Georgetown University, a think tank where experts debated weighty issues, such as whether it was proper to remove a person from a life-support system, or whether a young child should be allowed to donate a kidney to save the life of a sibling. When Bellows informed the others that the experts had agreed to consider their quandary and render an opinion, they each agreed it was a good idea, but no one was optimistic they would emerge with a clear resolution of their problem. The issues were too complicated.

On the morning of April 15 the director of the institute, two philosophers, an internist, and a geneticist who happened to know Dr. Jacobson, convened to consider the government's dilemma. Bellows didn't ask the experts to decide if the government *should* prosecute, but rather what were the implications if it *did* prosecute? He presented a factual summation of the case in a straightforward manner, unlike an emotional closing argument or an appeal to the jury. He laid out what he had learned from reviewing Dr. Jacobson's files, interviewing the former employees

and outlining the pros and cons of pursuing an indictment.

For two hours Bellows described the investigations conducted to date, telling them about the resorption cases and
their suspicion that Dr. Jacobson had fathered some of his
patients' children. Willetts was impressed with Bellows's
neutrality in presenting the facts, especially knowing the
prosecutor's inclination to indict.

From time to time the philosophers interrupted with
questions. How old were the children? Were most of them
living in the northern Virginia suburbs? How many were
boys or girls? They had conducted ethical exercises with
students many times before, but this wasn't a classroom
drill. This time the facts were real and the outcome would
be everlasting.

The panel said the government had an obligation
to inform the parents, whether Dr. Jacobson was indicted or not. The risk of consanguinity—the chance of the
children someday marrying one another—was too great to
ignore. The parents had to be told at any cost. A more dire
consequence would be to say nothing and face the risk
of genetic abnormalities if the children should meet and
produce offspring. Presumably some of the families already
knew each other. Maybe they were friends or had met
in Dr. Jacobson's waiting room. Perhaps some of them
had been supporters of the doctor during the medical-
board hearings. Even if the government dropped the case,
the panel concluded, the parents had to be told about the
biological father of their children. They said it was the
obligation of the U.S. attorney's office to do so.

Chapter Twenty-Eight

When Cecil asked Jim Tate to represent him in the impending criminal investigation, the attorney almost didn't accept the case. He realized he would be up against teams of government investigators who had been pursuing Dr. Jacobson for years—first the Federal Trade Commission and now the U.S. attorney's office—and he believed Cecil, or anyone else, didn't stand a chance. "I don't care if the person has ten million dollars," Tate would say. "They can't match the power of the federal government. Not even the mob."

Tate and his partner, Doug Bywater, who was a personal friend of Cecil's, had six offices in northern Virginia, and their practice primarily involved cases of personal injury, medical malpractice, and personal liability. They handled some criminal cases, but it wasn't their bread and butter. Yet Tate felt he had to help Cecil. While representing him in the previous cases he had come to consider Cecil a friend. "In my gut I believed him when he said those women were pregnant," Tate would say, "and I knew nobody else would."

Tate gave Bellows a list of Cecil's supporters—patients who owed their children to him and doctors who had known him for years. He implored Bellows to talk with them before deciding to pursue the investigation. He said he was so convinced of Cecil's innocence that he would open his files to the prosecutor and make available all his evidence and witnesses so Bellows could decide for himself if the doctor was guilty. "I'll treat you like a judge," Tate said, and felt certain the prosecutor would drop the case once he examined all the facts.

Jane Nelson set up appointments with Tate's witnesses

including several women who had supported Dr. Jacobson at the medical-board hearings and who had supplied affidavits on Cecil's behalf. Unknown to anyone outside the prosecutor's office, some of the women were insemination patients who were still grateful to the doctor for their baby, without suspecting his possible role in the insemination.

The women were effusive in their praise for Cecil, saying they would be childless without him. They had been given HCG, just like the women who had failed to conceive, and their children were living proof of the validity of Dr. Jacobson's treatments. They said he'd been compassionate, always available, and his prices were reasonable. They couldn't understand why the government was still hounding him. Some women even turned hostile and accused Bellows of trying to destroy a caring doctor just so he could further his own career.

Bellows also met with Cecil's medical colleagues, the "gray-hairs" who had known him since medical school and had been referring patients to him for years. They explained he might have been misguided about the effects of HCG, and certainly wasn't the wizard at reading sonograms that he considered himself to be, but he wasn't a fraud and didn't intentionally hurt people.

Dr. Jacobson's supporters were raising enough conflicting opinions that Bellows concluded he needed an impartial opinion. Dr. Marian Damewood of Johns Hopkins University had reviewed more of Dr. Jacobson's cases than anyone, first as a medical expert hired by the Federal Trade Commission, then for several patients who sued Dr. Jacobson. Bellows wanted to hear her opinion—was the way Dr. Jacobson treated patients fraud, or just poor medicine?

Armed with a list of nearly two hundred questions, he and Willetts went to Baltimore and asked Dr. Damewood embarrassingly simple things, like "How does a woman achieve pregnancy?" and "How is a pelvic exam done?" Dr. Damewood eased them through a beginner's primer on human reproduction. As much as they were impressed by the doctor's knowledge, they were awed by their own ignorance. Bellows realized he knew so little about a woman's reproductive process that it was remarkable he'd fathered two children. He had a vague sense that the egg and sperm got together and ended up in the uterus—Randy Willetts didn't know much more.

They moved on to more sophisticated topics, but the key question was Dr. Damewood's opinion on whether Dr. Jacobson's explanation of resorption made sense. The future of their investigation hinged on the doctor's answer. If she said that Dr. Jacobson's explanation was even remotely possible, then they would shut down the investigation.

Dr. Damewood explained that resorption sometimes occurs with twins. When the physician delivers a healthy child, he finds evidence of a dead fetus or leftover placenta.

To Bellows and Willetts the most important words were "sometimes occurs." They couldn't make a criminal-fraud case out of a medical phenomenon that "sometimes occurs." But as Dr. Damewood continued, she said the resorption of a single fetus was a vastly different situation. A single resorption was extremely rare. In fact, it was so rare, she had never seen one.

What about women who were twelve or fourteen or sixteen weeks pregnant, Bellows asked, women like Debbie Gregory or Chris Maimone or Vickie Eckhardt? Could that be possible?

Dr. Damewood said it was not only impossible, it was ridiculous. A fetus of three or four months could not resorb without a trace, she said, and pulled out a textbook to show them how a pregnancy should appear at different stages.

At fourteen weeks the fetus has arms and legs, she explained. It has ribs and a skull with placental tissue around it.

At sixteen weeks it looks like a tiny human being with all its structures defined. "It just needs to grow and gain weight."

At eighteen weeks it has a fully formed skeleton. The bones are in place. "It's almost life-sized at that point," she said.

The idea that something so large and so well developed could be resorbed by the uterus is absurd, she said. The uterus is not an organ that resorbs. "It doesn't resorb tissue and bleeding; otherwise, we would all resorb our menstrual periods," she said.

As they dissected Dr. Jacobson's methods for treating patients, Dr. Damewood pointed out the dishonesty of what he'd been doing:

* There was no correlation between a bruise and a resorbing fetus. A bruise was a person's own blood that was resorbing, but a fetus was a fully formed foreign tissue that wouldn't resorb.

* A D and C was not a dangerous procedure. A dilation and curettage is "very safe," she said. "The risks of serious injury or permanent damage are less than one percent." A much greater risk was leaving a dead fetus inside a woman where it could cause serious clotting disorders.

* Bleeding during pregnancy was not normal either. By prescribing progesterone, Dr. Jacobson would only stop the bleeding, he wouldn't treat the condition that caused the bleeding in the first place.

* Prescribing alcohol during pregnancy was hazardous. The liquor would ease cramping of the uterus, but it also could cause fetal defects.

* It wasn't easier for a woman to get pregnant immediately following a miscarriage, as Dr. Jacobson had told patients. Once a woman miscarries, the residual hormones prevent her from getting pregnant right away. "It's just like women not being able to conceive right after delivery," she said. "Women don't reproduce in litters."

* Dr. Jacobson could not diagnose a patient's condition without conducting a physical exam. A cardiologist wouldn't prescribe heart medication without assessing a patient's heart, so an infertility doctor shouldn't prescribe infertility medication without examining a woman's ovaries and reproductive organs.

Before their visit their medical knowledge was one step beyond how babies are made—now they could explain in great detail the benefits of hormonal support for pregnancies or the effect of progesterone on a defective corpus luteum. Bellows's list of badges of fraud was even longer.

Perhaps the foremost authority in the world on HCG was Dr. Glenn Braunstein, a professor at UCLA who had devoted most of his career to studying the hormone. Since 1964 he had authored more than 250 scientific papers about HCG and had even performed some of the FDA qualification work for the Abbott pregnancy test.

Bellows wrote him a lengthy letter, outlining the facts of the case and asking if Dr. Braunstein would provide background information about the uses for the hormone. The doctor called Bellows a few days later and volunteered to help. He said it was inconceivable that any doctor with even a perfunctory knowledge of medicine could fail to understand that HCG would trip a pregnancy test.

The doctor and prosecutor built an instant rapport over the phone—Bellows found him to be articulate and knowledgeable—and soon Dr. Braunstein was getting deeply involved in the investigation.

Bellows wanted Dr. Braunstein to review the files of all one thousand infertility patients, but the doctor said he didn't have time. Although he was fascinated by the case, he still had a medical practice to run and a slate of courses to teach at the university. So they compromised. Bellows sent him the records of patients whose surnames began with the letters *A, B,* or *C*—plus the files of women who had filed suit or were included in the FTC case.

Once again Willetts thought Bellows was getting side-tracked and wasting valuable time. They already had an expert medical witness in Dr. Marian Damewood, and bringing Dr. Braunstein onboard seemed like tremendous overkill. Bellows listened to Willetts and considered what he was staying, then ignored him and sent the material to Dr. Braunstein anyway.

In a few days Braunstein called back. He had reviewed the records of 151 infertility patients in the shipment Bellows sent him, and he couldn't believe what he'd found.

He would refer to Dr. Jacobson's methods as "reprehensible" and his use of HCG as "worthless," no better than "placebo therapy." He was not aware of any other doctor in the country who was using HCG like Dr. Jacobson. "It wouldn't work any better than giving sugar shots," he said.

Of the 151 patients he said 13 women had gotten pregnant, about a 12 percent pregnancy rate. He characterized it as "background noise." Even without any infertility treatment at all, he said between 12 and 20 percent of the patients should get pregnant.

Even worse, the method in which Dr. Jacobson was using the hormone actually interfered with a woman getting pregnant. "If you give HCG too early during the menstrual cycle, you can actually inhibit ovulation," he said. For a woman with no ovulatory defects, the repeated HCG injections could cause her to develop an inadequate luteal phase, meaning she wouldn't produce enough progesterone, and the implantation of the egg would be hindered.

"How many of the patients had received HCG injections?" Bellows asked.

"One hundred percent," Dr. Braunstein said. That fact alone told him that Dr. Jacobson had used the hormone "inappropriately." There was no way that every patient in an infertility practice would require HCG, but Dr. Jacobson had given it to women no matter what their problem. "Giving HCG under those circumstances is worthless," he explained.

From reading Dr. Jacobson's testimony at the disciplinary proceedings of the medical board, Dr. Braunstein noticed another significant development. Sometime during the mid-1980's, Dr. Jacobson had switched brands of pregnancy tests from the Organon to the Abbott test. He emphasized that the switch was important.

The Abbott test was one of the most sensitive on the market, he explained, about twenty to forty times more sensitive than the Organon test. By using a combination of the Abbott test and instructing a woman not to drink fluids the night before a test, Dr. Jacobson virtually ensured the test would be positive. He said there was no way a doctor, especially someone who was practicing infertility, could not have known the tests would be positive after an HCG injection, especially someone who had been repeatedly warned as Dr. Jacobson had been. The hormone didn't disappear overnight—its half-life was two days, meaning the HCG levels in a person's system would decrease by half every two days. If a woman had 1,000 units in her system on Monday, she would have 500 by Wednesday and 250 by Friday.

The half-life calculations also led Dr. Braunstein to another irrefutable fact that was hidden among the reams of medical records. He had no doubt that Dr. Jacobson had lied to a patient about the results of her pregnancy test.

He noticed in the case of one woman that Dr. Jacobson had told her she had a positive pregnancy test on July 6, 1982, using the Organon test. He had even written two plus signs on her pregnancy report to indicate the strength of the levels. But three days later her obstetrician had given her a blood test. According to the test results, her HCG level was less than ten.

Based on the results of the blood test, Dr. Braunstein said it would have been impossible for the woman to have passed an Organon urinary test three days earlier.

Bellows wasn't following him and asked him to explain.

Dr. Braunstein said the Organon test required a minimum of 1,000 units of HCG to turn positive, so by the time she was tested three days later, the half-life level would have been 250 units, at the very minimum. Even giving Dr. Jacobson the benefit of a fourth day, the level would have been 125 units. It would have been impossible for the woman to have tested positive on July 6, then register fewer than 10 units on a blood test three days later.

Dr. Braunstein was certain: Dr. Jacobson must have been lying when he told the woman that her test was positive.

Chapter Twenty-Nine

The woman who would become known as "Mary Smith" was one of Dr. Jacobson's staunchest supporters. The circumstances of how she was put in touch with the U.S. attorney's office would be as closely guarded as her identity, but it is known that in April 1990 "Mary Smith" and the prosecutor's staff met in a conference room at the U.S. attorney's office, and she became the first patient to reveal the truth about what Dr. Jacobson had been telling his insemination patients.

Two years earlier she had agreed to testify for Dr. Jacobson during the malpractice suits and had signed an affidavit explaining her appreciation for what he had done for her. "It is my belief that I would not have had this child without Dr. Jacobson's assistance." But the affidavit made no mention of the fact she conceived as a result of artificial insemination. It was made to appear that she conceived because of her HCG injections. Cecil's attorneys had written the affidavit for her, and she had merely signed it.

As soon as her daughter was born, she had suspected Dr. Jacobson might be the donor. She and her husband were Jewish, with dark features, but their daughter was fair-haired with a light complexion. They had asked him for a Jewish donor, and he assured them he had a "perfect match." They also asked him about the donor's track record and how many children he had sired. She was worried about the possibility that her child would unknowingly mate with a sibling.

As she would later explain, "He said that the donor had two children of his own, and that he would use him again for possibly two or three more." Dr. Jacobson had told her the donor was "amazingly similar" to her husband's physical characteristics. He described the donor as a "social worker" who was "musically inclined."

She didn't mention her suspicions to anyone about Dr. Jacobson being the donor. Normally, she would have discussed her problem with her family, or her closest friends, but the insemination had been such a closely guarded secret that no one was aware if it. "There was no one else I could go to," she would say, "because no one else knew about the circumstances of my daughter's birth."

Bellows said the only foolproof method to determine if Dr. Jacobson was the donor was with a DNA paternity test. He asked if the woman would submit to a blood sample.

"When?" Mrs. Smith asked. She was ready to take the test right away.

Bellows and Willetts contacted the FBI crime lab in Quantico, Virginia about conducting the DNA tests. Although the FBI had the country's largest DNA lab, and each year busted thousands of criminals by analyzing samples of blood, semen, or hair found at the scene of a crime, the bureau had rarely been asked to perform a paternity test before, and then only in rape cases. The lab director explained that an astute defense attorney could successfully challenge the DNA test results since the lab wasn't even accredited for paternity testing by the American Society of Blood Banks.

Bellows contacted several commercial labs before selecting Roche Biomedical Laboratories in Burlington, North Carolina. Roche assigned its top person, Gary Stuhlmiller, a former member of the Duke University faculty. Stuhlmiller had personally reviewed more than fifteen thousand cases of disputed parentage, but he'd never been asked to compare the blood of one father against a number of possible children.

On April 22 Bellows obtained a subpoena to compel Dr. Jacobson to donate a sample of his blood for comparison with his possible children.

* * *

A few days later Randy Willetts flew to Utah with another postal inspector, Dave Cyr. In Dallas they caught a connecting flight to Salt Lake City, on American Airlines flight number 1341. Only two postal investigators would realize, or even care, that 1341 was the statute number for mail fraud under which the government was investigating Dr. Jacobson.

They met Cecil the next morning at the LDS hospital in Salt Lake City. The meeting was carefully orchestrated by agreement between Bellows and Tate. The postal inspectors were under strict orders not to question the doctor. Willetts recognized the doctor from the pictures he'd seen on TV. Even so, Dr. Jacobson displayed his driver's license to identify himself so there was no question they were obtaining blood from the right man.

The lab technician withdrew forty milliliters of blood— about one tenth the amount taken during a normal blood donation—then Cyr and Willetts caught a flight to North Carolina. The next morning they met Gary Stuhlmiller of Roche Laboratories and gave him the blood sample. Then they went directly to the airport and boarded another flight for Virginia to supervise the drawing of blood from the first mother and her child.

The identity of the parents was more classified than military secrets. At all times Mary Smith would be referred to by her pseudonym. Even her daughter wasn't told the real reason she was being stuck with a needle. She responded with a wail, then wanted to know why the technician was calling her mother, "Mrs. Smith." From then on the routine was changed. The technician wasn't supposed to refer to the patients by any name at all.

The DNA testing normally took four to six weeks, but the lab could have preliminary results in about a week. Early tests revealed that Dr. Jacobson had an unusual antigen that would make it easier to determine quickly whether he was the father. The lab officials weren't told who, or for what, they were testing, only that it involved a "potentially sizable number of individuals" to be compared with the potential father known as "John Doe Number One."

DNA had been used for only a few years in paternity testing. Even as a crime-fighting tool it was relatively new. More unique to individuals than even fingerprints, DNA is found within the chromosome of cells and can be extracted from tiny amounts of blood, semen, or hair.

The genetic tests aligned DNA from the child with DNA from the parents, much like a zipper connecting two sides of a jacket. If one side didn't match the other, then Dr. Jacobson would be excluded and the comparison with that child would end. But as he continued to pass each test, the analysis would advance to the next stage—with an increased probability that he was the father.

Bellows didn't need to be reminded of the monumental mistake he'd made if the tests turned out to be negative. Already Dr. Jacobson and his attorney were making complaints about governmental misconduct. By midweek Bellows was checking his messages every couple of hours to see if the lab had called. He left a number where he could be reached at all times and grew more nervous with each passing day. Willetts, on the other hand, felt surprising calm. He had no doubt the tests would be positive.

By the end of the week Bellows couldn't wait any longer. He called the lab as soon as he got to the office Friday morning and left three messages. When the lab director finally called back, Bellows summoned Willetts and Jane to his office and put the call on his speaker phone.

Gary Stuhlmiller dispensed with the preliminaries and got right to the point. He said it looked like a match. Bellows, Willetts and Jane breathed much easier.

As the government prepared to notify the rest of Dr. Jacobson's donor insemination patients, Bellows was nagged by doubts. The news they were about to impart on the rest of the unsuspecting parents was so potentially explosive it could destroy the very fabric of their lives. Before proceeding further he wanted a second opinion to reassure himself that he wasn't making an irreparable mistake. He had once taken a philosophy course from one of the leading bioethicists in the country, Professor George Annas, of Boston University. Bellows later saw him described in a magazine article as a national expert on issues related to artificial insemination.

Bellows and Jane Nelson contacted Professor Annas one afternoon for advice, and Bellows provided the same description of the facts that he'd given to the scholars at the Kennedy Institute.

Professor Annas likened the situation to the case of an anesthesiologist who had been accused of sexually assaulting his drugged patients. The patients were unaware they had been assaulted. Did prosecutors have the right, or obligation, to inform them? The professor thought they did.

He thought the same held true for Dr. Jacobson's patients. The parents had a right to know. He felt even more strongly about it than the scholars from the Kennedy Institute.

Informing the parents about the sperm donor was like informing someone about a death in the family. It had to be handled with sensitivity and concern.

The Kennedy Institute suggested the government hire psychological counselors to assist in determining the best means of informing the families, and also to provide emergency counseling afterward.

Bellows and Willetts went to the Department of Justice and obtained a ten-thousand-dollar grant to hire a team of counselors—two psychiatric social workers, a psychologist, and a geneticist—to advise them.

They conferred with the counselors, trying to establish a protocol for contacting the patients. The government couldn't just burst in on the families and blurt out that Dr. Jacobson might be the biological father. The information had to be delivered delicately, and in stages, so the parents could be offered a hint of the news they were about to receive, then given an option of deciding how much, if anything, they wanted to know.

They had several options for contacting the families. They could go to the house and talk to the couples in person. It would be the most personal method, but it also could lead to an awkward situation, as the parents opened the door to find federal investigators on their doorstep.

Calling them by phone wouldn't be much better—it would force them to make a snap decision on whether to speak with a stranger on the other end of the line.

Finally, after days of haggling, they decided the best method would be to send a letter. Bellows lost count of the rewrites as he struggled to find the proper wording. He wanted to alert the parents without being too obvious in case the letter fell into the wrong hands.

Then they couldn't decide the best way to mail it. Should the letter be addressed to both the husband and the wife, or to just one of them? As far as they were concerned, the mother was the patient. Some couples might be divorced. And they couldn't always assume the husband had known about the insemination. What if he had objected to his wife being inseminated with another man's sperm, but she had done it anyway? Or what if the husband had insisted on being the donor, but since he had a sperm problem, the wife had secretly asked Dr. Jacobson to use another donor? With so many variables to figure, the only constant was the mother. She certainly knew whether she'd been inseminated, so they decided to address the letter just to her.

Willetts explained the best way to mail it would be certified mail with registered delivery to the addressee only, which meant the postal carrier would place it directly in the hands of the mother.

Bellows hoped it contained enough "red flags," as he called them, to tip off a parent without being too descriptive.

The Office of the United States Attorney for the Eastern District of Virginia, in conjunction with the United States Postal Inspection Service and the Federal Bureau of Investigation, is conducting an inquiry concerning Dr. Cecil B. Jacobson and his provision of treatment to his patients between 1976 and 1988.

As you know, Dr. Jacobson practiced in Vienna, Virginia, at his company, Reproductive Genetic Center, Ltd. Our inquiry concerns Dr. Jacobson's provision of infertility treatment and counseling.

Specifically, this inquiry concerns certain representations made by Dr. Jacobson to his patients, Dr. Jacobson's treatment methods, Dr. Jacobson's diagnoses of pregnancy and miscarriage, and a sensitive matter concerning Dr. Jacobson's Artificial Insemination by Donor ("AID") program.

Based on the material we acquired in the course of our inquiry, we have identified you as a former patient of Dr. Jacobson's. The purpose of this letter is to request that you (and your husband if you wish) agree to speak with us about the treatment you received from Dr. Jacobson. There are some specific subject matters which we believe it is important to discuss with you; however, due to their sensitivity, we are not referring to them more directly in this letter.

They decided to send the letter to only ten mothers, so they could evaluate the response. If there were problems, they could make changes before contacting the rest of the patients.

Three months after the meeting at the Kennedy Institute, the first letters were finally sent out on July 12, 1991. And it wouldn't take long to receive the replies.

The letters triggered mixed reactions. Some women picked up on the veiled intent and immediately realized what the government was trying to say. But most didn't have a clue. What was this "sensitive matter" the U.S. attorney's office wanted to discuss? What was so secretive that it couldn't be mentioned in a letter? Many women were afraid it involved the health of their babies.

Each mother was asked to contact Jane Nelson and arrange an appointment, but many wouldn't wait. They demanded to know what was wrong—now.

Conference calls were set up, and Bellows followed a carefully worded script. "We've learned something about Dr. Jacobson's donor insemination program," he would say. "But it would involve disclosing the possible identity of the donor." He made it clear that it didn't involve a health issue.

Each mother had the option to decline, but if she wanted to know more, the next question would be: "The government has information about the biological father of your child. Do you want to know more about it?"

Once again the mother was given the opportunity to hang up, but if she was still curious, then she had reached the point of no return. Bellows would reveal the suspicions about the doctor.

Only two mothers from the first group of ten didn't want to know. As the team of ethicists had predicted, most mothers, upon receiving the letter, suspected what the government was trying to tell them. The similarities between some children and the doctor were hard to miss.

One mother thought it was too risky that the letter had been mailed to her house. What if her child had opened it? The notification process was immediately changed, so that any woman whose child was more than ten years old would receive a letter hand-delivered by an FBI agent. The agent was instructed not to discuss the case, just hand the letter to the mother and leave. Then the rest of the letters were mailed out.

About a third of the parents didn't respond. Once it was determined the mother had received her letter, and it was clear she was not participating, she wasn't contacted again. Bellows thought it was important for the other parents to meet personally with him, Jane, and Willetts. That way the parents would know they weren't dealing with uncaring government bureaucrats, but rather with real people who had children of their own and who were concerned about the well-being of the donor families.

The meetings were carefully scripted according to a protocol set up by the therapists. Each mother was assured there was no health problem with her baby. Then she was advised that if she continued the discussion, she would be told the identity of the man who might be her sperm donor. Finally she was informed of the suspicions about Dr. Jacobson.

The reactions varied from fury and anger to shock and dismay. The decision to undergo artificial insemination had been so private that most couples hadn't even told their families. Now they were being told their doctor had tricked them.

A few parents weren't upset at all. One woman didn't care who had donated the sperm. Her child was healthy. Her family was happy. Nothing else mattered. Now she just wanted to be left alone.

But she was the exception. Most couples were devastated. Because so many women had not confided in anyone about the insemination, their normal network of confidants was broken. Rather than sharing this awful secret with a friend, or sister, or mother, the women had nowhere to turn.

The couples were told that a team of therapists and a geneticist was available for counseling and support. Although the government was paying for the counselors, Bellows wouldn't know which couples were seeking psychological help. He received coded bills that didn't identify the patients.

If the therapists thought the parents would be psychologically damaged by helping the government, they could encourage the parent not to testify, and the prosecutor's office would never know. The prosecutor's office made it clear to the therapists that their obligation was toward the families, not the government.

To ensure each couple's privacy, pseudonyms were assigned. Someone suggested they use colors, so the couples became known as John and Mary White, or Red, or Green, or Gray, although they stopped short of using exotic hues like burnt sienna. When they ran out of colors, they used precious metals—John and Mary Silver, and Ruby, and Stone. The couples were supposed to be referred to by the pseudonyms at all times, even in conversations among the prosecution team, in case someone might overhear them.

The conferences continued for weeks. At the conclusion of each meeting the parents were asked to give blood for DNA testing. Many parents needed time to think. They were concerned about compromising their privacy. Others preferred to live with doubt rather than with certainty.

In the end about half the couples who responded to the letter, and who learned the suspicions about the sperm donor, decided not to submit to blood testing. It wasn't known if the parents elected to drop out of their own accord or upon the recommendation of the government's counselors. One woman was surprised to learn the government would provide counseling for her even if she declined to participate. The therapy program was designated for victims, she was told, and she was considered a victim whether she testified or not.

The prosecutor's office was so sensitive to the patients' concern for privacy that no one involved would later reveal any details of specific conversation, but in the months ahead the women would describe years of lies and deceit. The following stories would eventually become public.

"Mary Jones" began her inseminations with Dr. Jacobson in 1973 at George Washington University. He claimed he was inseminating her with a mixture of sperm from her husband and a GWU medical student; then, when she returned years later to try again, he told her the same donor was available. During fourteen years of treatments she spent ten thousand dollars. When her child was tested, Dr. Jacobson was determined to be the donor.

"John and Mary Adams" were told their donor was in his late twenties to early thirties, about six feet tall, with a thin to medium build—not a middle-aged doctor weighing almost three hundred pounds. The Adams asked to have the same donor for each of their three children. They wanted the kids to resemble each other. Their two youngest children were tested. The older one was excluded, but the youngest was a match. Dr. Jacobson was determined to be the father.

"Mary Silver" was another of Dr. Jacobson's supporters, until she learned that he was her donor. She and her husband stayed with him so long that they had to borrow money for the inseminations. Their donor was supposedly from a pool of medical or seminary students who would resemble Mr. Silver's height, weight, muscle structure, even his intelligence. They had two children. Mrs. Silver later signed an affidavit written by Cecil's attorneys. "It is my belief that I would not have had these children without Dr. Jacobson's treatments." Dr. Jacobson was identified as the donor for both children.

"John Ruby," at six feet nine inches tall, wanted a tall donor like him. Dr. Jacobson claimed he found a six foot six inch former medical student who fit the bill. The donor had turned to theology after medicine, he said. The testing indicated it was really Dr. Jacobson.

Dr. Jacobson gave "John and Mary Stone" a list of eight qualifications for his donors.

1. He used only monogamous married men, with no history of venereal disease. They had to be making a conscious effort to be a donor, not medical students who sold their semen for profit.

2. The donor must have a history of bearing healthy children with no chromosomal abnormalities.

3. The donor's sperm must be freezable in case he moved from the area and the couple wanted more children.

4. He had to have sired an equal ratio of sons and daughters.

5. The donors were all highly intelligent businessmen, clergy, or professionals.

6. Females would be five eight to five ten. Males would be six feet tall or more.

7. The donors were screened for hereditary diseases like diabetes, hypertension, cardiac problems, and bowel cancer.

8. The donors had no dominant facial characteristics, like a large nose or ears.

The supposed donor for the Stones came from a "professional walk of life" and had a high IQ, Dr. Jacobson said. The Stones subsequently had three children. However, when the second one was born with "serious medical problems," they asked to use a different donor for their third child. All three children were tested. Dr. Jacobson was determined to be the donor for each one.

*   *   *

The donor for John and Mary Gray was supposedly tall and slender, like Mr. Gray. The DNA test showed the donor was Dr. Jacobson.

"Mary White" also signed an affidavit for Dr. Jacobson, stating she wouldn't have had her two children without his assistance. The donor for both was supposedly a tall man of medium build with dark-brown hair and eyes, just like her husband. The DNA testing proved Dr. Jacobson was the donor for one of them. The other child didn't match.

"John and Mary Green's" child had Down's. Dr. Jacobson told them the donor was from a pool of about fifty medical and seminary students and closely resembled Mr. Green, who was taller and considerably thinner than Dr. Jacobson. The testing determined Dr. Jacobson was really the donor.

Of the seventeen children whose tests would be made public, Dr. Jacobson was linked to fifteen of them. There would be considerable speculation about the other two. Cecil would claim he had a ready supply of donors, but his former employees said they never saw any donors at the clinic. Many people suspected that Dr. Jacobson sometimes used the semen of other patients. Whenever a new couple started treatments, he conducted a sperm analysis on the husband. And what happened to all that semen? Some people believed Jacobson kept the most potent batches and used them on days when his own well ran dry.

Chapter Thirty

Bellows suspected that if the investigation ever proceeded to trial, Dr. Jacobson's ego was so big that his attorney wouldn't be able to stop him from taking the witness stand. In anticipation of a showdown Bellows began to accumulate every statement Cecil had ever made about HCG, resorptions, pregnancy tests, or anything of any relevance to the case.

He got a paralegal, Jan Purvis, to categorize the doctor's depositions and testimony into various subject matters so he could compare Cecil's inconsistencies over the years. She spent six weeks dividing the material into binders. The end product was twenty-four volumes of "Jacobson Speaks." On the sensitivity of his pregnancy tests alone, Dr. Jacobson had contradicted himself no fewer than six times.

It seemed every day Bellows had a new list of priorities that was driving Willetts and Jane crazy.

One day Bellows heard about an infertility study conducted several years earlier for Congress by the Office of Technology Assessment. Researchers had sent questionnaires to physicians inquiring about the source of their sperm for artificial insemination. Two percent of the doctors who responded said they had sometimes used their own semen. When Bellows heard about the study, he wanted Willetts to drop everything and rush over with him to get a copy of the research. Maybe Dr. Jacobson was one of the respondents and had admitted using his own sperm. But the researchers said the data was confidential. Bellows threatened to get a subpoena, but the researchers said it wouldn't do any good. The raw data had been thrown away.

Another time Bellows decided to visit the scene of the crime. Several former receptionists had said it would have been impossible for Dr. Jacobson to leave the clinic, or for a sperm donor to enter, without being seen by the receptionist, but Bellows worried about being blindsided by a surprise revelation that there was a secret passageway into the doctor's office. Willetts had been to the clinic and assured Bellows there were no trapdoors, but Bellows, who from his training as a public defender had learned always to visit the scene of the crime, wanted to see for himself.

The clinic, much smaller than Bellows had expected, was still vacant after more than two years. For two hours he checked the windows and looked for hidden doorways, then wandered around the place. He sat in the middle of the floor and imagined what the clinic must have been like. Leaving nothing to chance, he brought his own camera with him, in case Willetts's camera didn't work, and shot six rolls of film. He finally assured himself it would have been impossible for Dr. Jacobson to leave, or for someone else to enter, without the receptionist seeing him. Willetts reminded him that's what the receptionists had been saying all along.

They had accumulated more than enough evidence to indict the doctor, but Bellows wouldn't stop. Willetts was a firm believer in leaving no stone unturned, but he also knew there could be an infinite number of stones. At some point they would have to put an end to the investigation, but it seemed every day Bellows was coming up with a new demand for information. Left to his own devices, Bellows would have used every resource of the U.S. attorney's office, the FBI, and the postal service. Even worse, he made everything a top priority, and every decision was discussed and debated to the point of exhaustion. They didn't make a move without considering the consequences, sometimes holding strategy sessions for days without reaching a solution. Most problems were resolved after Bellows and Willetts took opposite stands on an issue and worked toward the middle. On the rare occasions when they agreed on something from the outset, they reevaluated to find out why. But despite their differences, they respected each other immensely.

Bellows considered himself a cautious prosecutor and was impressed that Willetts was even more careful than himself. He'd worked with investigators who would recklessly collect evidence, then later have it thrown out of court. Their relationship wasn't combative, but filled with what they called "creative tension." Each was a strong-willed professional with a healthy respect for his own abilities who wanted things done his own way.

Jane and Willetts knew the best time to win a disagreement with Bellows was late on a Tuesday or Thursday evening. He was a single father who had joint custody of his two young daughters who stayed with him on those two nights and on weekends. The rest of the time he practically lived in his office. Willetts and Jane knew if they wanted something, he was most accommodating when he was rushing to pick up his daughters.

Early in the investigation Willetts made the mistake of giving Bellows his home phone number. One night Willetts was watching the eleven o'clock news, and was almost ready for bed, when the phone rang. "I don't believe it," he said to his wife. As he suspected, it was Bellows. The prosecutor had just spoken with a former employee they had been trying to find. She had moved out west, and Bellows wanted to interview her that night before she changed her mind about cooperating.

The next day Willetts was relieved when he saw Bellows transpose two digits of Willetts's phone number as he copied it onto a master list. Willetts didn't correct him, knowing he'd rarely get a full night's sleep if Bellows could reach him too easily.

Even after the DNA testing, there were no assurances the patients would testify. Of all the couples who had been initially contacted, only nine remained. The rest had decided not to participate. Jane was constantly fielding calls from the remaining parents who needed the reassurance of discussing their dilemma with someone they trusted. She spent hours on the phone with them, and often informed Bellows when he needed to drop whatever he was doing to spend time with a parent whose anxiety level was rising.

In late October, Bellows, Willetts and Jane met individually with the remaining patients and asked them to testify at trial. This was the point of no return. Bellows made it clear that once a person's name was listed in the indictment, even under a pseudonym, he would subpoena them to testify. He was almost pleading as he asked each couple for their help. He was beginning to prepare an indictment and their testimony was essential in proving Dr. Jacobson had deliberately lied to patients about the identity of the donor.

Although Willetts guaranteed each couple that they would be listed in the indictment under pseudonyms, no one could guarantee what the judge would do. Several couples emphasized that they would refuse to testify if they weren't allowed to use a fictitious name.

On November 19, 1991, Dr. Cecil Bryan Jacobson was indicted on fifty-three counts of fraud. He was accused of devising a bogus pregnancy scheme to defraud patients and obtain their money, then using the U.S. mail and interstate telephone calls to further his scheme. He was also accused of lying under oath during various sworn depositions throughout the malpractice cases and FTC proceedings. But the charges that attracted the most attention were the donor-fraud counts. The indictment read that shortly after an insemination patient arrived, Dr. Jacobson "went into the office bathroom and generated an ejaculate" that he used to fraudulently inseminate patients. "It was further part of the scheme," the indictment charged, "that defendant Jacobson falsely and fraudulently represented that he had numerous donors" and could match the donor's physical characteristics with a patient's husband. He fraudulently represented that he had a pool of carefully screened donors from a variety of occupations, then solicited twenty dollars in cash from each patient, ostensibly for the donor, and pocketed the money.

In all, he was charged with thirty-three counts of mail fraud, ten counts of wire fraud, four counts of travel fraud, and six counts of perjury. If convicted he faced up to 285 years in prison and five hundred thousand dollars in fines.

The indictment created a media storm. The public was captivated by the thought of an overweight doctor secretly using his own sperm on his patients. The story was picked up by virtually every newspaper and TV station in America, and news organizations from around the world dispatched reporters to Virginia. Hollywood production companies started sniffing around for a possible TV movie of the week. Jim Tate likened it to a school of sharks on a feeding frenzy. He'd seen only one media "gang bang" like it. He'd been at the White House for a luncheon meeting on the day the Iran-contra case broke.

Dr. Jacobson was formally charged a week later at the federal courthouse in Alexandria. He was taken to the U.S. marshal's office in the basement, where he was photographed and fingerprinted like a common criminal. As he stepped outside, he was mobbed by reporters.

He seemed startled as photographers jockeyed for position and reporters shouted questions. He apologized for keeping them waiting outside in the cold. "It's not been my decision," he said. "Nothing is my decision anymore."

"Are you hurt by these accusations?" a reporter shouted at him.

"Very much so," Cecil said. "But it hurts many people besides me. It hurts my patients. It's damaged my family and my friends." Worst of all, he said, women facing high-risk pregnancies now had nowhere to turn for help. He described himself as just a simple doctor who had devoted his entire life to helping couples have normal children, but now his reputation was destroyed and his freedom was in jeopardy.

Someone asked if his patients were aware they had gotten his sperm.

He skirted the question. "No one knows who got what sperm," he said. His donor program had always been anonymous—until the government invaded his files.

"Were you ever the donor?" another reporter asked.

Again he evaded the question and said all his donors were anonymous.

"Are you confident that the semen you gave them was clean and uncontaminated?"

He said only one patient during all his years of insemi-nations had given birth to a child that was "abnormal." His attorney stepped in to rescue him and said it was time to go. Tate tried to hustle him away, but Cecil wasn't ready to leave yet.

"What about the other charges?" a reporter asked. "You told people they were pregnant and they weren't?"

Dr. Jacobson said that wasn't the whole truth. "Many of them had miscarriages or absorptions," he said. "Those who stayed with the program have had babies. One day I would like to hear that story told."

Tate again tried to end the press conference before Cecil said something he would regret. "Ladies and gentlemen," Tate said, "please let Dr. Jacobson go to his car."

One reporter tossed a final question. He asked Dr. Jacobson how he felt about the indictment.

Cecil stopped to answer. "I don't understand how for practicing medicine I'm going to serve two hundred and eighty-five years. I can't comprehend that."

Once Dr. Jacobson was gone, the reporters turned to Tate. He called Dr. Jacobson a "pioneer and a genius." Someone asked about the accusations that Dr. Jacobson misled his patients.

"He did not mislead people," Tate shot back. "He made some mistakes in using HCG, and he didn't realize the pregnancy test was so sensitive." He said this shouldn't be a criminal case. "This is a man who has given his heart to his science to try to advance a field that very few people will touch."

"Does he now believe his theory was incorrect?" some-one asked.

"Absolutely not. And we will defend his theory at trial." He called the allegations about the sperm donor a cheap ploy to attract media attention. "Our position is that the sperm is clean and good and that these people have good children who are healthy. Why should they complain about the source of the sperm if Dr. Jacobson did his part and kept it anonymous?"

"You don't think this is a crime?" he was asked.

"Absolutely not," Tate said. "They're making up the laws as they go along."

"Is he going to testify?"

"Absolutely."

Chapter Thirty-One

Mary Johnson and Patricia James had never met and had little in common, but each woman had the same reaction when she heard the news about the indictment on the radio.

"I nearly fell on the floor," Mary Johnson would say. She suddenly suspected her son's problems with a wandering eye had been inherited from Dr. Jacobson.

Patricia James was awakened by a news report on her clock radio. "It hit me like a ton of bricks," she would say. Suddenly there was an explanation for why their twins didn't resemble either her or her husband. She sprang from the bed and turned off the radio, then went into the bathroom and began shaking uncontrollably.

Her husband had heard the news too. "It was like things clicked," he would say. The children sleeping in the other room weren't his children.

"That day, and for a lot of days afterward, it was like being at the eye of the storm," he would say. "If there is a death in the family, it's not a unique experience. You know you can get through it. Even though it can be devastating, you have a frame of reference with which to deal. But this was something we had no frame of reference for. It was something that was so foreign to our ethics and our morality. We were dealing with inconceivable things."

They were already scheduled to go away for the weekend with friends. They spent most of the time by themselves, on long walks, trying to decide what to do next. Should they contact the U.S. attorney's office? Did they want paternity tests? What would they do once they had the information?

Patricia said it was John's decision. She would abide by whatever he believed was right. As she would say,

"We talked about it, and talked about it again, thinking about the consequences of each step." Above all they had to protect their children. Jokes were already making the rounds about Dr. Jacobson's being "The Sperminator" and "The Father of his Country." They knew how cruel other children could be. Keeping the twins' identity secret was essential.

After days of gut-wrenching discussion John decided he couldn't go through the rest of his life with the constant doubt. For better or worse he wanted to know for sure. Patricia contacted an attorney to act as go-between with the U.S. attorney's office. For the time being they didn't want the prosecutor's office to know their names in case either of them changed their mind.

When Mary Johnson heard the radio broadcast, she remembered her husband's tasteless joke after the insemination that Dr. Jacobson had probably used his own sperm. For the next few nights, as the news of the indictment dominated the evening news, Mike would come home to find her sitting in front of the television set, working the remote control like a madwoman, looking for every morsel of news.

Sometimes their son wandered into the room while the news was on. They deliberately didn't chase him away, not wanting to alert him that anything was wrong. Soon enough he would lose interest and wander off to watch cartoons on another TV set in the next room.

Bill could see it eating away at his wife. She couldn't get enough of the case. She scoured the newspapers every day, even the supermarket tabloids that were carrying stories about "The Sperminator."

Always short-tempered, now her fuse was even shorter. She yelled and slammed doors. The house was a mess. She punished her son for minor transgressions. "Before all this started," she would say, "I spanked him because he was bad. Now when I spank him, I have to stop and think if it's because of what he did, or because of everything that's gone on. Am I actually taking it out on him when I'm the one who went to Jacobson in the first place?"

She couldn't live with the uncertainty about the donor. When she told Bill she wanted to know for sure if Dr. Jacobson was the father, he told her to forget it. "It's over and done with," he said. "You're just going to make a big stink." But Mary feared she'd been deceived—and she wanted to get even.

He tried to talk her out of it, but he knew from experience that once she made up her mind, he couldn't stop her.

"If you feel that strong about it," he relented, then it was fine with him. "But after all this is over, I don't want to hear another word about it."

She called the U.S. attorney's office and decided to have herself and her son tested.

When Randy Willetts saw Jesse Johnson, he had no doubt how the test would turn out. Jesse's resemblance to the other children was uncanny. Willetts entertained him with tricks while Mary's blood was drawn; then it was Jesse's turn, and he started crying.

"I'm so sorry," he told Jesse. Mary thought he was going to cry. "He felt so bad when they took his blood," she would say.

The samples were sent to the Roche testing facility in North Carolina. When the preliminary results were returned, the probability Dr. Jacobson was the father was 99.79 percent. It increased to 99.99 percent when the final results came in.

When Randy Bellows heard the description of the Jameses' twins, he knew right away they were Dr. Jacobson's. It was too late to include their case in the indictment, but he could still arrange for paternity testing, and he guaranteed he could ensure their anonymity. This was the first known instance in which Dr. Jacobson had substituted his sperm for a husband's sperm, and it was clear the Jameses would attract even more media attention than the other parents. So Bellows offered them a unique arrangement. If the Jameses decided to undergo testing, he would allow them to control use of their test results. Even if the tests pinpointed Dr. Jacobson as the donor, the Jameses could decide whether or not to testify. It was a deal a prosecutor didn't ordinarily make.

The Jameses were astute enough to realize they needed professional advice in dealing with the decisions they were about to make. "We were absolutely clueless about what to do," Mr. James would recall.

They consulted the government's psychologist, but Patricia didn't agree with the counselor's recommendation to tell the children the whole story as soon as possible. They sought out a psychologist of their own who worked with an in-vitro fertilization program and began attending regular sessions.

They went for the paternity testing on a Tuesday, and the results were due on Friday, the day after Thanksgiving. To complicate matters, they had house guests for the week and vainly tried to hide the turmoil in their lives.

That week *Time* magazine published a story about Dr. Jacobson. Although Patricia had seen him only a handful of times, and probably wouldn't have recognized him on the street, she couldn't miss his photograph. The resemblance to her children was unmistakable. She couldn't believe what the doctor had done to her family.

On the night before the test results were due, John went into the children's bedroom and watched as they slept. He spent a long time sitting in the dark and listening to them breathe, remembering the times he'd changed their diapers, watched their talent shows, attended their sporting events, shared their victories, and nursed their wounds. Until now there had never been a doubt about his being their father. "It was probably the hardest I ever cried in my life," he would say.

Bellows called the next morning. John took the call in the bedroom and Patricia got on an extension phone downstairs. The preliminary tests confirmed their worst fears. Dr. Jacobson was the biological father. Probability was 99.68 percent for one child, and 99.63 percent for the other.

Patricia came up to the bedroom and they held each other, crying in one another's arms. It was official. John felt like an outsider to his family. The children he had raised since birth might as well have been the neighbor's children. They were like strangers to him in his own home. When he told Patricia how he felt, she wouldn't tolerate it. "There's a difference between being a father and being a sperm donor," she said. "I don't ever want the word 'father' used in the same breath as Jacobson. He may have been the sperm donor, but he's not the father."

They didn't permit themselves much time for pity before composing themselves to greet their houseguests who were waiting downstairs. They tried to appear as if nothing had happened. It was a performance they would learn to perfect in the years ahead.

The revelation that a doctor had the audacity to use his own sperm on patients sparked an ethical and philosophical debate. Cecil's former boss at the Eastern Virginia School of Medicine, Dr. Anibal Acosta, was contacted by *The Washington Post* and said Dr. Jacobson had violated virtually all ethical and medical standards. "The donor is not supposed to know the recipient to protect the child from any problems in the future," Dr. Acosta said. In the past some children had suffered "severe identity problems" when their mothers had fought legal battles with biological fathers whose identities were revealed.

Dr. Robert J. Stillman, director of the infertility program at George Washington University, said the allegations against his predecessor were even more disturbing because Dr. Jacobson had been so well respected. "The academic work he had done, including the first use of amniocentesis in the country, was a well-known breakthrough," Dr. Stillman told *The Washington Post*. "But one who makes a breakthrough and publishes scientific articles has a greater responsibility to maintain the ethics and patient-care responsibilities."

Dr. Arthur Caplan, director of the Center for Biomedical Ethics at the University of Minnesota, said children faced a "serious risk" of passing genetic diseases to their own children if they unknowingly mated with a sibling. He believed each donor parent who had been affected should be provided with the identity of all the other children so they wouldn't accidentally mate. But another ethicist strongly disagreed. Rolf Peterson, a professor of psychology at George Washington University, recommended individual counseling for the parents. "The child is their child, regardless of who the donor is—that's the way it ought to be."

Despite Dr. Jacobson's claims that fresh semen was most desirable, fertility researchers said he actually ran a medical risk by not using frozen sperm. Some infectious diseases, like HIV, cannot be detected immediately, and the semen must be frozen for several months before it can be tested.

When no one rose to Cecil's defense, his attorney was left to speak up for him. "This is a criminal case, not a medical-ethics case," Jim Tate said to whoever would listen. "What's the crime? If Dr. Jacobson were the donor, and I don't admit that he is, what is the crime if the sperm is clean and good and disease free?"

Chapter Thirty-Two

Cecil told his lawyer he was more concerned with possible retribution from the Church than going to jail for 285 years. Under Church law anyone convicted of a crime involving moral turpitude could be excommunicated. If he pleaded guilty to fraud, it could lead to an automatic expulsion from the Church. For reinstatement he would face a period of repentance and humbling. He told his attorney that he would rather take his chances with prison than lose his standing as a Mormon. The government offered him a plea bargain, but it wasn't much of a deal. He could plead guilty in exchange for a prison sentence of up to fifteen years. Cecil turned it down flat.

As a bishop, Tate appreciated Cecil's position. Tate realized that Cecil had his share of detractors within the Church. "I'm sure there were probably some people in the Church who didn't like Cecil, just because of his personality. He was a lightning rod. He's hardheaded, he's opinionated, but he's got a forgiving spirit."

Still, the members of his stake in Virginia rallied around him. Mormons were accustomed to persecution for their beliefs. They fasted before court appearances, and many of his Brothers and Sisters called him in Utah to offer their support.

When the Jacobsons' close friend, Carol Terry, visited them in Provo that fall, she noticed that Cecil's wife was feeling the pressure. Outwardly Joyce was keeping a cheerful façade for the sake of the children, but Carol knew she was terrified of the possibility of losing her husband to prison.

In the kitchen one day Carol put an arm around her friend and asked how she was doing. Joyce broke down crying. "I don't know how I'm going to support the kids," she said, sobbing.

Cecil saw her outburst. "Now, Joyce, we shouldn't burden our friends with our troubles," he scolded her.

His lawyer, meanwhile, was having a difficult time getting Cecil to focus on the case. "It took me forever to get Dr. Jacobson to teach me what he knew," Tate would say. Even Cecil sometimes found his theories difficult to describe. "I don't know how to explain it," he told Tate one day, "but I'm telling you it works." The proof was in the hundreds of women he'd helped to have children.

They held long discussions about the rationale behind Cecil's medicine, and the more Tate heard, the more he started to believe that Dr. Jacobson could have been right all along. Before becoming a lawyer Tate was a chemical engineer who had been trained to believe that every action had a scientific reason behind it. As he listened to Cecil's explanations of timed intercourse, early pregnancies, and theories on resorption, they began to make perfect sense to him. "It was just so simple," Tate would say. "There came a time when I said, 'This man's a genius.' I haven't had the pleasure of working with many geniuses in my time, but Dr. Jacobson was one of those people. The fact is, Doc Jacobson was right. And I've got to find somebody who agrees with him."

As Tate reviewed the proceedings from Cecil's earlier legal difficulties, before he was retained as Cecil's personal legal adviser, he was discouraged at the basic assumption under which Cecil's insurance company had defended him. Tate thought they could have done a better job of trying to uphold Cecil's treatments as sound, rather than caving in and admitting the treatments were bogus and the women were never pregnant. Instead of finding legitimate medical experts to bolster him, they had hired a psychiatrist to examine him.

"When I read those depositions, I almost cried," Tate would say. "Here's a man who's clearly a genius. He's right in his medicine. And his own lawyers are abandoning him. They're trying to explain why he's crazy. I really felt sorry for Dr. Jacobson."

He brought in two assistants and an investigator to work full-time on the case. Attorney Don Criswell was assigned to locate doctors to help Cecil. Lisa Hagin was supposed to find satisfied patients. Tate categorized the patients into three groups. "You had people who were totally selfish and didn't care about anybody but themselves. People who were totally unselfish and wanted to help Dr. Jacobson. And people who wanted revenge. The government got virtually every one of them who wanted revenge," he said. But many patients, especially the donor patients, would have a different opinion. They couldn't believe the gall of Cecil's attorneys for asking them to help.

Cecil's previous search of the medical literature had found nothing to support him. If he was as far ahead of the medical field as he and his attorney believed, it was clear the rest of the world hadn't caught up yet. Apart from an obscure scientist in South Africa, it seemed no one had been studying HCG. Then one of Tate's assistants found a recent article in a European medical journal by a physician from Ireland who was conducting some experimental work with HCG. And for the first time it appeared that Cecil might have a fighting chance.

Dr. Robert Harrison of Dublin, Ireland, was as qualified a medical expert as the defense could hope to find. He was head of the academic ob/gyn department for the Royal College of Surgeons in Ireland and also chairman of the World Health Organization's task force on infertility. He'd been working with HCG for nearly thirty years and had recently published a study that showed the hormone had a beneficial effect in preventing miscarriages.

Tate went to visit him in Dublin a few weeks after the indictment and told him how Cecil was being persecuted for using HCG on patients. Dr. Harrison was appalled. He was aware of Cecil's reputation as a pioneer in amniocentesis and knew many of the scientists with whom Cecil had collaborated at Cambridge. He'd even met Cecil four or five times at medical seminars over the years, although he doubted that Cecil would remember him.

He agreed to review each patient's case. From the scant

summaries the defense supplied him, he thought Dr. Jacobson's care for the women seemed perfectly sound. When Tate returned to America, he thought he'd found the answer to their prayers. As he told Cecil, "If Dr. Harrison has the perseverance to go through a criminal case, you've got a major ally."

Cecil and "Robbie" Harrison were like kindred spirits. When Dr. Harrison flew from Dublin to Virginia a few weeks later to review Cecil's files, it became a mutual admiration society as they discussed their theories of treating infertility and complimented each other on their work.

Dr. Harrison didn't have time to go through all one thousand infertility cases, so he examined most of the files that Dr. Braunstein, the UCLA expert on HCG, had reviewed for the government. He retreated to a conference room at Tate's law office and spent the rest of the weekend reviewing the records for 118 patients. He set up twenty-two parameters for each patient, such as the woman's age and how long she had been seeing Dr. Jacobson. What was the cost of her treatment and her reason for seeking help? He made note of how long each patient received HCG shots after getting a positive pregnancy test, and he charted the final outcome, making note of how many women eventually got pregnant.

It appeared to him that many of the women had been pregnant, just as Dr. Jacobson had diagnosed. Otherwise, there was no way to explain how some women got positive pregnancy tests sixteen or eighteen days after their last HCG injection. The shots couldn't have influenced the tests, he said. Conversely, some of the government's own witnesses had negative pregnancy tests soon after receiving HCG injections. One woman had a negative test only two days following an injection.

He showed Tate the file of one woman who had received blood/pregnancy tests at intervals of two to four days after HCG injections. The HCG levels ranged from 20 units to 125 units, meaning each would have been negative under the Organon test, and most of them would have been negative, or at least borderline, under the Abbott test. Dr. Harrison said the results would have confirmed Cecil's belief that the injections would not cause a false-positive result.

He characterized Cecil's practice as the "skid row" of infertility, because so many patients were old or were referred by doctors who had given up on them. Yet he said the "problem cases" that the government was focusing on, constituted only about 4 percent of Dr. Jacobson's patients, not enough to warrant concern.

As he reviewed the sonogram photos, he also thought he saw evidence of some pregnancies. The pictures were poor-quality photocopies, but he felt certain he saw tiny embryos in about a half dozen of them and suspected he saw pregnancies in a "large number" of others. He knew of an expert in England who could examine the photos. The defense attorneys got copies of the originals from the U.S. attorney's office and sent them to London via one-day transatlantic delivery.

Dr. Stuart Campbell was a world-renowned sonographer from Britain who practiced at King's Hospital in London. He was editor in chief of the *Ultrasound Journal* and was known and respected by many of the radiologists who had been ridiculing Cecil's sonograms for years. He agreed to review the photos and resolve the new suspicions that they contained images of young pregnancies.

Dr. Campbell was also somewhat of an expert on the timing of ovulation. The hospital where he worked had been using HCG for years to stimulate ovulation, and recently Dr. Campbell had been doing some amazing work in the field. Employing some of the most advanced sonographic equipment in the world, he was able to spy on the changes occurring deep within a woman as her ovulation approached. He could actually watch a uterine follicle ripen with the onset of ovulation, then watch it collapse afterward. He hoped his studies would provide new information about the timing of ovulation.

Tate explained to him that, in a much more primitive way, Dr. Jacobson had been doing the same work for more than fifteen years. He had been predicting ovulation with his temperature charts. Dr. Campbell was impressed. "Tremendously advanced thinking," he called it.

Of even more interest to the defense, however, was Dr. Campbell's research on resorption. He was preparing to publish a paper in the *British Medical Bulletin* entitled "Disappearing Gestation Sacs." He had scanned 140 early pregnancies between five and thirteen weeks and discovered that 27 percent of the sacs had disappeared. That's exactly what Cecil had been saying for years. Resorption was much more common than anyone realized, and now a noted British physician was finally documenting it. For the first time Cecil had not one, but two world-class physicians on his side. Tate only wished he had found them sooner. Time was running out.

Dr. Campbell took part in a blind study of the sonograms, not knowing the names of the patients or the age of the supposed pregnancies when the scans were taken. He only checked if the images contained evidence of a pregnancy. He was given 180 sonograms, which included each of the prosecution's witnesses, and divided them into four categories:

Definite—100 percent chance of pregnancy.
Probable—75 percent chance of pregnancy.
Possible—50 percent chance of pregnancy.
No—He could not diagnose pregnancy
          from the photograph.

Dr. Campbell reported he found evidence of pregnancy in twenty-four of the images, which contradicted every radiologist who had previously seen the sonograms and reported nothing was there.

He said five contained "definite" views of a pregnancy— Chris Maimone, Susan Dippel, Judith Dowd, Mary Sutphin, and Vickie Eckhardt.

Five were "probable"—Debbie Gregory, Chris Maimone, Judith Dowd, Mary Sutphin, Vickie Eckhardt.

And fourteen were "possible"—Debbie Gregory, Chris Maimone, Barbara Mull, Nina McClain, Marilyn Lewis, Jean Blair, Vickie Eckhardt, and Charlotte Gooch. Some women had more than one "possible pregnancy."

He marked the back of each photo and sent them back to Tate. As required Tate later notified the government about the existence of his two expert witnesses, then sat back and hoped the prosecutors wouldn't figure out how much weight their testimony would carry. He had a sense that Bellows believed Cecil's Dublin physician and British sonographer were some backwater quacks who were signing on as hired guns to testify for the defense, and he hoped the prosecution wouldn't realize their significance until it was too late.

Chapter Thirty-Three

Protecting the anonymity of the donor witnesses was so essential that Randy Bellows took the extraordinary step of asking the judge to close the courtroom during the trial. Such a request was well beyond his authority, so he petitioned the top levels of the Justice Department for approval. He argued in court papers that disclosure of the identities would "profoundly and permanently" alter the children's lives.

The children, who ranged in age from four to fourteen, were old enough to read their parents' names in the newspapers or hear their names on television, he said, and he included statements from two of his consultants, psychologist Richard Rosenfield and child psychiatrist Kenneth Kaplan, who contended the children would suffer "significant psychological harm" if their identities became known.

The Washington Post immediately objected. In court papers the newspaper said it recognized the potential dangers of disclosing the identities and already determined it would not identify any children or their parents; but to close the trial to the public was a violation of the First Amendment.

Tate had plenty to say, too. He called the government's request another ploy to drum up controversy and taint his client. "These people were happy with their lives. The children were doing great, and here the government comes in and unloads all this on them." He claimed the closed-courtroom request was an attempt by the government to "cover up what they've done." He also said that the pseudonyms would compromise the doctor's right to a fair trial by suggesting to the jury that the alleged crimes were so horrifying that the witnesses couldn't be identified.

Tate filed his own legal papers and requested the indictment be dismissed on the grounds the government was guilty of "gross misconduct" by intruding into the lives of the patients. "The right to investigate the possibility that a crime has been committed is not an unlimited one, and certainly does not allow prosecutors to wreak havoc on families and create wrongs where none existed," he wrote.

"The government initiated the blood testing of Dr. Jacobson without any valid belief that a crime had been committed since no federal or state statutes makes it a crime for a doctor to inseminate his patients with his own semen."

Tate maintained that most of the parents apparently agreed with him. He noted that of the seventy-eight children identified to him by the government, only twelve underwent testing, and only ten parents had agreed to testify. For the rest who decided not to cooperate, he claimed, "the damage has already been done." Virtually every woman who ever went to Dr. Jacobson for artificial insemination was now aware of her possible donor, despite Dr. Jacobson's best efforts to keep it anonymous.

He also contended that the prosecutor's office was being manipulated by the attorney who had represented most of the women who sued Dr. Jacobson. He maintained privately that Bob Hall was the Svengali pulling the prosecutor's strings. Some of Cecil's friends claimed Hall had an ulterior financial motive for keeping the case alive by trying to drum up more business. Tate asked the court to order Hall to disclose how much money each of his sixteen clients received from the lawsuit settlements.

Tate's accusations put Bellows on the defensive. He went to great lengths to defend the cautious manner in which the patients were approached. He told of hiring a psychologist, two social workers, and a geneticist to help guide the prosecutor's office before the first couple was contacted. The letter to patients was crafted to contain enough "red flags" that parents could decide for themselves how much they wanted to know. And the Kennedy Institute had warned him that informing the parents was vital.

As the case progressed toward trial, Bellows came under personal attack from Cecil's supporters. One of them wrote a letter to the editor of *The Washington Times*, in which he said the donor children could have suffered a much worse fate than being the offspring of Cecil Jacobson. "They could have been parasites and noncontributors such as . . . Assistant U.S. Attorney Randy Bellows."

Portions of the medical community blamed Bellows for the heat they were taking for not exposing a member of their fraternity. Some doctors believed that if Cecil had been a handsome, well-conditioned athlete, there wouldn't be such an uproar about his using his own sperm. He was being prosecuted, some believed, for a practice more common than the self-righteous medical community would care to admit. "Cecil wasn't an angel," one doctor would say. "And no doubt he made some serious mistakes. But as far as I'm concerned, the villain is the prosecutor."

Bellows was reviled by Cecil's friends at their Monday-night dinners and replaced reporter Lea Thompson and attorney Bob Hall as the chief villain. At various court hearings on the case, they told whoever would listen that Bellows was a glory seeker who was being manipulated by Hall.

Carol Terry said that she heard Bellows was a low-level "gofer" at the U.S. attorney's office until he seized an opportunity to make a name for himself. According to her version, Bellows had been transporting some papers from one office to another when he accidentally came across some confidential documents about Cecil. He decided to capitalize on the discovery and was now prosecuting his "first big case," she said. When she told the story to people, she reported it as fact.

Ells Knudson accused Bellows of having a personal connection to the case. He claimed that one of Bellows's friends was a disgruntled patient and Bellows was acting out of revenge. Ells said he was so disgusted he couldn't force himself to repeat Bellows's name. "I'd have to brush my teeth," he said.

When Willetts's wife, Susan, later attended court one day to watch the result of her husband's work, she would unknowingly select a seat among a group of Cecil's friends. When Ells asked why she was there, she pointed to her husband sitting at the prosecution table. Ells recognized Willetts. Randy was "a nice young man," Ells said, which was more than he could say for "that other one," in reference to Bellows.

At a hearing shortly before Christmas, Judge Cacheris denied the government's request to close the courtroom. He ruled, however, that the patients could testify under the aliases the government had given them. He cited the "significant psychological harm" that could result if the parents and their children were identified.

The judge also agreed to restrict questions during the trial that might reveal the identity of the children. And the judge warned both sides to stick to the facts and avoid sensationalizing details of the case, which were sensational enough already.

At the conclusion of the hearing Bob Hall walked up to Randy Bellows and introduced himself. Although they had spoken many times on the phone, they had never met. Just then Tate and Dr. Jacobson walked up.

Bellows pointed to Hall. "This is the man who's designing our prosecution," Bellows needled Tate.

Unamused, Tate said he believed it. Dr. Jacobson kept walking, his head down, without looking at anyone.

In the hallway outside, the reporters converged on the doctor and his attorney, peppering them with questions. Cecil took a deep breath, ready to answer, but Tate cut him off.

"Cecil, we're not talking to the press today," the attorney said.

Dr. Jacobson took a step backward as the reporters continued to toss questions. Tate headed them off as Cecil walked off by himself, practically unnoticed, and got into a waiting car.

He was driven to the U.S. attorney's office around the corner by private investigator Jim Wilt. All his files were under lock and key at the prosecutor's office, and whenever he wanted to inspect them, he had to make an appointment. While he was waiting to review the records, some reporters showed up to interview the U.S. attorney.

Although privately at war with the media, Cecil showed no animosity. He asked if the reporters knew a cameraman none of them had ever heard of and name-dropped some stories about "my good friend" Willard Scott, the *Today* show weatherman. "I've known Willard since we were kids," he said. "Nice man, fine fellow. Good kids."

Someone asked if Cecil had seen the story the previous night on *PrimeTime Live* about the latest genetic research on homosexuality. A researcher had linked homosexuality to impulses from the brain.

Cecil showed his disapproval. "People are always trying to make something complex out of something that is so simple," he said, and totally discounted the study—without knowing anything about it. He said British researchers had proved that homosexuality was caused by child abuse: "It's all in the parenting," he said, and called the notion that the brain was responsible preposterous.

He started to compare the situation to his own—he had been treating infertility with simple methods, while everyone else was trying to make it into something complex—but just then a secretary interrupted him and announced the prosecutors were ready to see him.

At least for a few moments Cecil was back in his element. He was the center of attention. He was name-dropping about famous people he claimed were his friends and pontificating about science and medicine in a room full of people. Then he was jolted back to reality and trudged off to the prosecutor's office to view some of the evidence the U.S. government was compiling to put him in prison for the rest of his life.

From Dr. Jacobson's viewpoint the initial press reports were overwhelmingly negative. Tate's office was besieged with calls as the media clamored for interviews with Dr. Jacobson. There weren't enough hours in the day for Tate to answer all the media and prepare Cecil's defense, so he hired a public-relations specialist, Jane Pierce, to handle the reporters.

Pierce was supposed to polish Cecil's public persona. Tate had noticed how poorly Cecil had handled the press on the courthouse steps. When asked a question, he didn't know when to stop talking. "You can't just talk about everything in the world," Tate told him. "You have to focus on things." Pierce was supposed to teach Cecil how to organize his thoughts before responding to questions. Tate assured him it was no different from corporate executives taking lessons in media relations. At the very least they had nothing to lose. The coverage was so negative, Tate said at one point, "We have nowhere to go but up."

They selected one newspaper, *The Washington Post*, and one television program, *PrimeTime Live*, as outlets for their media strategy. Dr. Jacobson told *Washington Post* reporter Robert Howe, who covered the federal courthouse beat in Alexandria, that his treatment of infertility had begun years earlier as a means of helping women avoid abortions. He'd grown despondent at continually recommending abortions for women who carried a fetus with birth defects, he said, so he sought ways to prevent genetic abnormalities through his fertility treatments. He had believed he could regulate a woman's ovulation and create the ideal circumstances for conception through hormones, artificial insemination, and other treatments to "lessen the number of defective fetuses."

When the reporter contacted other fertility experts, they said the treatments described by Dr. Jacobson could prevent some miscarriages, but they were unaware of any evidence the treatments could avert serious abnormalities, as Dr. Jacobson claimed they could. When Bellows read the paper the next day, he thought Cecil was trying to court public favor from right-to-life groups.

Dr. Jacobson tried another approach when he agreed to do an interview with Sylvia Chase, correspondent for the ABC newsmagazine *PrimeTime Live*. For weeks Cecil's publicist had negotiated with associate producer Jaclyn Levin about a sit-down interview.

The defense made available some of the happy patients for interviews. One man said his wife had suffered four miscarriages before consulting Dr. Jacobson, then had two children. "We were oh-for-four with Mother Nature," he said. "But we were two-for-two with Dr. Jacobson. I think those are pretty good odds." A woman said it was ridiculous to believe Dr. Jacobson deceived his patients for money. Her veterinarian charged more for treating her dog than Dr. Jacobson charged for infertility treatments. The defense started to arrange an interview with their medical expert, Dr. Harrison, but then decided otherwise. The prosecution still didn't know how crucial he could be.

Cecil was carefully prepped for his on-camera appearance. He obviously had been coached by his publicist, Jane Pierce, and his attorney's assistant, Lisa Hagin. Throughout the interview he kept referring to Sylvia Chase as Jane or Lisa.

His image also experienced a thorough makeover. No longer was he the arrogant doctor who denied making mistakes. Now he was apologetic and conciliatory. He admitted he'd erred in reading ultrasounds. And he blamed his problems on not realizing that his pregnancy tests were sensitive to the HCG injections. During the course of the interview he apologized seven different times.

"I have never knowingly lied to a patient," he said.

"I have misinformed out of ignorance."

"I admit I made mistakes."

"I regret the hurt and pain I've caused people. I have never done it knowingly. I have certainly not done it willfully. To my knowledge, as God is my witness, I have never harmed or lied to anyone."

But he didn't offer any apologies when he talked about his donor insemination program. For the first time he made a public confession about being a donor.

"Did you inseminate patients with your own semen?" Sylvia Chase asked him.

"I will not deny in some cases I was the donor," he said.

"The government says there are at least seventy-five children out there sired by Dr. Cecil Jacobson."

"I would greatly doubt that," he said.

"What would sound reasonable?" she asked.

"I don't know. And I probably can't find out."

He said more doctors use their sperm than people realized. "Who else is reliable enough to produce the semen when you need them? Who else cares about patients?"

Sylvia asked if he'd ever thought twice about using his own sperm.

"I felt it was an expression of good medical sense," he said, and blamed the government for destroying his patients' families. "They have violated the very tenet of donor insemination, which is the donor will not know about his children, and the children will not know about the donor.

"What fault did I have in being a donor?" he asked.

When Bellows learned about the interview, he rushed to the Justice Department to get permission to subpoena the network's tapes. He wanted to use the doctor's statements against him during cross-examination. The subpoena called for the network to allow prosecutors to view the unedited tapes, but the ABC attorneys made it clear the network would not relinquish the tapes or transcripts of the interview. Not even the President of the United States got such a privilege. Bellows basically had a choice. He could wage a bitter fight for the tapes or prosecute Dr. Jacobson. He wouldn't have time to do both. He decided to drop the subpoena and get on with his case against Dr. Jacobson.

Even after the indictment Bellows wasn't satisfied with the progress of the investigation and wanted more. Willetts thought Bellows was going too far again when he suddenly wanted to drop everything else and conduct a scientific experiment of HCG. More than a year earlier the Federal Trade Commission had hired Dr. Marian Damewood of Johns Hopkins to test the effect HCG had on pregnancy tests, but Bellows thought they needed their own study. The FTC's study wasn't designed to stand up as evidence at a criminal trial. Now he wanted Dr. Damewood to collect the urine from her in-vitro patients at Johns Hopkins and have Dr. Braunstein do the analysis at UCLA.

Willetts and Jane Nelson thought it was unnecessary. Any medical expert could testify that an injection of HCG would cause a woman to test positive. Another study seemed like overkill. Willetts argued that too many things could go wrong. Jane agreed with him. She thought they were getting too involved with a side issue that was stealing time from more important matters. Besides, if the study somehow supported Dr. Jacobson, the prosecutors would be obligated to notify the defense. Let the defense do their own study, they argued.

But Bellows thought it was important. They discussed it for hours, until it finally dawned on Willetts and Jane that Bellows planned to have the tests conducted whether they agreed with him or not.

Willetts was sent out to buy forty tests from Organon and forty from Abbott. An ambitious Abbott salesman later called the postal service wanting to know if they planned to renew their order, as if there were an outbreak of pregnancies at the post office.

Bellows sent letters to Dr. Damewood and Dr. Braunstein, setting out rigorous rules on preserving the chain of custody. He told them how to treat the material, wrap it, and ship it across the country. The urine was collected from women in the Johns Hopkins in-vitro fertilization program who received an HCG injection before ovulation; then it was freeze-dried and placed in special containers for shipment across the country to Dr. Braunstein in California.

He tested each sample against an Abbott test and an Organon test. To no one's surprise all registered positive on the Abbott test. But not all of them were positive on the less-sensitive Organon test. One was negative.

Dr. Braunstein tested the negative sample again, this time for specific HCG levels, and discovered it contained less than five hundred units, still more than enough to trip the Abbott test. He told Bellows it was further confirmation that Dr. Jacobson's switch from the Organon to the Abbott test would guarantee that women had positive results.

Following the success of the experiment, Bellows was primed for more investigating. No one had ever examined all of Dr. Jacobson's infertility files. Dr. Braunstein had studied a portion of them, and the defense's expert was conducting a similar study, but no one had examined all 1,011 of them.

Bellows wanted to know how many women had gotten pregnant. How many had suffered miscarriages? How many got HCG? And how many resorbed?

Willetts and Jane thought there wasn't enough time. The date for the trial was rapidly approaching, and there were still too many loose ends without taking on a new project at the last minute. To conduct an accurate analysis, an investigator would need to work full-time to design a computer spreadsheet and input the data.

They had already decided to avoid a statistical battle with Dr. Jacobson. No doubt he would be inflating his success rates, and they didn't want the trial to develop into a battle of dueling statistics. Even so, Bellows thought a statistical review would be important. He saw how Dr. Jacobson and some of his defense team were going through the files in the conference room, and he was worried about being blindsided.

Shortly before the trial he hired Dr. Damewood to begin compiling an analysis of Dr. Jacobson's 1,011 infertility patients. She closeted herself in a conference room at the U.S. attorney's office and eventually became the only medical expert ever to examine all his records. Even Willetts would admit it was well worth the effort.

Chapter Thirty-Four

Amid the atmosphere of an armed camp, jury selection began at the federal courthouse in Alexandria, Virginia, on Monday, February 10, 1992. Courthouse observers hadn't seen security so tight since the trial of political extremist Lyndon LaRouche. Security guards stood at the staircase leading to the second-floor courtroom and turned back reporters and spectators during jury selection. The judge didn't want the crush of reporters to come into contact with the potential jurors who filled the courtroom.

Because the case had attracted so much media attention, the jury pool was much larger than normal, yet every one of them had already heard about the case. Several people had decided that the doctor was guilty and were eliminated from sitting on the jury. Within two and a half hours, much faster than expected, a panel of eight men and four women were seated.

Bellows had spent more than two weeks preparing his opening statement to the jury. Working late at night, after putting his daughters to bed, he wrote five drafts and circulated them for critique. He believed that most cases were won or lost on the strength or weakness of an opening statement, and he decided to hold nothing back. He wanted the jury to understand immediately the horrors Dr. Jacobson's patients had been through.

"Ladies and gentlemen," he told the jury, "this is a case about a deceitful, cunning, and—above all else—cruel betrayal of trust." He said he wasn't using such descriptions lightly. "Even such strong words are inadequate to describe what this man did to the women," he said.

For the next forty-five minutes he described a man he

called a "master in manipulating women" and accused him of luring his patients into a complex "web of deceit."

Dr. Jacobson had used his prestige as a doctor and medical pioneer to prey upon women during the most vulnerable time of their lives, putting his patients through an "emotional hell" while making money each step of the way. He said Dr. Jacobson was motivated by money and an "ego that knew no bounds."

"As you will learn, this defendant did not have the training nor the expertise, nor the credentials to do what a real infertility specialist does. So the defendant simply pretended to be an infertility specialist. And not a run-of-the-mill infertility specialist, but a fertility specialist with spectacular results."

He led women to believe they were pregnant, and to bond with their babies, when he knew the children did not exist and, finally, "through the most brutal of charades," told them their children had died. "Week after week after week, this man pretended that he was observing a growing, healthy, wonderful baby." Women went home and prepared for the birth of their children, only to later learn it was all a hoax.

"You will learn that this man caused numerous women to have surgery, to have general anesthesia, to have surgical instruments inserted into their reproductive organs to remove what they believed to be dead fetuses—when in fact there were no fetuses at all." He said the jurors would be hearing from women who had gone through more than forty bogus pregnancies, and from their doctors, who confirmed there were no babies.

Some had three or four nonexistent pregnancies without being referred to their own doctors, he said, but when women were truly pregnant, he promptly sent them to their gynecologist.

But worst of all, he said, was the betrayal of trust. "This man was not only their doctor, but their friend. The man they called Cecil. The man who had cried with them. Who even suggested that he pray with them. If Dr. Jacobson had told them their fetus had reabsorbed, then it reabsorbed."

He said the evidence would show that this wasn't the

case of a doctor who made innocent errors. "This is a case about fraud, about a chain of lies and deceit that are so carefully linked, so carefully structured, and so cunning that no accident or negligence could possibly account for them."

But he said nothing would so ably demonstrate Dr. Jacobson's willingness to lie to his patients than what he routinely told his donor patients. "You will also learn that the defendant had another kind of fraud in his medicine chest," Bellows said. He decided that for certain women he would become the father of their children. "He coolly lied to these women and their husbands. He told not just one lie, but lie upon lie. And in doing so he took from these women and their husbands the right to choose in the single most important decisions of their lives."

He claimed his donors were young medical students and had sired only a limited number of children. "In truth the donor was the defendant himself," Bellows said. "The donor program consisted of one participant. The defendant himself."

But his scheme unraveled on the evening of February 15, 1988, Bellows said, when a local television station broadcast "Conception or Deception?"

"Suddenly these women began to consider the possibility that they had never been pregnant at all." And the secrets of Dr. Jacobson's donor program eventually came to light.

Nearly two dozen patients sued, the Federal Trade Commission obtained a permanent injunction against him, and the Virginia Board of Medicine launched an investigation. As his pursuers closed in, Cecil shifted his assets to a family company, then lied about it under oath. He lied about many things as he attempted to cover his tracks, but now it was too late. "Today begins a day of reckoning," Bellows said. "A final accounting for this defendant, and for the many women he deceived for over a decade."

Tate seemed surprised by the aggressiveness of Bellows's opening remarks. In comparison his statement to the jury was flat and unemotional. He worked without notes, at times stumbling and forgetful. At one point he stopped and apologized to his friend. "Sometimes my memory fails me," he said. "Dr. Jacobson, if I mess up on something, please don't get mad at me, but I will do my best."

He introduced Cecil's wife and father to the jury and asked them to stand up. He said they had come all the way from Provo to support Cecil. He described Dr. Jacobson's accomplishments, beginning with his work at the university, and listed his awards, accolades, and honors. He disputed Bellows's assertions that the trial was about accusations of fraud. In reality Dr. Jacobson was being prosecuted because he dared to buck the medical establishment and opposed established theories of medicine. While studying at Cambridge he'd become convinced that drugs and surgery did more harm than good. HCG wasn't some "big, bad, evil hormone," Tate said, but rather a natural approach to treating infertility.

"Unfortunately, medicine is not something that's exact. Unfortunately, some women did not get pregnant. If Dr. Jacobson has a fault, it was that he tried too hard."

His motive wasn't money, Tate argued. Quite the contrary. When patients got behind in their bills, he didn't charge them for their visits. At Christmas he sometimes cleared their accounts as a present. If his fees for amniocentesis had been equal to the Blue Cross–Blue Shield average, Tate said, he would have made more money on amnios than all his infertility work combined.

Medicine was a series of choices, he said. Dr. Jacobson had chosen a natural approach over prescribing powerful drugs and surgeries. He used temperature charts while others used extensive tests and endometrial biopsies. He believed in giving HCG to stimulate ovulation, while others prescribed laparoscopies and bored holes in a woman's abdomen.

He prescribed a harmless hormone, HCG, rather than drugs with serious side effects. He used urinary pregnancy tests rather than more expensive blood tests, which took longer to get results. He believed in ultrasounds rather than pelvic exams. He believed in natural resorption versus a surgical dilation and curettage. He believed in fresh semen rather than using frozen semen.

Tate acknowledged that Dr. Jacobson sometimes used his own sperm, but not nearly as often as the government claimed. Even so, it wasn't illegal. "Nor was there anything wrong with it," he said.

He blamed Cecil's problems on the initial TV broadcast and the ensuing publicity. Doctors who would have supported him were afraid of being tainted by the bad publicity. Various investigative agencies capitalized on the media attention and began investigations. But when some of his most strident supporters called the TV station to complain that the story was not an accurate portrayal of their doctor, they were ignored.

Afterward Cecil's medical practice was ruined. His insurance company abandoned him and settled the malpractice claims rather than fight them. Dr. Jacobson went into a deep depression. He went back to Utah to do research and get on with his life, but other investigators continued to hound him.

But this time he was fighting back. For the first time the world would hear Dr. Jacobson's side of the story. "I submit to you, that when this case is done, we're going to have a lot of ob/gyns come in here and talk to you." Veteran doctors will say that resorptions occur. "But the most conclusive thing of all," Tate said, "is that Dr. Jacobson's treatment worked. His theory and ideas that he developed at Cambridge worked. The indictment says that it's a bogus way to treat people. But we're going to prove to you that it worked."

As he later told reporters on the courthouse steps, "I think we'll prove in this trial that Dr. Jacobson had one of the most successful infertility practices in the history of the world."

The courtroom was packed for the beginning of the trial, and security remained tight. Cecil's friends grabbed a section of the courtroom for themselves. His wife and father sat up front, surrounded by his friends, fellow Church members, and former patients.

On the other side were the husbands of the women who would be testifying. They were present to offer moral support—and take one more look at the doctor who had done so much to shatter their lives.

In the middle were reporters from all over the world, from newspapers, television stations, and national magazines. A New York-based freelance writer for an English paper shuttled between the Jacobson trial and the Jeffrey Dahmer trial in Milwaukee. A reporter for *The London Observer* considered the story "offbeat enough" that his readers would be interested. Other reporters from Australia and Japan would cover portions of the trial.

Around the courtroom U.S. marshals were stationed to keep a watchful eye on the proceedings.

The prosecution's first witness was Debbie Gregory, and her selection was no accident. Of all the patients, Bellows thought she most conveyed the sense of injury and damage, but he was concerned that she had told her story so often that she would become programmed and emotionless. She told him not to worry. "I'll be ready," she said.

On the witness stand she described her two years of treatments, explaining her exhilaration upon being told she was pregnant, and her despair when told she'd lost another one. She described the stress of living in constant fear of losing one baby after another. Whenever she started bleeding, he told her to drink beer and vodka to ease the cramping and gave her progesterone suppositories to stop the hemorrhaging. "With all this bleeding, and having never been pregnant, I was sure every time something happened, I was losing the baby," she said.

Her testimony was having a powerful effect on the jury. She started crying as she described the day Dr. Doppelheuer informed her she wasn't pregnant. The judge interrupted her testimony. "Mrs. Gregory, are you able to go on?" he asked. "Do you want a recess?"

"No, I'm fine," Debbie said. "I'm sorry."

The jurors hung on her every word as she described her relationship with the man she had trusted. "He was my doctor. He was my friend," she said. "We saw him so often. We brought him birthday presents." And through it all she believed what he'd been telling her. "He was a medical doctor who had extraordinary credentials, and we trusted him. It was a very good relationship."

On cross-examination Dr. Jacobson's attorney couldn't dent her testimony. He tried to show Debbie had been satisfied with the doctor's fees and never suspected him of gouging her. He even tried to show that she might have been pregnant. But then he made what appeared to many to be an error. He inferred that Debbie didn't have anything to complain about. She already had sued the doctor and won a substantial amount of money. "Would you tell us how much you were paid?" he asked.

Before she could answer, the judge called both attorneys to the bench. The settlements were supposed to be confidential, the judge said, and he asked Tate what he was driving at. Tate said he was trying to show that Debbie and the other women had profited by complaining against Dr. Jacobson. Bellows didn't object. He knew how the women would react.

When the cross-examination continued, Tate asked again how much money Debbie received. She said that after attorney's fees she and her husband got $183,845.

"Mrs. Gregory," Bellows asked on redirect questioning, "did this money compensate you for what Dr. Jacobson did to you?"

"No, it did not," she said. "The emotional damage that was done to myself, my husband, my family, and my friends—you cannot compensate that with money." She said she hadn't gone to him to win a malpractice suit; she went to him for a baby.

Debbie left the courtroom in tears, and Steven met her in the hallway. They embraced as reporters milled around; then Steven took her to the privacy of the witness room.

As one resorption patient after another followed Debbie to the witness stand, the defense tried to paint them as frustrated women who were lashing out at a caring doctor because of their own failure to become pregnant. Rather than acknowledge their own infertility problems, they blamed Dr. Jacobson. Tate pointedly asked each woman how much money she had won in malpractice settlements, as if the money should have appeased them. Each said the money wasn't important and she would gladly trade it for a baby.

When Mary Sutphin testified, she was grilled about the $125,000 settlement she had gotten from Dr. Jacobson's insurance company. She said she wasn't even aware how much money she had received.

Tate didn't believe her. "You don't remember something important like that?" he asked accusingly.

"Sir, that's not important," she said. "I went to Dr. Jacobson to have a child, not for money."

Along with the resorption patients were a succession of doctors who had treated dozens of Cecil's patients over the years. Dr. Richard Falk testified that after seeing eight to ten of Cecil's nonpregnant patients, the pattern became so predictable he barely needed to examine a patient's medical records. Just knowing she had gone to Cecil Jacobson was enough to know she most likely had never been pregnant. Before coming to court Dr. Falk said he'd asked the Columbia Hospital for Women, where he worked, to do a statistical study about the probability of resorptions. Of more than ten thousand pregnant women who had been treated at the hospital, he said, not one had ever absorbed a fetus.

Dr. Douglas Lord recalled how he had tried to warn Dr. Jacobson about his mistakes a decade earlier, after three women came to him with nonpregnancies. Dr. Lord said he had called Cecil to offer help, but Cecil had told him to mind his own business. He quoted Cecil as telling him, " 'You don't know what you're talking about. I have always been ahead of the rest of the people. I know what I'm doing. You're wrong.' "

After court Dr. Lord said he had no problem testifying against his former professor. "He makes our profession look bad. He makes us all look bad. I think what he did was quite unethical. He did a great deal of harm to these patients. These are desperate people and he took a lot away from them."

Another obstetrician, Dr. Michael Hotchkiss, testified

that he also contacted Dr. Jacobson after diagnosing a patient as not pregnant. While the patient was still in his office, he called Dr. Jacobson to ask why Cecil had misled her. "He told me that he knew what he was doing and that she was pregnant," the doctor testified.

His partner, Dr. Ronald Zielinsky, testified that he had performed a D and C on the woman who was supposedly ten to twelve weeks pregnant. He would have expected to remove a substantial amount of tissue from the uterus, but he retrieved only about one cubic centimeter. His operative report even stated that he'd tried with great difficulty to remove more tissue, but there was nothing else there.

"Do you have a specific recollection of this D and C?" Bellows asked him.

"Yes, I do," he said.

"Why is that?"

He said he was "very upset" about performing the procedure on a woman who wasn't pregnant.

When Tate questioned Dr. Zielinsky, he suggested the doctor had made a mistake and had actually missed whatever tissue was there.

"When you do a D and C," Tate asked, "you are scraping the uterus, isn't that so?"

"That's correct," Dr. Zielinsky said. "It's a blind procedure."

In this case, Tate said, "you could have missed some tissue, couldn't you?"

The doctor conceded he might have missed some tissue, "but not a hundred grams' worth."

During the course of the trial nearly thirty doctors were scheduled to testify. Sometimes partners in the same medical practice were pitted against each other. Dr. Doppelheuer was testifying for the prosecution, while his three partners were subpoenaed for the defense.

Physicians testified that treating the nonpregnant patients had been an emotional experience for them, as well as for the patient. Dr. James Haddock of Annapolis said that when he broke the news to his patient Susan Dippel that she wasn't pregnant, it was one of the most difficult things he'd ever done.

Chapter Thirty-Five

John and Patricia James nervously watched the news accounts of the trial every day, hoping nothing would surface about their twins. Less than a month before the trial they had made the decision to testify, but only on the stipulation that they be provided additional safeguards to protect the identity of their children.

They wrote a letter to Bellows and expressed their concerns. "After very careful consideration we have decided that we are willing to testify in the criminal prosecution of Dr. Jacobson. However, we have very significant concerns for our children, who are unaware of any aspect of this situation."

Bellows petitioned the judge to provide additional protection for the couple. He sought to exclude "irrelevant detail" from being disclosed in court. He asked that the children not be identified by their gender, age, or even general location in the metropolitan area where they lived. "They live in a close-knit community and are well-known in their neighborhood and school," Bellows told the judge. The James's testimony was essential, Bellows said, because "it is direct proof that his infertility practice was permeated by fraud."

Dr. Jacobson's attorney objected, but the judge granted the prosecution request. The Jameses realized their court appearance would be so emotional that their children would pick up the signals that something was wrong. They both decided to take off the week from work and arranged for the children to stay with friends, then checked into a hotel near the courthouse under another name.

Randy Willetts, working with the U.S. marshals, had

devised elaborate precautions for the donor witnesses to get in and out of court undetected. A makeup artist was hired to alter the patients' appearances. Corridors at the courthouse were blocked off so the witnesses could be whisked into the building.

He didn't want the parents to appear anywhere near the courthouse unless in full disguise, so he arranged to have them meet at his office at the Merrifield, Virginia, post office. The parents could enter the building like a typical postal customer, undistinguishable from the thousands of people who bought stamps or mailed letters there every day, and disappear into the bowels of the building to assume their wigs and makeup.

The witnesses began to assemble at Willetts's office shortly after dawn on the day they were supposed to testify. Mr. and Mrs. James considered renting a car in case reporters were staking out the parking lot and getting license numbers. They made a couple of passes around the lot, saw it was clear, and then blended in with the stamp-buying public.

When they got to Willetts's office, the artist was already working on some parents. Some parents had come from out of town and were booked into hotels under new pseudonyms in case an enterprising reporter tried to find them.

Mrs. James was fitted with a red wig that looked so hideous, she rejected it for a floppy blond number that wasn't much better. Her husband got a really bad toupee. When the artist began making her up, he asked her some questions about her role in the case. It was small talk more than prying, but it made her uncomfortable, and she complained to one of the postal inspectors.

When it was Mary Johnson's turn, she was given a "Marilyn Monroe wig" as she called it. When she checked herself in the mirror, she wasn't impressed. "It's awful," she said. Looking around the room, she noticed the others appeared just as bizarre, decked out in garish makeup and ill-fitting wigs. One man's wig was so small, his hair was sticking out the sides. "Don't do it," his wife was telling him. Some people decided they looked so foolish, they didn't wear any makeup at all. One parent had a Polaroid camera and offered to take some pictures. Several of the couples posed and laughed at how ridiculous they looked, which helped to ease their tension.

When the disguises were complete, they were taken to the basement in twos and threes, then loaded into vans with darkened windows with one postal inspector driving and another riding shotgun. When they got to the rear of the courthouse, they pulled up to the loading dock and the deputies jumped out to check for photographers, then opened umbrellas to shield the parents from view and hustled them inside.

The parents were taken to a judge's vacant chambers, where they were given magazines, doughnuts, and coffee and told to make themselves comfortable. When Bellows and Willetts walked in, they didn't recognize many of them.

Bellows had issued instructions for the parents not to discuss the case, so they sat together in awkward silence. They didn't know each other except by pseudonym and probably would never see each other again, yet they all had one terrible thing in common: they were the parents of a dozen half siblings. One by one they began to loosen up and started to discuss the thread that bound them— their children.

They compared their children's talents and afflictions— some were athletes, others had musical abilities, and many had physical problems. Mary Green said her daughter was born with Down's syndrome. Mary Johnson explained her son was born with a wandering eye and underwent surgery to correct it. Several of the others said their children had eye problems too. Mrs. James kept to herself, sitting off to the side, doodling on a notepad, not interested in sharing anything about herself or her twins.

The first donor witness to testify was Mary Johnson. A large placard with her alias was attached to the witness stand so the attorneys wouldn't refer to her by her real name. One slip and all the precautions were for naught.

As arranged, the judge told everyone to remain seated and ordered the sketch artists to leave, but as Mrs. Johnson was walking into the courtroom, she came face-to-face with an artist on his way out. For a moment they stared at each other until a marshal stepped between them and spun Mary around to face the wall.

When she walked into the courtroom, wearing her ridiculous wig and her overdone makeup, everyone turned to stare. She felt terribly self-conscious as she moved to the witness stand to be sworn in. She panned the courtroom, to the jurors, who were staring at her and making her uncomfortable, to the familiar faces at the prosecution table, who made her feel reassured, then to Dr. Jacobson, and she felt herself flush.

"I was okay until I saw him," she would say, "and then it was just rage. I got hot—real hot inside."

She wondered how she would react when she saw him, not knowing whether she would want to cry or to scale the witness stand and punch him. But now, facing him from across the courtroom, she gritted her teeth and clenched her fist. He stared back at her. "He looked me right dead in the face," she would say. For all her bravado and bravery, for all her vows that "Your ass is mine," or "I'm gonna get even," or "I'm gonna hang you," she was suddenly a quivering mess. She started shaking so violently, she thought her wig would fall off, and her heart was pounding so loudly, she thought the microphone would pick it up. Then Randy Bellows stepped up and started talking to her and eased her through her testimony.

She explained she had gone to Dr. Jacobson for artificial insemination because her husband was sterile. She was talking so softly, Bellows asked her to speak up. The judge suggested she move closer to the microphone.

"I'm just nervous," she said. "I'm sorry."

She tried to move the chair closer to the microphone, but it wouldn't budge, so she moved to the edge of her seat and leaned closer.

Bellows asked her to describe what Dr. Jacobson had told her about the donor.

"He explained to us that the donor was a GW University student who was not from this area. He said the person was fertile because he had children. The person was happily married and was a religious person and that he was free of disease."

She said it had been important that the donor resemble her husband, so their family wouldn't question why the child didn't look like the father. She explained that Dr. Jacobson assured them he had a "perfect match" for her husband.

"Do you see Dr. Jacobson in the courtroom?" Bellows asked.

Mrs. Johnson looked directly at the doctor. "Yes, I do," she said.

"Does Dr. Jacobson bear any resemblance to your husband?"

"None whatsoever."

She said they also had discussed the importance of retaining anonymity between her and the donor. "We were scared of blackmail," she said. She was concerned the father would try to claim his child someday or threaten to inform their families of what they had done. She also was concerned the donor had sired too many children. "I was worried about the children growing up and dating and possibly marrying each other."

"Did Dr. Jacobson make representations to you about limiting the number of children for a particular donor that he was using?" Bellows asked.

"Yes, he said he only used his donor two to three times."

"If you had known that the donor had been used to father numerous children, would you have proceeded to go through the donor insemination?"

"No," she said.

"Was it your assumption in the way he presented this to you that the donor was someone other than Dr. Jacobson himself?"

"Yes."

"If Dr. Jacobson had told you that he would be the father, that he would be inseminating you with his own sperm, would you have permitted yourself to be inseminated by him?"

"Absolutely not," she said defiantly.

* * *

When Jim Tate rose to question her, he smiled and introduced himself. He referred to her medical records and noted she didn't have much to complain about. "You were fortunate to be able to get pregnant right away and have a child, is that correct?"

"Yes," she agreed. "He said I was good for his statistics because he got me on the second try."

He noted from her testimony that Dr. Jacobson had told her the truth. He'd promised her a donor who was fertile, free of disease, and was married with children. She agreed it was all true.

"I take it throughout the course of your treatment you were treated fairly by him?" Tate asked.

"I felt it was wonderful."

"How did you feel when you had the baby, did you feel wonderful then, too?"

"I was thrilled," she said. "He gave me a miracle I was told I would never have."

"Is the child fine and healthy?"

She struggled to find an answer. She thought of her son's eye problems and knew the court had ruled the health of the children would not be discussed. If she blurted out that her son had birth defects, she suspected the judge would strike it, or maybe declare a mistrial. "I have a happy child," she said finally. It was the only answer she could think of.

Bellows had selected Mrs. Johnson as the first donor witness for a specific purpose. He anticipated the defense would be trying to attack the government for intruding into the lives of the parents, but no one had intruded on Mary Johnson or her husband. She had voluntarily come forward after hearing about the indictment. But Dr. Jacobson and his attorney obviously didn't realize this as Tate began laying the groundwork for his portrayal of the prosecutor's office as the evil invaders who had violated the doctor's pledge of anonymity.

Tate pointed out that Dr. Jacobson had never broken his vow to keep the identity of the donor secret. It was the government's fault, he said, not Dr. Jacobson's. "Did he keep his promise?" Tate asked.

"To my knowledge, yes he did."

"Did he ever notify you that he was the father of the child, or that his sperm was used?"

Mrs. Johnson said he did not.

He asked her to explain how she had been notified about the identity of the donor.

Before answering she glanced quickly at Bellows and saw just the hint of a smile. The trap had been baited and the defense was stepping into it.

She said she'd been listening to the radio when she heard news of Dr. Jacobson's indictment and had called the prosecutor's office.

Tate interrupted her. Obviously she had made a mistake. "You must have known about it before then," he said.

"What do you mean?" she asked coyly.

"Didn't somebody notify you that they suspected Dr. Jacobson might have been the donor in your case?"

"No, they did not," she said. "In fact, I contacted the state's attorney's office the morning I found out from the radio. I contacted Mr. Bellows."

Tate quickly backpedaled and tried to salvage the situation. He pointed out that at least Dr. Jacobson hadn't violated his pledge of confidentiality. "To this day Dr. Jacobson has never told you who the donor was for your child?"

She agreed he hadn't.

"Did they tell you anything about the characteristics of Dr. Jacobson's sperm? Did they tell you there was anything wrong with it?"

"The only thing they ever mentioned was there was a Down's syndrome child involved. They thought it came from the mother's side, but it put enough of a scare into me that I needed to find out if my child carried that same gene."

"Does it really matter to you who the donor was, Mrs. Johnson?"

"Yes, it does," she said.

"Do you think the sperm is important in the fatherhood? Do you think that's who the father is?"

"No," she said. The person whom she considered the father was her husband. "His daddy is at work right now," she said.

When Tate was finished, Bellows got up to ask a few more questions. He asked her to describe her contacts with the government. "Mr. Tate seemed to be suggesting that Mr. Willetts or myself or somebody else from the government put some ideas in your head." Had anyone misled her or made her feel uncomfortable? he asked.

"The government has been nothing but helpful," she said, and thanked the prosecutors for stopping Dr. Jacobson. "This man could still be out there doing this and putting more brothers and sisters out for my child."

When Mrs. Johnson was excused, she left the witness box and stared directly at Dr. Jacobson as she walked away. In the hallway she passed the next witness, the woman she knew as Mary Green, and gave her a thumbs-up.

For the better part of two days the parents of the donor children told of being lied to and deceived by Dr. Jacobson.

Mary Green, the mother of the Down's child, told the jury how Dr. Jacobson wanted her to masturbate after each insemination and had offered her the use of his office when her husband was out of town. "I wouldn't have thought he used his own sperm," she said. "I would have thought he was using a donor he had screened thoroughly."

John Stone explained how his wife had asked for another donor when their second child was born with a "health problem"; then they later discovered Dr. Jacobson had sired all three of their children. "How dare he decide that he knew better than myself and my wife what was good for us, and what was not good for us?" he said.

John Ruby, all six foot nine inches of him, explained that Dr. Jacobson had promised to get a donor as tall as he was. "He broke our trust. I trusted him that he was getting a donor like he said he was."

Tate tried to show that each parent was completely satisfied with Dr. Jacobson's care until the government encroached on them. But each parent said they had no complaints with the way the prosecutor's office treated them and were only thankful finally to know the truth.

Patricia James was on and off the witness stand so quickly, it seemed like a blur. Before her testimony Tate approached the bench and told the judge that Dr. Jacobson was not conceding he had fathered her twins. Although the doctor admitted being a donor in some of the cases, he denied he had switched sperm with Mrs. James's husband. Tate claimed the government's DNA testing was flawed and announced the defense had done its own testing, which disputed the government's results.

Mrs. James wasn't privy to the conversation at the judge's bench. She was training her gaze on Dr. Jacobson. She had spent so little time with him so many years before, that she might not have recognized him if she hadn't seen his picture so often in the newspaper. She wanted to look him in the eye and somehow make him realize the damage he'd done to her family. But he wouldn't look at her. He averted his gaze, pretending to shuffle papers on the table and glance at his attorneys, or at the jury—anywhere but at her. She felt cheated. He wouldn't even give her the satisfaction of looking her in the eye.

She looked past him, to his wife sitting in the gallery. They made eye contact for a moment; then her attention was drawn to the woman sitting beside Mrs. Jacobson. The woman was shaking her head disapprovingly, as if to condemn Patricia for testifying against the doctor. "I found it unbelievable that she would have done that," Mrs. James would later say.

When Bellows began questioning her, she was amazed at her calmness. "Did you and your husband ever discuss donor insemination with Dr. Jacobson?" Bellows asked.

"It was never discussed," she said. If she had wanted donor insemination, she would have consulted her own health maintenance plan.

"Was there ever any discussion with Dr. Jacobson about mixing your husband's sperm with the sperm of a donor, then inseminating you with it?"

"No," she said. "We never would have allowed it. We would have been out of the office in about half a second."

"Did you authorize Dr. Jacobson to insert his own sperm into you?"

"No," she said. She stopped to glare at him again. But he still wouldn't return her gaze.

The defense let her go without many questions, and she rushed to find her husband. He had decided not to sit in the courtroom during her testimony, partly because someone might recognize him, but mostly because he feared he wouldn't be able to contain himself when he saw Dr. Jacobson.

They were driven back to the post office and got out of their disguises, then emerged into the sunlight and fresh air, as if a great weight had been lifted. As they walked toward the parking lot, they were no different from the other people who were mailing letters. Their secret was still secure.

Back at the hotel Patricia took a long hot shower. She stood under the torrent of water for a long time, as if she could wash away all memories of the day. She and her husband called to check on the kids, then ordered room service. They shared a bottle of wine as they watched the six o'clock news and were relieved that her testimony had been too late to make the news.

Bellows called to say how much he appreciated their decision to testify. Her testimony had strengthened the case, he said, and he pointed out that the defense had handled her cautiously. "They didn't know what to do with you," he said.

Although it was only Wednesday, they remained at the hotel until Friday. They needed time to think things through and start the painful healing process that would last for years. Although it seemed the worst was over, they would discover it was only the beginning. Preparing for the trial had consumed their energy and diverted their attention, but now they would have to face the damage inflicted on their family—and mend the deep wounds of a father who had recently learned he had no biological connection to his children.

Chapter Thirty-Six

Each morning Dr. Jacobson arrived early before court and fought the gauntlet of reporters who blocked his way into the building. In the evenings a bailiff helped clear a path for Cecil, his wife, and his father. They had nothing to say to the press. Cecil's attorney did the talking as he fielded questions on the sidewalk and tried to put the best spin on that day's damaging testimony.

His family and friends also took up his cause, trying to generate sympathetic stories. His friend Carol Terry complained one day that she had written letters to the newspapers about what she perceived as the negative coverage. "These women had pain when they went in to see Dr. Jacobson. He didn't cause their pain. I'm sure in ten years there won't be any more pain, and they'll be able to relax," she told reporters. She blamed Dr. Jacobson's plight on Randy Bellows and reporter Lea Thompson, who were only trying to further their careers at Cecil's expense. Then she blasted attorney Bob Hall, saying he had whipped his clients into a litigious frenzy so he could get rich off their legal fees.

Her husband stood quietly by her side. "I really do worry about trial by media," he said calmly. "The government can make up anything they want against anyone. I have no faith in the judicial system anymore."

One reporter covering the trial was Charles Sherrill, Washington bureau chief for Bonneville Communications, a chain of TV stations owned by the Mormon Church. The headline-grabbing case of an LDS doctor from Utah was big news in Cecil's home state, and each day Sherrill's stories were broadcast on the Mormon-owned station in Salt Lake City.

The fact that Cecil was a Mormon had no bearing on Sherrill's stories. He reported each day's events neutrally. Cecil's friends had never been especially warm to him, but after the first few days of the trial he noticed relations were becoming even cooler. During a break one day Ells cornered Sherrill and complained about his reports. He accused Sherrill of doing a "hatchet job" on Cecil the night before and said he would have expected better treatment from "our Utah people."

"What do you mean by that?" Sherrill asked. His stories had been no more nor less critical of Cecil than anyone else's, but Ells didn't see it that way. "I would have thought you would have seen things more sympathetically," Ells said. "I would have expected the reporters around here to be biased," he said, "but not our Utah people."

Cecil's friends also were upset with the coverage by Lee Davidson, Washington reporter for the Church-owned *Deseret News* in Salt Lake City. Sherrill was sitting with Davidson at the trial one day when one of the women in Cecil's entourage turned around and accused him of writing a "lousy piece yesterday." She said a friend in Utah had read it to her.

One of the few media outlets they cooperated with was *People* magazine. One day after court Cecil went off with a reporter and photographer for a photo session along the Potomac River. He didn't talk to *People* magazine, but his wife did. She said her husband had only been trying to help people and never considered himself the father of his insemination children. "The father is the person there when the baby is born and who nurtures the baby. The sperm doesn't make the father," she said. "Anyone who got his sperm is lucky."

The story also quoted one of his insemination patients, Carol Franda, who accused the government of destroying the donor families. "This is tearing families apart. It's hurt the grandparents who loved and doted on these children. Why burst their bubbles?" She even posed for a bizarre photo with her teenage son concealed behind a fencing mask. Despite the questions about her son's parentage, she said she decided not to have him tested. "To tell your child you want him to be tested would be horrible. Your child would know you are questioning his paternity, and the one thing a child trusts is that you are his parent."

In the next few days Joyce Jacobson went on a mini-media blitz, even agreeing to do an interview with a new producer from WRC-TV, the station that they believed had caused Cecil's troubles. Producer John Rosson asked her how she felt about her husband using his own sperm on patients.

"I don't see a problem with that," she said. "I don't consider my husband to be the father of those children." She said many other doctors were donors, too, but wouldn't admit it. She was curious as to how the allegations about her husband's donor program came to light. "I don't know how people could figure out he was using his own sperm in the office," she said. The lab techs and receptionists had no contact with patients. If they had been doing their jobs, they should have been too busy to see the things they were claiming to have seen, she said. "Donors are no one's business. I didn't think it was my business. I never thought about it or considered it, because it wasn't my business."

As the trial continued, the prosecution called three receptionists who had worked at the clinic from its inception until the mid-1980's.

Rene Bushman, the secretary-receptionist from 1977 until 1980, said she never saw anyone at the clinic who could have been a sperm donor—and later came to suspect that Dr. Jacobson himself was the donor. She said she'd felt uncomfortable about it. "I didn't like it," she said. Sometimes Dr. Jacobson would leave the office and say he was going to meet the donor down the hall, but in time he stopped leaving the clinic and started going into the bathroom before patients arrived.

Mary Whitten, who was the receptionist during the early 1980's, said her supervisor first mentioned the possibility that Dr. Jacobson was his own donor, and afterward Mary started paying closer attention when he went off to the bathroom. "On the days when there would be an insemination, I would observe him going to take the vial and going to the rest room," she said. It usually happened twice a

week, about three or four o'clock in the afternoon, about
an hour or two before the insemination patients arrived.
She said he remained in the bathroom longer during the
afternoons than during the mornings.

Launi Robertson, the receptionist between 1982 and
1985, had met Dr. Jacobson through the Church and had
known the Jacobson family for years. She was a close
friend with one of Cecil's daughters.

Randy Bellows asked her if there ever came a time when
she concluded that Dr. Jacobson was generating his own
sperm for use with donor patients.

She said her suspicions had started when some of the
other women in the office had mentioned it; then she
noticed for herself that Dr. Jacobson stayed longer in the
bathroom during his afternoon breaks than at other times
of the day. She could see both bathrooms from the receptionist's desk and noticed that Dr. Jacobson normally went
into the bathroom before the insemination patients arrived.
Afterward semen specimens would appear in the lab.

"And Dr. Jacobson hadn't left the facility?" Bellows
asked.

"Correct," she said. He couldn't leave without passing
her desk, she said.

"Is it a fair statement that it was common knowledge
that he was doing this?"

"Basically, I suppose so," she said. She never saw another man drop off a semen specimen, and since she also
handled the mail, she never saw any checks paid to donors.
Once in a while the twenty-dollar fees that Dr. Jacobson
received from the insemination patients were recorded in
the office deposits that she filled out every night.

On cross-examination Tate's partner, David Axelson,
asked Launi if she ever kept a record of how long Dr.
Jacobson was in the bathroom. "Or was this just a sub-
jective guess?"

She said she never kept track.

"You never timed it?" he asked.

She said she didn't, but sometimes she noticed he was
taking an extra-long time, especially while the insemination patients were in the waiting room.

*   *   *

One of the spectators during the trial was Dr. Marian Damewood, who had been hired by the U.S. attorney's office to listen to the testimony. Shortly before the trial she had concluded her examination of Dr. Jacobson's entire patient load. Now Bellows wanted her to testify about what she'd found.

She explained that Dr. Jacobson had treated all his patients the same, no matter what their ailment. Whether it was endometriosis, problems with the cervix, or improper ovulation, Dr. Jacobson treated them with HCG. Even if it was the husband's problem, the wife still got HCG. He routinely diagnosed his patients as having a "major risk of fetal defect" whether the woman's problem was an ovarian cyst, herpes, or smoking. He even made the same diagnosis for women in their twenties who didn't have a high risk of Down's syndrome or other fetal defects.

But she had noticed one clear distinction. A woman who was truly pregnant, and who eventually delivered a baby, was referred to her obstetrician in the first trimester, she said, but the ones who eventually suffered a resorption never got referrals, no matter how far along they progressed.

She said it hadn't taken her long to notice what she called a "repetitive, recurrent pattern." After the first ten charts, and certainly by the first fifty, she could open a file and predict what would happen to the patient. "You could see that a patient would come in, at some point she'd get HCG shots. At some point she got pregnancy tests while she was getting HCG. Then she had positive pregnancy tests for a while. Then she had multiple sonograms. Then something was going to happen before she came to the point of amniocentesis. I never noticed any patient having an amniocentesis on a nonpregnant uterus."

"What is the significance of that?" Bellows asked.

"It shows that it must have been clear that these women were not pregnant," she said. Otherwise a doctor who was negligent or sloppy would have mistakenly done an amniocentesis on a woman he thought was pregnant. Performing an amnio on a nonpregnant woman, she explained, could cause serious damage to the woman's bladder and bowel.

"In your opinion, was Dr. Jacobson's conduct haphazard or organized?"

"Very well organized," she said.

She hadn't calculated the miscarriage rate, but knew the number of failed pregnancies was "staggering" and the number of resorptions were "unheard of in human reproduction." The numbers were so high, she said, that, "there's really no way that these could have been legitimate pregnancies. It was hundreds." If anything like that had happened at Johns Hopkins, it would have set off alarms that something was seriously wrong.

She said Dr. Jacobson's prescriptions of alcohol and progesterone suppositories would have served no useful purpose, except to mask a woman's menstrual period, and actually could have caused more harm than good. And there was no sound medical basis for telling one woman after another that a virus had killed her baby. "In fact, it's a very serious statement to make because it makes the patient feel it's her fault that she had the miscarriage."

"In your practice," Bellows asked, "are you aware of any physician other than Dr. Jacobson who was giving women just HCG, and as many as one hundred shots?"

"No, I have never seen anyone give that much HCG." She said she was aware of some European studies that tested the effectiveness of HCG by itself, but they indicated that the hormone was better used in combination with fertility drugs. Other studies, she said, had demonstrated that HCG sometimes was effective in treating habitual-abortion patients. "But that's not what we're talking about here. These patients weren't habitual-miscarriage patients." At least not until they started with Dr. Jacobson, she added.

Tate tried to attack Dr. Damewood as a hired witness for the prosecution who was profiting handsomely from Dr. Jacobson's case. She was making two hundred dollars an hour to review Dr. Jacobson's records and sit in the courtroom, after already selling her services to the FTC and the malpractice attorneys who had sued the doctor. Dr. Damewood said she hadn't profited from her work.

The money had gone to Johns Hopkins University, she said, and she didn't keep any of it.

He tried to lay the foundation for the upcoming defense theory that the women really had been pregnant and only Dr. Jacobson was astute enough to have realized it. He asked if she would change her mind about Dr. Jacobson's practice if she discovered that some of the women really had been pregnant. What if some of the sonograms contained views of pregnancies? he asked.

She said it wouldn't matter if a couple of women had actually been pregnant. "To do this to even one patient is unheard of."

He asked her about a Harvard study done in collaboration with the University of Colorado that had been published earlier in the year showing that 57 percent of all tubal pregnancies were resorbed.

She was aware of the study, she said, but it bore no resemblance to what Dr. Jacobson had been telling his patients. The resorptions were very early pregnancies, she said, when the embryos were no bigger than a pin. Even so, the resorptions occurred in the fallopian tubes, not in the uterus.

"Yes, ma'am, but if it could resorb in the fallopian tubes, why couldn't it resorb in the uterus as well?" Tate asked.

"That's a very good question," she said. "The answer is, the uterus is not an organ that absorbs." If it did, women would absorb their menstrual periods.

Tate tried to show that the government had managed to locate every disgruntled patient, whereas the silent majority of patients had been pleased with Cecil's care. Wasn't it true, he asked, that only twenty patients fit the category of questionable pregnancies and resorptions that the government was harping on?

"Absolutely not," she said. There were many more than twenty. "There were hundreds and hundreds of women. The women we have seen in this courtroom are just the tip of the iceberg," she said. "It got to the point where I could take a stack of charts and open them up and expect to see these pregnancy sheets with all the stuff written on them."

Tate tried again. What if it could be shown that only 4 percent of the women actually had questionable pregnancies and resorptions? "Would that change your opinion?" he asked.

"It's extremely unlikely that four percent represents the nature of this problem."

Tate said his expert's analysis showed that 30 percent of the women had children. "Isn't that true, Dr. Damewood?"

She said she hadn't compiled specific numbers, but she knew that many of the women were pregnant before they got to the clinic.

Tate tried one last time to get her to admit that Dr. Jacobson's treatments weren't as bad as the government was contending. If anything, the mistakes were nothing more than a difference of medical opinion. There was no right and wrong. "I guess you recognized from studying his records that Dr. Jacobson was doing what he thought was right, and not necessarily what everybody else was right doing?"

"I disagree," she replied. "I think he had a purposeful pattern. He knew exactly what he was doing. He is a very intelligent person." From reviewing his records she believed he had engaged in a well-thought-out scheme.

The government's other medical expert, Dr. Glenn Braunstein, had also spent dozens of hours reviewing the boxes of material Bellows had sent him. All of Bellows's dealings with Dr. Braunstein had been by telephone until shortly before the trial, when the doctor attended a medical seminar in the Washington area. Bellows had expected to meet a nerdish little man who had devoted his entire life to studying an obscure hormone, but he was surprised to meet a tanned, healthy southern Californian who seemed right out of central casting. Bellows thought he was a dead ringer for actor Alan Alda.

Dr. Braunstein was anxious to tell the jury that he thought Dr. Jacobson had deliberately defrauded his patients, but as the government's expert witness he wasn't permitted to offer an unsolicited opinion. He could testify about whether Dr. Jacobson's treatments met the routine standard of care rendered by infertility doctors, but Bellows told him he couldn't offer his opinion unless the defense asked him, which seemed unlikely at best.

Dr. Braunstein told Bellows he felt frustrated by the legal constraints on his testimony. When he took the witness stand, he confined his testimony to Dr. Jacobson's use of HCG and explained that prescribing HCG for women who had never been examined was "reprehensible," and that relying on temperature charts after HCG injections was "absolutely worthless." Any doctor with an iota of training should have known the injections would trip a pregnancy test. Yet he was unable to describe how he really felt about Dr. Jacobson's practice.

On cross-examination Tate attacked Dr. Braunstein's review of the patient files and attacked the HCG study he'd conducted with Dr. Damewood. He accused them of using the Johns Hopkins in-vitro patients as "guinea pigs," but Braunstein pointed out that the women had been volunteers who already were receiving HCG injections and only donated their urine.

For nearly an hour Tate tried to weaken Dr. Braunstein's testimony but succeeded only in getting the HCG expert to admit that a single HCG shot wouldn't trip a pregnancy test after fifteen or sixteen days.

Before wrapping up his questioning Tate said he couldn't understand how anyone could believe Dr. Jacobson had been deceiving his patients, not when he gave each couple their sonograms to take home and referred each woman to her own obstetrician. "How in the world can the woman be deceived if she is seeing her OB the whole time?"

Dr. Braunstein said he had an opinion. He sat up straight and squared his shoulders, as if he'd been waiting for this all day. "I think that Dr. Jacobson's action represents a purposeful pattern of deceit, and I will be happy to go through chapter and verse why I think that."

Tate quickly changed the subject, but it was too late. Not only had the jury heard the medical expert's opinion, but Tate had made an even bigger blunder. He had provided the government an avenue to get their medical expert's opinion into evidence. Bellows was quick to pounce on the opportunity during his redirect examination.

"Dr. Braunstein, since Mr. Tate has opened this door, can you explain what you meant when you said a few moments ago that you had formed an opinion that Dr. Jacobson had acted in a purposeful pattern of deceit?"

For the next ten minutes Dr. Braunstein analyzed Dr. Jacobson's entire practice for the jury, from the moment a patient walked in the door until she was told her baby had resorbed.

On resorption of a second-trimester fetus, he said, "It just doesn't happen."

On Dr. Jacobson not knowing HCG injections would trip a pregnancy test: "That's just beyond the fathom of my understanding."

And his thoughts after a detailed study of Jacobson's practice: "This was a purposeful pattern of deceit on these women," he reiterated, in case the jury had missed it the first time.

As the doctor continued uninterrupted, Bellows stood at the podium, amazed at the glorious opportunity he'd been afforded by the defense blunder. Tate sat at the defense table unable to stop him.

Dr. Braunstein concluded by saying of Dr. Jacobson, "He was tricking people into thinking that they were pregnant when they were not. To me it's beyond belief."

After five days of testimony from fifty-six witnesses the government rested its case. Some of the final witnesses spoke of Dr. Jacobson's attempts to shield his property from the patients who were suing him, and his lies under oath to conceal those transactions.

The final witness was Gary Stuhlmiller, who had supervised the paternity testing at Roche Laboratories. He explained the elaborate DNA testing procedures which showed that Dr. Jacobson had fathered fifteen of the seventeen children.

Besides linking a father with a child, he said the tests also provided a "very large measure" of protection against a man being falsely accused of paternity. Under conventional testing Dr. Jacobson was determined to be the father in each case with a certainty ranging from 90 to 99 percent. But under DNA testing the probability in each instance was 99.99 percent. "Roche can never issue one hundred percent probability," he said.

Bellows asked if he'd calculated the likelihood of another man having fathered all of the fifteen children.

"Yes, I did," Stuhlmiller said.

"What is that calculation?" Bellows asked.

"Approximately one in twenty-eight trillion," he said.

The defense wasn't taking the results of the DNA testing at face value. Before Stuhlmiller even took the stand, the defense attacked the results of the government's testing. During a recess Tate presented the prosecution with the results of the defense's independent testing of Dr. Jacobson's blood sample. And the report claimed that the government's lab had misread or misanalyzed one of the doctor's genetic markers.

Stuhlmiller called it a "technical complication" and said the testing his lab had conducted was actually more conservative and afforded further protection from false accusations than what the lab hired by the defense was advocating.

"The results were essentially the same as ours," Stuhlmiller said. Only five of the fifteen children were affected, and the discrepancy would have no affect on the "paternity index" of the children, which he said was still 99 percent certainty for each of them.

"Dr. Stuhlmiller, is it fair to say this issue is a red herring?" Bellows asked.

The defense objected before Stuhlmiller could answer, and the judge sustained the objection. As Bellows rested his case, he wondered what other surprises the defense would throw at him.

Chapter Thirty-Seven

D r. Jacobson and his attorneys managed to keep the existence of their first witness a secret until shortly before she was scheduled to testify. She was an insemination patient known as "Frances Redd." She lived overseas, and ironically Willetts had gone to great lengths to find her, tracking her down through a foreign embassy. Shortly after the indictment Frances Redd had written a letter to Cecil's attorney complaining about the way the government notified her.

> To brand Dr. Jacobson as a criminal is wrong and a callous attempt to demean our greatest gift of joy for which he alone is responsible. Dr. Jacobson has not committed fraud, he has kept his pledge of anonymity to us. It doesn't matter if he were the sperm donor. I feel sadness that his service in helping high-risk pregnancies such as mine have been terminated and that other women cannot turn to his help in having babies. I also believe that the U.S. government has greatly abused its authority and taxpayers' tolerance in this case.

Tate had secretly approached the judge and used Mrs. Redd's information to support his allegations of governmental misconduct, but a few weeks before the trial the judge had ruled it was a matter for appeal and not to be considered by the jury. Still, Tate wanted to show the government had relied on lies and scare tactics to bias the insemination patients unfairly against Dr. Jacobson.

Mrs. Redd explained to the jury that she underwent twenty inseminations before she conceived her son, and each time she received an HCG injection. "He thought there was no real reason if I were in good health and ovulating regularly that even at age forty-one or forty-two I could not have a child."

She had made no special requests for a donor. Her main concern was the anonymity. She was afraid that a disgruntled employee or another patient could get into the records and discover she had been inseminated. "Dr. Jacobson assured me that would not be the case," she said. His records were coded so that only he could understand them. "And I greatly commend him for that," she said. No one had known she'd been inseminated until the government breached the confidentiality.

"I take it, then, you were happy with Dr. Jacobson's services?" Tate asked her.

"Both my husband and I remain eternally grateful to him," she said.

"Let me ask you, did there come a time this past year when you received a communication from some agency of the United States government in reference to your child?"

She said she had received a fax the previous summer asking her to contact the district attorney's office.

"Do you recall who it was you spoke to at the United States attorney's office?"

"I spoke with Mr. Randy Bellows."

"At the time that you had this conversation with him, did you keep notes so you have an accurate recollection of what was said?"

"Yes, I did. Mr. Bellows told me that ten former patients of Dr. Jacobson had undergone blood testing, and in at least seven of those cases for which he had results, Dr. Jacobson was the biological father. Mr. Bellows told me he thought there to be as many as seventy to eighty children." She said he had been "somewhat vague" in explaining that some of the children had health problems, except to say there was the risk of sibling marriage and Dr. Jacobson had fathered a Down's syndrome child. She said he blamed it on a "rare defective trait" in Dr. Jacobson's sperm. "He also told me that the children fathered by Dr. Jacobson had two commonalities. One was fatness and the other was high intelligence."

"Up to this point in time," Tate asked, "had you felt that you had been damaged in any way by Dr. Jacobson?"

"I have not been damaged in any way," she said.

"I take it Mr. Bellows informed you what his laboratory said the results were."

"Yes," she said. "There was a very high probability that Dr. Jacobson was the sperm donor."

Tate asked her to describe her son. She said he was slim and of average intelligence. "I say this without a mother's pride," she said. "I think I have an unusually handsome child."

"Does your child resemble Dr. Jacobson?"

She didn't know whom he resembled. "My son doesn't look too much like my husband or me, and yet some people say he looks like my husband and some people say he looks like me. So it's very interpretive. But it doesn't make a tinker's damn worth of difference. He is a beautiful child."

"Let me ask you," Tate said in conclusion, "do you feel that Dr. Jacobson kept his pledge of anonymity?"

"Very much so," she said. "That's the major reason why I'm here today."

The defense didn't wait long to spring their next surprise. They produced their own paternity-testing expert to attack the government's DNA testing. Jerome Mayersak, a urologist from Minnesota, traveled to courtrooms around the country disputing DNA paternity results. It seemed that whenever Roche conducted a paternity test, Dr. Mayersak was hired by the opposition to refute it.

Bellows questioned his qualifications and tried to portray him as a "hired gun," but Mayersak said he wasn't even getting paid to help Cecil. They had known each other since George Washington University, and Dr. Mayersak said he had the utmost respect for him. It was the only pro bono case he was handling, he said.

Mayersak had reviewed the government's tests and claimed they weren't performed correctly. The lab should have conducted a "double-blind test," he said. Rather than running Dr. Jacobson's blood sample once and comparing it against everyone else, the lab should have conducted each test separately. Also, the lab didn't conduct the same number of tests on everyone and should have run one test for sixty-five hours, not forty-eight. He also suggested the lab should have tested Dr. Jacobson's parents to ensure the tests weren't skewed because of traits unique to a Mormon "subpopulation."

Bellows characterized the defense testing as a "red herring" designed to mislead the jury. In the end the judge denied the defense's attempt to throw out the DNA testing. He said the jury could decide for themselves which expert to believe—the one for the government or the one for the defense.

For the rest of the next two days Cecil's friends, colleagues, and fellow Mormons marched into court and defended his honor. They told of babies they wouldn't have had, and a scoutmaster who did good deeds; of a good friend who was always eager to help and a doctor who wrote off his fees if a patient couldn't pay. There was a woman who'd been exposed to radiation as a teenager and had been given no hope of having children, until Cecil inseminated her and she had a son. Another woman had tried unsuccessfully to conceive for fifteen years until consulting Cecil, then delivered a baby. An Annandale, Virginia, woman said she went to Cecil when she was miscarrying and he told her not to have a D and C. The next month he did a sonogram and discovered another embryo. She'd been carrying twins and didn't know it. If she had gone to another doctor and gotten a D and C, she wouldn't have her nine-year-old son. One woman said she had gotten pregnant right away through Dr. Jacobson's treatments and had a child, but when she wanted a second baby, he'd been run out of business. Since then she had been treated by a series of other doctors who were unable to help her.

One patient said she had a miscarriage and resorption, just like the unhappy patients. She had passed a pregnancy test twenty-three days after her last HCG injection, which the defense contended proved that she must have been pregnant and resorbed. Dr. Jacobson never guaranteed success, she said. "I am convinced that we have the child because of Dr. Jacobson."

When Tate passed the witness, Bellows had only a few questions. He said he could understand her appreciation of Dr. Jacobson but asked if her attitude would be the same if she had been led to believe that she was three or four months pregnant, then learned she wasn't pregnant at all. "Is it fair to say your feelings for Dr. Jacobson might be significantly different?"

"I think that if my experience had been an experience of failure rather than success, I would not be as thankful to Dr. Jacobson as I am," she said.

Several witnesses testified that Dr. Jacobson's prices were always reasonable and his fees were the cheapest around. One woman said he charged her only two hundred dollars for an amniocentesis while another doctor had charged eight hundred dollars.

The defense hired an accountant to analyze the clinic's financial records. He said Cecil's fees were less than the Blue Cross–Blue Shield average for the metropolitan Washington area.

Many of those who testified for Cecil were prominent Washingtonians. One was a judge and another was President Reagan's pollster, who called Dr. Jacobson "a person of great honesty and trustworthiness." But they were on and off the stand so quickly that the jury didn't realize their prominence. After a while, Judge Cacheris found the witnesses repetitious and wouldn't allow many more.

Of all the people who had worked for Cecil over the years, the defense found only one to testify on his behalf. His longtime assistant, Elizabeth Vosbeck, had run the amnio lab for him since the clinic opened and staunchly defended him every time an investigator had tried to interview her. But Tate didn't ask her to defend her boss this time. Instead he had a more unusual line of questioning. He asked her to describe Cecil's feelings about abortion.

Before she could answer, Judge Cacheris cut her off. "I don't think that's an issue in this case," he said.

Tate asked to approach the bench. He told the judge he was trying to show his client would have done anything to prevent a woman from having to undergo an abortion. "He had a very strong bias about trying to save pregnancies to the point that it affected everything he did," Tate said.

Bellows objected, saying it was only a tactical smoke screen aimed at the media. "There was a story in the paper about a month or two ago where he talked about being antiabortion," Bellows said. "It seems to me this is designed to elicit some support from any jurors who might be prolife."

The judge said he wouldn't permit testimony about the abortion issue, but if Tate wanted to demonstrate Dr. Jacobson's attitude about saving fetuses, "I'll let you ask it that way."

Bellows argued that any discussion at all of the doctor's attitude about abortions could lead to even more explosive testimony. He said the U.S. attorney's office had discovered evidence in the doctor's files that he had been using amniocentesis for sex selection. Women came to him for amniocentesis so they could abort a fetus if it wasn't the gender they preferred.

"I don't believe there's any evidence of that," Tate shot back.

Bellows disagreed. "First of all, I can represent to you and to the court that we have amniocentesis files where the patients specifically came there for the purpose of sex selection."

The judge settled the dispute before it went any further and said the doctor's position on abortion was off-limits, and so was the evidence about his using amnio for sex selection.

Since the beginning of the trial Jim Tate had been boasting about the stable of medical experts who were prepared to support Dr. Jacobson's methods. Doctors who had been referring patients to Cecil for years filed into court and described him as an honest and sincere physician who would never defraud a patient. Even those doctors whose patients had experienced some of the nonpregnancies thought Cecil's mistakes were of the head, not of the heart. Sometimes he tried too hard and was blinded by his own exuberance, they said, but his successes far exceeded his failures.

Several of these doctors also shared Cecil's belief in resorption. One compared a resorbing fetus with a cancer that disappears after radiation or chemotherapy treatments. "I'm sure that a pregnancy can go in the same way," he said. On cross-examination, however, he conceded that the skull and bones of an eighteen-to-twenty-week fetus couldn't possibly resorb.

Cecil's staunchest and most distinguished defender was his former department chairman, Dr. James Sites, who described Cecil's character as excellent. "He has always been honest, fair, and very approachable," Dr. Sites told the jury.

Tate asked him to compare the controversy over Dr. Jacobson's infertility treatments to the debate caused two decades earlier by Cecil's amniocentesis work. Dr. Sites said the medical community had called amniocentesis "wild" and "unjustified" and said "it would result in abortions and infections and termination of pregnancies."

"Did Dr. Jacobson stand up to the criticism at that time?" Tate asked.

"Yes, he stood up to it, very much so."

"Did there come a time when he received similar criticism for another study on the genetic effects of radiation?"

Dr. Sites didn't recall all the details but remembered that Cecil's diagnosis of chromosome abnormalities was disputed at the time he released his research, but he was exonerated over time. He said Cecil had stubbornly defended his findings until he was proved to be correct.

On cross-examination Dr. Sites admitted that after five doctors from Fairfax Hospital complained to him, he had tried to warn Cecil that his treatments were way off base. He told Cecil to stick with genetics counseling and get out of infertility.

How did Dr. Jacobson respond? Bellows asked.

"His reaction was, 'My success rate is as good as anyone else's,' " Dr. Sites said, "and that he would continue."

Each night after court Bellows worked on what he considered to be the crucial point of the trial—the cross-examination of Dr. Jacobson. He had been anticipating the showdown for months. His "Jacobson Speaks" collection of depositions, hearings, newspaper clippings, and relevant statements had expanded to 23 volumes. He was getting to know more about Dr. Jacobson than the doctor knew about himself.

One evening as he was preparing his questions, it suddenly dawned on him that he was concentrating on the wrong man. The jury would see Dr. Jacobson for what he was. The key to the defense's case was their medical expert from Ireland, Dr. Robert Harrison, who was expected to testify the next morning. Bellows didn't know much about Dr. Harrison except that he'd done some studies on HCG and had impressive credentials. Bellows had come across the studies months earlier in some of the research material Dr. Damewood had provided him. Later he'd been surprised that Dr. Jacobson had been able to land him as a witness. Since then the defense had managed to keep the substance of Dr. Harrison's testimony a closely guarded secret.

It was already after ten P.M. when Bellows closed his "Jacobson Speaks" notebook and turned his attention to the next day's witness. He worked well into the night preparing for the Irish physician, who was suddenly looming as the most serious threat to the case.

From the moment Dr. Robert Harrison walked into the courtroom, he was Bellows's worst fears come true. He was a red-haired little leprechaun of a man who charmed the women on the jury and delighted the men. He spoke in a lilting accent that had the jury, and even the judge, chuckling along with him.

As part of his duties for the World Health Organization, Dr. Harrison had inspected infertility clinics around the world, and now, after examining Dr. Jacobson's practice, he thought it was as good as any he'd ever seen—and better than most. He said Dr. Jacobson was a misunderstood genius.

Dr. Harrison was the only defense witness who had inspected Dr. Jacobson's infertility files, and he went into great detail explaining the methodology of how he'd analyzed the patients' records. Whenever he made a point, he glanced toward the jury to make sure they were listening and sprinkled his answers with Irish colloquialisms that kept the jurors entertained, especially a woman in the front row. She seemed quite smitten with him and giggled whenever he crinkled his nose or said something amusing.

He explained he had analyzed 118 cases and found 61 of the women had gotten pregnant, a rate of 51 percent, which he characterized as "excellent." Of them 37 patients had delivered babies, a rate of 31.4 percent. Again he described the percentage as well above average.

The success rates were even more remarkable, he said, considering the type of patients Dr. Jacobson was treating. The average woman was thirty-two years old, and many were considerably older. Yet he said only four percent of the patients he studied could be classified as resorbing pregnancies. Extrapolated over his thousand patients, he said it would mean forty women had undergone resorptions.

Dr. Harrison was surprised to hear there was any controversy about Dr. Jacobson's use of HCG. He said he'd been using the hormone since the 1950's and '60's with great success and no in-vitro program in the world could function without it. He was also surprised that Dr. Jacobson was being criticized for his bias against D and C's. "It's an unnecessary risk to the patient," he said, and could delay subsequent attempts to get pregnant.

In fact he agreed with almost everything Dr. Jacobson had done—diagnosing pregnancies with urinary tests and prescribing alcohol to ease cramping. He couldn't even fault Dr. Jacobson for not knowing that HCG would trip an Abbott pregnancy test. He said he'd never read the package inserts either.

For the most part Dr. Jacobson's attorney didn't need to question Harrison. He was a one-man show. He said Dr.

Jacobson's treatment regimen was well thought out, not a scheme as the government's doctors were claiming. "To me a scheme means it's a bit underhanded, it's a bit nefarious. I prefer to say it's a planned approach." And apart from two menopausal women who probably shouldn't have been treated, he thought Dr. Jacobson was practicing "perfectly good medicine." He didn't understand how some of the women who were complaining had received money from malpractice lawsuits because he couldn't see that Dr. Jacobson had done anything wrong.

Dr. Harrison's testimony attacked the heart of the government's case and raised doubts about everything the government's medical experts had said. Not only was he staunchly defending Dr. Jacobson, but he had solid credentials behind him.

When it was Bellows's turn to cross-examine him, he asked Dr. Harrison if he'd read the indictment against Dr. Jacobson.

"I scan-read it," he said, "but I didn't read it through totally."

"So you are testifying here today on Dr. Jacobson's behalf, but you have not read the criminal charges lodged against him?"

"I don't feel myself testifying on Dr. Jacobson's behalf," he corrected the prosecutor. "I came here to discover the truth," he said. "I'm not on any side whatsoever. My only interest is the patients' welfare and how they were treated."

Bellows asked if Dr. Harrison had listened to the testimony of the resorption patients or had read any of the transcripts from their previous legal proceedings.

"No," he said. He had read everything that was given to him, but he didn't recall receiving anything about the malpractice cases.

"In terms of what was presented to you in Ireland, was it your understanding that Dr. Jacobson was being criminally prosecuted for using HCG in a particular manner?"

"Yes, I think so," he said.

"Now, Doctor, you said something in your testimony— and I wrote it down—that Dr. Jacobson practiced very good medicine. Was that your testimony?"

"Yes."

He asked whether that statement was based on looking at Dr. Jacobson's records.

"Yes, Dr. Jacobson's records," he agreed.

"And, Doctor, is it fair to say that you accepted at face value what Dr. Jacobson was saying?"

"I accepted at face value what was written down in the notes," he said.

So if Dr. Jacobson wrote that a fetus was growing each week, "you accepted that's what Dr. Jacobson was seeing?"

"Not necessarily," he said. "I felt it was important to see a fetal heart, and that's what I looked for in the notes to see if somebody had written down, 'fetal heart seen.' "

"So if Dr. Jacobson wrote on his files that he detected an embryo heart, or got a positive pregnancy test on a certain date, you accepted that was true?"

"I considered it might be true, but then I went to look for the photographic evidence." He said he studied the ultrasounds.

Bellows drove home the point again. "If you are coming into court and relying on Dr. Jacobson's files and have not heard the witnesses or their doctors, isn't it true that the only way you can do that is to rely that the files are accurate?"

He said that was correct. "I don't think it would be right for me to talk to twenty-one ladies, although I would have loved to." He smiled, as if he'd cracked a joke, and looked to the jury for their reaction. Previously they had been laughing with him, but they weren't smiling anymore.

"Your assumption is that Dr. Jacobson had not faked the pregnancy tests, had not put false information into the file intentionally?"

"That's right," he said.

He referred Dr. Harrison to the donor patients who had received Dr. Jacobson's sperm. Their files stated they had been inseminated with the husband's sperm.

Dr. Harrison said the notation was made to preserve the patient's anonymity.

"I'm not asking you why he did it," Bellows said icily. "It's false information, is it not?"

Dr. Harrison agreed. "It's false."

"Don't you think it would have been relevant for you to listen to the women who are accusing Dr. Jacobson of having committed fraud upon them?"

He said he would have preferred to hear their testimony, but he was busy in Ireland.

The questioning became contentious as Bellows described several of the cases. He asked the doctor what he thought about women who had advanced pregnancies that disappeared virtually overnight. Dr. Harrison wasn't ready to concede Dr. Jacobson had been wrong, and tried to find plausible explanations. Despite his earlier description of himself as a seeker of truth, he was coming off as a blind defender, and the jury noticed it.

Bellows pointed out that several doctors had warned Dr. Jacobson that his injections were causing false pregnancy tests, but he ignored them. And six doctors had performed D and C's on women who were not pregnant. "Would that suggest to you that Dr. Jacobson was intentionally deceiving his patients?"

"It's a possible interpretation," Dr. Harrison admitted. But they were only six patients out of more than a thousand, he noted. "The thing that surprises me," Dr. Harrison said, "is that I examined one hundred eighteen files, and I examined them very thoroughly. And I didn't find evidence of widespread problems such as you're suggesting."

"But, Doctor, you based your examination on Dr. Jacobson's files."

"Yes."

"You didn't hear the women who testified in court?"

"No."

"You didn't hear what he was representing to them, or the evidence of what happened when they went to their gynecologist?"

"Right."

In the beginning Dr. Harrison had been very confident of himself as he laughed and joked with the jury, but after Bellows got through with him, he was stumbling and frantically searching for documents to support what he was saying. When the trial recessed for lunch, he was so flustered that he was sweating and muttering to himself as he left the courtroom. Bellows had taken a world-renowned infertility specialist and reduced him to sounding like a quack.

On the way out of court Dr. Harrison apologized to Dr. Jacobson. Cecil responded angrily that the prosecutor should be ashamed of himself for beating up on a fine man. "He's spending more time on our witnesses than we are," he snapped.

When the jury returned from lunch, their reaction toward Dr. Harrison was considerably colder. They weren't laughing with him anymore, and the woman who had seemed so smitten with him took a seat toward the back.

When Dr. Jacobson's other European expert testified later in the day, he, too, seemed to be everything the defense could have hoped for—and more.

Dr. Stuart Campbell had examined 180 sonograms and said he found evidence of pregnancy in 25 of them. He showed the jury slides of what happens to ovarian follicles when a woman ovulates and said it was "perfectly logical" to prescribe HCG before ovulation and in the early days after conception.

He told the jury about his research on HCG—he'd found that in 28 percent of the early miscarriages the sac disappeared, and in most of them no D and C was necessary. The sac resorbed by itself.

His testimony couldn't have supported Dr. Jacobson any better. At the prosecution table Bellows marveled at how the defense had procured such a legitimate expert to testify so credibly for them, but after listening a while longer, he thought he suspected how.

As Dr. Campbell explained his criteria for examining the sonograms, he said he'd conducted a blind study, with no knowledge of the patient's name or the age of the pregnancy. He'd simply examined each photograph and reported on what he saw.

For Susan Dippel he was "absolutely certain" he saw a gestation sac with an embryo.

For Judith Dowd he said he didn't see an embryo, "but there's no doubt in my mind that is a gestation sac."

For Vickie Eckhardt he said he saw a gestation sac with a "very, very tiny embryonic egg within it."

It was remarkable how his interpretations were so different from what all the other sonographers had found.

Prosecutor David Barger, who had been assigned to assist Bellows during the trial, conducted the cross-examination, and as soon as he started, it became clear why Dr. Campbell's interpretation was vastly different from everyone else's. He'd been virtually blindfolded as he studied the sonograms, unmindful of the names, ages, medical histories, or even the length of the supposed pregnancy. So when he was studying a sonogram photo, he didn't know whether it was supposed to be the view of a pregnancy at three weeks or three months. He assumed most of the sonograms were views of six-to-eight-week pregnancies. Dr. Jacobson's machine wouldn't have detected a pregnancy much earlier than that, he said.

"What would you say if Dr. Jacobson were claiming to diagnose pregnancy at five weeks, or four weeks? Would you have a hard time accepting that as accurate?"

"Definitely," he said. He'd used a similar machine in "the old days" and knew it wasn't sophisticated enough to detect very early pregnancies.

Barger referred him to the case of Barbara Mull, the former nurse from Winchester, Virginia. Dr. Campbell has described her sonogram as containing a "possible" pregnancy. But Barger told him that two doctors had diagnosed her as menopausal. Dr. Campbell said he wasn't aware of that. "I can only say what I'm seeing on these photographs," he said.

"You weren't given any information at all as to what diagnosis Dr. Jacobson was making on a supposed pregnancy?"

"None at all," he replied.

"If Dr. Jacobson is looking at the same picture you're looking at, and he is telling a woman she's fourteen, fifteen, eighteen weeks pregnant, obviously that doesn't reconcile with some of the sonogram pictures you looked at?"

"I quite agree," he said. "That would not reconcile."

"Were you given any of the affidavits or statements of these women to see what Dr. Jacobson was telling them?"

"No," Dr. Campbell said.

"Would you be interested in looking at those files since they haven't been available to you?"

Dr. Campbell said he would. They started with one of Debbie Gregory's sonograms that Dr. Campbell had marked as a possible pregnancy. "In your opinion how far along is Debbie Gregory in that pregnancy?"

Dr. Campbell said it was a very early pregnancy, or she may have already miscarried.

"Was there any way Debbie Gregory could have been sixteen or seventeen weeks pregnant at that time?" the prosecutor asked.

Dr. Campbell looked shocked. "Not in that image," he said. "Not in that image."

Barger referred him to the next Polaroid, when Debbie was supposed to have been eighteen weeks pregnant. He said that five days after this scan was taken, Dr. Jacobson had told Debbie that "Junior is doing fine."

Again Dr. Campbell seemed surprised. He said he couldn't see evidence of an eighteen-week pregnancy. At best it was the view of a pregnancy that had failed many weeks earlier, but he wouldn't concede there was no pregnancy at all.

"But this would be wholly inconsistent with Dr. Jacobson's diagnosis that 'Junior is doing just fine'?"

"Yes," Dr. Campbell admitted. "That's inconsistent."

Barger asked him about one of Chris Maimone's sonograms. Dr. Campbell had marked it as "definite." Barger told him that Chris was supposed to be fourteen weeks pregnant when the ultrasound was taken. Dr. Campbell looked at the photo again and said it wasn't likely.

He said the circles Dr. Jacobson had drawn on the photo were consistent with what a fourteen-week pregnancy should look like, but the actual image wasn't.

Barger gave him the sonogram taken by Dr. Peter Dunner a day after Dr. Jacobson told the Maimones their baby was fine. It clearly showed an empty uterus. Dr. Campbell studied it and said the early pregnancy had probably died and was in the process of resorbing. But Barger told him the circumstances of how the photo was taken.

"Well, that's clearly a mistake," Dr. Campbell said. "There's no two ways about it."

"There's another possibility, isn't there, Doctor?" Barger asked.

Dr. Campbell agreed. "The possibility is that he was trying to persuade the woman she was pregnant when she was not," he said.

As Dr. Campbell left the courthouse, a group of reporters caught up with him outside. With the first question he tried to distance himself from the trial. "I don't know much about this case," he said. "I was only summoned from England to testify about the ultrasound." He said he believed Dr. Jacobson had made some "honest mistakes" and didn't appear to be deliberately defrauding anyone. There weren't enough cases to indicate a conspiracy, he said. "Four cases out of many hundreds doesn't sound like a conspiracy," he said.

Someone pointed out that many more than four cases were involved. There might be hundreds.

"I think I've said enough," he answered, and hurried away.

Chapter Thirty-Eight

On February 25, two weeks into the trial, Dr. Jacobson took the stand in his own defense. In a sense he was in his element, talking about himself and his accomplishments. Only this time, instead of pontificating in front of an attentive audience, he was making a last-ditch effort to save himself from prison.

He seemed supremely confident, even cocky, as he walked to the stand, especially for a man who had so much riding on his performance. He had a lot of damaging testimony to counteract. His European medical experts had been turned against him. His attempt to cloud the DNA testing didn't work. Now it was up to him.

His attorney led him through a rendition of his glory days, beginning with his pioneering genetics work at George Washington University. He described his awards, faculty appointments, and research projects. The intent was to demonstrate his vast medical knowledge and experience, but he was coming across as self-serving. Then he finally began answering the accusations against him.

He said there was nothing sinister about the way he treated patients. He never realized that HCG would affect a pregnancy test, and he didn't switch to the Abbott test because it was more sensitive. "It was an easier test for people to read. It reacts with a definite plus or minus."

As for not listening to his friends over the years who had tried to warn him about his mistakes, he said he felt "foolish." He'd been sitting in court for nearly two weeks, listening to people say terrible things about him in front of his wife and father, but what bothered him most was that people had scoffed at his religious beliefs.

"I have been ridiculed in this court for praying with patients. That offends me greatly because I think there are sources of help that may be much more effective than doctors." He said his belief in resorption wasn't misguided either. "All the guys with the gray hair" had seen it happen, he said. "I wonder why it's such a controversy."

He insisted his real problem wasn't erroneous pregnancy tests or misread sonograms, but a poor choice of words. "Reabsorption" was a common condition that occurred with animals, but what he'd been describing for all those years was really called a "missed abortion."

Tate asked him about allegations that he prevented women from seeing their own obstetricians or getting a D and C.

He showed a flash of anger. "I didn't tie anybody up and prevent them from seeing a doctor or having a D and C," he said. He still believed that the dilation and curettage caused more harm than good. "How this allegation got in here, I don't understand, because anyone that would look at my records knows that I gave monthly pelvic examinations to women I put on Clomid," he said. "Sir, I don't have a scheme. I didn't perpetuate a scheme. I didn't design a scheme."

"Did you guarantee anybody that they were going to get pregnant?" Tate asked.

"You can't guarantee anybody anything," he said. "I told them that I would do the best I could to give them the best service I knew how. And if I couldn't, I'd be willing to refer them somewhere else."

"Dr. Jacobson, did you treat any of your fertility patients differently from any of the other fertility patients as you saw them?"

"No, sir." He said he applied a basic three-step approach on all his patients. In fact he denied he operated an infertility clinic at all. "It was a reproductive genetics center," he said.

"Was your purpose in giving these women HCG shots to fake the pregnancy so the women could think they were pregnant?" Tate asked.

"That's not only insulting, that's ridiculous," he sputtered. "I was using HCG not for a scheme, but to try to help women who were losing babies to maintain them." He admitted that he'd made some mistakes in reading ultrasounds, but denied he gouged patients by performing too many of them.

"Did you ever deliberately lie about what was on the ultrasound?" Tate asked.

"Absolutely not," he said. "I'm not proud of misreading ultrasounds. That hurts me very much for the impact on the patients. But I felt I was doing a credible job."

He testified throughout the afternoon, until the hour was getting late, and the judge recessed the trial for the day. Overnight he and his attorney apparently worked on his testimony. When he came back the next morning, his answers were more succinct and to the point, and they quickly moved through each allegation in the indictment. He said he prescribed alcohol only in small quantities so it would cause no harm, and denied that his failure to order D and C's was part of a cover-up. "I did not have a scheme," he insisted. "I had the same treatment program for everyone." The reason he experienced so many resorptions, he said, was due to the HCG and progesterone he gave his patients, and he did multiple sonograms only on difficult pregnancies.

"Would you do ultrasound sonography on your patients so you could run up a bill?" Tate asked.

"That's insulting. The answer is no," he said. "I saw those people more frequently for medical reasons, sir, not to increase their bill." He said he never held himself out to be an obstetrician or a primary-care physician, or even an infertility specialist. "I was a reproductive geneticist," he said proudly.

"Did you ever tell your patients not to go to their obstetrician?"

"No, sir."

"Did you discourage them from seeing their obstetrician at the very early stages of pregnancy?"

"No, sir." He said he treated some patients, like those whose fetuses were microcephalic, until they delivered, but he sent the vast majority of women to their doctors after their second month. He denied he ever got angry with anyone for consulting another doctor, nor did he argue with other doctors who tried to warn him about his mistakes.

Tate said one allegation in the indictment accused him of coaxing patients to tell other people in the waiting room that they were pregnant.

Dr. Jacobson said he was an "enthusiastic individual" who celebrated with his patients, and he couldn't prevent other patients from overhearing.

Tate asked if Dr. Jacobson had ever told a patient he didn't want any "boo-hoos" if she miscarried?

"I'm afraid that could be me," he said. " 'Boo-hoo' is not something I'd use, but I would try to explain to them that there's no guarantee you can get pregnant."

Finally, after several hours on the witness stand, they got to the part most spectators had been waiting for. He was asked about his insemination program. "Could you just tell the court and the jury what you did in your donor insemination program?" Tate asked.

"Well, I'll get very personal in this, if you don't mind," he said. He admitted he had been a donor for other doctors when he was a medical student; then, after becoming a doctor himself, he started performing his own inseminations.

"Did there come a time when you became a donor for your own practice?"

"In very isolated circumstances, yes."

"Could you tell the court and the jury why you did that?"

He said that sometimes his donor didn't show up, or the frozen semen wasn't compatible with the patient, so he began using his own sperm while at the university, then increased the practice when he moved his clinic to Virginia because it was more difficult to get the donor's semen delivered. He veered into an exhaustive explanation about dairies and cattle and the problem in freezing a bull's semen. Tate brought him back on track and asked him to describe the procedures he used for collecting sperm from his donors.

He said he had many donors over the years, mostly medical students. "We always requested that they collect the sperm in the privacy of their own home." The donors never visited the clinic, he said, and none of his staff ever met them. He would leave the office, usually at lunchtime, and meet the donors elsewhere in the building. He didn't specify where.

"Did you feel that everything you were doing was correct and on the up-and-up?"

"Absolutely."

"Could you tell us what it was you told these patients?"

"The most important thing is that the donor was fertile, and that the semen was clean and safe." He denied he ever told anyone he could match a person's height or skin coloration. Genetics don't work that way, he said. "I tried to explain to them that's very hard to predict," he said. "I never gave any of the specifics that I heard here."

Tate asked him what happened to the twenty dollars each patient gave him for the donor.

"I used it for other reasons," he said.

"You kept it?"

"Yes."

"Is the government correct that you didn't report that on your taxes?"

"That's correct."

"Was there a reason for that?"

He said he was concerned about the anonymity. "Plus the amount was not that much." He said he used the money for "petty cash."

Tate quickly ran him through the perjury charges against him. He denied that he'd lied to anyone under oath; then he concluded with a statistical explanation of his practice.

In the three months leading up to trial, he said he'd visited the U.S. attorney's office eight or ten times to inspect his medical records and tabulate his success rate. While most doctors could report only a 20–30 percent success rate, Dr. Jacobson said 75 percent of his patients who followed his program for six months or more got pregnant, and 48 percent gave birth. According to his statistics he was the most successful infertility doctor in the world.

* * *

At the prosecution table Bellows was furiously making notes of Cecil's testimony. From the doctor's contradictions and inconsistencies it seemed he had been attending a different trial. When it was Bellows's turn to question him, the prosecutor rose slowly from his seat and walked to the podium, carrying a condensed version of his "Jacobson Speaks" notebook, trying to show the jury that Dr. Jacobson had a more sinister side than the kindly professor they had just heard.

He began with the statistics Cecil had compiled. "I notice there's a category missing," Bellows said to him. Where was the category for patients who'd been told they were pregnant when they weren't? And with that he set the tone for a spirited battle that continued throughout the day.

"Now, Dr. Jacobson, what I'm going to try to do during the hour or two we spend together is try to focus on the subject matter of this indictment—whether or not you lied to your patients. If I understand your testimony, you never lied to anyone?"

Dr. Jacobson agreed. "To the best of my knowledge I have never lied to anyone."

"Let's just start by talking about the times when you were under oath." He asked Cecil about his deposition with Bob Hall more than two years earlier when he denied he was his own sperm donor.

Dr. Jacobson said he'd been trying to avoid revealing the name of a specific donor. "I gave a medically correct answer to that question," he said.

Next the prosecutor asked about the time Cecil had denied under oath that he had any signature authority for the Jacobson-Ziff partnership. Cecil insisted that what he'd said that day was correct.

Bellows presented him with bank documents showing Cecil had guaranteed loans, transferred money, and signed checks for Ziff, but Cecil refused to acknowledge that he had any responsibility or signature authority over the account, even when shown a certified document that proved otherwise. His arrogance wasn't enhancing his credibility for the jury.

Next Bellows asked him about the doctors who had
tried to warn him about his mistakes. He either disputed
the versions the doctors had told in court or denied having
the conversations at all.

With each new area of inquiry Bellows was exposing
Dr. Jacobson as someone who couldn't separate fact from
fiction. And the doctor wasn't helping his own cause by
refusing to concede even basic facts.

"Do you admit that you fathered the child of the
Jameses?" Bellows asked.

"Absolutely not," Dr. Jacobson said.

"Do you concede that you fathered the child of Mary
Johnson?"

Dr. Jacobson said he would have to consult his records.

Bellows asked if he admitted to fathering any of the
donor children. Cecil took credit for just one. The daughter
of Mary Green, the Down's syndrome baby.

The inquisition continued throughout the afternoon, as
Bellows hammered Dr. Jacobson for seeing fetuses that
weren't there and guaranteeing women he could get them
pregnant. He denied he had guaranteed anything to anyone. "I cannot 'guarantee' a pregnancy," he said. "That's
not a word I would use." He even denied that he'd portrayed himself as an infertility specialist.

"So if these women went to you because they believed
you were an infertility specialist, they were simply mistaken?"

Dr. Jacobson said he saw only people who had "genetic
problems with early reproduction."

"Doctor, do you concede that some of the women who
testified in this court were not pregnant when you were
telling them they were pregnant?"

"There are some women where I probably made a mistake," he said. "And for that I'm very sorry. But the vast
majority were, in fact, pregnant."

Bellows pointed out that Dr. Jacobson had never
acknowledged an error before. Not during all the civil
cases and medical-board hearings had he ever conceded

a mistake. Bellows suggested he knew the reason. "In the civil cases you were being charged with negligence and, therefore, couldn't admit it," he said. "But here you're being charged with fraud, and strategically, it's the smart thing to do? Isn't that correct?"

"That's highly insulting," Dr. Jacobson replied, then further damaged his already shaken credibility when he tried to misrepresent the findings of his British sonography expert, Dr. Campbell. He claimed that when Dr. Campbell had written "No" on the back of each sonogram photo, he'd actually meant that the photo was not readable. Bellows showed him one of Debbie Gregory's sonograms. Cecil had drawn the outline of an embryo on it. "Turn it over and tell us what Dr. Campbell wrote on the back," Bellows instructed him.

Cecil looked at it and said Dr. Campbell had written the sonogram was unreadable.

Bellows again told him to read "exactly" what Dr. Campbell had written, but Cecil refused.

Finally Bellows showed the jury that the word "No" was scrawled on the photo, meaning Dr. Campbell had seen no pregnancy. Cecil continued to insist that "No" actually meant "Not readable."

As the afternoon drew to a close, Bellows attempted to tighten the noose and present the government's version of a motive. "Dr. Jacobson, is it not correct that your amnio business, your bread and butter, began a steep decline between 1982 and 1986?"

"That's wrong," Cecil said.

But wasn't the doctor having financial problems, and wasn't he in default on a six-thousand-dollar-a-month computer lease in Utah, at the same time he began injecting women with HCG three times a week?

Cecil denied it.

"Every time you gave a woman an injection or sold her a bottle of HCG, you made a profit, is that correct?"

"Yes, I did," Dr. Jacobson conceded, but the price also included his time.

"There was no time involved when you sold a woman five bottles of HCG to take home and have administered by her husband."

"Mr. Bellows, I resent very much what you're implying." Whenever a woman took a bottle home, it was for her convenience, he said.

But wasn't there a tremendous markup in selling a ten-dollar bottle of HCG for twenty-five dollars, and a three-dollar pregnancy test for thirty-five dollars?

"I don't know how much we were paying," he said.

Before concluding his questioning Bellows had one more surprise for the doctor. He asked him again to estimate how many women he had inseminated with his own sperm. Cecil estimated "around thirty patients."

Bellows produced a document that Cecil had written for a deaf couple, on which he claimed his donor had sired "fifty-plus" children.

Cecil said that's not what he'd meant. "I work with handicapped people quite a bit," he said, and had to be "quite cryptic" when he transmitted information to them. He said he'd actually meant that his donor program had produced fifty-plus children.

He denied he routinely used his own sperm, or that he had fathered fifteen of the seventeen children in this case. He also disputed the testimony of his former employees who said he lingered in the bathroom before the insemination patients arrived. "I never realized my bathroom was so closely watched," he said.

Bellows asked about each of the misrepresentations he'd made to his patients—that he could provide a Jewish donor, or a tall donor, or a donor who resembled the husband. Dr. Jacobson said he never told his patients any of those things.

The judge noted that the questioning was taking a long time and told Bellows to begin wrapping it up.

Bellows quickly went through the case of each patient, pointing out the lies she'd been told and asking Dr. Jacobson to offer explanations.

Cecil denied he ever told a woman that her baby was sleeping, or told a woman to disregard laboratory blood-test reports, or told a patient he'd seen a fetal penis, or measured a fetal heart rate of 120 beats per minute in a woman with an empty uterus. He was denying practically everything the patients had said. And his denials were sounding hollow. Although Bellows still had another two hours of questions, he concluded the cross-examination, but not before the doctor's credibility was completely shattered.

Yet as Cecil left the stand, he seemed confident that he'd done a good job. He had shown the jury a glimpse of the intellectual doctor his patients had trusted, although on cross-examination Bellows believed the jurors had seen another side of the doctor's personality—the arrogant, condescending physician who lied to patients and led them to believe they were pregnant when they were not.

Chapter Thirty-Nine

After nearly three weeks of testimony from 110 witnesses, the jurors would admit to feeling "baffled" as they began their deliberations. The jury foreman would compare the deliberations to deciding fifty-two separate trials, one for each count of the indictment. The law was complicated; just the instructions from the judge had taken an hour and forty-five minutes.

Most of the jurors weren't any closer to making a decision than they had been when the trial started. Before beginning their consideration of the charges, the jury tried to determine Dr. Jacobson's intent. "We kicked it around for two days before we even started dealing with what the charges were," a juror would say. One juror believed the doctor had been practicing good medicine. Another thought he'd been on the verge of a dramatic infertility breakthrough. Others were convinced he was a fraud, but most still weren't sure.

They started with the insemination charges, then moved on to the accusations of fake pregnancies, as they meticulously reconstructed the medical history for every patient. They made charts and hung them on a board, then compared the doctor's clinical notes with the testimony of the patients and the medical experts. They became convinced that an early pregnancy could resorb, but the key question was whether a fourteen-week pregnancy could disappear without a trace. They searched through the evidence for a photo of a fourteen-week-old fetus to see how well the bones and skull were developed. Bellows had tried to introduce one into evidence, but the judge had sustained a defense objection because it didn't depict an actual fetus. The jurors asked the judge to send them a photo, but he declined and instead sent them a note explaining they had to consider only the evidence before them.

The next day the jury asked for sonogram photos for the woman known as Mary Jones. They wanted to inspect the photos from July 1987 and said it was a "personal request" from the jury foreman, Dan Richard.

Bellows said he would be glad to let them see the photos, except the woman didn't have a baby in 1987. Her child was born in the late 1970's. He offered to clarify the facts for the jurors. But Tate argued that the jurors should interpret the evidence for themselves, without any help from the attorneys. The judge agreed and sent a note: "I regret that I cannot answer your question. All the evidence has been submitted to you by the parties. You should decide this case on the basis of the testimony and evidence submitted to you."

Otherwise there was no indication of how the jurors were leaning as their deliberations lasted into the fourth day. Cecil was encouraged that the jury was taking so long. On the morning of the fourth day his attorney had an extra bounce in his step as he greeted the reporters. "I don't want to predict what they're gonna do, but I suspect the government gets more nervous every day they're out."

Bellows surprised himself with his calmness. He realized there was nothing more he could do, and for the first time in months he was taking leisurely lunches and leaving work early, shortly after the jury recessed for the day. Willetts, whose normally laid-back style contrasted with Bellows's tenseness, was a nervous wreck. He was confident they had won the case but realized that each day the jury remained in deliberations wasn't a good sign.

Finally, on the afternoon of the fourth day, the jury sent out a note. They had reached a verdict.

Both sides were hastily assembled. Because the deliberations had dragged on so long, few of the patients or spectators were still there. The judge instructed everyone to remain seated until after the jury had announced its verdict and left the courtroom. No matter what the decision, he said, he didn't want any outbursts.

When the jury filed in and was seated, the judge asked

the foreman, "Have the members of the jury reached a verdict?"

"Yes, we have," he said.

The judge told Dr. Jacobson to rise and face the jury as the clerk read the verdict.

"We the jury find the defendant, Cecil Jacobson, guilty as to Count One. Guilty as to Count Two. Guilty as to Count Three." The clerk continued to read all of the fifty-two verdicts. The decision was unanimous. He was found guilty of every charge.

Dr. Jacobson was reeling as he left the courtroom, as if someone had punched him. His father, hobbling on a cane, supported him as they walked outside. "I'm obviously in shock," Cecil said. "I had total reliance in the justice system of this country. I spent my total life trying to help women have children. It's a shock to be found guilty trying to help people."

He seemed on the verge of tears. A reporter asked if he was surprised at being found guilty on all the charges.

"I was astounded I was found guilty on any of the counts. I have not perpetuated a scheme. I have not in any way tried to harm or hurt people. I have obviously made some mistakes, but my entire career was to try and help women have children. Some were hurt by problems that I obviously did not recognize early. And for that I'm very sorry. It's an absolute shock that I can be found guilty of something I didn't do."

When the jurors came out, they explained they had "agonized" over their decision. None of them had enjoyed their work. Most believed that Cecil was a good man who wasn't motivated by money but, rather, had misled the women to enhance his own ego and reputation. He must have known the hormone would affect a pregnancy test. He must have known a fourteen-week fetus couldn't resorb. He must have known the women were not pregnant when he claimed they were. He was too adept at using sonograms during amniocentesis to mistake a fully formed fetus in the womb. The only question they couldn't decide was why.

For one woman the key piece of evidence was Dr. Jacobson's own testimony. "We knew he was lying," she would say. He'd lied about so many things, how could they believe him when he said he didn't know his pregnancy tests were affected by HCG?

"I think he was a good man and did a lot of good," one of the other women on the jury said. "But there was overwhelming evidence that he went wrong somewhere and he mistreated a lot of women."

"I think that lying to your patients is reprehensible," the jury foreman said.

"Do you think he did it for the money?" a reporter asked.

"He did it for some kind of gain, whether it was money or acknowledgment. He definitely did something wrong." He remarked that the entire saga had produced no winners, only losers. "The ladies lost. They didn't get pregnant. Dr. Jacobson lost. Everybody lost."

Chapter Forty

Dr. Jacobson's sentencing was scheduled for May 8, 1992, two months after the trial. A group of Church members fasted for him the night before and prayed for leniency.

Cecil arrived early and walked silently through the sea of TV cameras accompanied by his father and some friends from his old neighborhood. His wife had stayed behind in Provo to care for their children. She had attended the trial for the sake of the jury, but now she would rather stay where she was needed—with her family.

Cecil selected a seat in the back row. Silently, he stared straight ahead, sometimes closing his eyes as if in prayer, and ignoring the patients who had come to see him finally get punished.

Only one insemination patient dared to attend, the one known as Mary Johnson, who ignored the risk of being recognized so she could witness the sentencing for herself. Her psychiatrist had told her it would be therapeutic. Before court her cover was nearly blown when she ran into Dr. Jacobson and the swarm of reporters following him into the courthouse. They stood face-to-face for a moment, and he started to say something to her. "Oh, shit," she thought, fearing they would attract attention. But Dr. Jacobson caught himself and pretended not to notice her. She turned quickly and walked away, before anyone recognized her. When she entered the courtroom, Willetts did a double take, then looked away before anyone noticed.

By the time the proceedings began, spectators were lined two deep in some places along the wall. Bellows asked for a ten-year sentence. This wasn't a typical white-collar fraud case, he told the court, the dollar figures didn't begin to measure the patients' loss. "The court has never had a white-collar crime in which the victims suffered more grievous injuries," he argued.

Tate pleaded for the judge's indulgence. "I doubt the court will sentence as many men who have done as much good for people as this man," he said.

Then Dr. Jacobson stood up to have a last word. He lumbered slowly to the podium and addressed the judge. "I was totally unaware of the anger, anguish, and hate that I caused until these proceedings," he said.

"I'm sorry. As God is my witness, I never intended to harm anyone. I ask for their forgiveness so the healing process can begin. I truly did not wish to hurt these people, I only wished to help." He mentioned the hardship that a prison sentence would inflict on his family—and himself. "I'm not a young man. A sentence of this extent is like a life sentence," he said. "I ask the mercy of the court." Then he stood silently to accept his fate.

Ninety people had written letters to the judge on Cecil's behalf, including his friends, colleagues, and fellow Mormons, even U.S. senator Orrin Hatch. Judge Cacheris said he was taking the letters into account as he assessed punishment, but he was also considering the cruel psychological injuries inflicted on the victims.

"I have not seen a case where there has been this degree of emotional anguish and psychological trauma," he said. He would never forget the women who testified about suffering such depression and anguish over the loss of their children. Others had wasted their childbearing years. "It affected every aspect of their lives," he said. "They blamed themselves for killing those babies."

As the doctor stood before him, he sentenced Cecil to five years in prison, without parole, and fined him $116,000. With time off for good behavior he could be out in four years and five months.

Cecil had nothing to say as he left the courthouse. His father stopped long enough to denounce the government's case as a "witch-hunt" and said the women who complained about his son were "gold diggers" who were seizing an opportunity to make money from civil suits. "This has not broken our family apart," he said. "It's brought us together."

Most of the patients felt the sentence was adequate. They would have preferred a longer prison term—one woman suggested castration——but generally they were satisfied. Mary Johnson tried to slip away unnoticed. Only Rob Howe, of *The Washington Post*, recognized her. He walked up and quietly said hello. "What do you think?" he asked, low enough so no one could hear.

"It was fair," she said. "I don't think anything will ever really make me happy with it. But it was fair."

When Howe walked away, Mary was approached by a reporter from a London newspaper who was doing a wrap-up piece on the case. He asked if he could speak with her a moment. She said she didn't know anything—she was just a friend of one of the witnesses—and walked away.

The verdict and sentence were a hollow victory for most of the patients. Nothing had changed. Most women still didn't have a baby. The insemination patients now knew the identity of their donor. Families had been torn apart. As the juror said, there were no winners, only losers.

The man known as John James felt like the worst loser of all. He'd lost the connection to his family. The twins he thought were his children weren't his—for some reason Dr. Jacobson had substituted his own sperm—and now it was as if he was living with strangers. He looked at his children with "an asterisk," he said, and constantly thought about what Dr. Jacobson had done. He found it difficult to work, he couldn't sleep. He didn't smile anymore. He was gaining weight and, for the first time in his life, developed high blood pressure. "I am not the same person I was before. My personality is much different. My friends know it. My colleagues know it." He couldn't go ten minutes without thinking about it. "He is an ever-present, unwelcome visitor in our lives," John would say.

His wife worried about him. They underwent counseling, not only to deal with their own emotional trauma, but also for advice on how to inform the children. They worked with their therapist for months and devoted their summer vacation to breaking the news. They went on a cruise so the children wouldn't associate their home with receiving the unpleasant news.

John and Patricia explained they had gotten help in conceiving and there had been a "mix-up"—they were careful not to characterize it as a mistake. Then they revealed that John was not their biological father. They didn't mention Dr. Jacobson, and the children didn't ask about the donor.

The children seemed to take it well. John assured them he loved them, whether or not he was the biological father, and said that nothing about their relationship would change. But in the coming months there were indications each child was reacting differently. One seemed to repress the information, while the other rebelled.

One child asked if Patricia had gotten pregnant the first time she had intercourse with John. "Don't you remember we talked about this?" Patricia said.

The other child was constantly seeking reassurance that John still loved them. But once, after John punished them, the child blurted out, "You're not my father," implying that John didn't have to be obeyed.

The Jameses and four other donor couples sued Dr. Jacobson. His insurance company settled each of the cases out of court, except the Jameses' case. Dr. Jacobson continued to deny he was the biological father of their children or had switched the sperm, despite the government's DNA tests, which showed a 99.99 percent probability. The attorneys hired by Dr. Jacobson's insurance company fought the suit by attacking the Jameses' use of pseudonyms, and a local judge ruled that the couple would have to testify in public without anonymity if they insisted on pursuing the suit. The Jameses were so livid, they decided to appeal the judge's ruling.

John was put through the indignity of undergoing a psychiatric exam. Then, during a deposition, despite an agreement not to identify the family by name, Dr.

Jacobson's attorney constantly inserted their identity into the record. At one point he even insinuated that the children weren't Dr. Jacobson's offspring, but maybe were the result of Mrs. James's infidelity. As the court reporter was leaving and packing up his stenography machine, he turned to John and said sympathetically, "I've been in this business for a long time and I've heard a lot of stories, but I've never heard anything like this."

When Dr. Jacobson was deposed by the Jameses' attorney, William "Sandy" Snead, Cecil admitted that his own wife had been aware that he was a donor, and he also had discussed it with the leaders of his Church. He said the Church elders had given him permission to be a donor, even for his own patients, but not for inseminating single mothers. "The only restriction that was placed," he testified, "was a reservation that I should not participate as a donor in single parents."

He said he didn't feel it was medical malpractice to use his own sperm and said he didn't remember the Jameses at all. "It's been years," he said. "I've only seen them four times in my office." He said he would have gotten to know them better if Mrs. James had had an amniocentesis. "That is the time when you really get close to your patients," he said.

John often wondered how Dr. Jacobson could think his sperm was so much more exceptional than everyone else's that he should be his own donor. "It has to be some godlike megalomania that causes him to feel that his sperm, his genetics, are so far superior to anyone else's." He also wondered if the doctor's motive was somehow related to his religious beliefs. "It wouldn't surprise me if there is some religious aspect to this," John would say.

He didn't know much about the Mormon religion, except that Mormon men often felt superior to women and believed in large families and spreading the Mormon seed. "It wouldn't surprise me if they believed it's their job to populate the earth."

Other patients were having the same suspicions. One patient researched the Mormon doctrine to better understand the doctor who had defrauded her and, after the trial, sent anonymous faxes to the local and national media to trumpet what she had found. She had been a witness for the government but was upset that prosecutors had skirted what she believed to be the true motive behind the insemination cases. "It is my contention that Dr. Jacobson's Mormon belief was a driving force in the acts he committed," she wrote. She had discussed her suspicions with Randy Bellows while she had been interviewed at the U.S. attorney's office, but Bellows said the government wouldn't be exploring the doctor's religious beliefs. She called it "high-tech polygamy" and claimed Dr. Jacobson had been trying to populate the earth with his own children as part of a misguided religious conviction.

Her theory was endorsed by two university professors who also studied the possible religious overtones of Dr. Jacobson's case. Anson Shupe, a sociology professor at Purdue University, and his partner, Roger D. Edwards of Indiana University, had written several books and articles about Mormonism. They reviewed the courtroom testimony and interviewed several participants in the case and suggested that Cecil's artificial-insemination program was "an outlaw interpretation" of Mormon teachings. Mormons were taught they could become gods in the hereafter and beget spirit children with their spirit wives. The sociologists suggested that with extra children on earth it would take Dr. Jacobson less time to populate a new spirit world in the next life over which to preside as a god. They said the motive would seem absurd to non-Mormons who were not familiar with Mormon teachings, and they expected the Mormon hierarchy to "cry foul." Nevertheless, they presented their study, entitled "The Strange Case of Dr. Cecil Jacobson: Mormonism, Theology, and Deviance," on August 20, 1992, at a meeting of the Association for the Sociology of Religion held in Pittsburgh. They said the religious motive made as much sense as anything else.

But when Patricia James thought of her two children, she didn't want to accept the idea of a religious overtone.

She wanted to believe that Dr. Jacobson thought he was helping couples have children, and it didn't matter how the pregnancy was accomplished. But the possible religious aspect scared her. "It's scary because that means he's got some kind of hold on these kids," she would say. "And there can't be any attachment."

Chapter Forty-One

Epilogue

Dr. Jacobson continued living with his family near Provo, Utah, as his attorneys appealed his conviction to the highest courts in the nation.

The Virginia State Board of Medicine revoked his medical license soon after his conviction on the fraud charges. Then his insurance company, after paying off millions of dollars in lawsuits, filed suit against him, claiming it was no longer responsible for paying patients he had defrauded. Dr. Jacobson battled the insurance company and won. A judge ruled the company was still liable to pay damages to the remaining insemination patients who sued.

John and Patricia James finally settled their case against Dr. Jacobson, after an appellate court ruled they could testify under pseudonyms. Their settlement was the last of nearly thirty lawsuits that had been filed against him.

Many of those women who sued, after undergoing years of emotional turmoil and bogus pregnancies, fared much better once they left his care.

Chris Maimone consulted the in-vitro clinic where her doctor, John Doppelheuer, had initially referred her. After a few months of treatments, she conceived a son, Christopher.

Jean Blair, who was told by Dr. Jacobson that she resorbed seven children, quickly conceived two babies, Travis and Kaitlyn, after consulting another infertility specialist.

Renea and Louis Jennings, who had withdrawn their names from the Fairfax County adoption list after being told by Dr. Jacobson that Renea was pregnant, later moved to Tennessee, where they adopted a son.

Susan Dippel got pregnant almost immediately after she

left Dr. Jacobson for another doctor, then gave birth to a son, Matthew.

But others, like Vickie Eckhardt, never managed to conceive. Even after moving to Maine with her husband, Bill, she refused to give up hope and continued treatments at an in-vitro fertilization clinic not far from Dr. Jacobson's former clinic. But after several years of unsuccessful treatments, she finally gave up. She blamed Dr. Jacobson for robbing her of five years of valuable time during which she could have been seeking legitimate help elsewhere.

Dr. Jacobson's story was made into a TV movie that aired in February 1994. Less than two weeks later Judge Cacheris ruled that Cecil had been free on bond long enough.

On February 18, 1994, Dr. Jacobson reported to a minimum-security federal prison in Florence, Colorado, about thirty-five miles south of Colorado Springs, to begin serving his five-year sentence. With good behavior he will be eligible for release after four years and five months of his term. A prison spokeswoman said he will be treated like any other prisoner. Despite his notoriety he will work alongside other inmates in the prison kitchen or maintenance area earning twelve cents an hour.

Before Dr. Jacobson went off to prison, Debbie Gregory and her husband, Steven, became one more casualty of the doctor's misguided infertility program. Their marriage finally collapsed under the constant stress that had begun with their infertility treatments six years earlier. Following their divorce, Debbie moved in with another man and soon afterward got pregnant. She gave birth to a daughter she named Emma. Two months later she got pregnant again. Despite her years of treatments with Dr. Jacobson, and his diagnosis that she had a "major risk of fetal defect," it turned out Debbie didn't have an infertility problem at all. She got pregnant twice, without the help of any so-called infertility experts, and had two uneventful deliveries.

About the Author

Rick Nelson, 42, is an investigative producer in Washington, D.C. for the ABC Newsmagazine *Prime Time Live*. He has won more than two dozen journalism awards for investigative reporting while working for newspapers and television stations in Florida, Colorado, Texas and Washington, D.C, including the prestigious Peabody Award, two Sigma Delta Chi awards, the George Polk Award, two Emmys and is a five-time winner of the Investigative Reporters and Editors award. His first book, *The Cop Who Wouldn't Quit*, about a Houston murder case, was published by Bantam in 1984. He lives in Maryland with his wife and two children.

DON'T MISS
THESE CURRENT
BANTAM BESTSELLERS